AKIRA

KATSUHIRO OTOMO

BOOK FOUR

KC
KODANSHA
COMICS

A Kodansha Comics Trade Paperback Original

AKIRA Volume 4 © 1987 MASH•ROOM. All rights reserved.
English translation copyright © 1987 MASH•ROOM /Kodansha Ltd.
First published in Japan in 1987 by Kodansha Ltd., Tokyo.
Publication rights for this English edition arranged through Kodansha Ltd., Tokyo.

Published in the United States by Kodansha Comics, an imprint of Kodansha USA Publishing, New York.

Kodansha Comics is a registered trademark of Kodansha Ltd.

ISBN 978-1-935429-06-7

First edition: October 2010
Printed in the United States of America

10 9 8 7 6 5 4 3 2

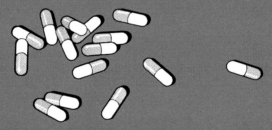

Translation and English-language adaptation: Yoko Umezawa, Jo Duffy
Graphics adaptation and sound effects lettering: David Schmit/ Digibox, Editions Glénat
Digital lettering and additional graphics adaptation: Digital Chameleon, Dark Horse Comics
English edition cover design and art direction: Lia Ribacchi, Mark Cox

MASH•ROOM staff: Yasumitsu Suetake, Satoshi Takabatake
Original series editor: Koichi Yuri
Original cover design: Akira Saito/Veia
Editor for this edition: Naoto Yasunaga, Takeshi Katsurada

AKIRA
PART 4

ケイI

Kei I

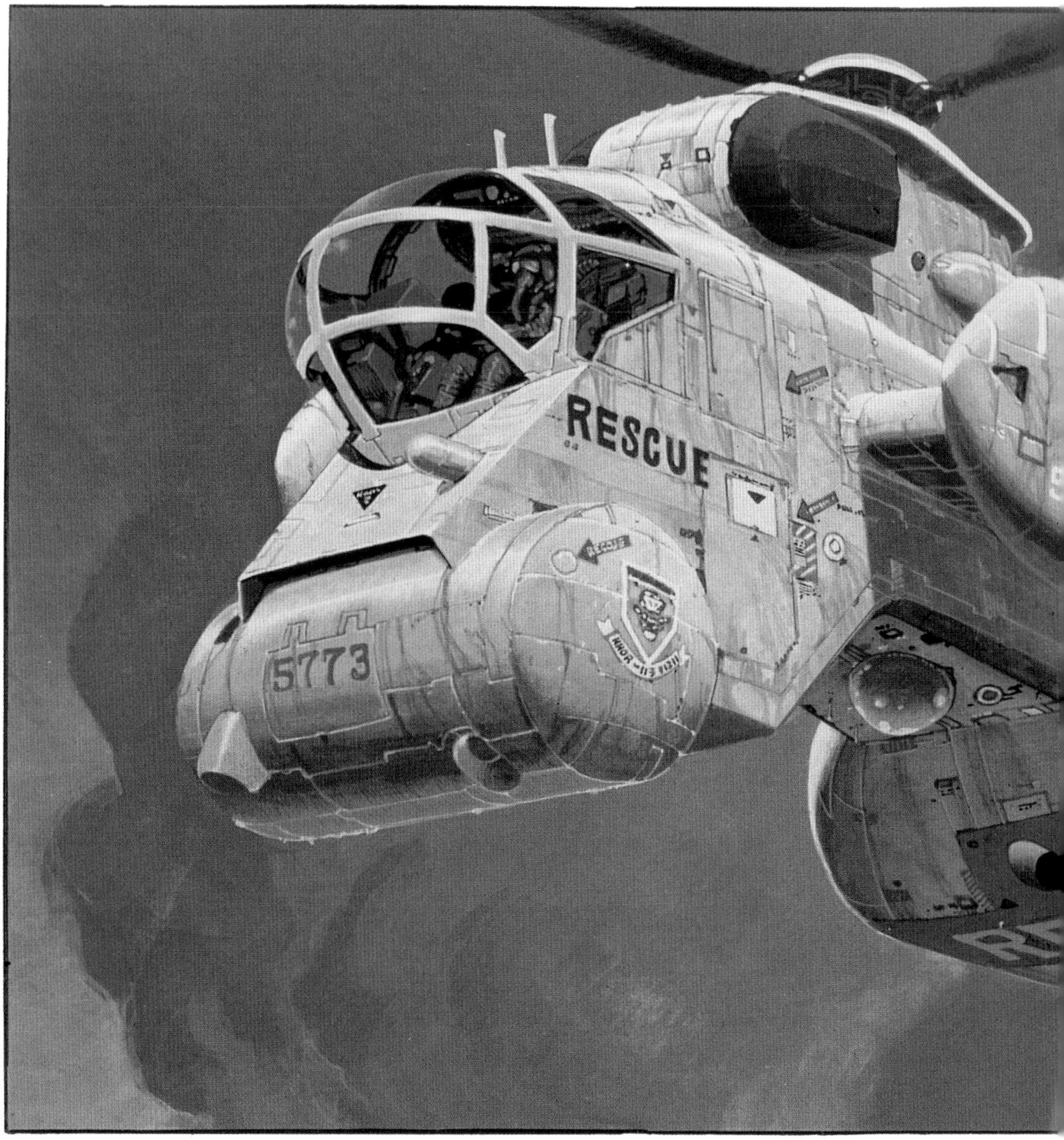
RESCUE
5773

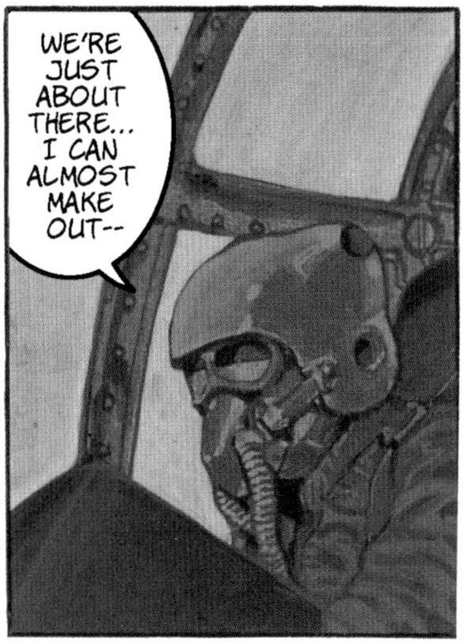
WE'RE JUST ABOUT THERE... I CAN ALMOST MAKE OUT--

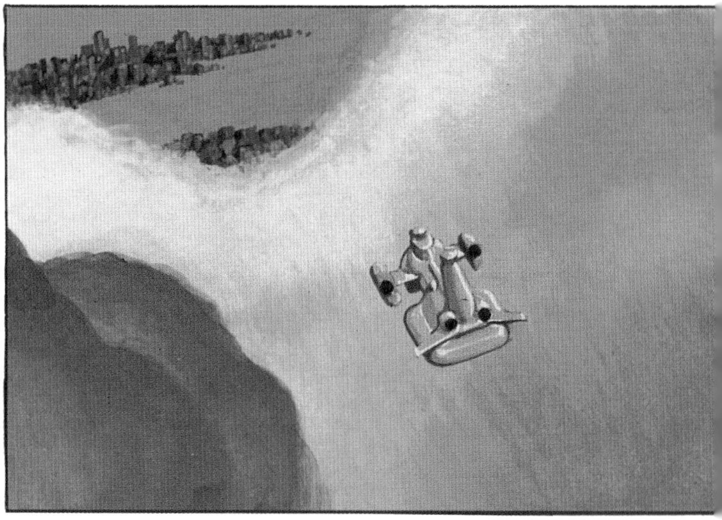

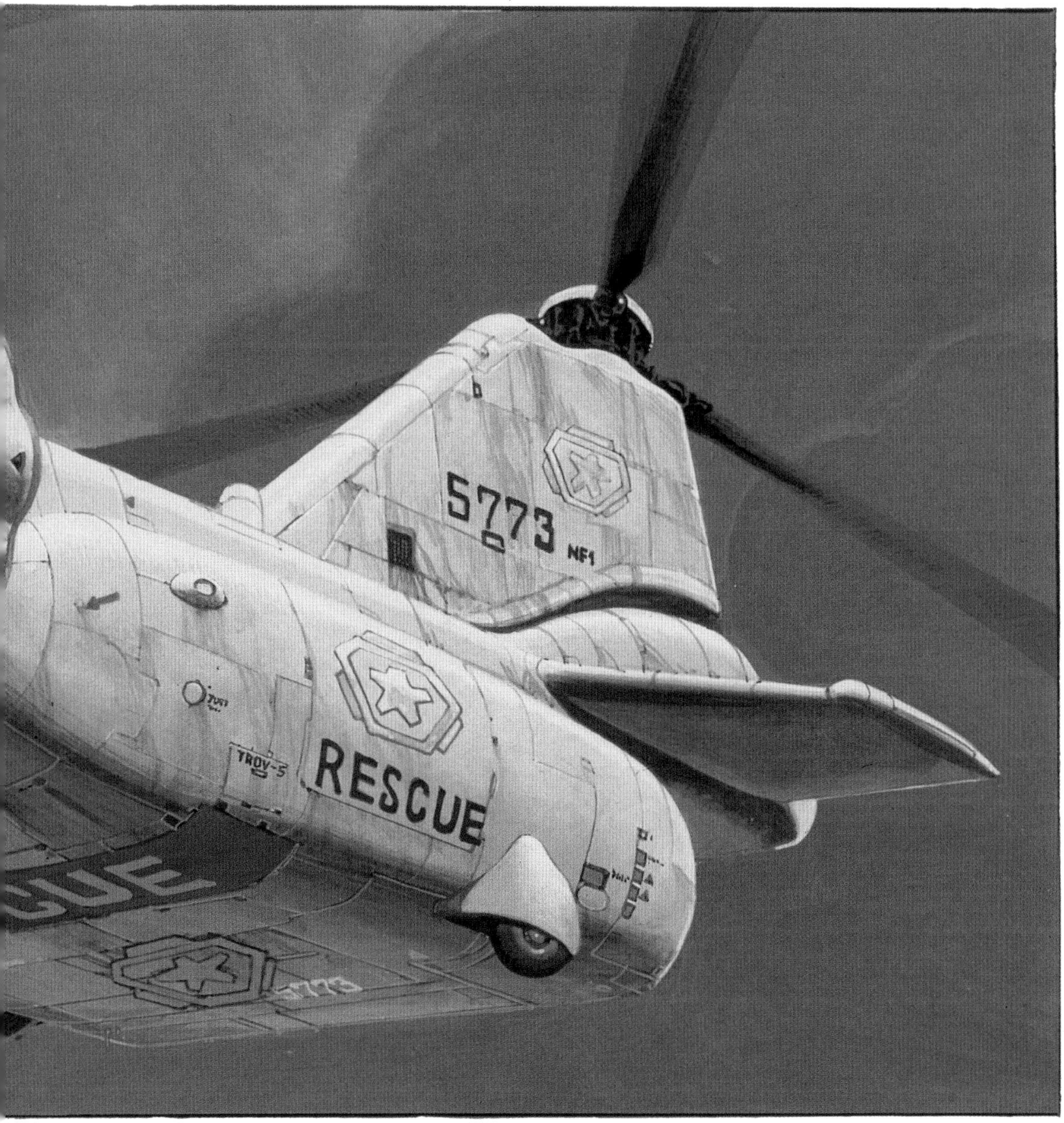
5773
NF1
TROV-5
RESCUE

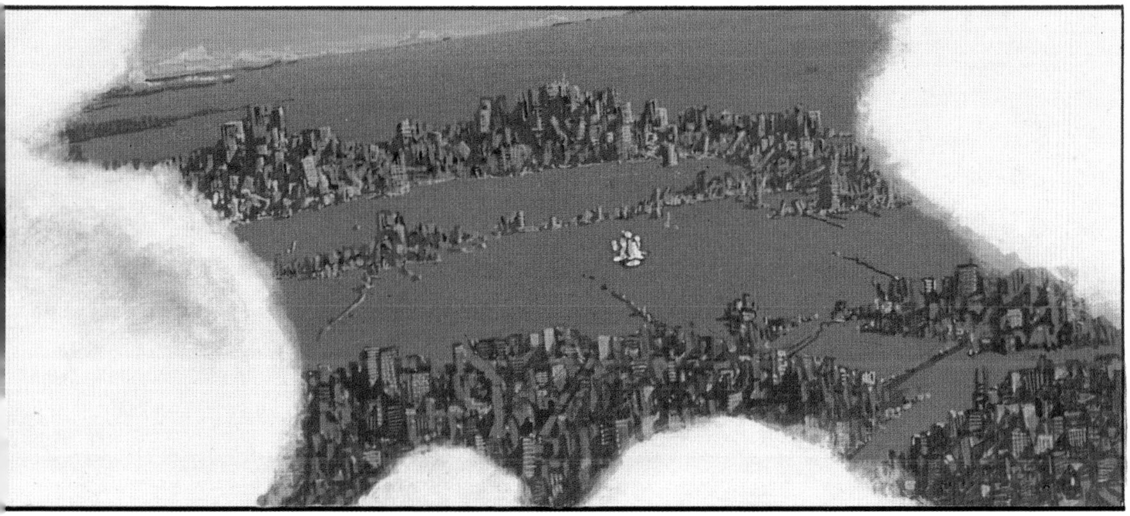

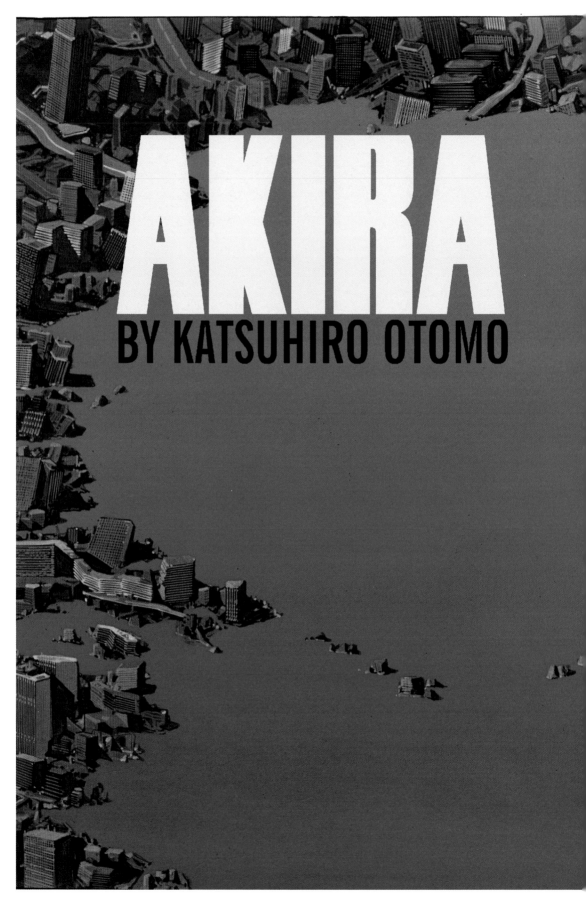

AKIRA
BY KATSUHIRO OTOMO

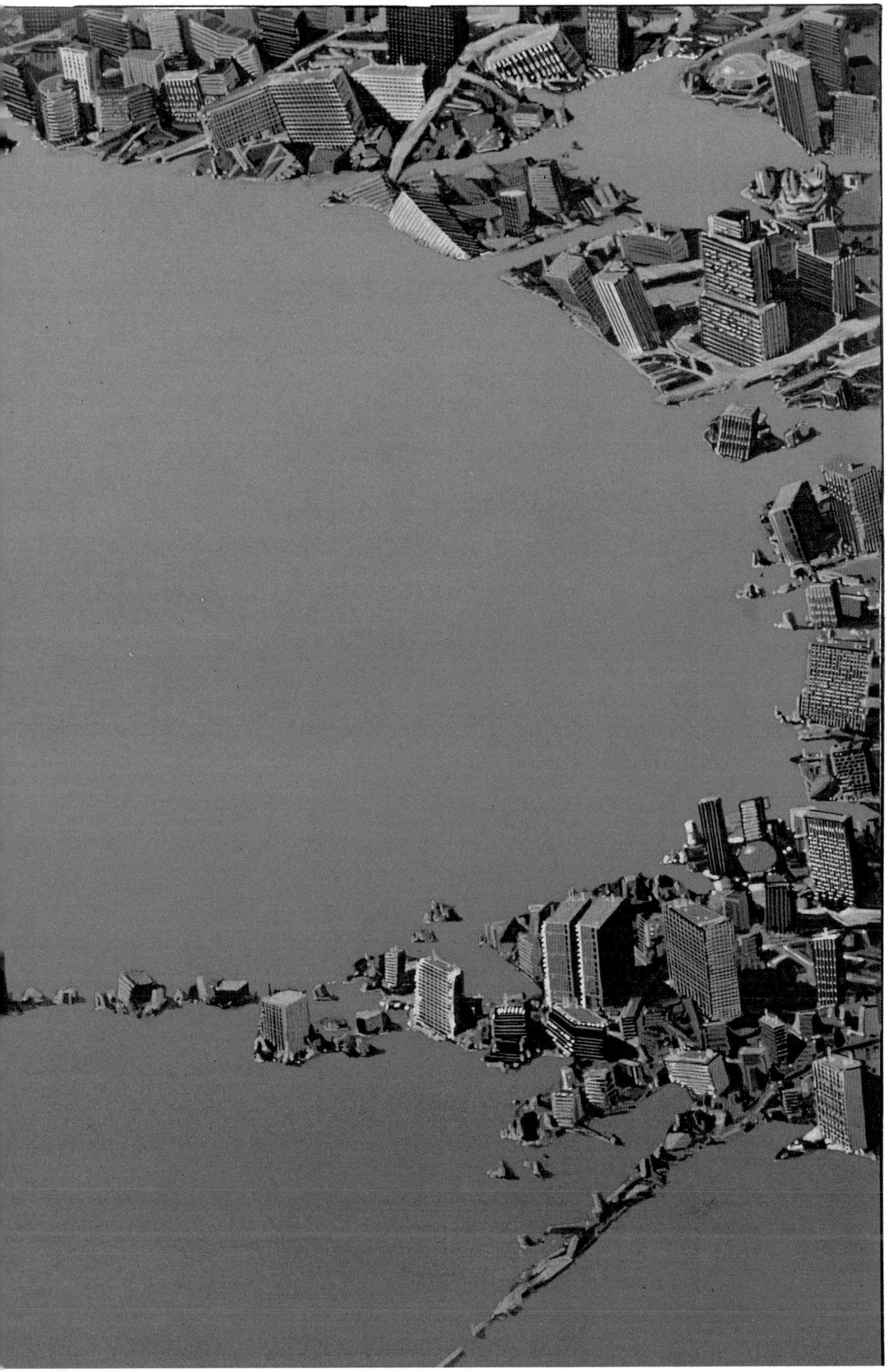

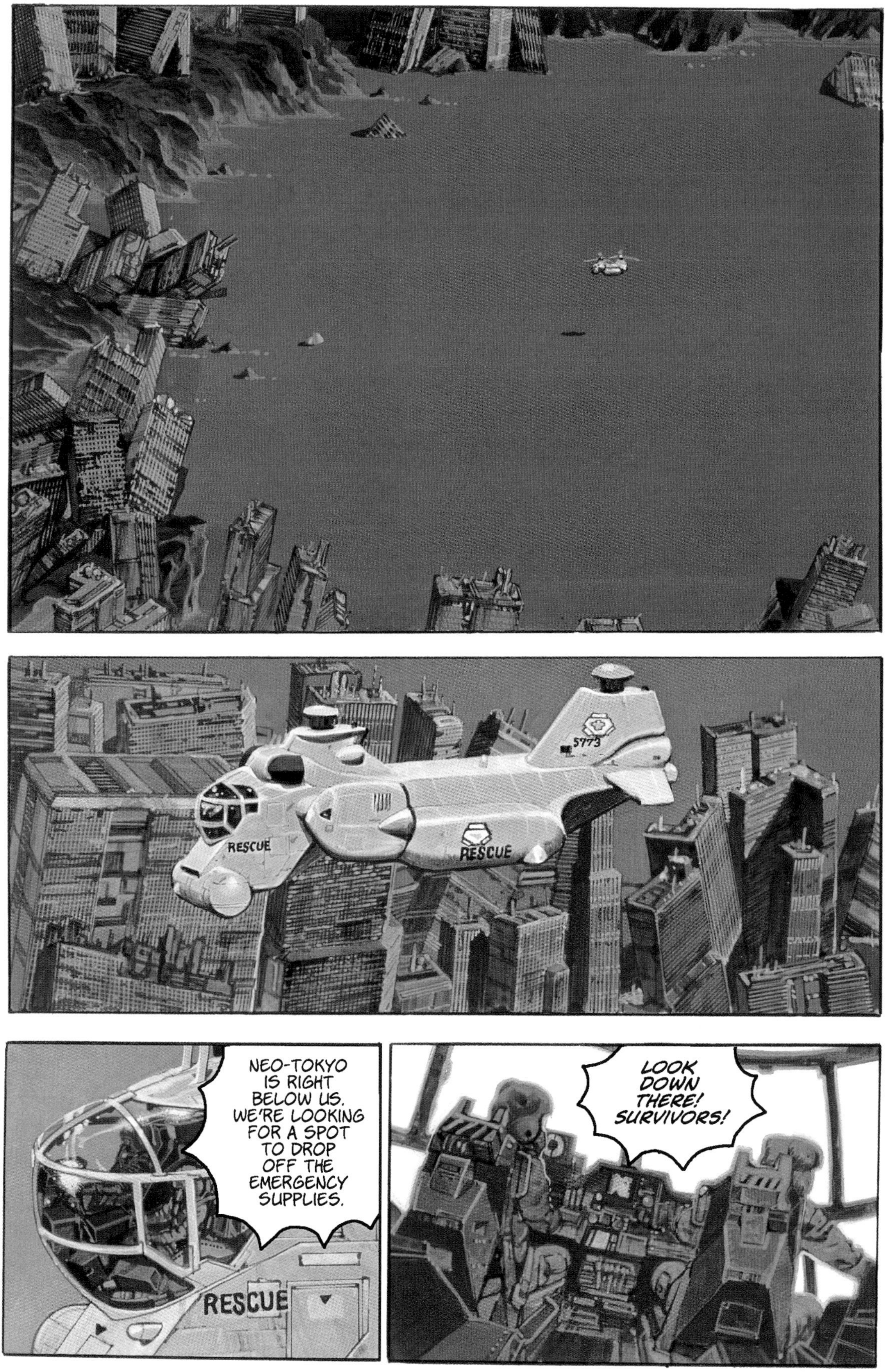
5773
RESCUE
RESCUE
NEO-TOKYO IS RIGHT BELOW US. WE'RE LOOKING FOR A SPOT TO DROP OFF THE EMERGENCY SUPPLIES.
RESCUE
LOOK DOWN THERE! SURVIVORS!

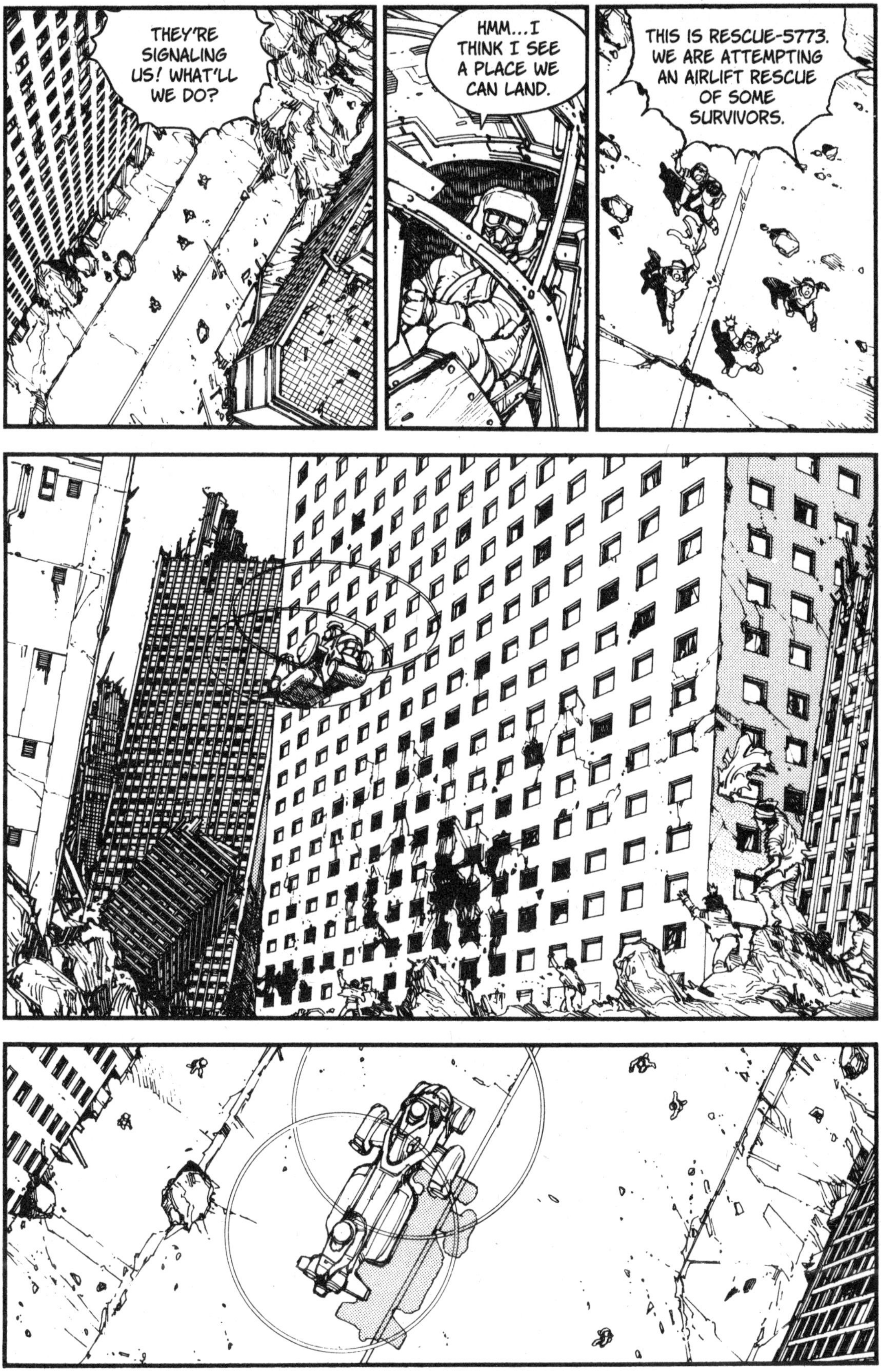
THEY'RE SIGNALING US! WHAT'LL WE DO?
HMM...I THINK I SEE A PLACE WE CAN LAND.
THIS IS RESCUE-5773. WE ARE ATTEMPTING AN AIRLIFT RESCUE OF SOME SURVIVORS.

OUR FIRST PRIORITY IS FOR THE RESCUE OF THE INJURED. STAY CALM--OTHER HELICOPTERS WILL COME FOR THE REST OF YOU.

WE'RE LEAVING YOU FOOD AND MEDICAL SUPPLIES AND TWO-WAY RADIOS. KEEP TUNED FOR BULLETINS AS YOU WAIT.

KEEP BACK! WE'VE ALREADY SAID WE CAN ONLY ACCOMMODATE THE WOUNDED!

DON'T YOU UNDERSTAND?!

THEY WON'T LISTEN! TELL THE PILOT TO TAKE OFF!

FREEZE!

WHA--?!

TCHiK

IN THE NAME OF THE EMPIRE, I HEREBY REQUISITION THIS VEHICLE! GIVE IT UP, AND NO FUNNY BUSINESS!

WHO ARE YOU GUYS?!

"REQUISITION"...?

"EMPIRE"...?

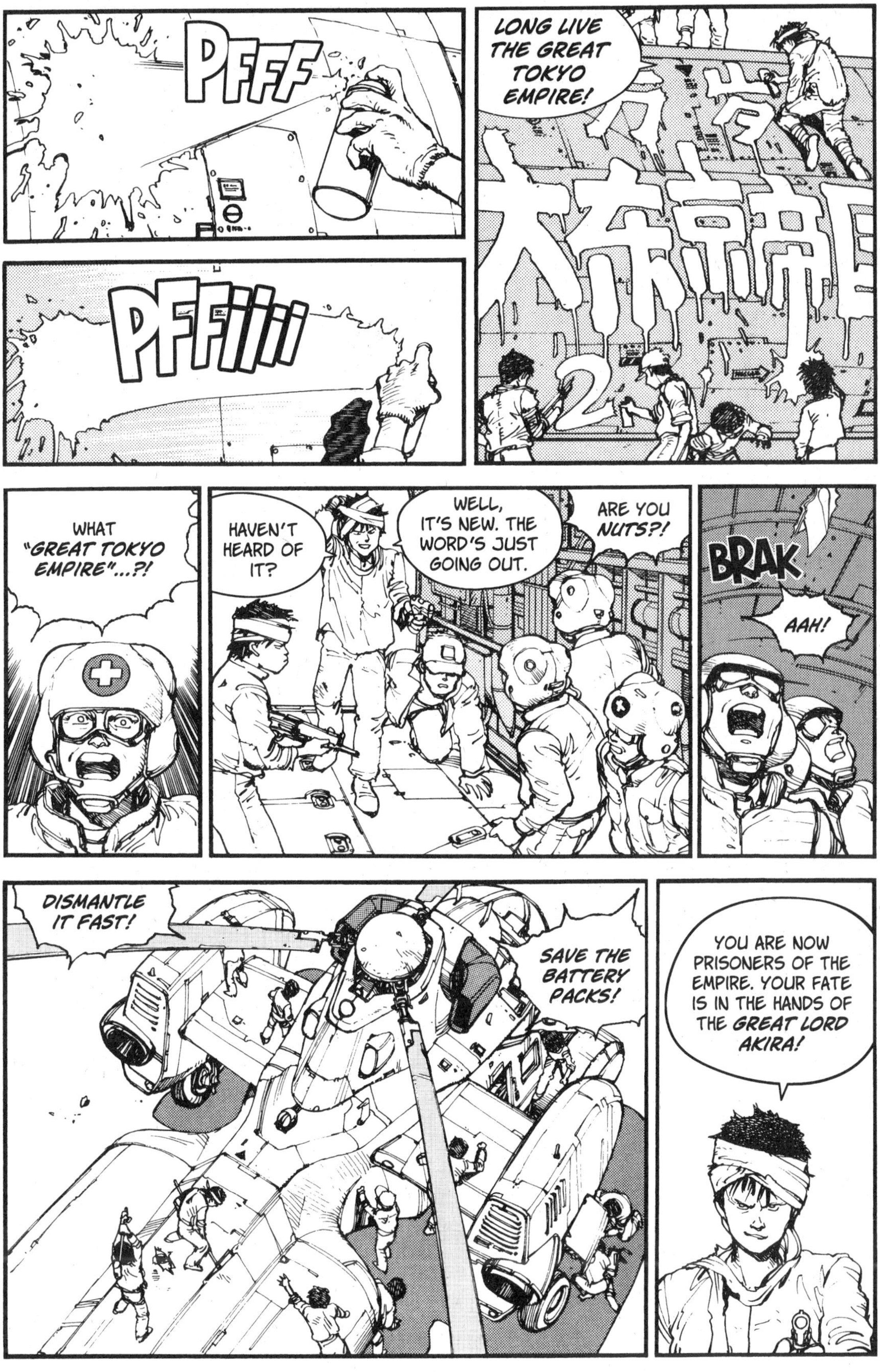
PFFF
PFFiiii
LONG LIVE THE GREAT TOKYO EMPIRE!
WHAT "GREAT TOKYO EMPIRE"...?!
HAVEN'T HEARD OF IT?
WELL, IT'S NEW. THE WORD'S JUST GOING OUT.
ARE YOU NUTS?!
BRAK
AAH!
DISMANTLE IT FAST!
SAVE THE BATTERY PACKS!
YOU ARE NOW PRISONERS OF THE EMPIRE. YOUR FATE IS IN THE HANDS OF THE GREAT LORD AKIRA!

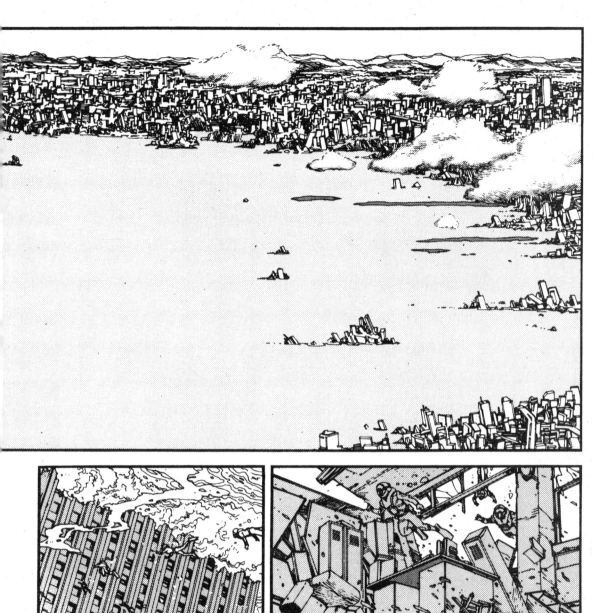

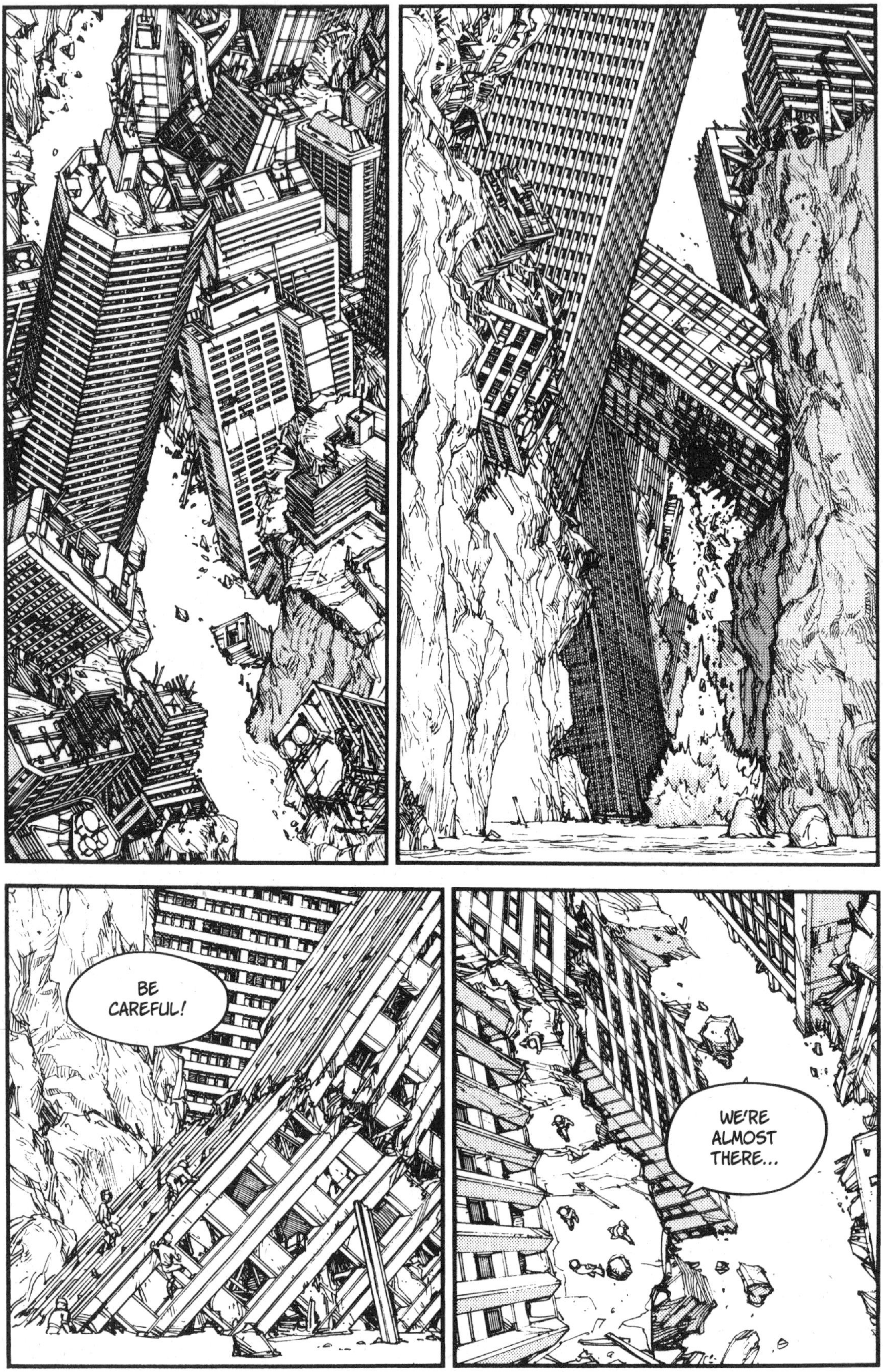
BE CAREFUL!
WE'RE ALMOST THERE...

HMM...

TAKE COVER!

WHAT GOES *UP* MUST COME *DOWN*...

HUNH?

TSHAF

≥HMPH!≥

HEY! WHAT'RE YOU...?

SPLOF

OKAY! LET'S MOVE!

SRAAP

15

HERE'S WHERE WE DIVIDE INTO PAIRS.

NO CONTACT UNDER ANY CIRCUMSTANCES BETWEEN THE VARIOUS TEAMS. IF ANY OF US CROSS PATHS...

...WE ACT AS STRANGERS. IF YOUR BUDDY DIES, CARRY ON THE MISSION ALONE. THE MISSION IS ALL THAT MATTERS!

RELAY AS MUCH INFORMATION AS POSSIBLE ABOUT AKIRA TO HEADQUARTERS. NOW, CLEAR OUT!

EH?

VOON

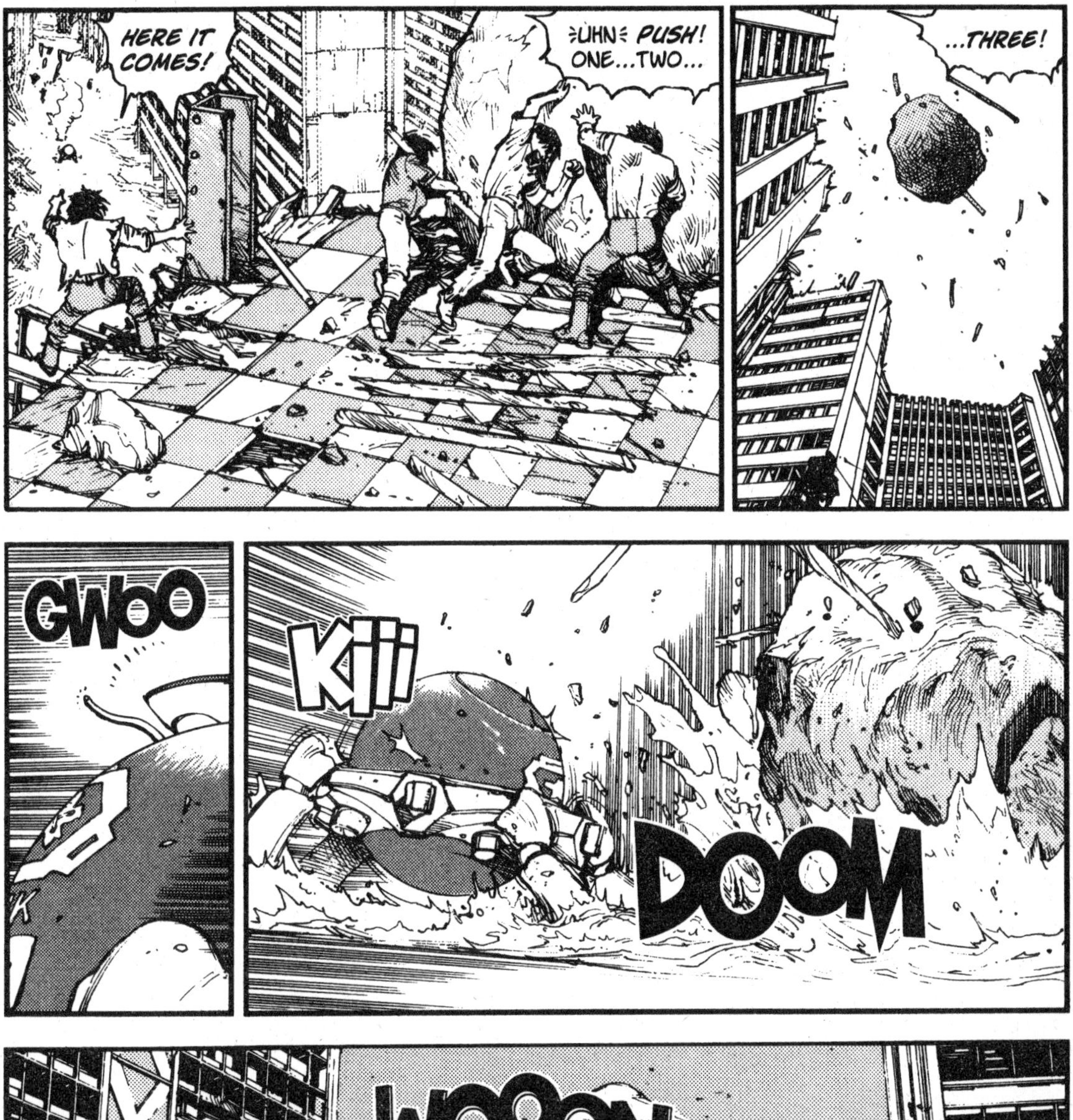
HERE IT COMES!
UHN PUSH! ONE...TWO...
...THREE!
GWOO
KIII
DOOM
WOOON

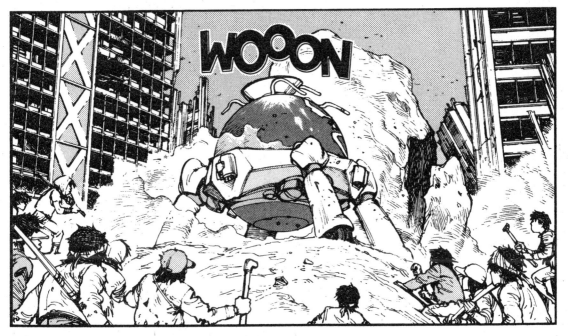

ATTACK !!

SUCK ON THIS!

RETREAT!

YIPE!

YAUGH!

THAT WAS ONE OF THE ARMY'S *CARETAKER* ROBOTS.

ORDINARY RIOTERS SHOULD NEVER HAVE BEEN ABLE TO TAKE IT. THIS WAS A *PLANNED* ATTACK.

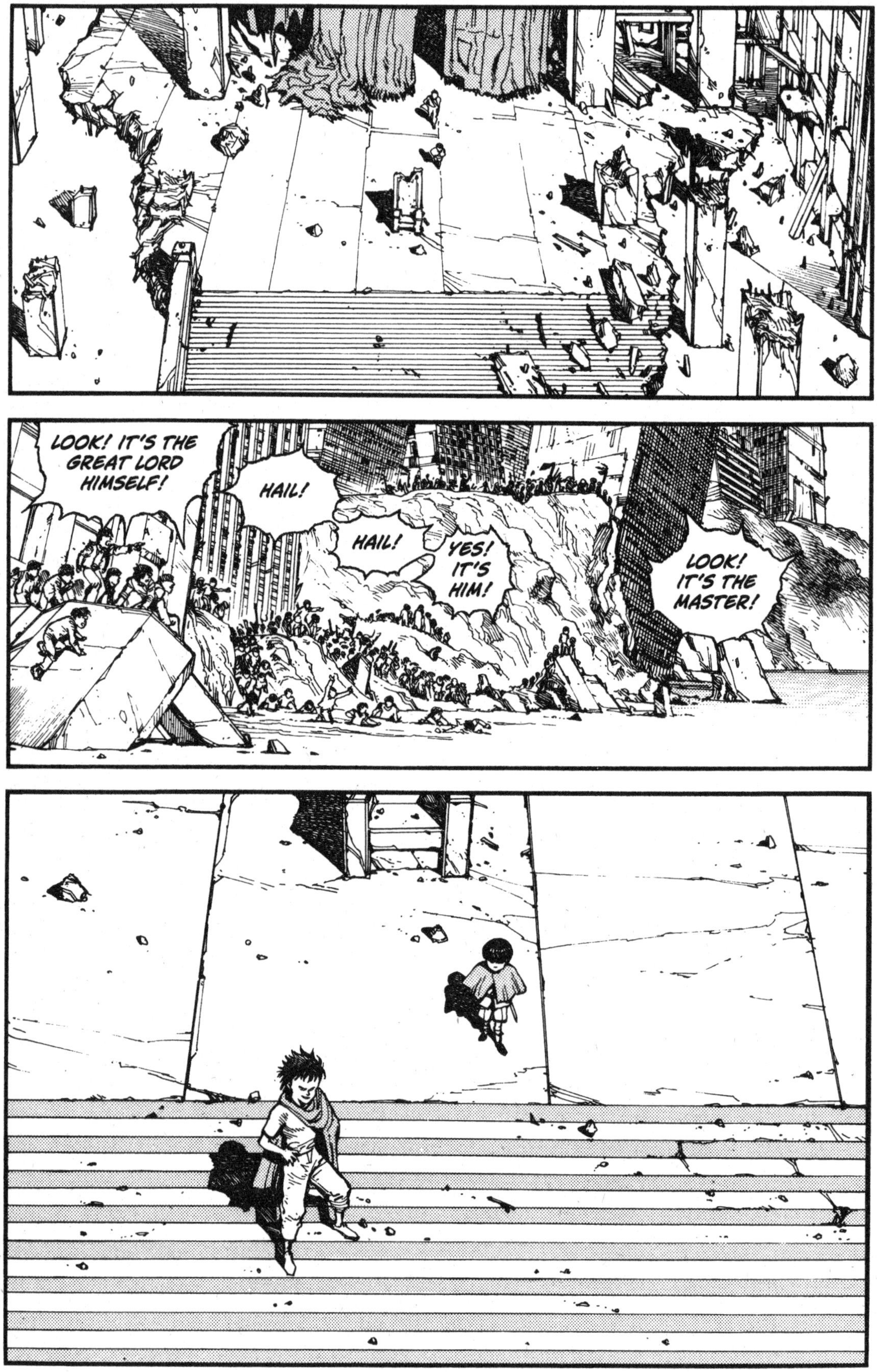
LOOK! IT'S THE GREAT LORD HIMSELF!
HAIL!
HAIL!
YES! IT'S HIM!
LOOK! IT'S THE MASTER!

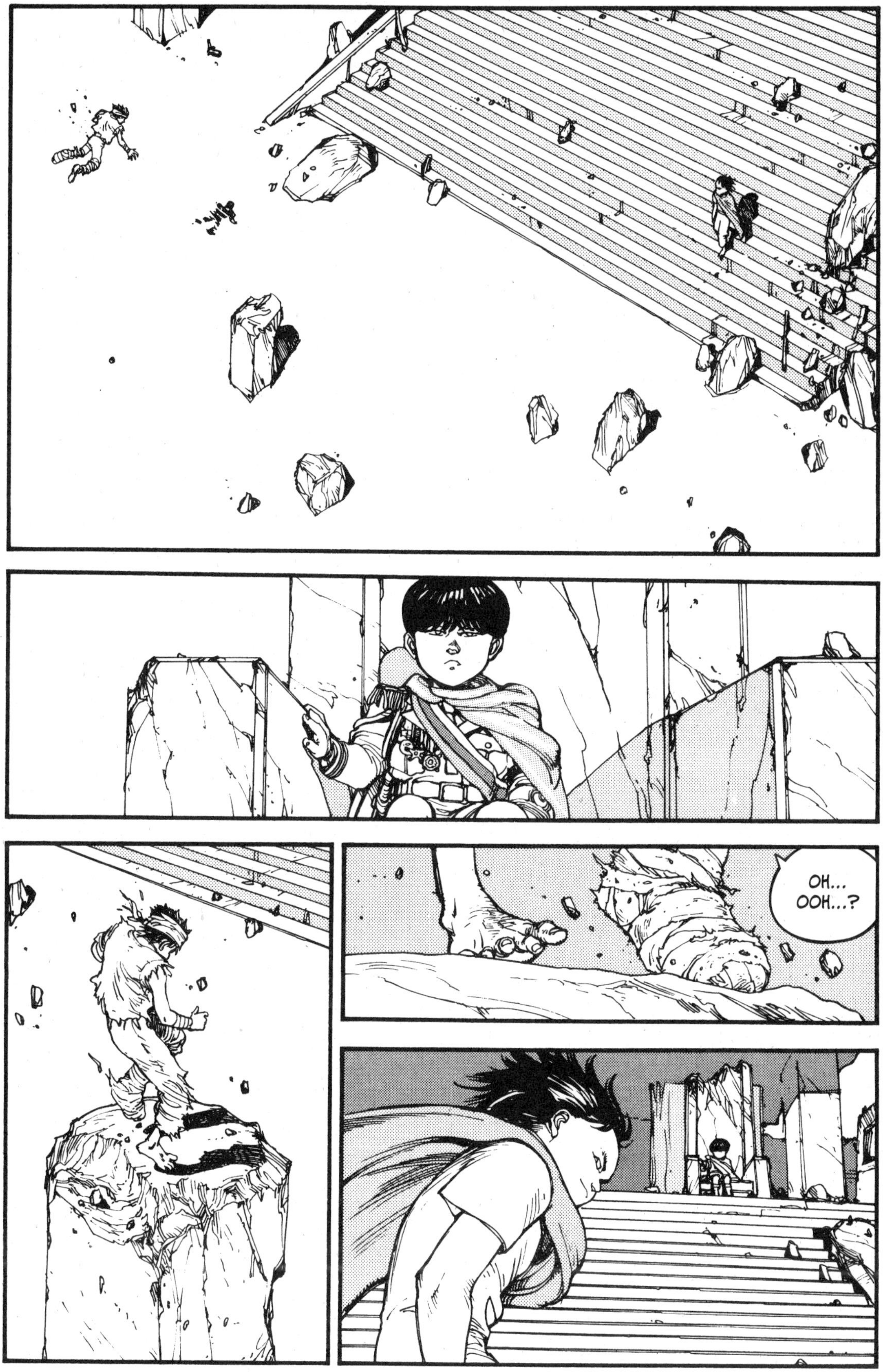
OH...
OOH...?

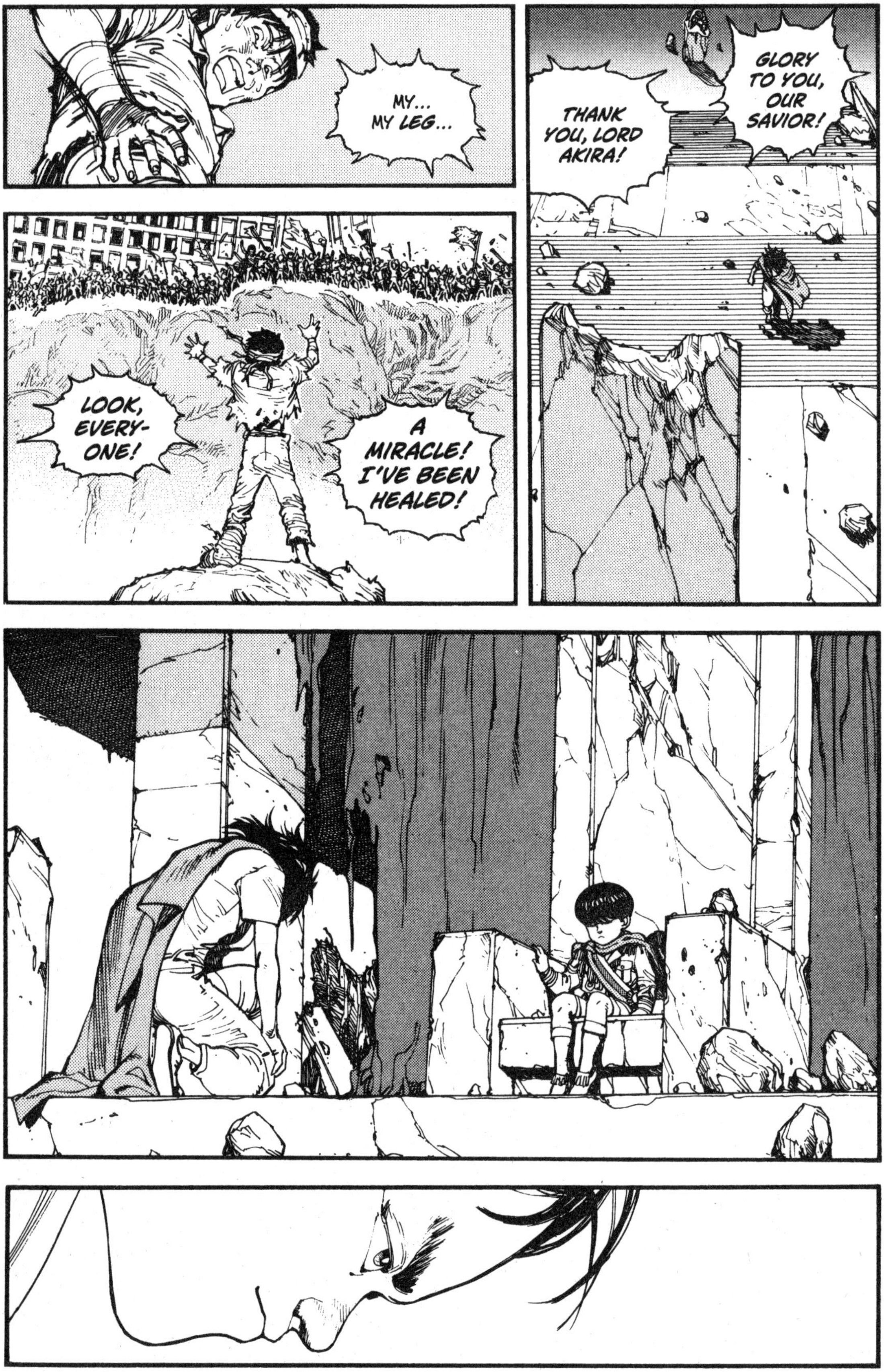
MY... MY LEG...
LOOK, EVERY-ONE!
A MIRACLE! I'VE BEEN HEALED!
THANK YOU, LORD AKIRA!
GLORY TO YOU, OUR SAVIOR!

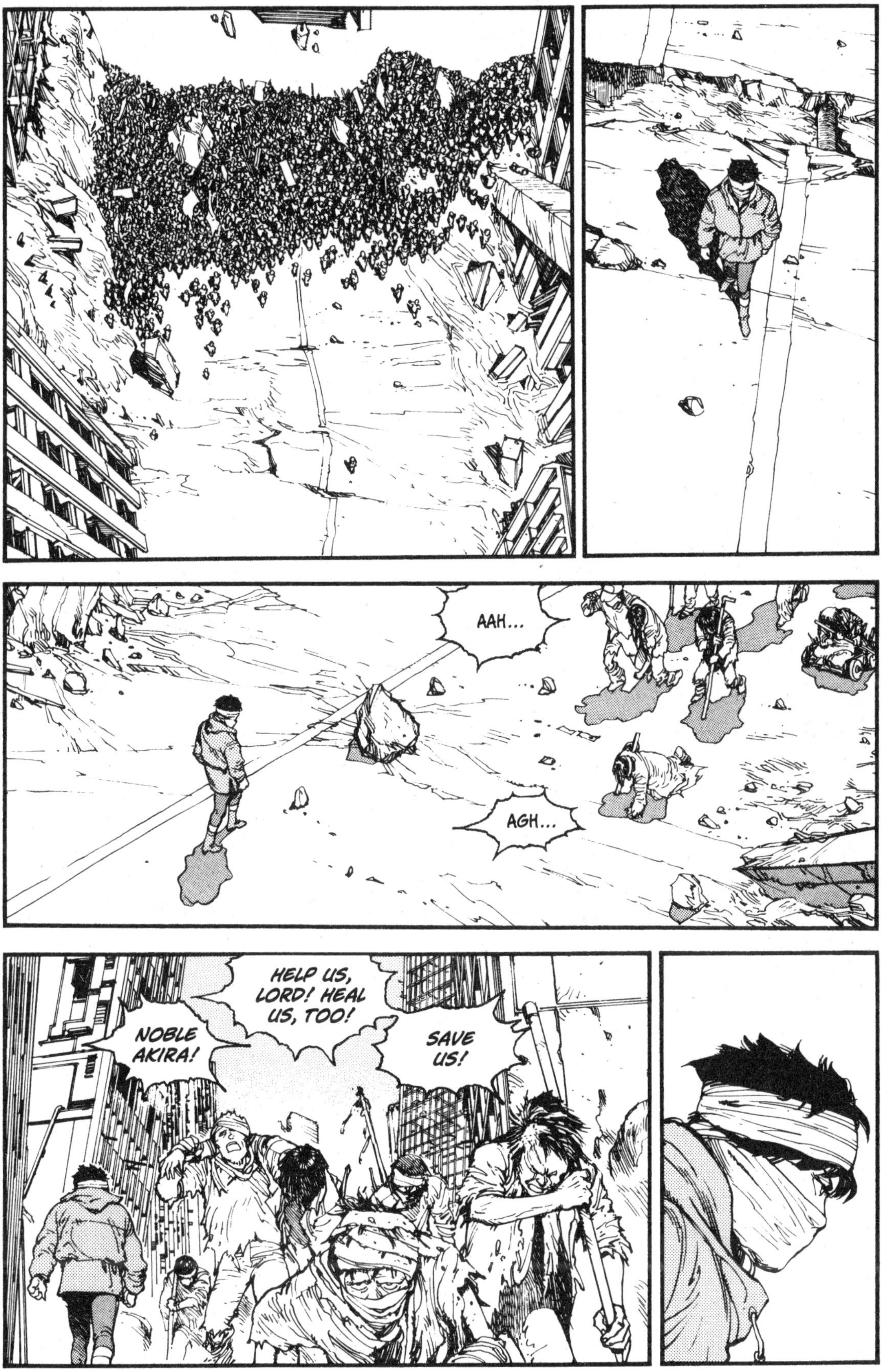
AAH...
AGH...
NOBLE AKIRA!
HELP US, LORD! HEAL US, TOO!
SAVE US!

HEH HEH
HEH!

...

LOOKS LIKE
WE GOT OUR-
SELVES A PIECE
OF ASS!

HOO-HO-
HAH!

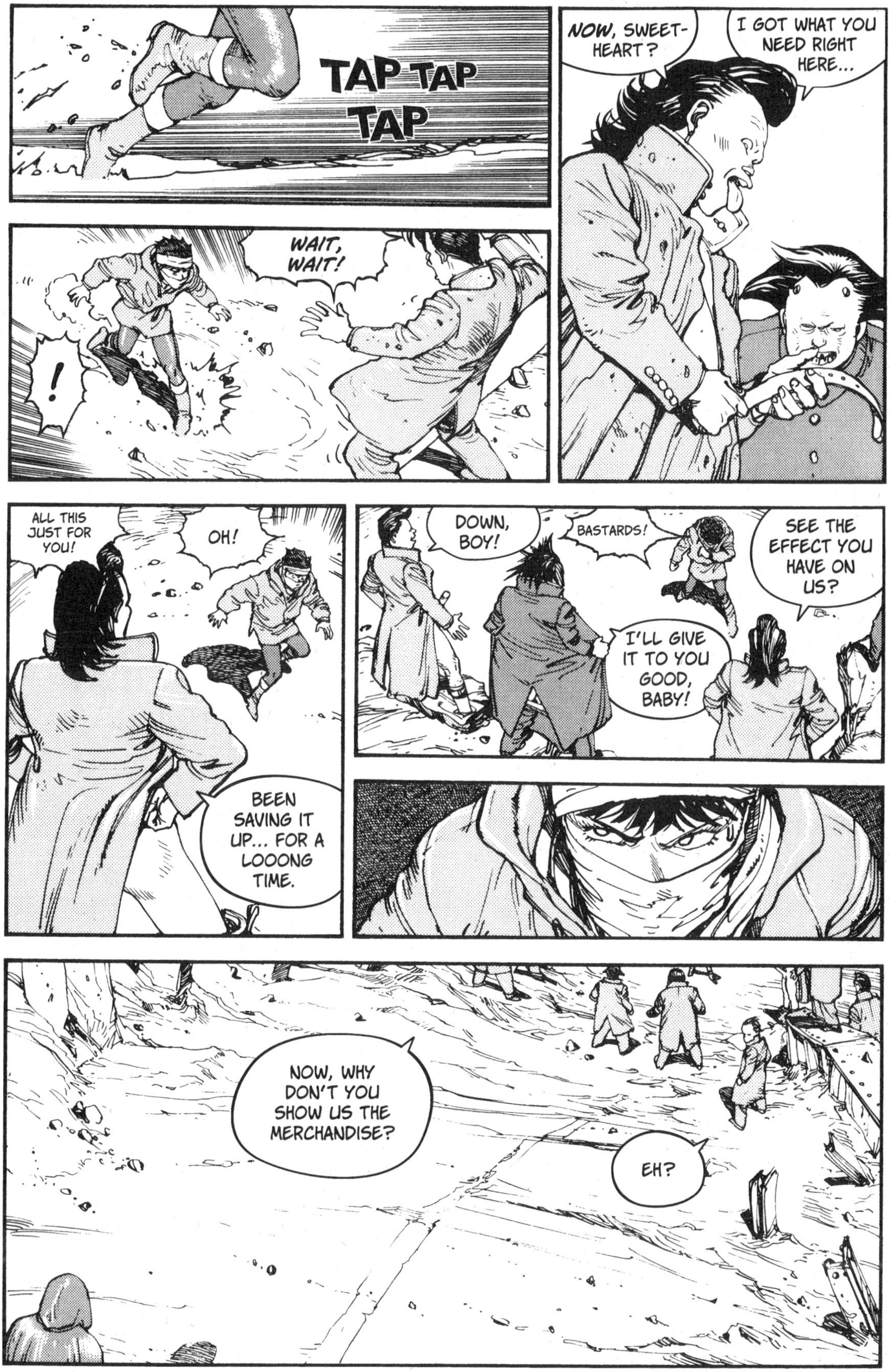
TAP TAP TAP
WAIT, WAIT!
!
NOW, SWEET-HEART?
I GOT WHAT YOU NEED RIGHT HERE...
ALL THIS JUST FOR YOU!
OH!
BEEN SAVING IT UP... FOR A LOOONG TIME.
DOWN, BOY!
BASTARDS!
SEE THE EFFECT YOU HAVE ON US?
I'LL GIVE IT TO YOU GOOD, BABY!
NOW, WHY DON'T YOU SHOW US THE MERCHANDISE?
EH?

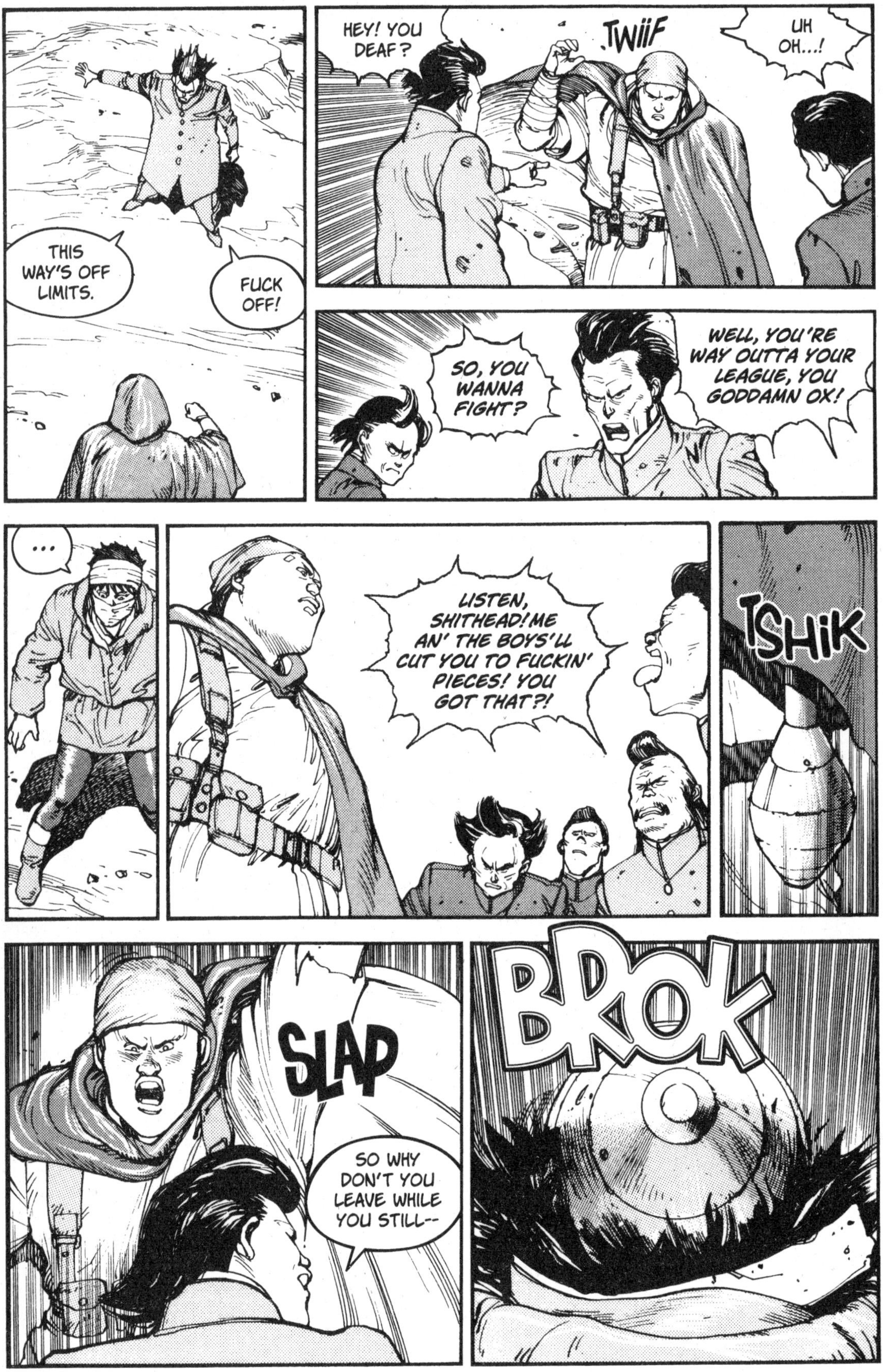
THIS WAY'S OFF LIMITS.
FUCK OFF!
HEY! YOU DEAF?
TWIIF
UH OH...!
SO, YOU WANNA FIGHT?
WELL, YOU'RE WAY OUTTA YOUR LEAGUE, YOU GODDAMN OX!
...
LISTEN, SHITHEAD! ME AN' THE BOYS'LL CUT YOU TO FUCKIN' PIECES! YOU GOT THAT?!
TSHIK
SLAP
SO WHY DON'T YOU LEAVE WHILE YOU STILL--
BROK

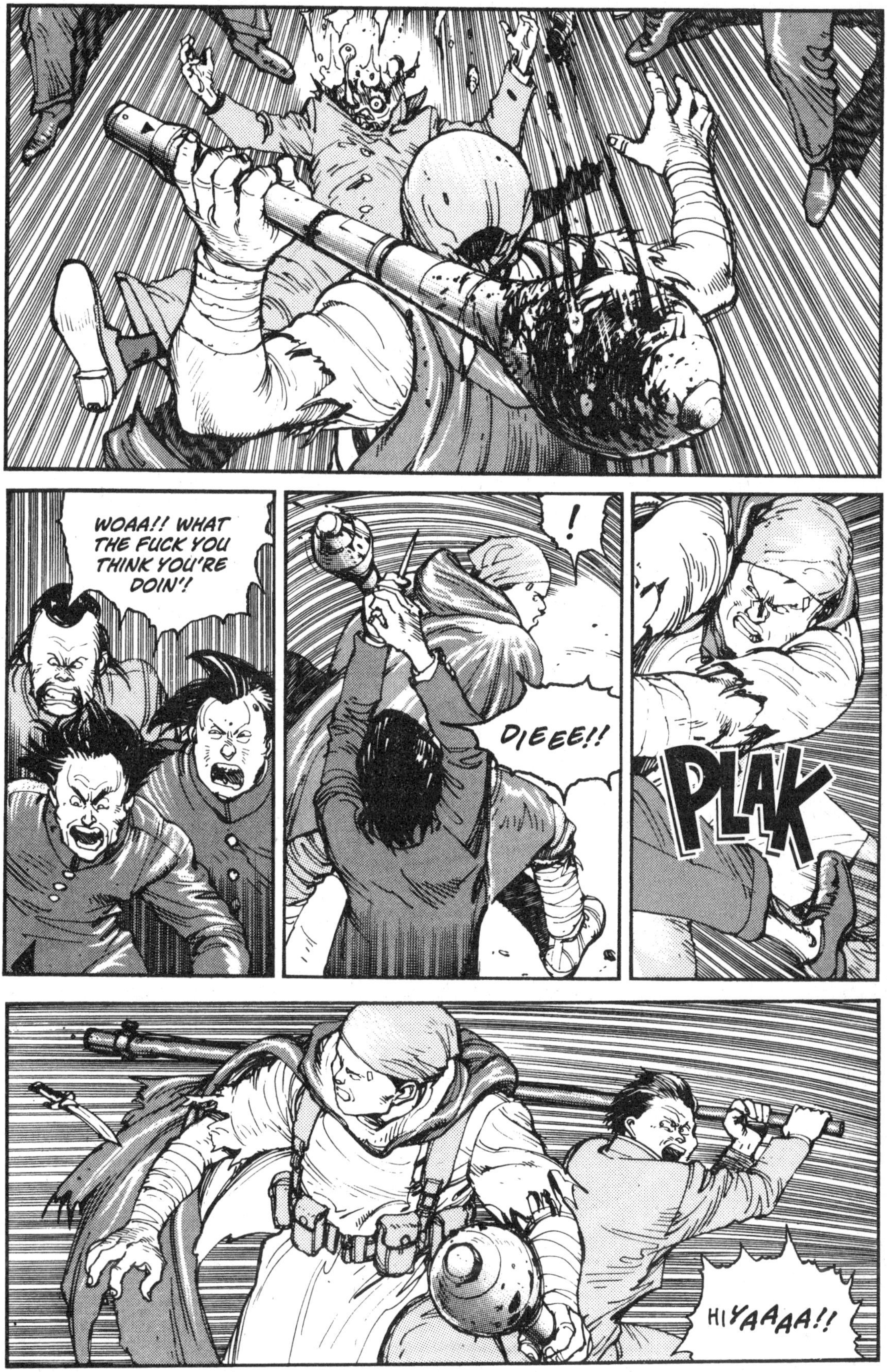
WOAA!! WHAT THE FUCK YOU THINK YOU'RE DOIN'!
!
DIEEE!!
PLAK
HIYAAAA!!

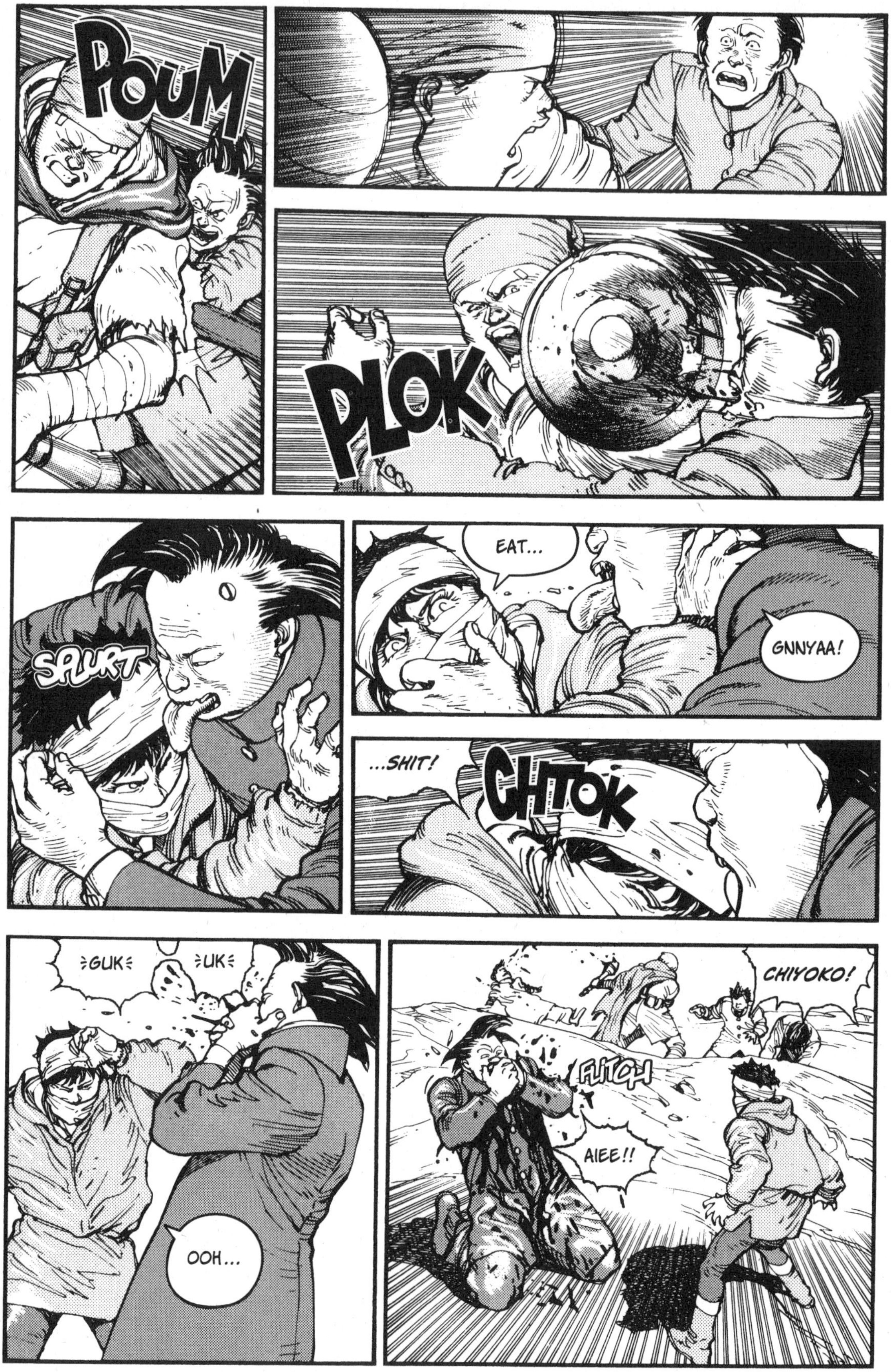
POUM
PLOK
SPLURT
EAT...
GNNYAA!
...SHIT!
CHTOK
GUK
UK
OOH...
CHIYOKO!
FLITCH
AIEE!!

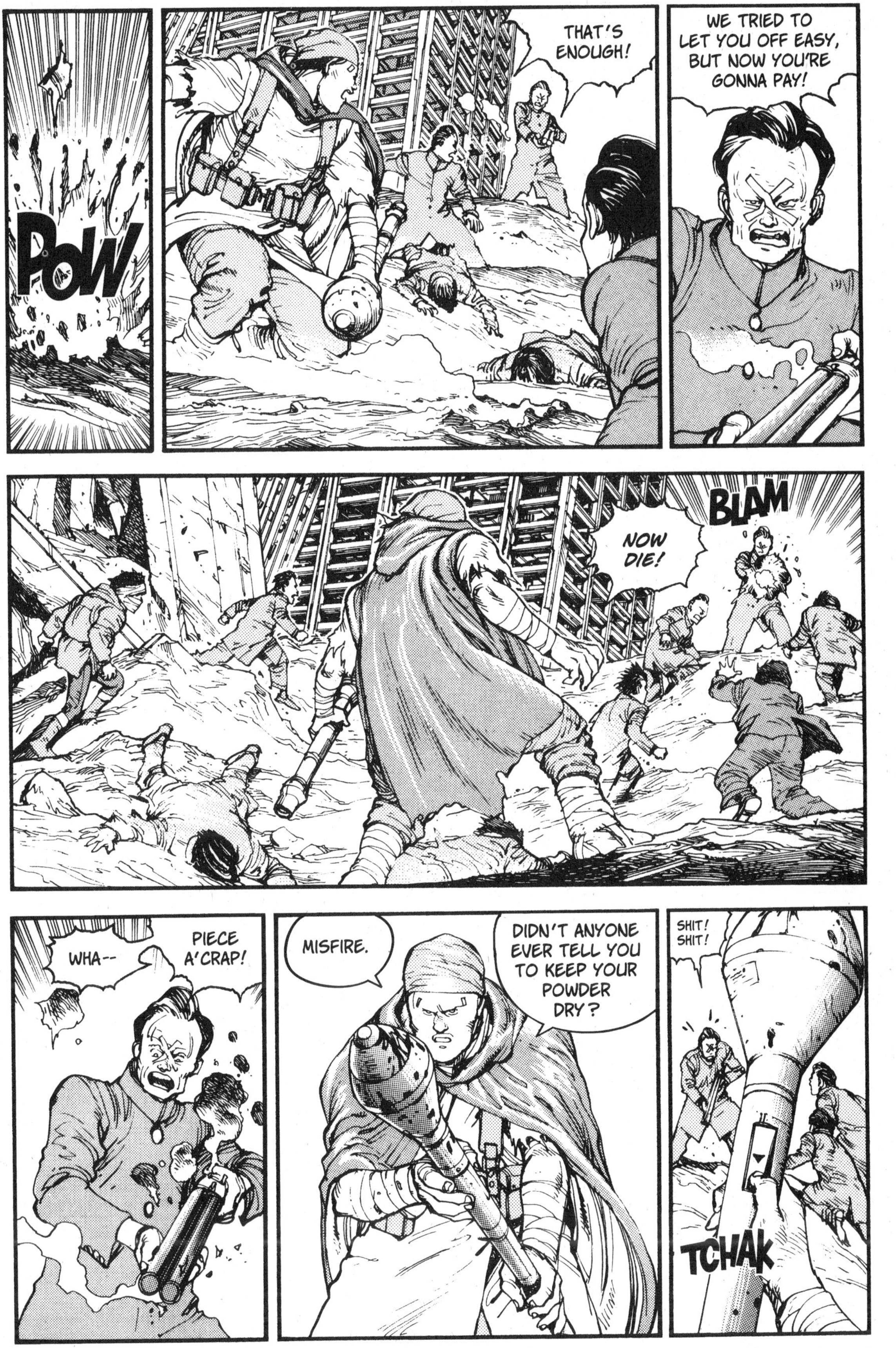
POW
THAT'S ENOUGH!
WE TRIED TO LET YOU OFF EASY, BUT NOW YOU'RE GONNA PAY!
NOW DIE!
BLAM
WHA--
PIECE A'CRAP!
MISFIRE.
DIDN'T ANYONE EVER TELL YOU TO KEEP YOUR POWDER DRY?
SHIT! SHIT!
TCHAK

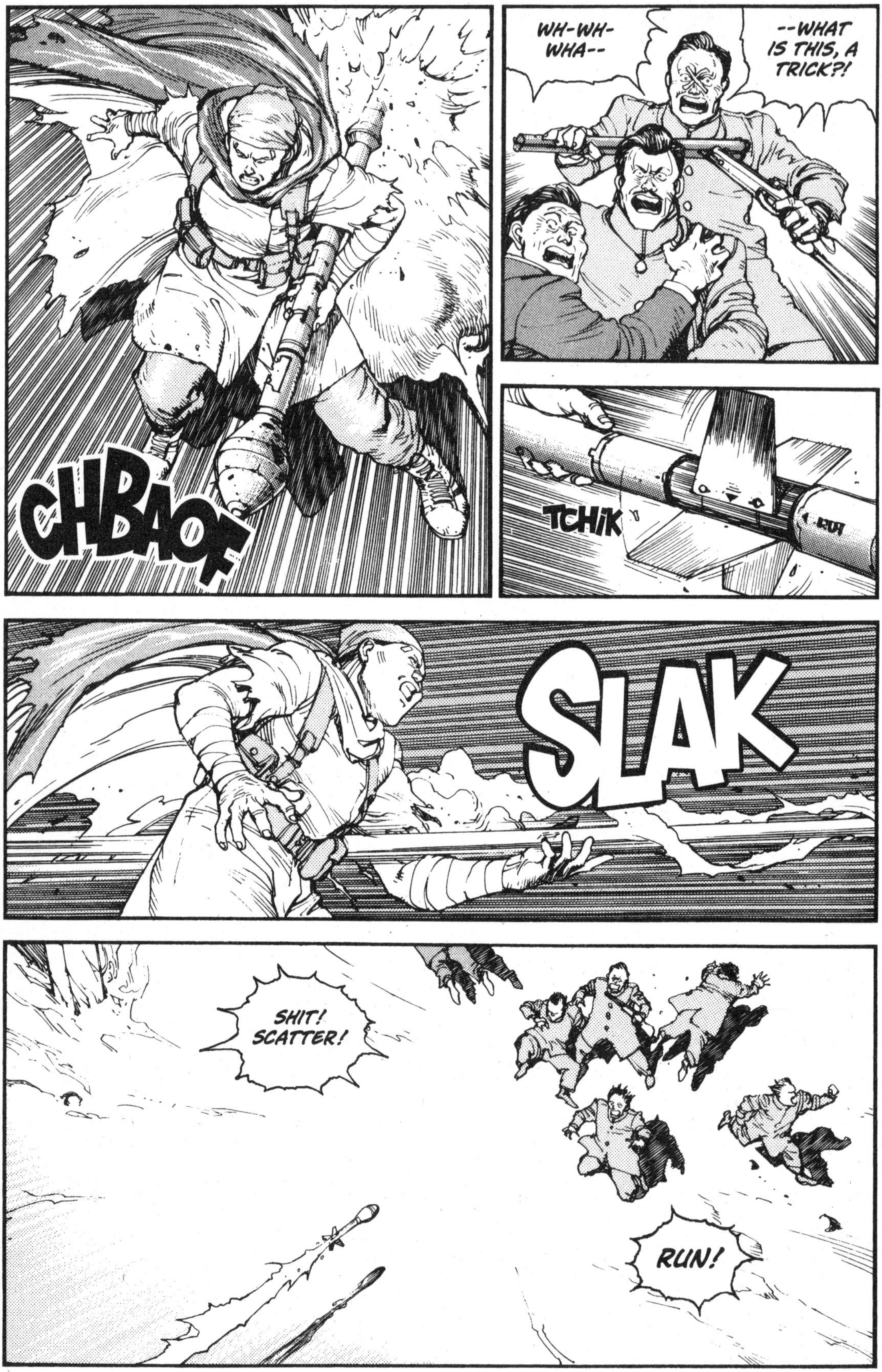
CHBAOF
WH-WH-
WHA--
--WHAT
IS THIS, A
TRICK?!
TCHIK
SLAK
SHIT!
SCATTER!
RUN!

BOOM

I'M OKAY... JUST A LITTLE SICK TO MY STOMACH.

YOU ALL RIGHT, KEI?

THESE CREEPS MAKE WE WANT TO *PUKE*...

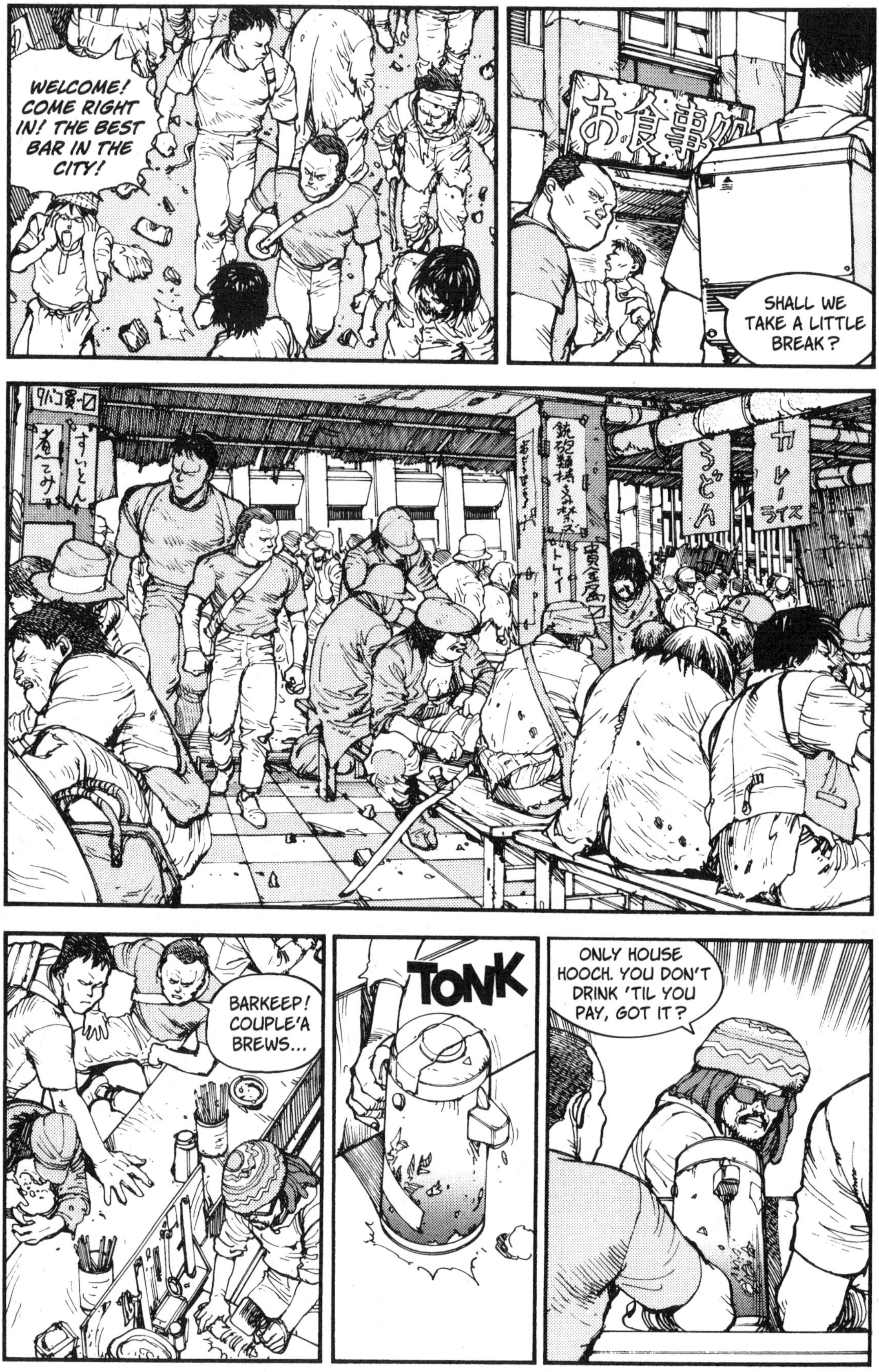
WELCOME! COME RIGHT IN! THE BEST BAR IN THE CITY!
SHALL WE TAKE A LITTLE BREAK?
うどん
カレーライス
BARKEEP! COUPLE'A BREWS...
TONK
ONLY HOUSE HOOCH. YOU DON'T DRINK 'TIL YOU PAY, GOT IT?

OKAY... HOW MUCH?

THAT *PAPER'S* NO GOOD AROUND HERE!

WHERE HAVE *YOU* BEEN?

BROM

SHOW ME SOMETHING OF *VALUE*...

WE ACCEPT SOLAR CELLS... ANTIBIOTICS... TOBACCO... SHOES...

SOMETHING LIKE *THESE*...

BLINK

HOW ABOUT...

...THIS?

NOT BAD. YOU'LL EVEN GET SOME *CHANGE*.

KEEP IT. MAYBE YOU CAN TELL ME WHAT'S BEEN GOING ON.

MY FRIEND AND I ARE A LITTLE BEHIND THE TIMES. WE ONLY CAME OUT OF THE SHELTER YESTERDAY.

YEAH, SO...?

WHAT IS THIS "GREAT TOKYO EMPIRE" I KEEP HEARING ABOUT? I GET THE FEELING IT'S NOT JUST SOME JOKE.

YOU'RE TALKING ABOUT THAT GROUP IN THE WESTERN DISTRICTS--THEY WORSHIP SOME KID... *AKIRA*, I THINK THEY CALL HIM.

SOUNDS LIKE SOME KIND OF MESSIAH. THEY SAY HE CAN PERFORM MIRACLES.

EH, JUST ANOTHER NEW CULT TO FLEECE THE SHEEP...

AKIRA...

ALL I KNOW IS WHAT I HEAR, BUT PEOPLE SAY HE'S GOT AN OLDER KID WITH HIM...

...CALLED *TETSURO* OR *TETSUO*...SOMETHING LIKE THAT. THEY'RE OUT TO BUILD A PERFECT WORLD. PERFECT FOR *THEM*, ALL RIGHT...

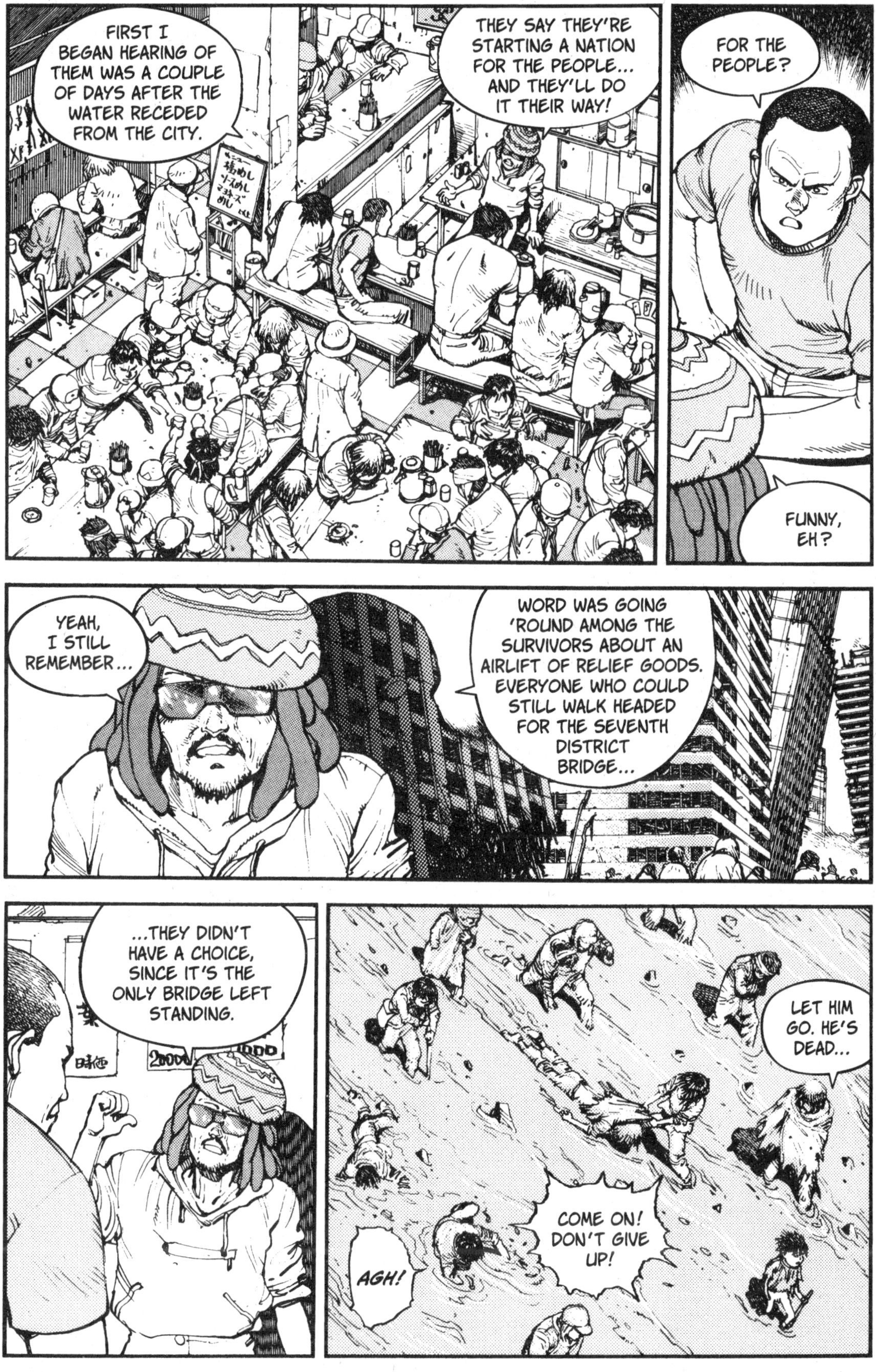
FIRST I BEGAN HEARING OF THEM WAS A COUPLE OF DAYS AFTER THE WATER RECEDED FROM THE CITY.
THEY SAY THEY'RE STARTING A NATION FOR THE PEOPLE... AND THEY'LL DO IT THEIR WAY!
FOR THE PEOPLE?
FUNNY, EH?
YEAH, I STILL REMEMBER...
WORD WAS GOING 'ROUND AMONG THE SURVIVORS ABOUT AN AIRLIFT OF RELIEF GOODS. EVERYONE WHO COULD STILL WALK HEADED FOR THE SEVENTH DISTRICT BRIDGE...
...THEY DIDN'T HAVE A CHOICE, SINCE IT'S THE ONLY BRIDGE LEFT STANDING.
LET HIM GO. HE'S DEAD...
COME ON! DON'T GIVE UP!
AGH!

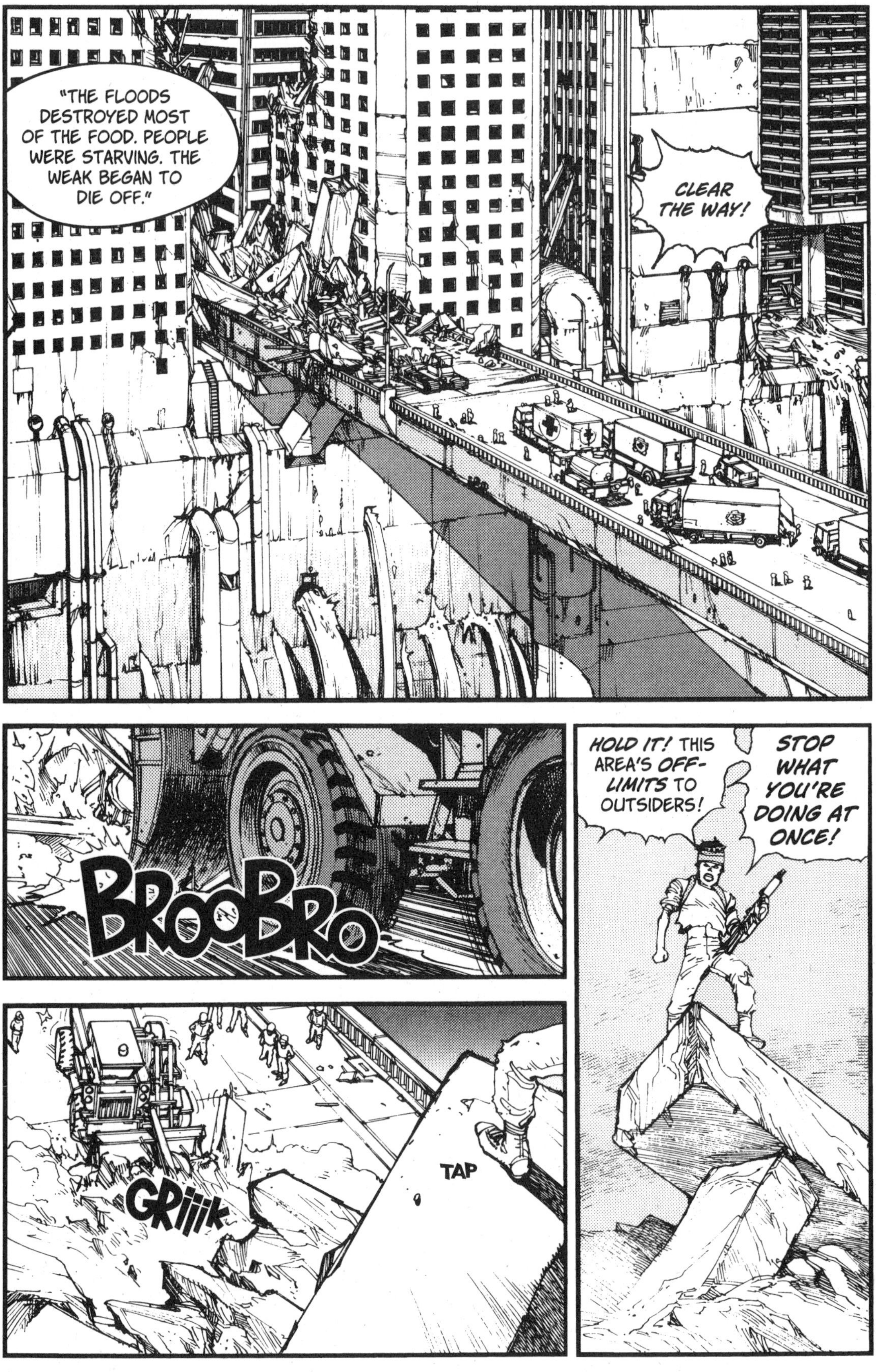
"THE FLOODS DESTROYED MOST OF THE FOOD. PEOPLE WERE STARVING. THE WEAK BEGAN TO DIE OFF."
CLEAR THE WAY!
BROOBRO
GRiiiik
TAP
HOLD IT! THIS AREA'S OFF-LIMITS TO OUTSIDERS!
STOP WHAT YOU'RE DOING AT ONCE!

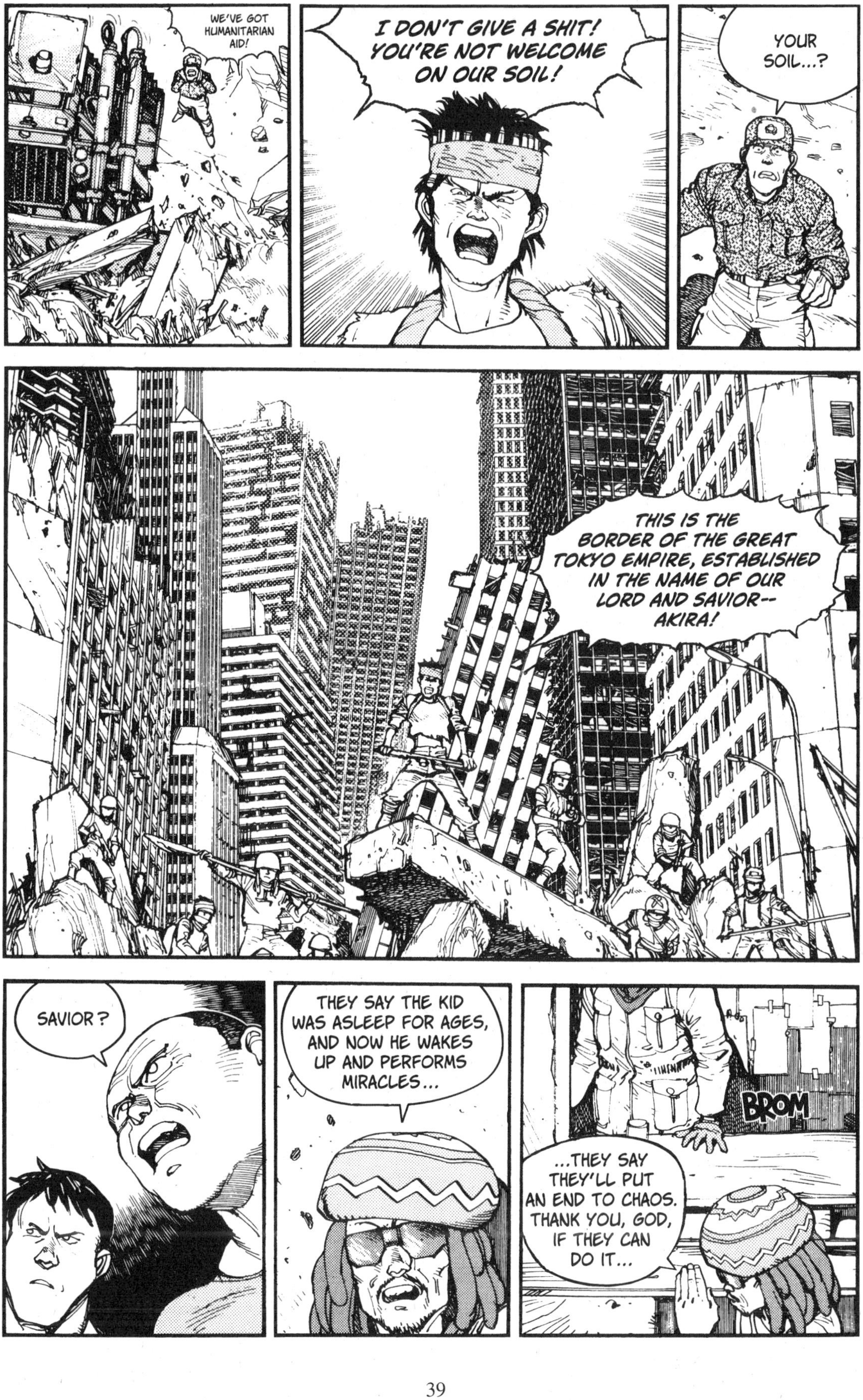
WE'VE GOT HUMANITARIAN AID!
I DON'T GIVE A SHIT! YOU'RE NOT WELCOME ON OUR SOIL!
YOUR SOIL...?
THIS IS THE BORDER OF THE GREAT TOKYO EMPIRE, ESTABLISHED IN THE NAME OF OUR LORD AND SAVIOR-- AKIRA!
SAVIOR?
THEY SAY THE KID WAS ASLEEP FOR AGES, AND NOW HE WAKES UP AND PERFORMS MIRACLES...
BROM
...THEY SAY THEY'LL PUT AN END TO CHAOS. THANK YOU, GOD, IF THEY CAN DO IT...

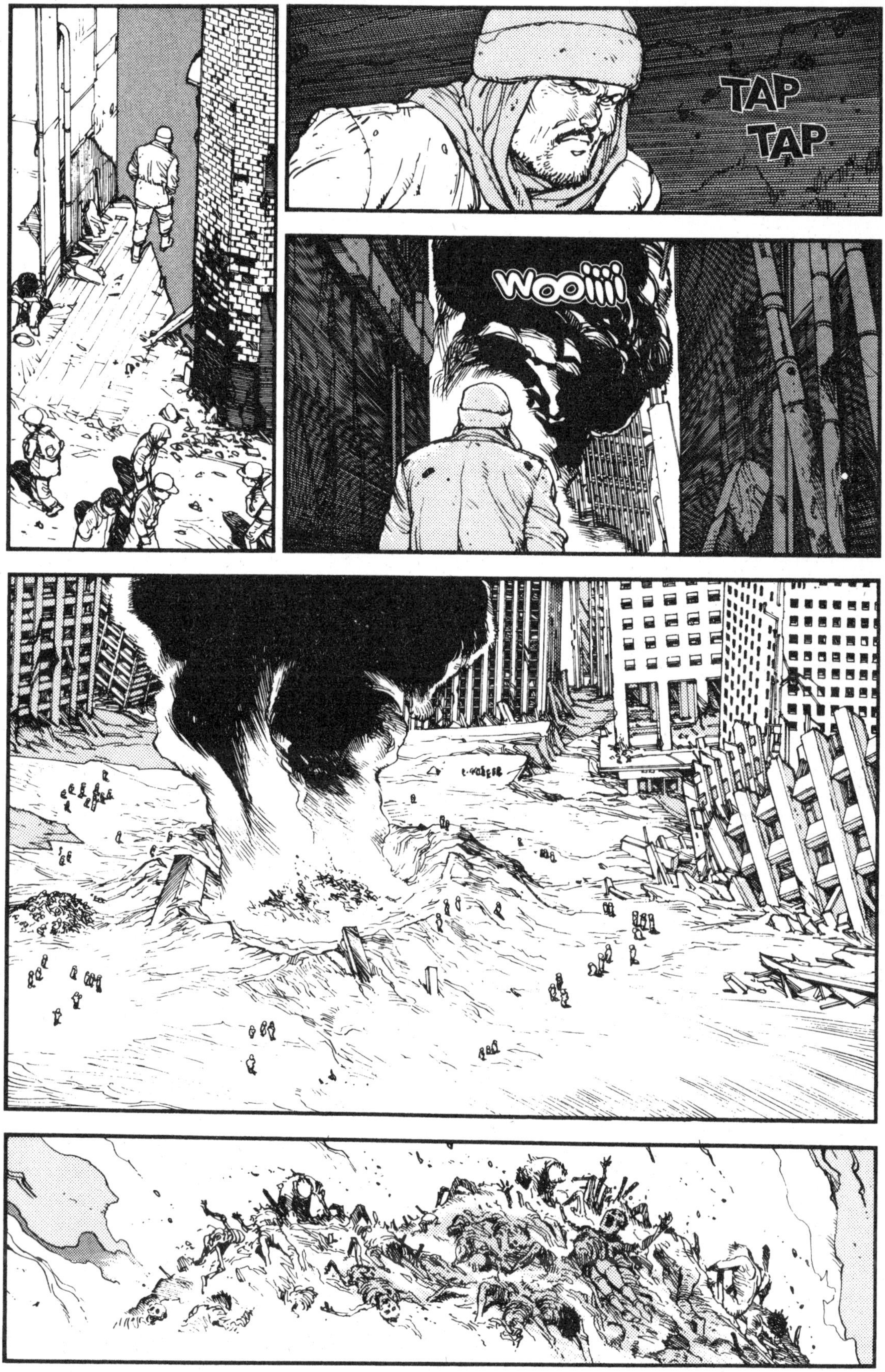
TAP
TAP
Wooiiii

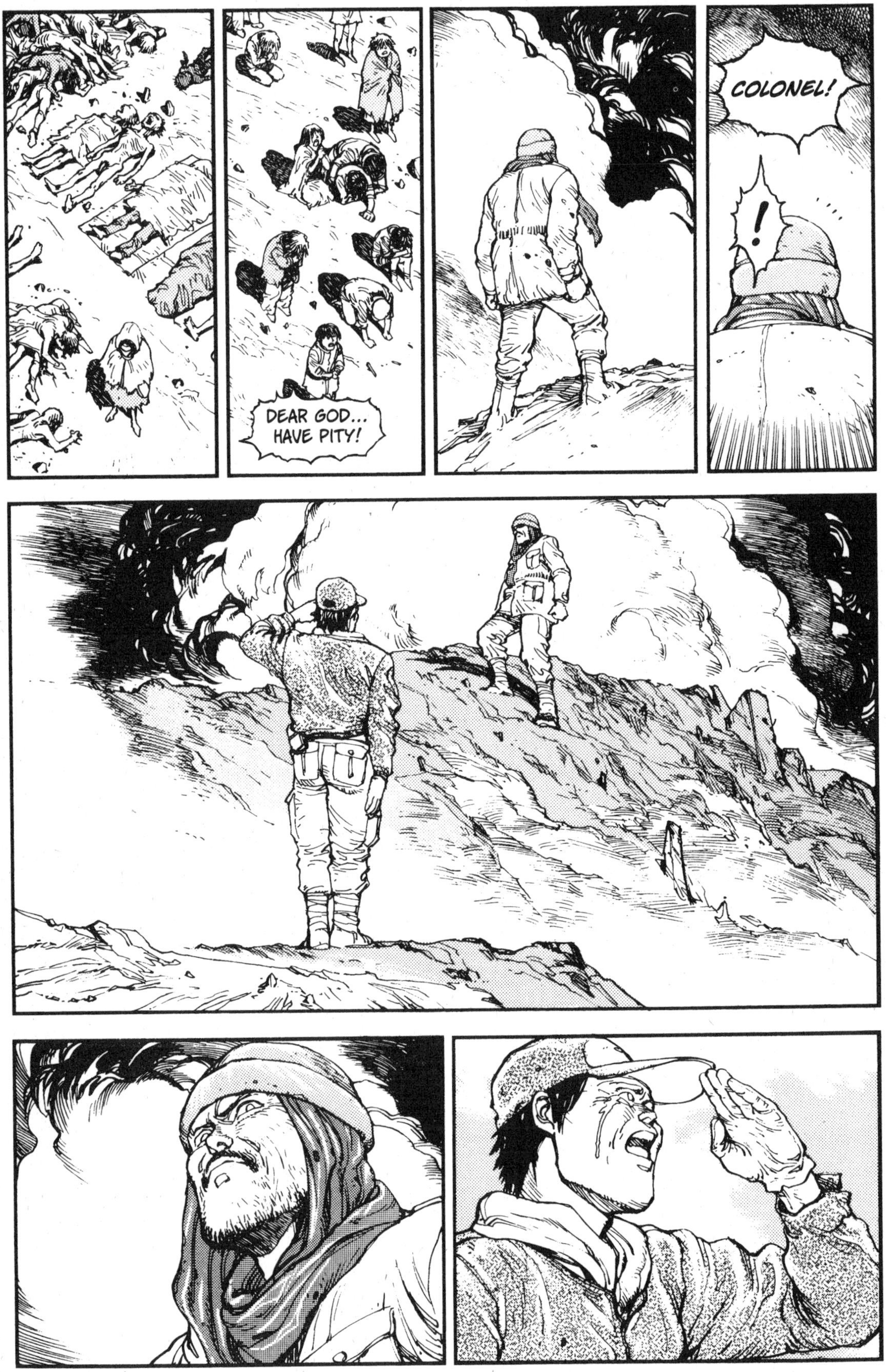
DEAR GOD... HAVE PITY!
COLONEL!
!

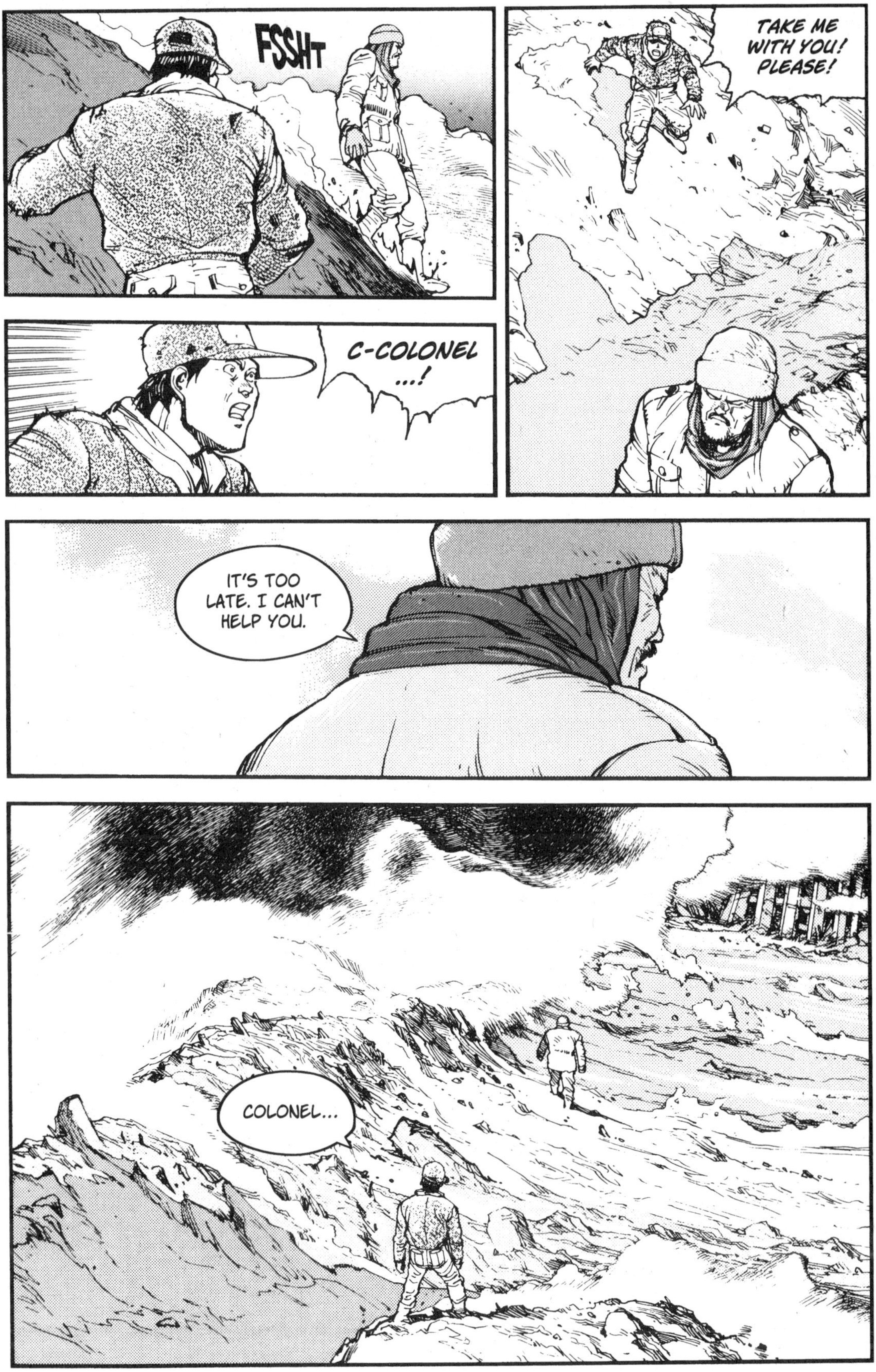
FSSHT
C-COLONEL ...!
TAKE ME WITH YOU! PLEASE!
IT'S TOO LATE. I CAN'T HELP YOU.
COLONEL...

SO FAR, SO GOOD. NO ONE'S TAILING US.

HOW'RE WE DOING?

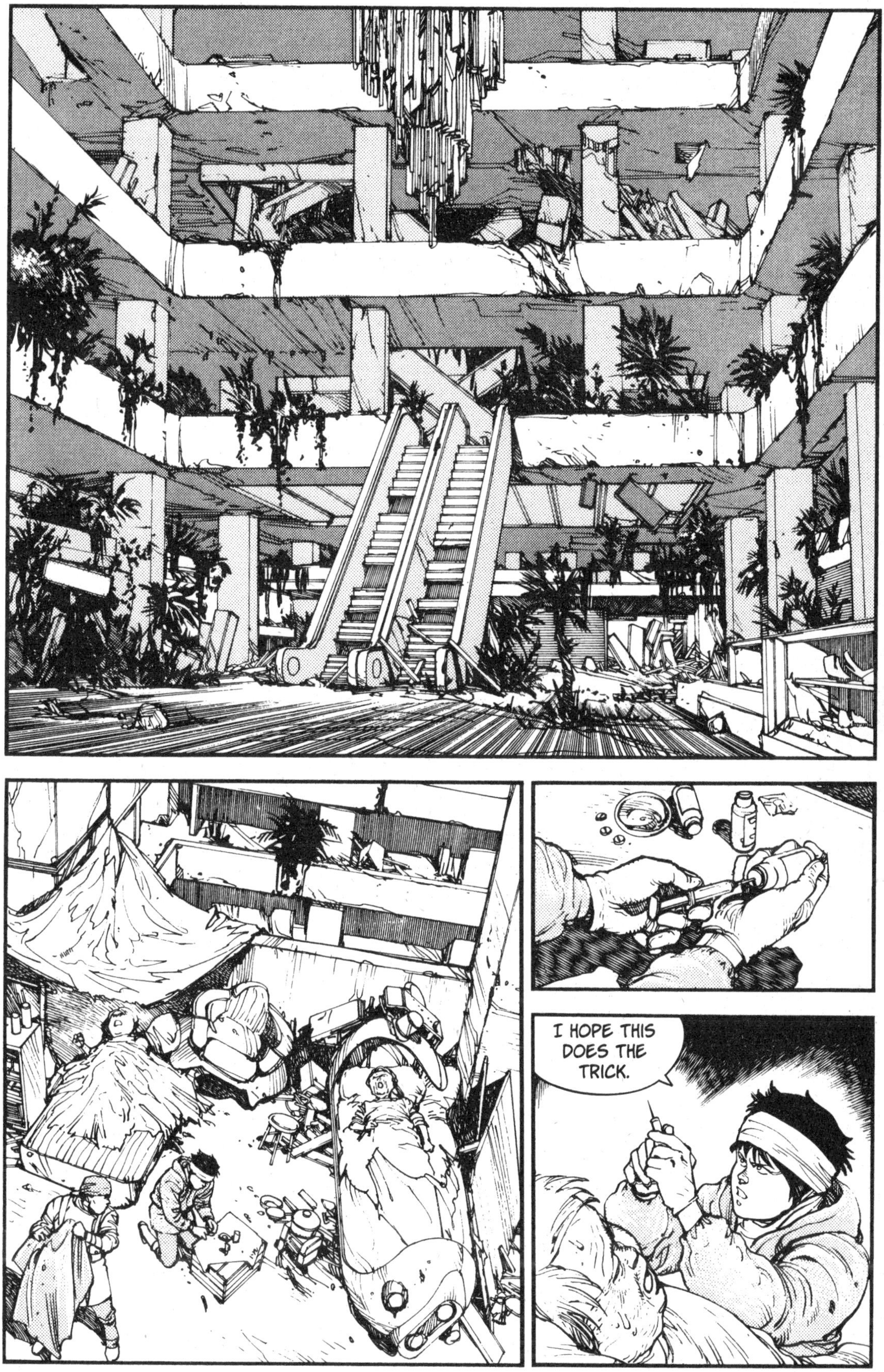
I HOPE THIS DOES THE TRICK.

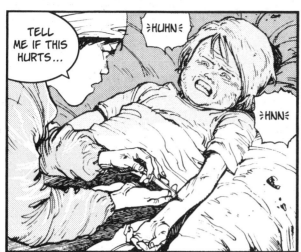

TELL ME IF THIS HURTS...

≋HUHN≋

≋HNN≋

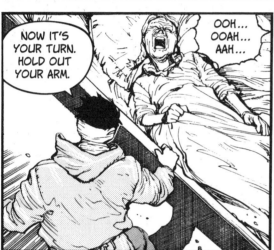

NOW IT'S YOUR TURN. HOLD OUT YOUR ARM.

OOH... OOAH... AAH...

IT'S ALMOST GONE...

THIS IS ALL I HAVE...

WHAT?! WHAT ARE YOU TRYING TO TELL ME?

...N-NU...

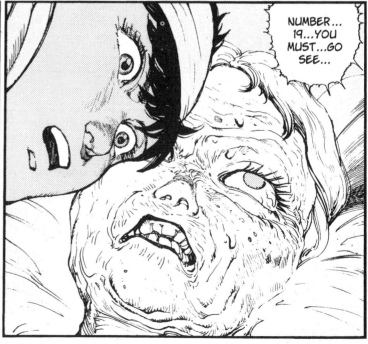

NUMBER... 19...YOU MUST...GO SEE...

NUMBER 19?!

TALK TO ME!

TELL ME WHAT DO DO?!

LADY MIYAKO...?

LORD AKIRA IN THE WEST VERSUS LADY MIYAKO IN THE EAST. SHE'S BEEN TAKING IN THE WOUNDED AND OFFERING RELIEF TO DISASTER VICTIMS...

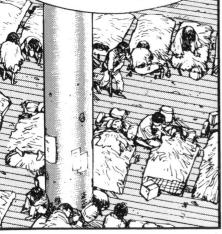

"THE SICK, THE HUNGRY, THE HOMELESS, STREET KIDS...SHE HELPS 'EM ALL. HER POPULARITY IS GOING THROUGH THE ROOF... SHE'S GETTING A LOT OF DEVOUT FOLLOWERS, AND HER INFLUENCE IS INCREASING..."

"SOME EVEN SAY SHE HAS SUPERNATURAL POWERS, TOO..."

"I DON'T KNOW WHETHER IT'S TRUE OR NOT..."

"...BUT NOW THERE'S *TWO* TOP DOGS IN NEO-TOKYO."

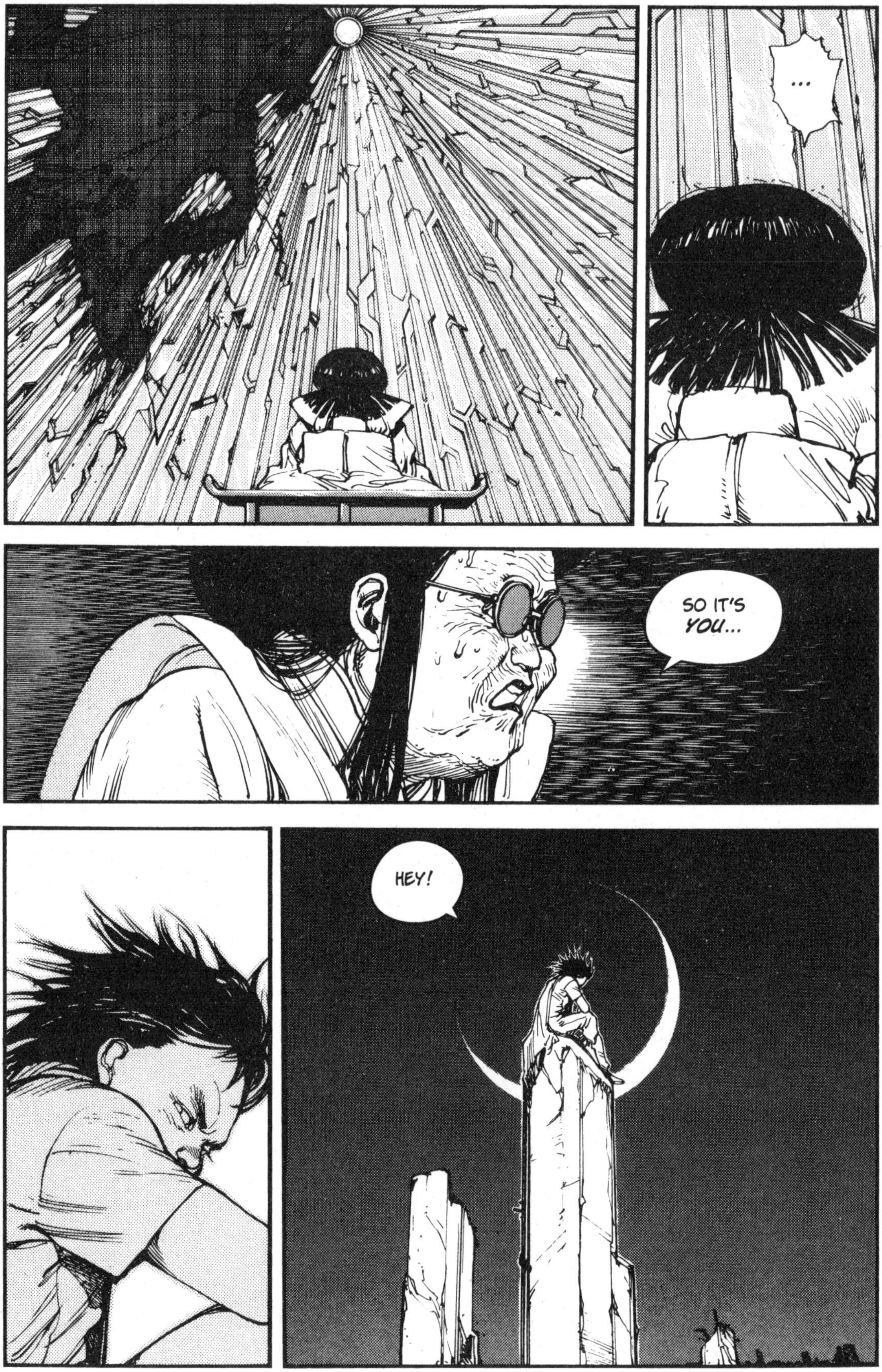
...
SO IT'S YOU...
HEY!

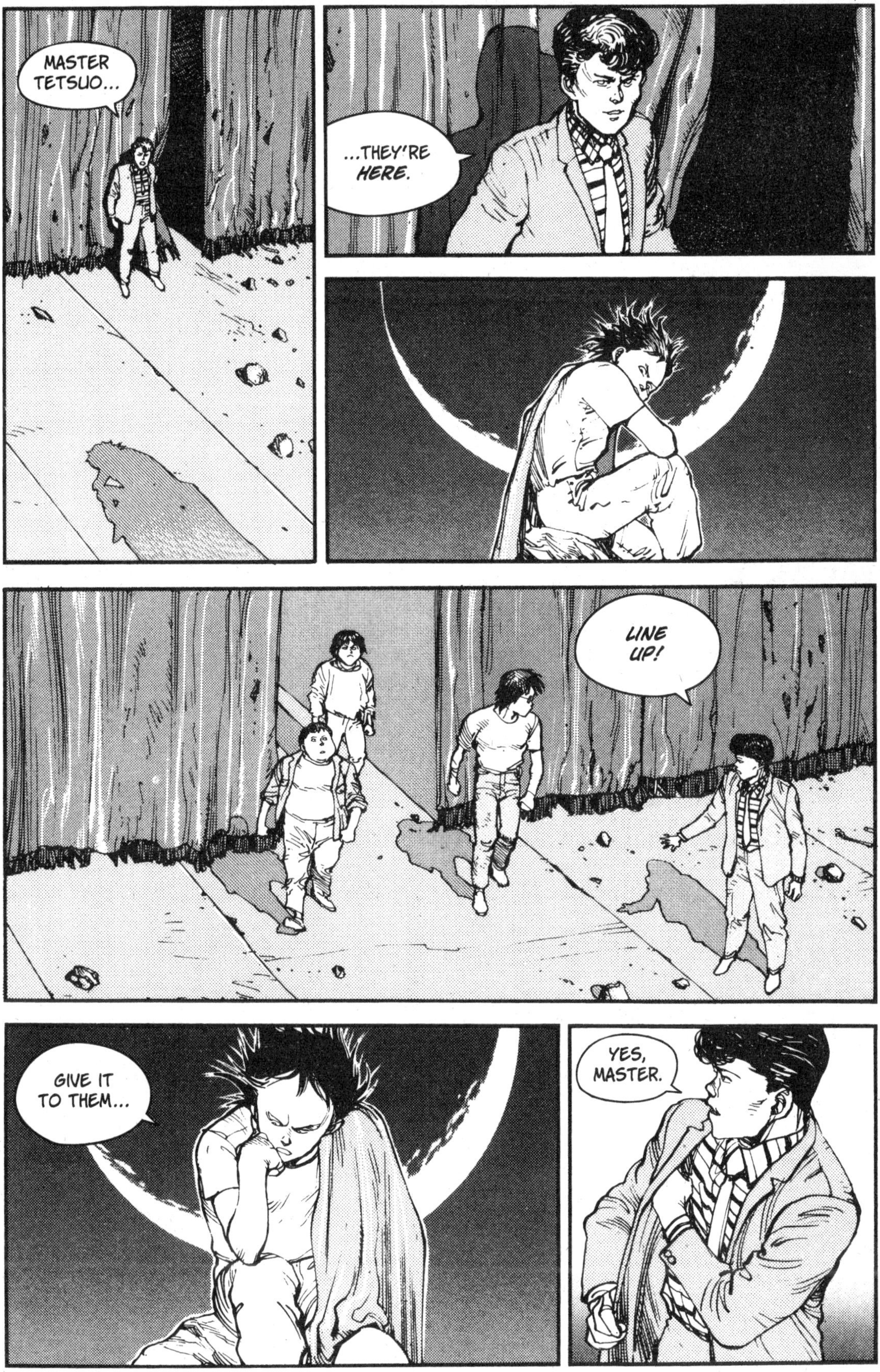
MASTER TETSUO...
...THEY'RE *HERE.*
LINE UP!
GIVE IT TO THEM...
YES, MASTER.

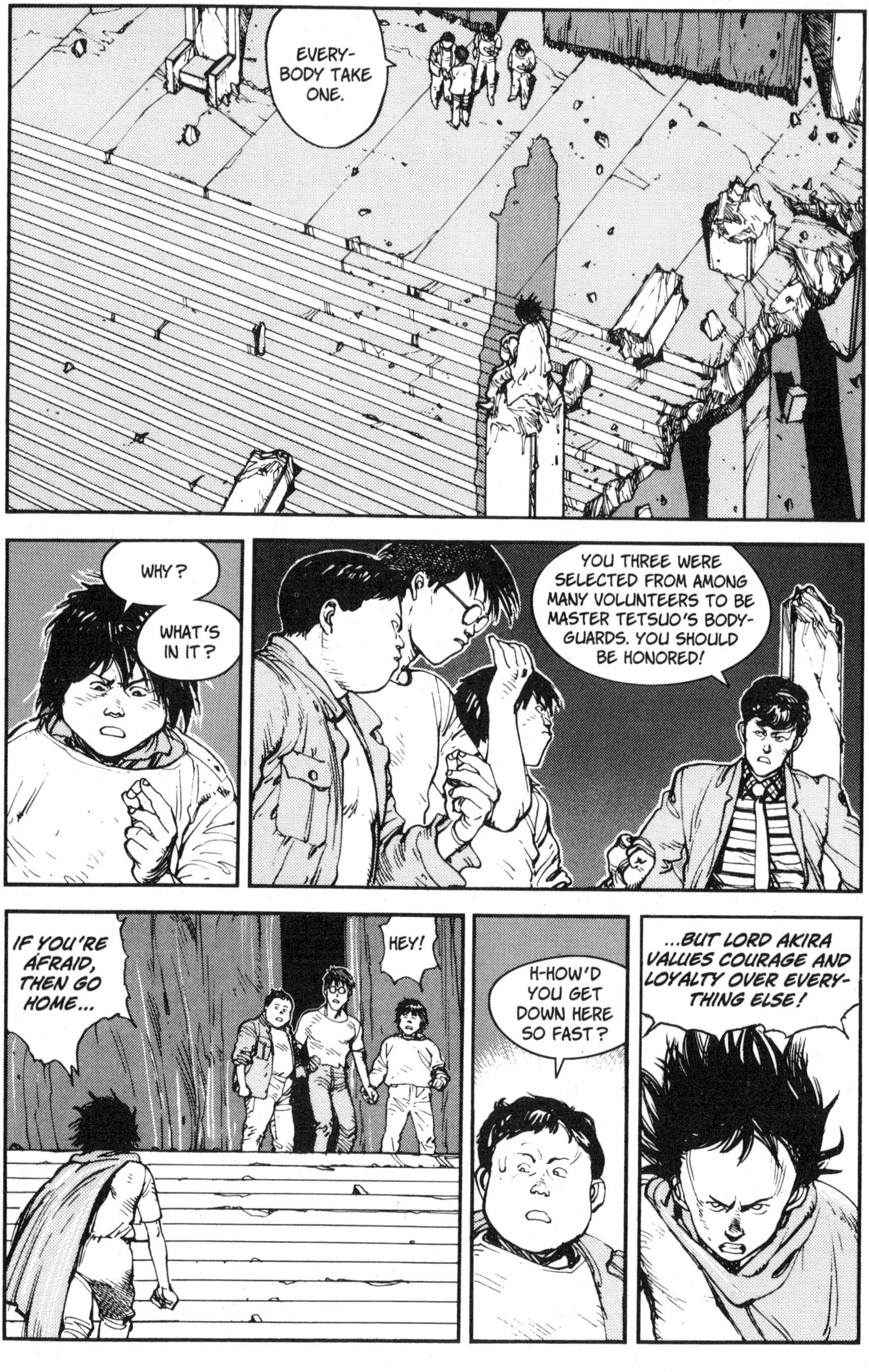

EVERY-BODY TAKE ONE.
WHY?
WHAT'S IN IT?
YOU THREE WERE SELECTED FROM AMONG MANY VOLUNTEERS TO BE MASTER TETSUO'S BODY-GUARDS. YOU SHOULD BE HONORED!
IF YOU'RE AFRAID, THEN GO HOME...
HEY!
H-HOW'D YOU GET DOWN HERE SO FAST?
...BUT LORD AKIRA VALUES COURAGE AND LOYALTY OVER EVERY-THING ELSE!

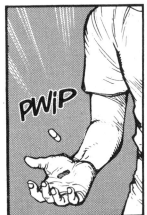

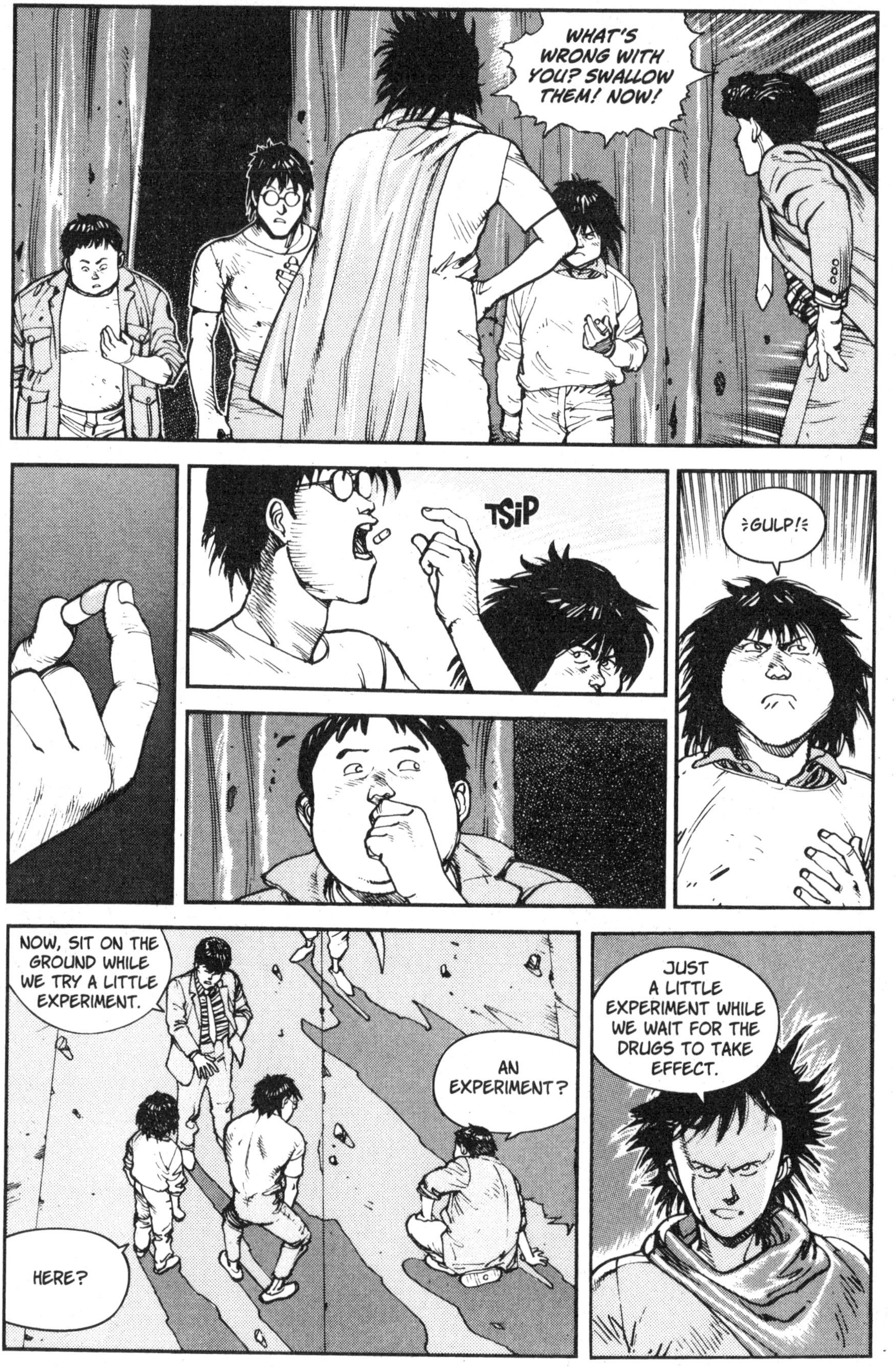
WHAT'S WRONG WITH YOU? SWALLOW THEM! NOW!
TSIP
GULP!
NOW, SIT ON THE GROUND WHILE WE TRY A LITTLE EXPERIMENT.
HERE?
AN EXPERIMENT?
JUST A LITTLE EXPERIMENT WHILE WE WAIT FOR THE DRUGS TO TAKE EFFECT.

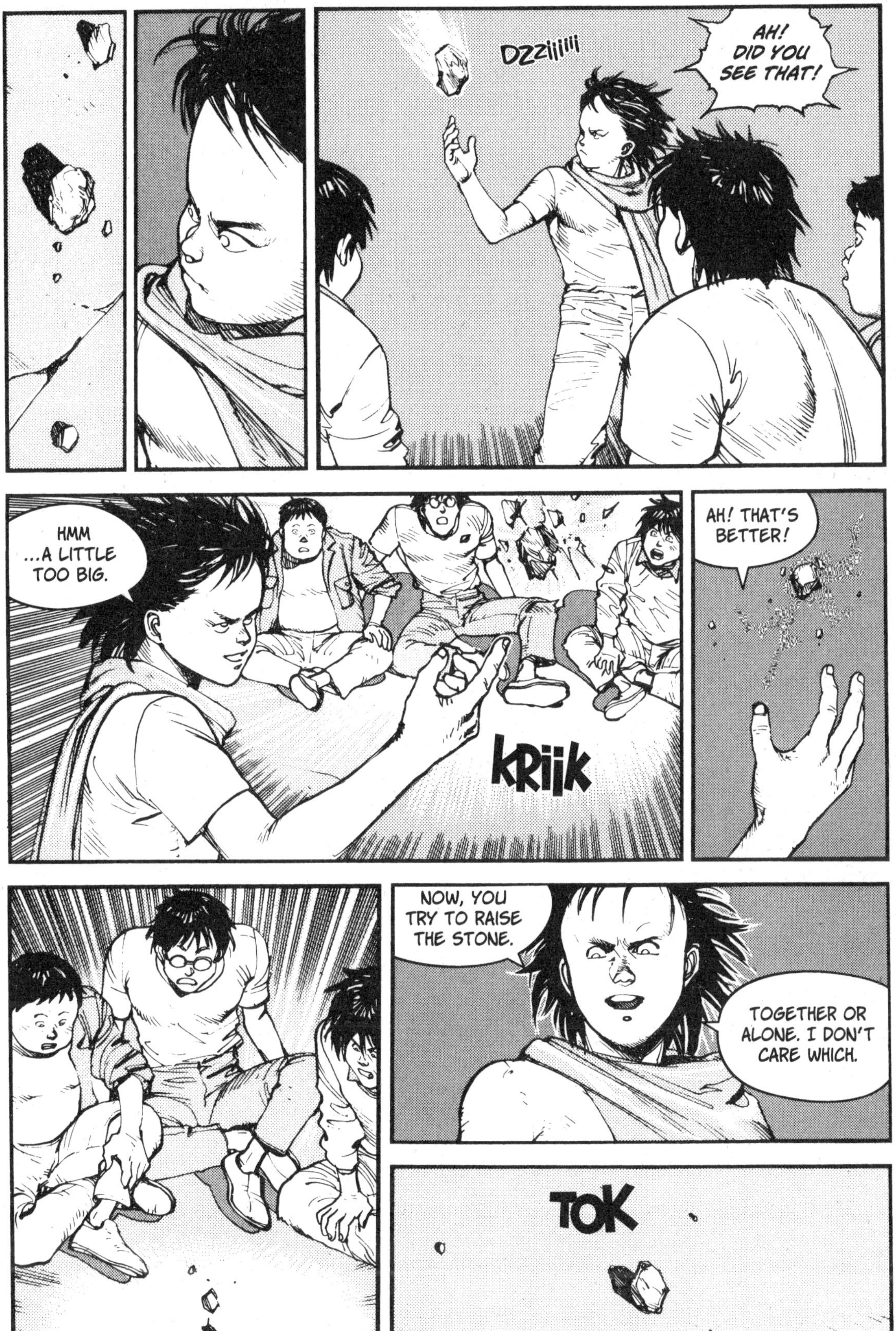
DZZiiiii
AH! DID YOU SEE THAT!
HMM ...A LITTLE TOO BIG.
KRiiK
AH! THAT'S BETTER!
NOW, YOU TRY TO RAISE THE STONE.
TOGETHER OR ALONE. I DON'T CARE WHICH.
TOK

EMPTY YOUR MIND. TRY TO FOCUS THE POWER OF YOUR SPIRIT.

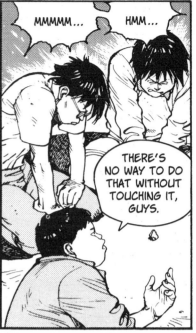

MMMMM... HMM...

THERE'S NO WAY TO DO THAT WITHOUT TOUCHING IT, GUYS.

HMMM...

I MEAN, SURE, I'VE BENT A SPOON OR TWO IN MY TIME, BUT A STONE--

≈UHN≈

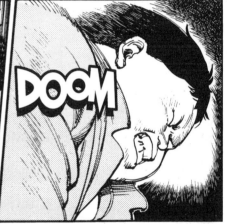

DOOM

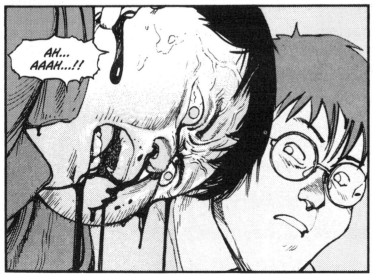

AH... AAAH...!!

DODOM

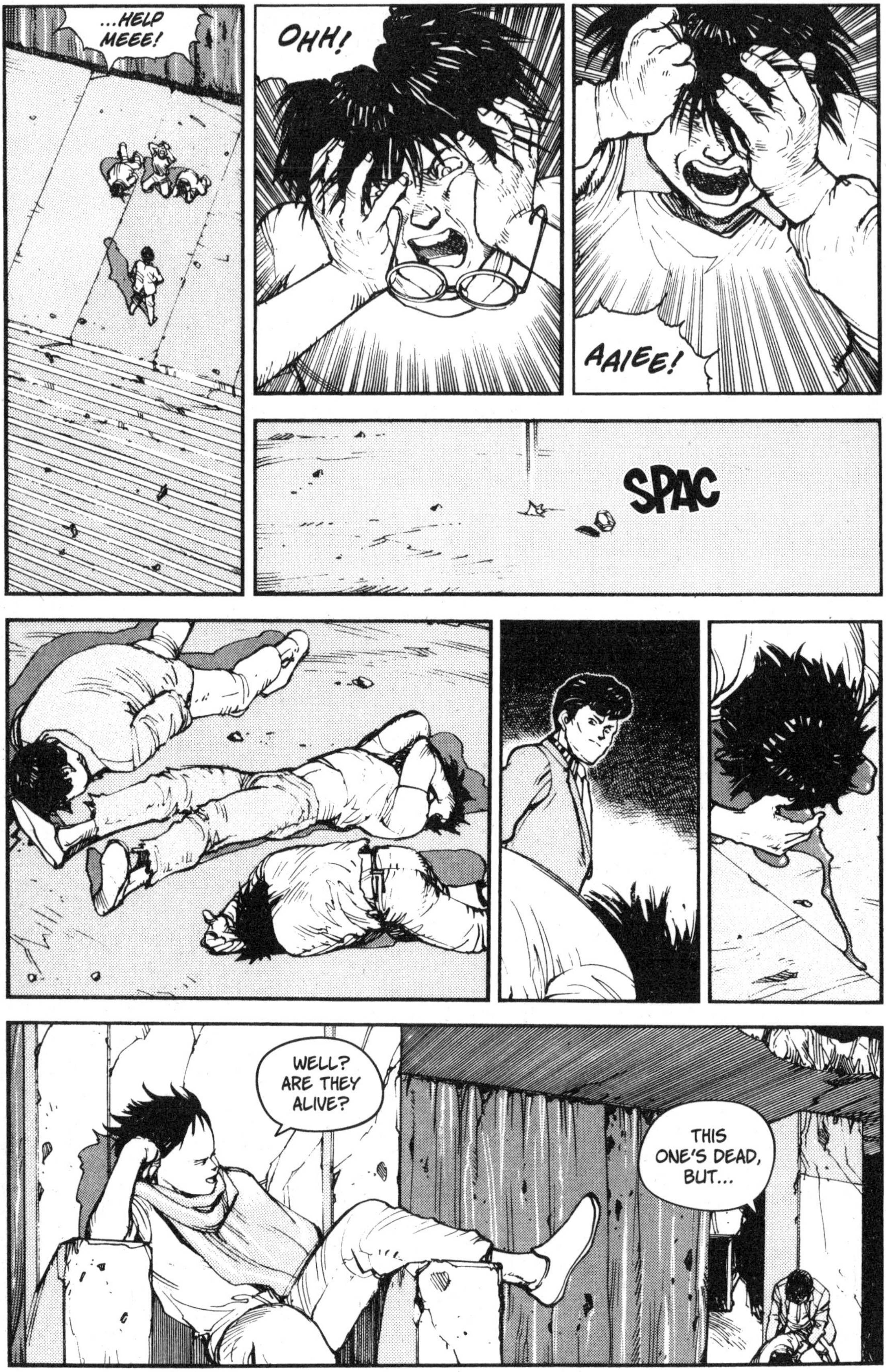

...HELP MEEE!
OHH!
AAIEE!
SPAC
WELL? ARE THEY ALIVE?
THIS ONE'S DEAD, BUT...

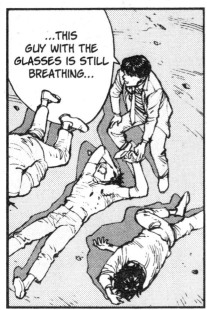

...THIS GUY WITH THE GLASSES IS STILL BREATHING...

GUESS HE WAS THE ONLY ONE WHO LEVITATED THE STONE, EH?

IF HE HASN'T BECOME A COMPLETE *VEGETABLE*...

...GIVE HIM THE DRUG AND BEGIN HIS TRAINING.

HE MIGHT COME IN HANDY.

YES, SIR.

VOOF

TAP TAP

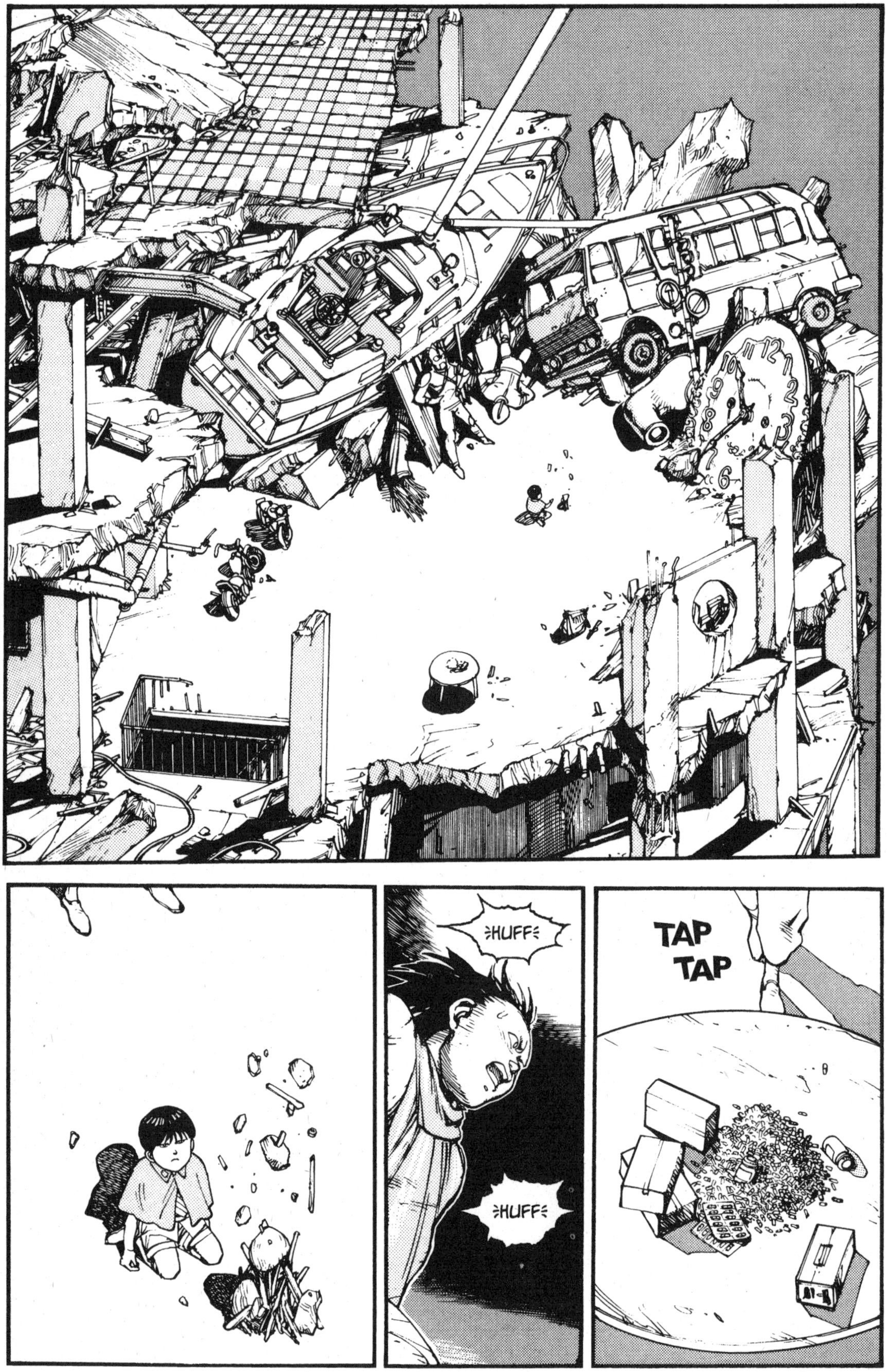
HUFF
HUFF
TAP
TAP

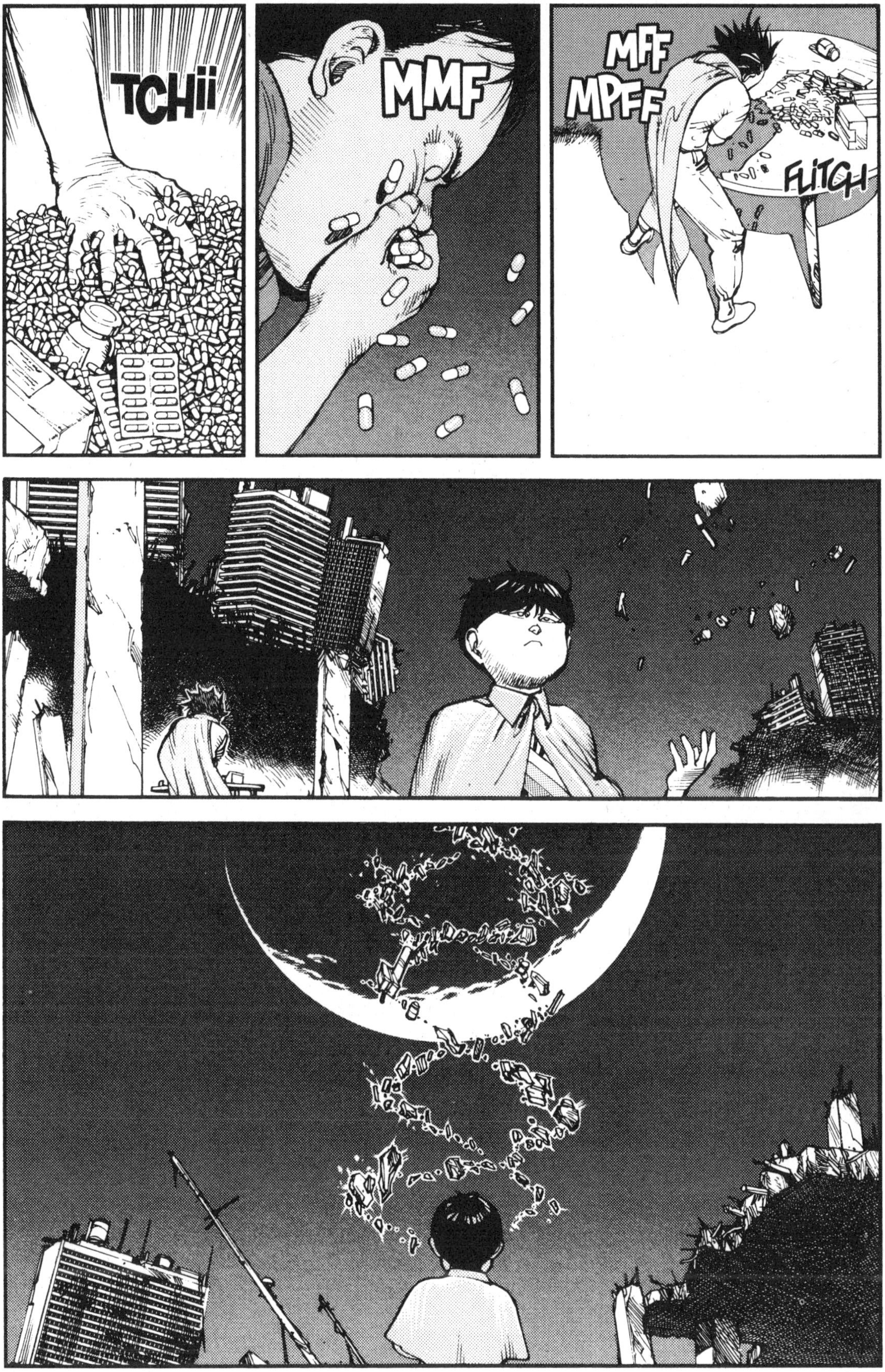
TCHii
MMF
MFF
MPFF
FLITCH

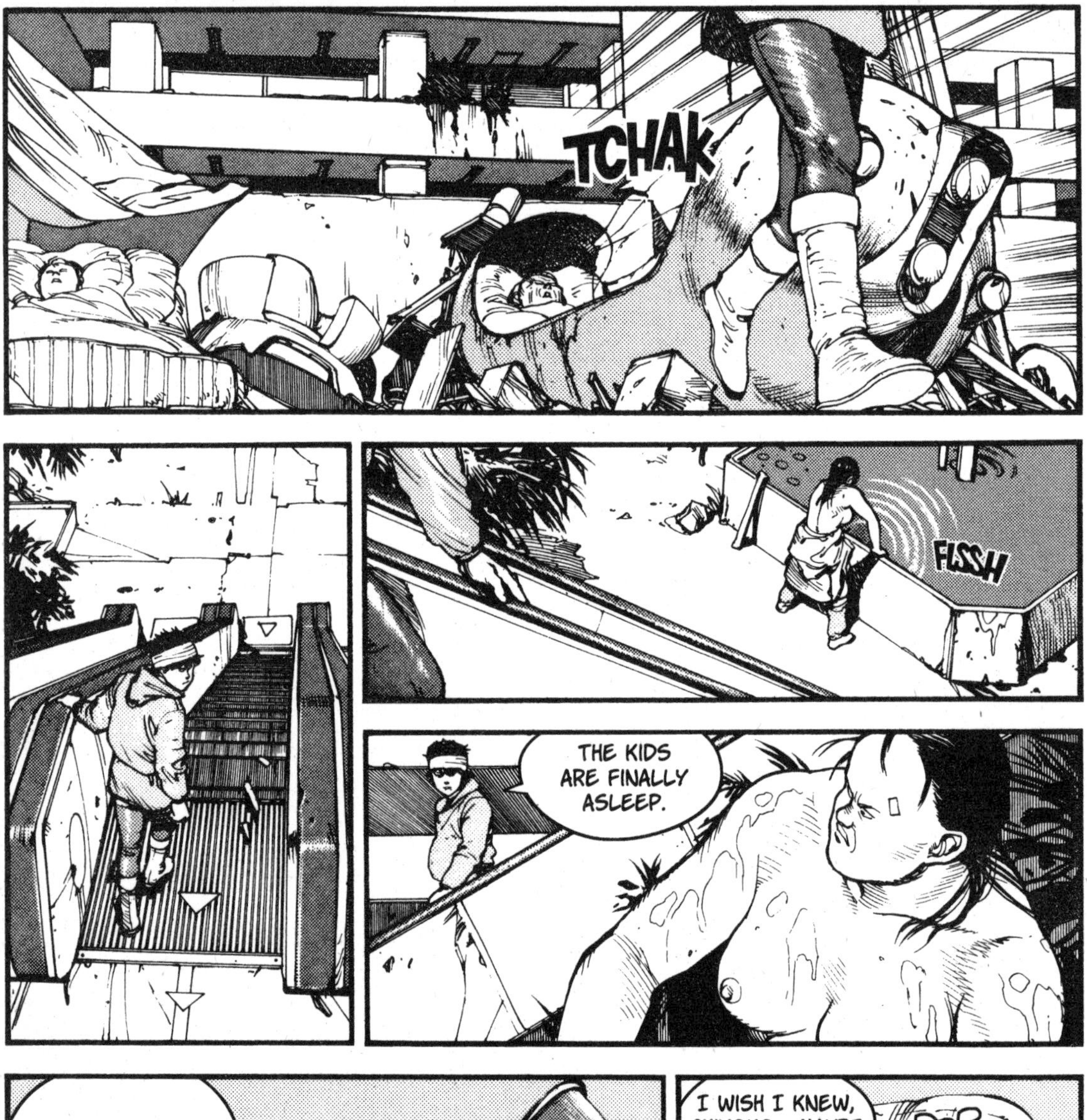
TCHAK
FLSSH
THE KIDS ARE FINALLY ASLEEP.
HOW LONG DO YOU THINK THE DRUGS'LL HELP THEM?
SPLOOSH
I WISH I KNEW, CHIYOKO... MAYBE TWO DAYS.
SPOF

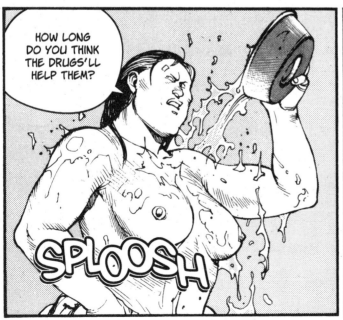

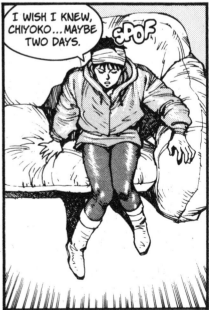

DID YOU FIND OUT ANYTHING MORE ABOUT THIS "NUMBER 19"?

NO. ALL THAT SHE SAID WAS THAT I SHOULD ASK NUMBER 19 FOR HELP.

KEI, THE WHOLE CITY IS IN RUINS. HOW ARE WE EVEN GOING TO *FIND* THIS NUMBER 19?

WE DON'T EVEN KNOW WHAT IT IS... A THING, A PERSON, DEAD, ALIVE...

I KNOW WHERE TO GO...

ARE YOU CRAZY? THAT'S IN *LADY MIYAKO'S* TERRITORY! ARE YOU SURE...?

YES, THERE'S NO MISTAKE. THAT'S WHERE WE'LL FIND NUMBER 19...

SO LET'S NOT WASTE ANY MORE TIME!

KLANK

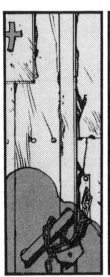

SHAK
SHAK

I'M WORRIED ABOUT WHAT MAY HAPPEN TO THOSE KIDS WHEN THE DRUGS RUN OUT...

STRRRR

WHO'S THERE?

YO!

RYU!!

HEH! MY HEAD'S GOIN' 'ROUND N' 'ROUND...AN' IT WON'T STOP ...HEH HEH!

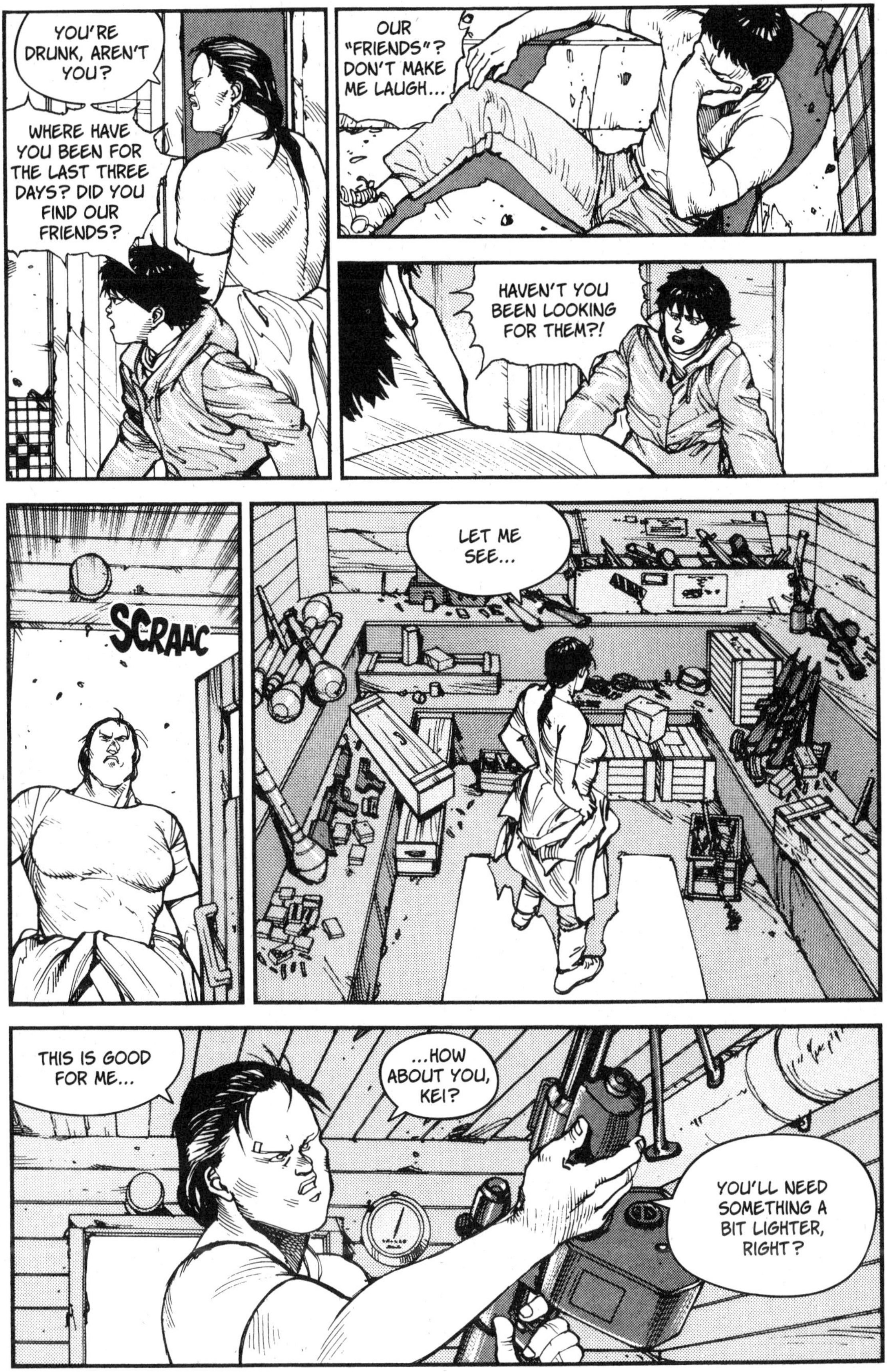

YOU'RE DRUNK, AREN'T YOU?
WHERE HAVE YOU BEEN FOR THE LAST THREE DAYS? DID YOU FIND OUR FRIENDS?
OUR "FRIENDS"? DON'T MAKE ME LAUGH...
HAVEN'T YOU BEEN LOOKING FOR THEM?!
SCRAAC
LET ME SEE...
THIS IS GOOD FOR ME...
...HOW ABOUT YOU, KEI?
YOU'LL NEED SOMETHING A BIT LIGHTER, RIGHT?

EH?

OHH!

PWARF

KEI...

RYU!

WHY DON'T YOU TAKE A COLD SHOWER AND COOL OFF?!

...

...

BUT... CHIYOKO!

COME WITH ME. WE DON'T HAVE TIME TO SCREW AROUND.

TAP TAP TAP

OUR... FRIENDS...

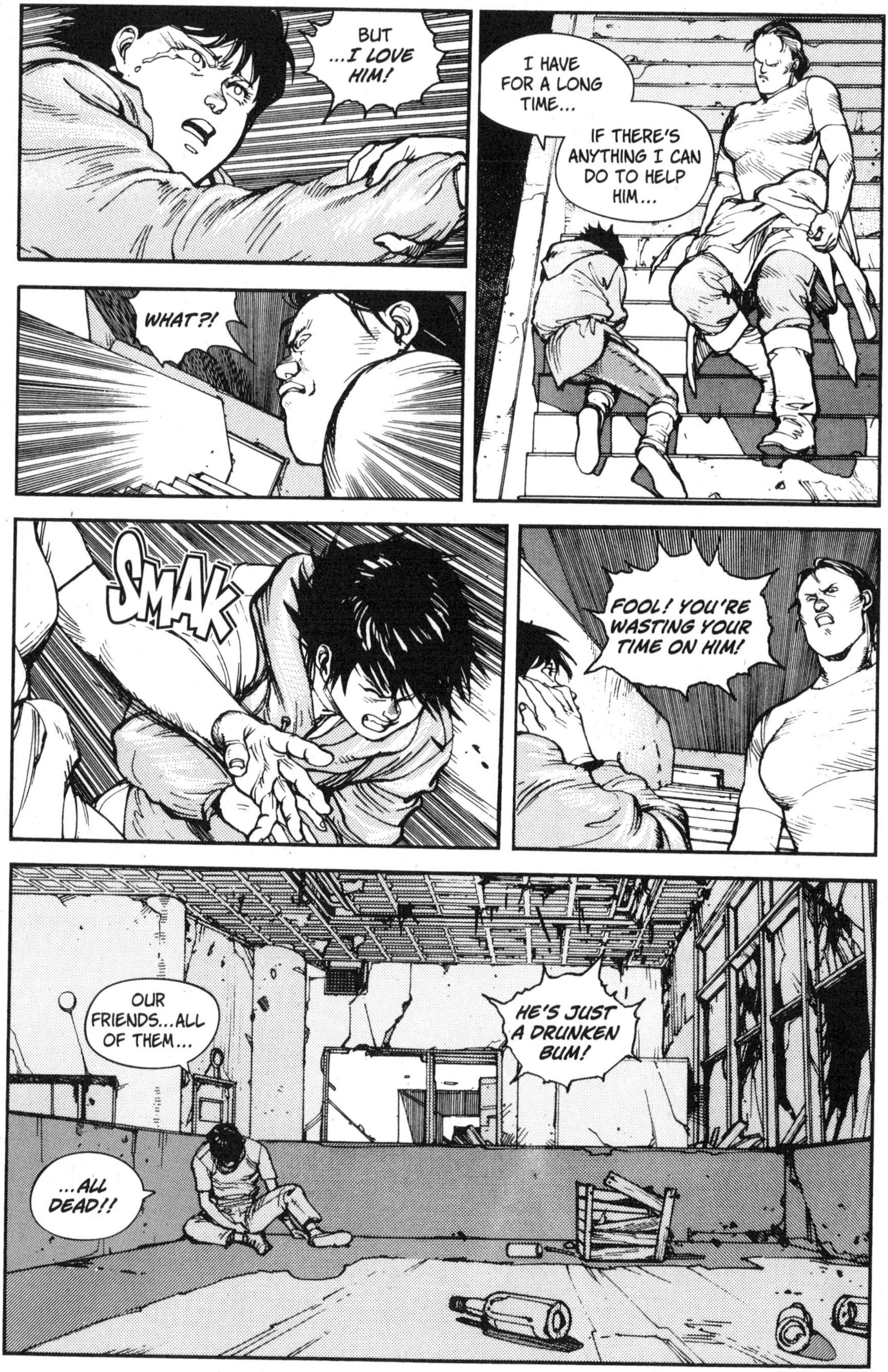
BUT ...I LOVE HIM!
I HAVE FOR A LONG TIME...
IF THERE'S ANYTHING I CAN DO TO HELP HIM...
WHAT?!
SMAK
FOOL! YOU'RE WASTING YOUR TIME ON HIM!
OUR FRIENDS...ALL OF THEM...
...ALL DEAD!!
HE'S JUST A DRUNKEN BUM!

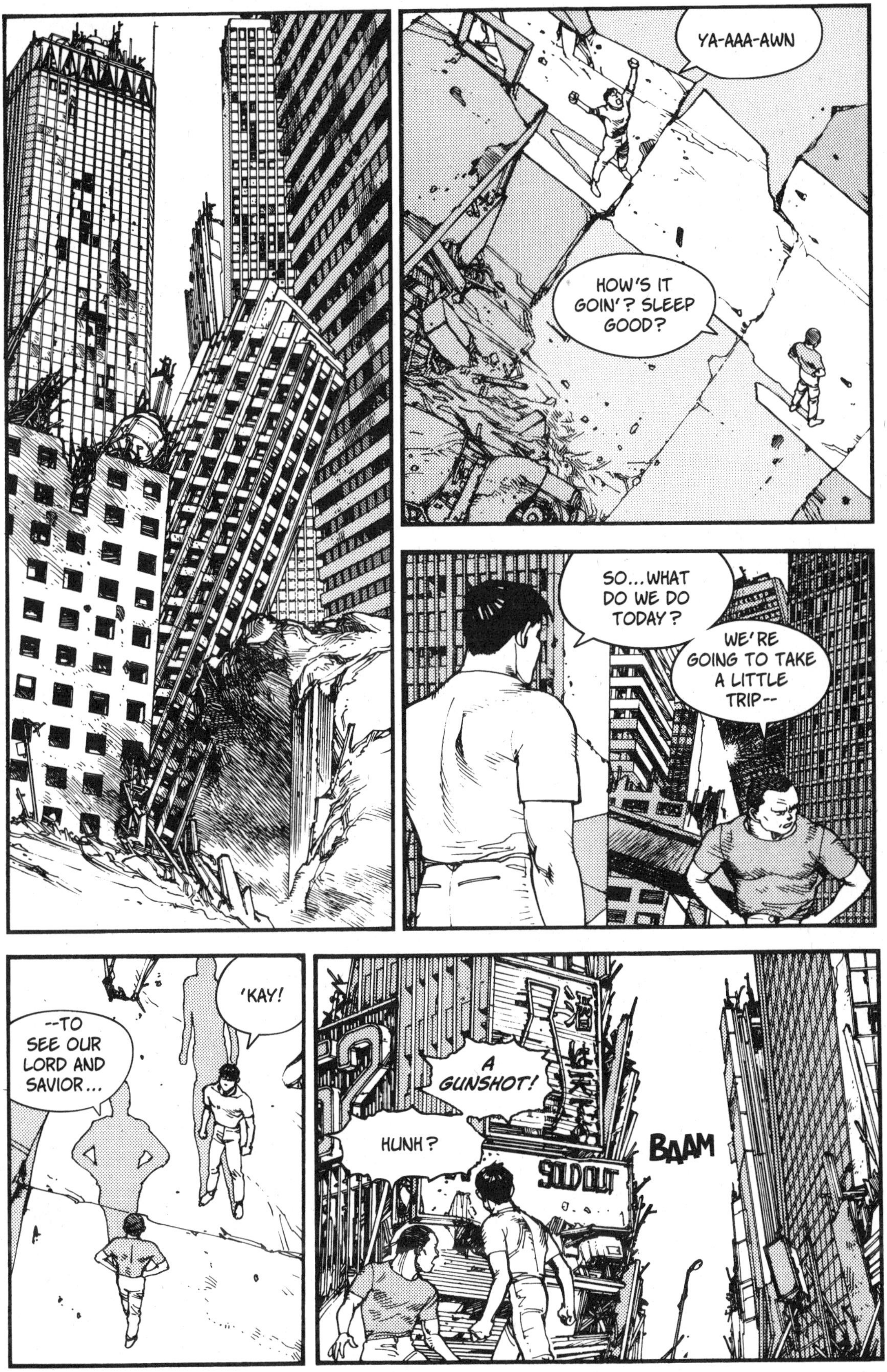
YA-AAA-AWN
HOW'S IT GOIN'? SLEEP GOOD?
SO... WHAT DO WE DO TODAY?
WE'RE GOING TO TAKE A LITTLE TRIP--
--TO SEE OUR LORD AND SAVIOR...
'KAY!
A GUNSHOT!
HUNH?
BAAM
SOLD OUT

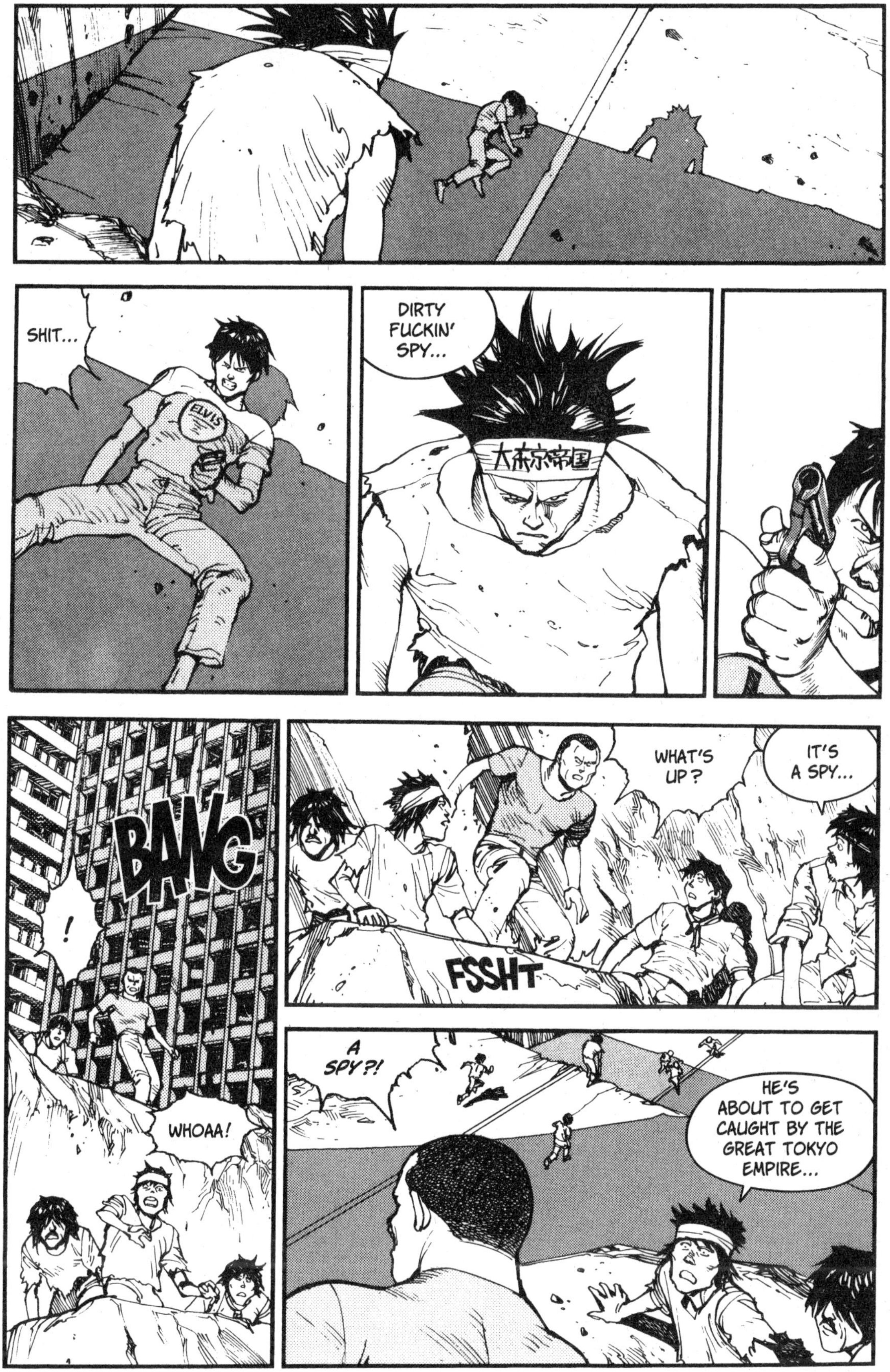
SHIT...
DIRTY FUCKIN' SPY...
大东京帝国
BANG
!
WHOAA!
WHAT'S UP?
IT'S A SPY...
FSSHT
A SPY?!
HE'S ABOUT TO GET CAUGHT BY THE GREAT TOKYO EMPIRE...

WELL? DID YOU TAKE HIM ALIVE?

...

GOOD JOB! GET SET FOR A PUBLIC EXECUTION!

OVER HERE! GET A MOVE ON!

HEY! DON'T WANNA MISS THIS!

PACK OF DOGS!

LISTEN TO ME!

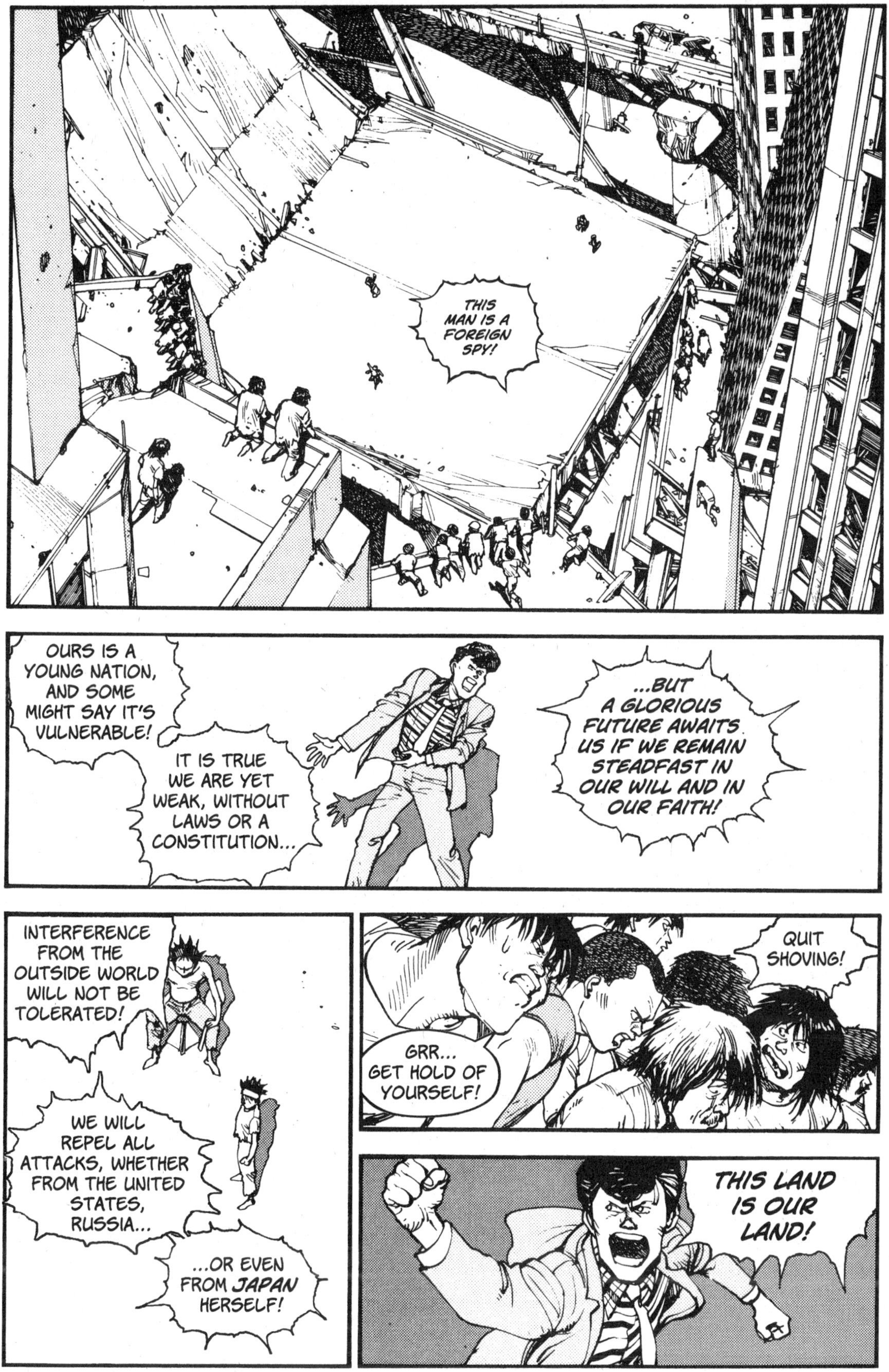
THIS MAN IS A FOREIGN SPY!
OURS IS A YOUNG NATION, AND SOME MIGHT SAY IT'S VULNERABLE!
IT IS TRUE WE ARE YET WEAK, WITHOUT LAWS OR A CONSTITUTION...
...BUT A GLORIOUS FUTURE AWAITS US IF WE REMAIN STEADFAST IN OUR WILL AND IN OUR FAITH!
INTERFERENCE FROM THE OUTSIDE WORLD WILL NOT BE TOLERATED!
WE WILL REPEL ALL ATTACKS, WHETHER FROM THE UNITED STATES, RUSSIA...
...OR EVEN FROM *JAPAN* HERSELF!
QUIT SHOVING!
GRR... GET HOLD OF YOURSELF!
THIS LAND IS OUR LAND!

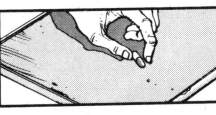

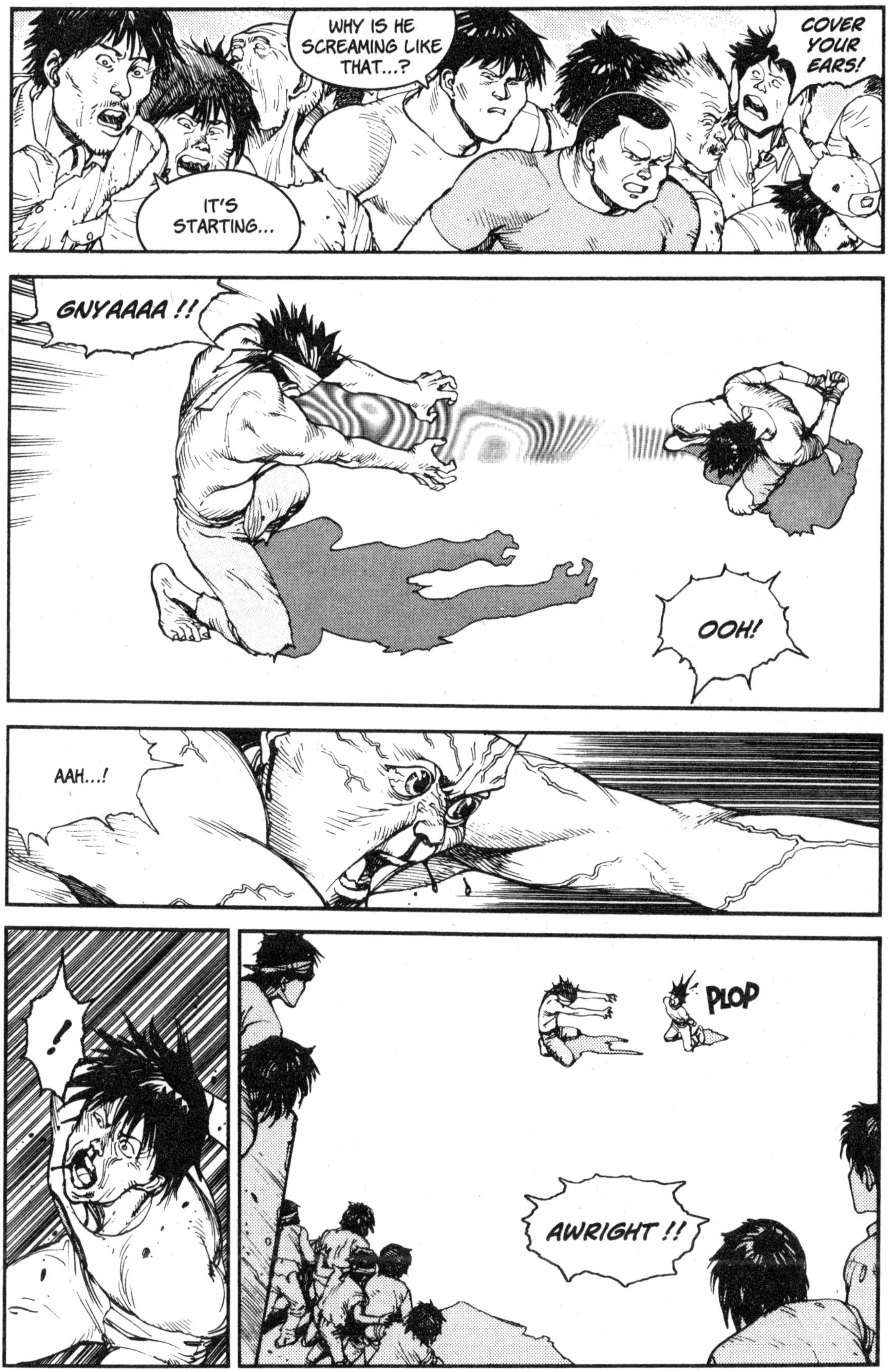
WHY IS HE SCREAMING LIKE THAT...?
IT'S STARTING...
COVER YOUR EARS!
GNYAAAA !!
OOH!
AAH...!
!
PLOP
AWRIGHT !!

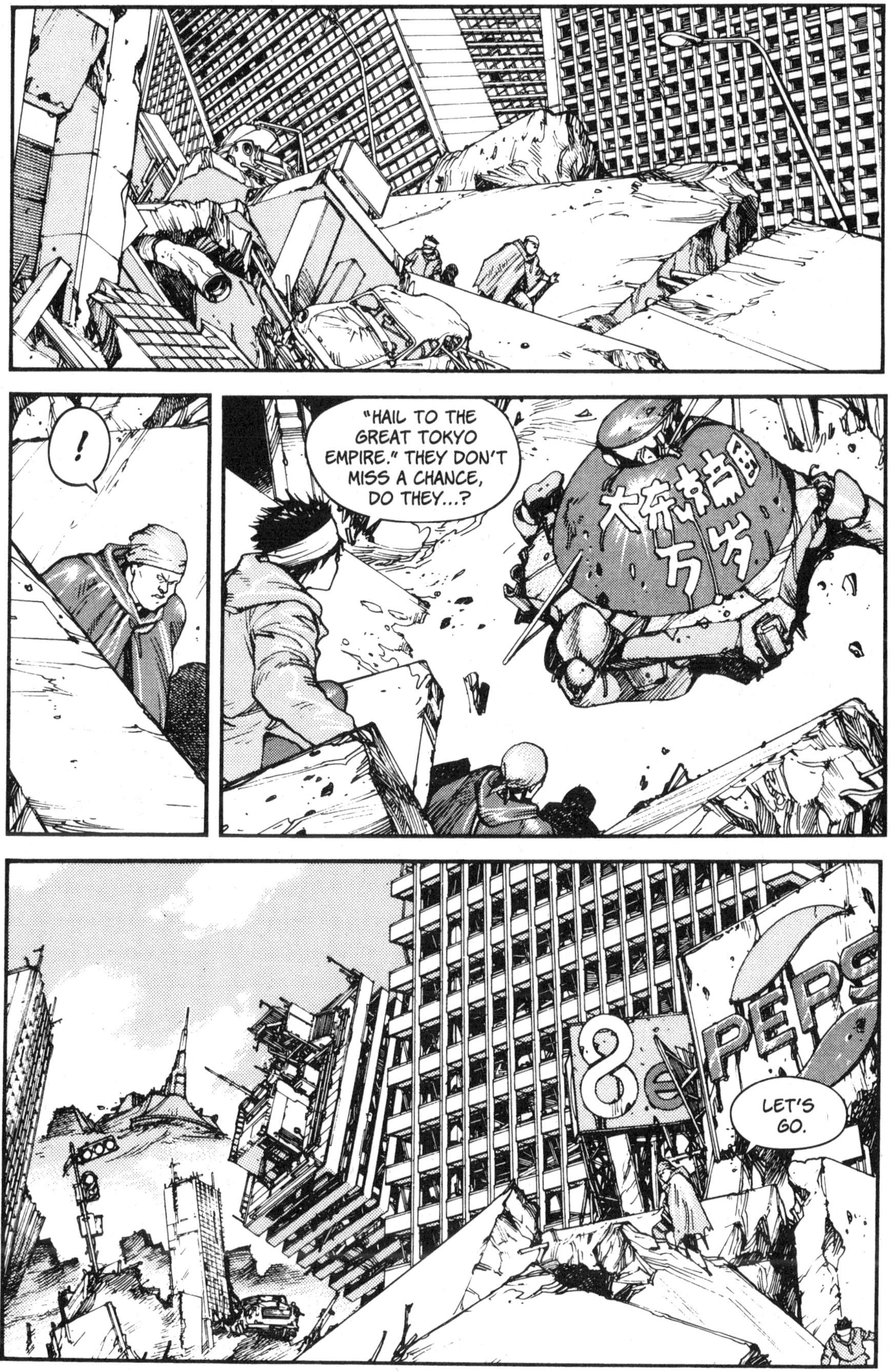
!
"HAIL TO THE GREAT TOKYO EMPIRE." THEY DON'T MISS A CHANCE, DO THEY...?
LET'S GO.

LINE UP TO COLLECT YOUR RATIONS.

≈KOFF≈

≈KOFF≈

Hiii

FINDING THIS NUMBER 19 IS GOING TO BE TOUGH. WE DON'T EVEN KNOW IF WE'RE LOOKING FOR A MAN OR A WOMAN...

I DON'T THINK NUMBER 19 IS AMONG THE SICK.

WHAT DO YOU MEAN?

YOU SAID WE SHOULD LOOK HERE...

WE'RE IN THE RIGHT PLACE... BUT I DON'T THINK NUMBER 19 IS ONE OF THESE PEOPLE. JUST A FEELING...

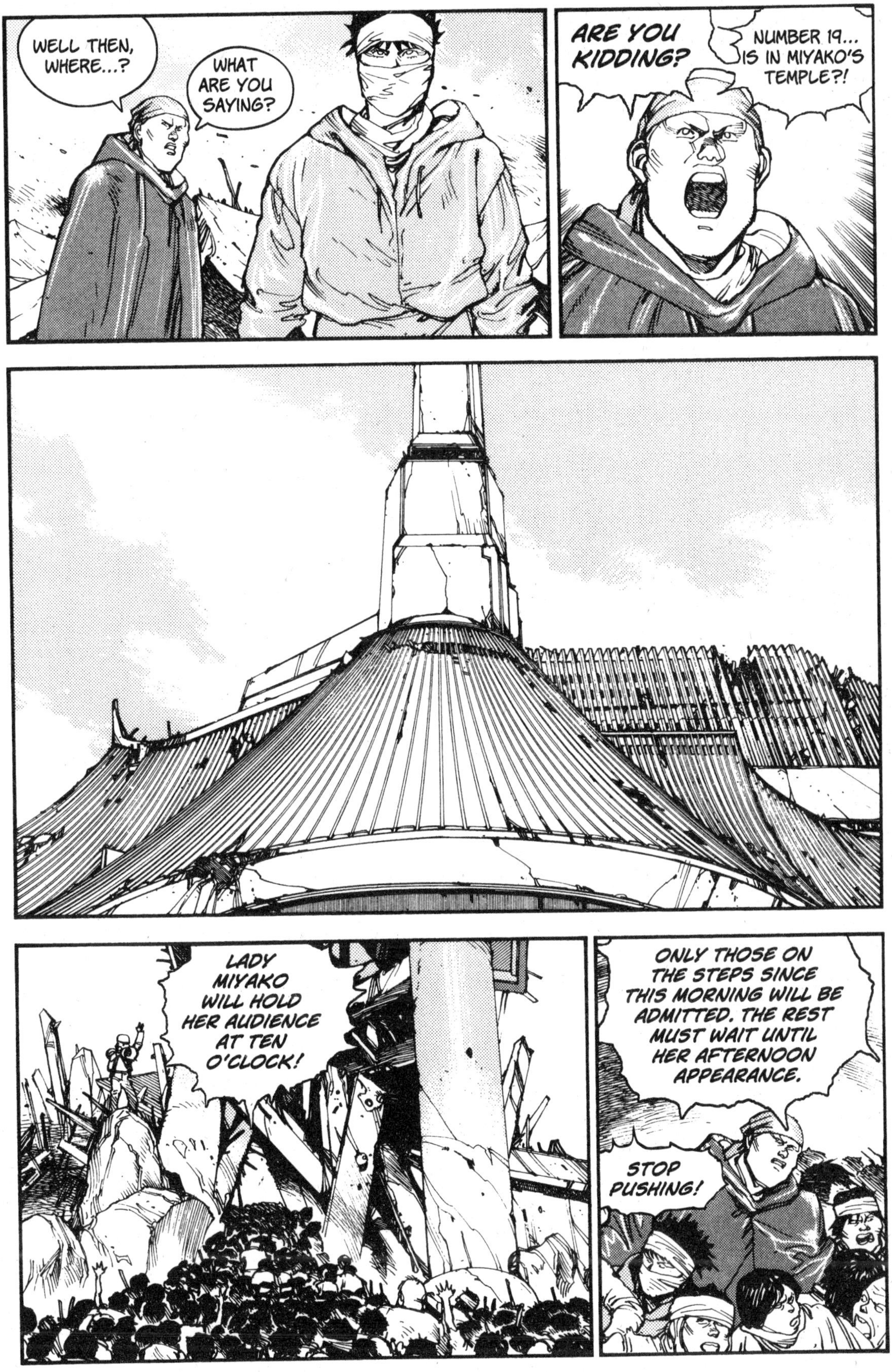
WELL THEN, WHERE...?
WHAT ARE YOU SAYING?
ARE YOU KIDDING?
NUMBER 19... IS IN MIYAKO'S TEMPLE?!
LADY MIYAKO WILL HOLD HER AUDIENCE AT TEN O'CLOCK!
ONLY THOSE ON THE STEPS SINCE THIS MORNING WILL BE ADMITTED. THE REST MUST WAIT UNTIL HER AFTERNOON APPEARANCE.
STOP PUSHING!

PLEASE STOP SHOVING! STAY CALM!

YOU WILL ALL GET YOUR TURN!

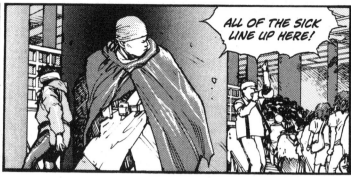

ALL OF THE SICK LINE UP HERE!

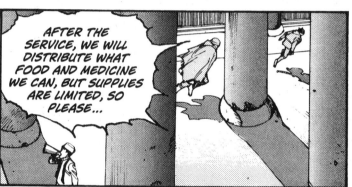

AFTER THE SERVICE, WE WILL DISTRIBUTE WHAT FOOD AND MEDICINE WE CAN, BUT SUPPLIES ARE LIMITED, SO PLEASE...

LOOKS LIKE THE COAST IS CLEAR.

THIS WAY.

KEI! HOW DID YOU ...?

I DON'T KNOW HOW I KNOW...

...BUT I KNOW THIS IS THE WAY!

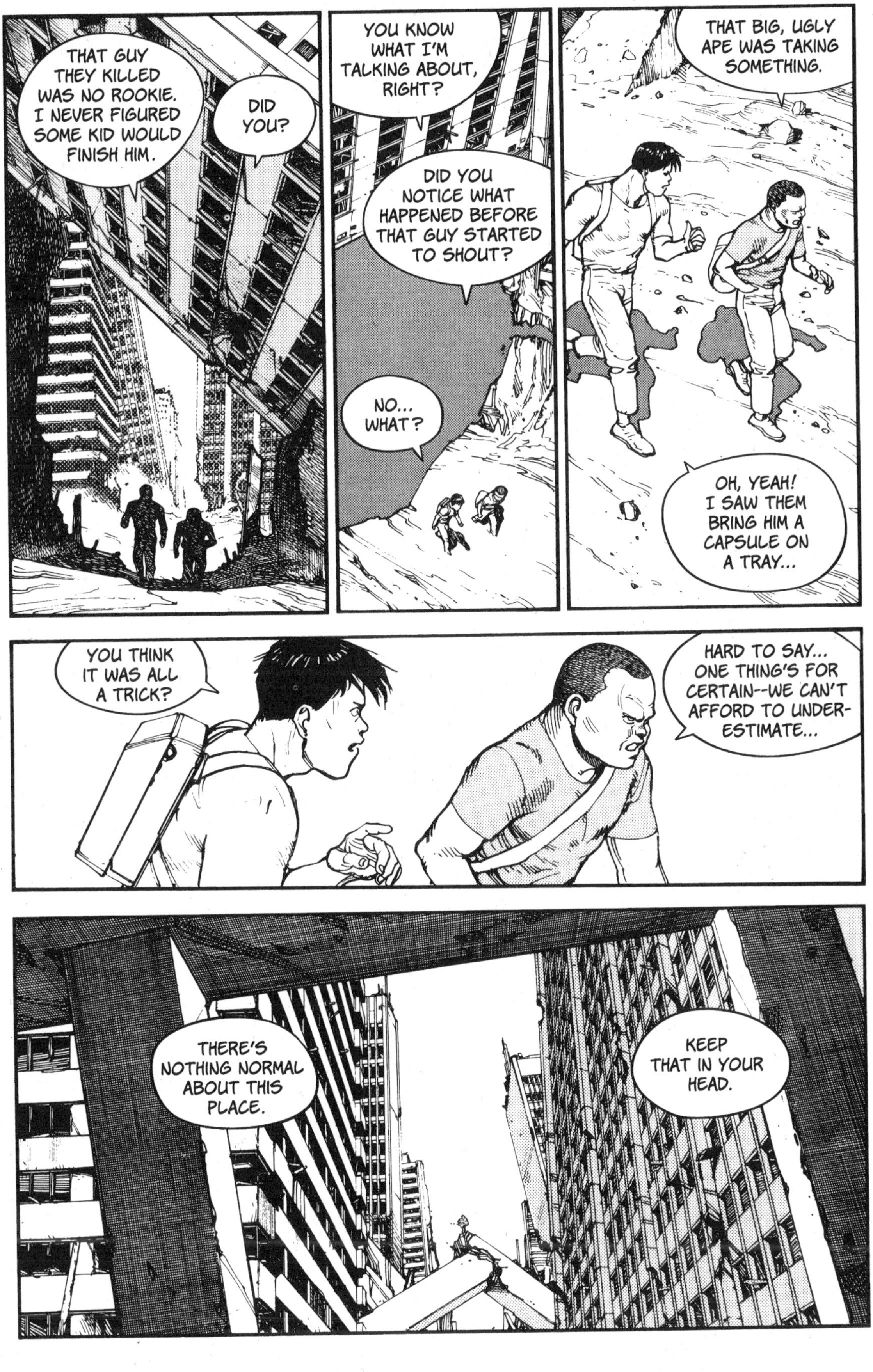
THAT GUY THEY KILLED WAS NO ROOKIE. I NEVER FIGURED SOME KID WOULD FINISH HIM.
DID YOU?
YOU KNOW WHAT I'M TALKING ABOUT, RIGHT?
DID YOU NOTICE WHAT HAPPENED BEFORE THAT GUY STARTED TO SHOUT?
NO... WHAT?
THAT BIG, UGLY APE WAS TAKING SOMETHING.
OH, YEAH! I SAW THEM BRING HIM A CAPSULE ON A TRAY...
YOU THINK IT WAS ALL A TRICK?
HARD TO SAY... ONE THING'S FOR CERTAIN--WE CAN'T AFFORD TO UNDER-ESTIMATE...
THERE'S NOTHING NORMAL ABOUT THIS PLACE.
KEEP THAT IN YOUR HEAD.

I SEE TWO MEN. THEY CARRY BOXES ON THEIR BACKS...

...BOXES WITH ELECTRONIC DEVICES...

BE WARNED!

...I SENSE THAT THEY ARE FAR MORE DANGEROUS THAN THE LAST ONE...

I SENSE THEIR HATRED!

HURRY! THEY'RE RIGHT HERE!

WHAT THE F...?!

CHILL OUT! HE'S TRYING TO PROVOKE US!

I SEE THEM RUNNING DOWN AN ALLEY!

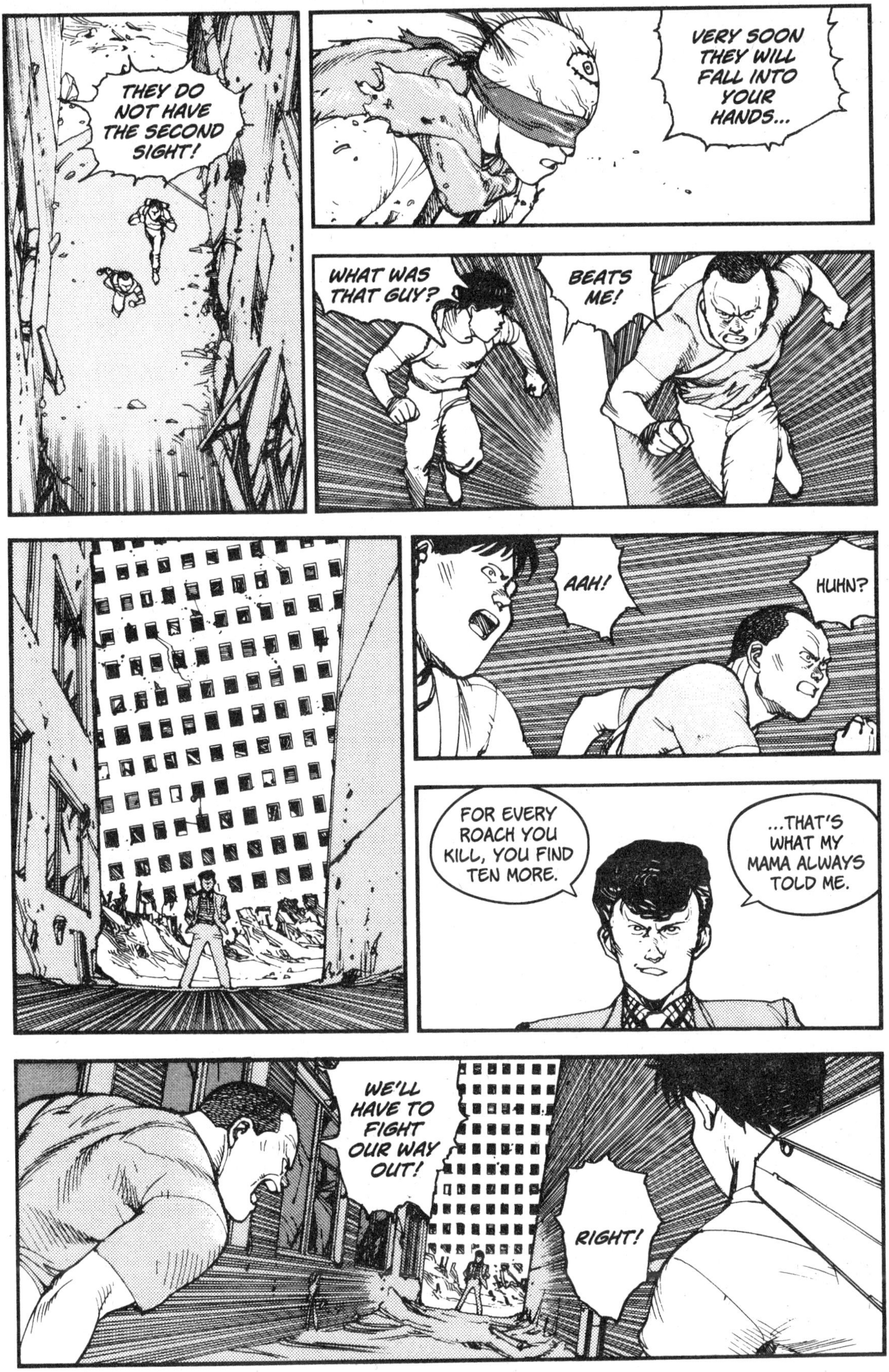
THEY DO NOT HAVE THE SECOND SIGHT!
VERY SOON THEY WILL FALL INTO YOUR HANDS...
WHAT WAS THAT GUY?
BEATS ME!
AAH!
HUHN?
FOR EVERY ROACH YOU KILL, YOU FIND TEN MORE.
...THAT'S WHAT MY MAMA ALWAYS TOLD ME.
WE'LL HAVE TO FIGHT OUR WAY OUT!
RIGHT!

ZZiNG

!

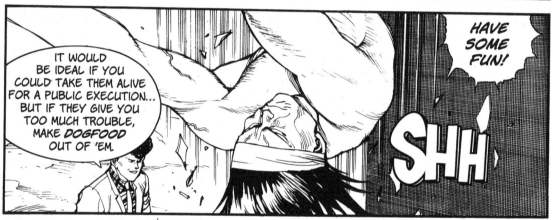

IT WOULD BE IDEAL IF YOU COULD TAKE THEM ALIVE FOR A PUBLIC EXECUTION... BUT IF THEY GIVE YOU TOO MUCH TROUBLE, MAKE *DOGFOOD* OUT OF 'EM.

HAVE SOME FUN!

SHH

SHLiK

ALL RIGHT YOU BIG MONKEY-- BRING IT ON!

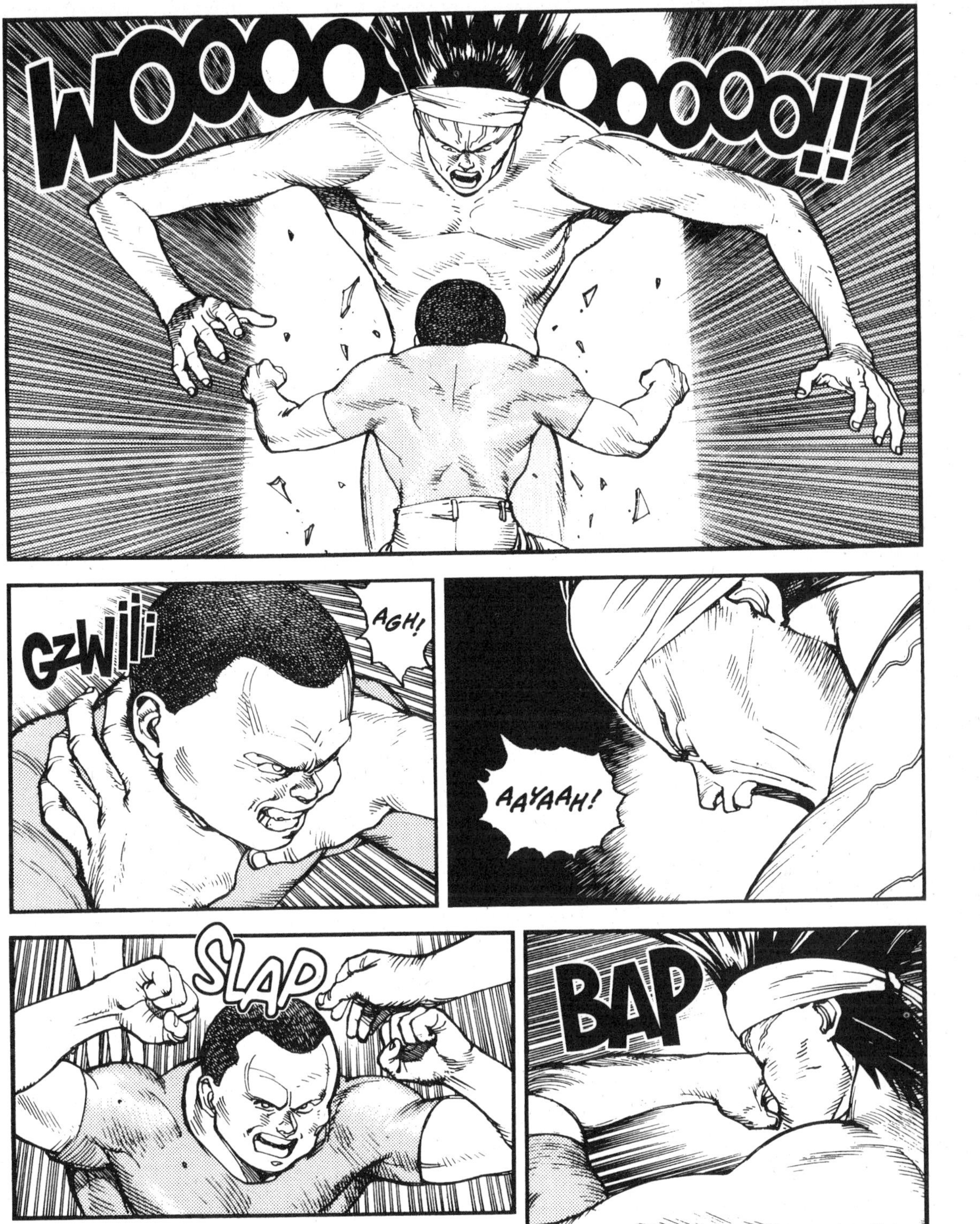
WOOOOOOOOOO!!
GZWiii
AGH!
AAYAAH!
SLAP
!
BAP

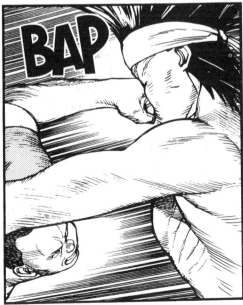

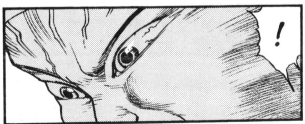

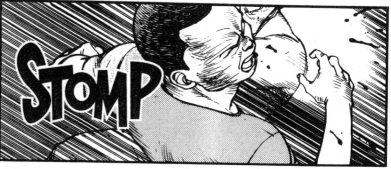

84

BOK

UHNN!

POUM

GURK

OOH!

...AH...

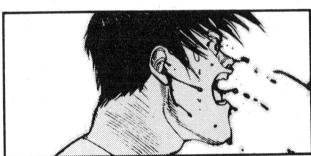

NO!

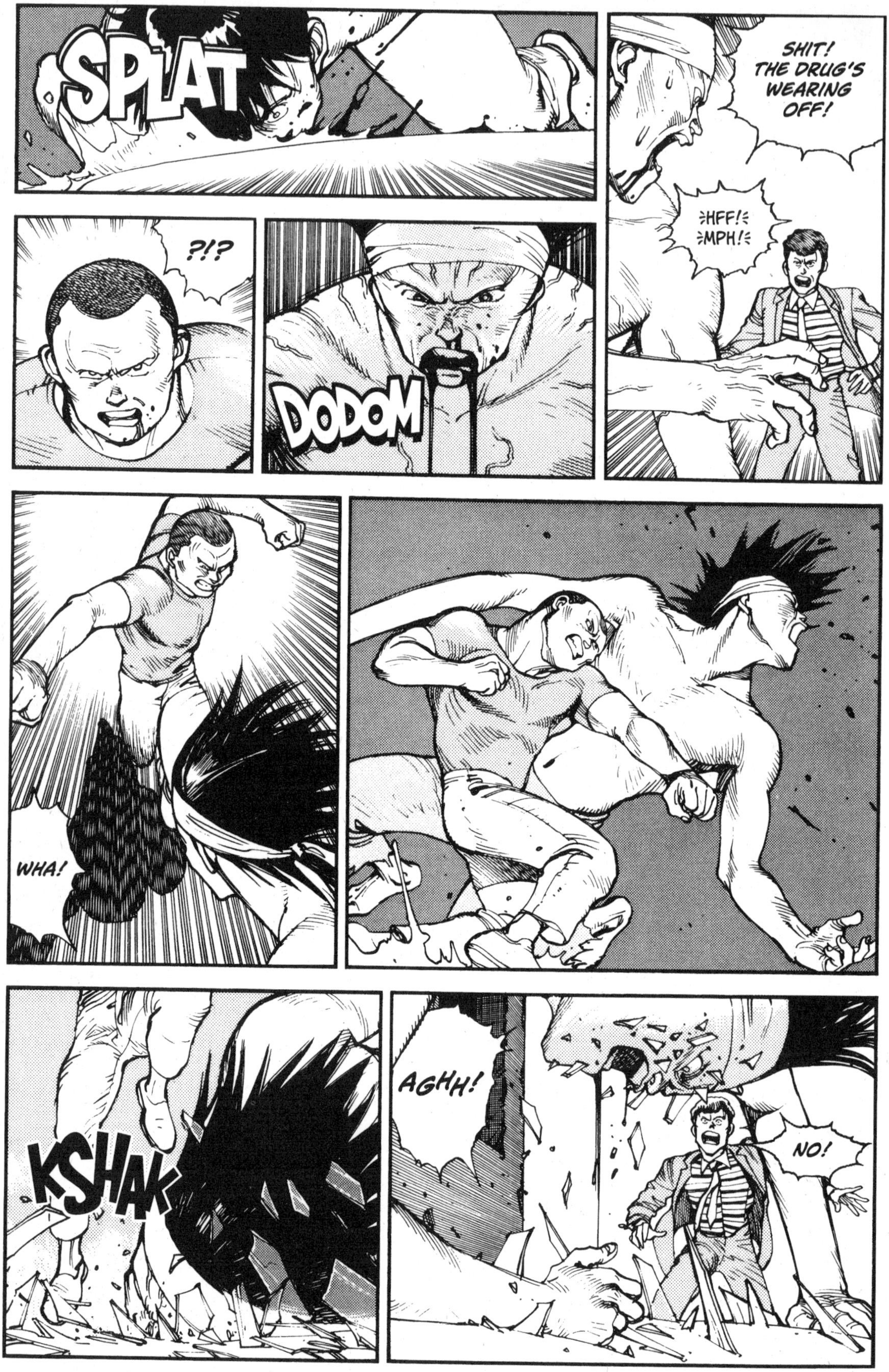
SPLAT
SHIT! THE DRUG'S WEARING OFF!
HFF! MPH!
?!?
DODOM
WHA!
KSHAK
AGHH!
NO!

GYAAAH!

HAI--

--YAH!

SWAP

KRUSH

POUTCH

HEY! TALK TO ME!

SONUVA--

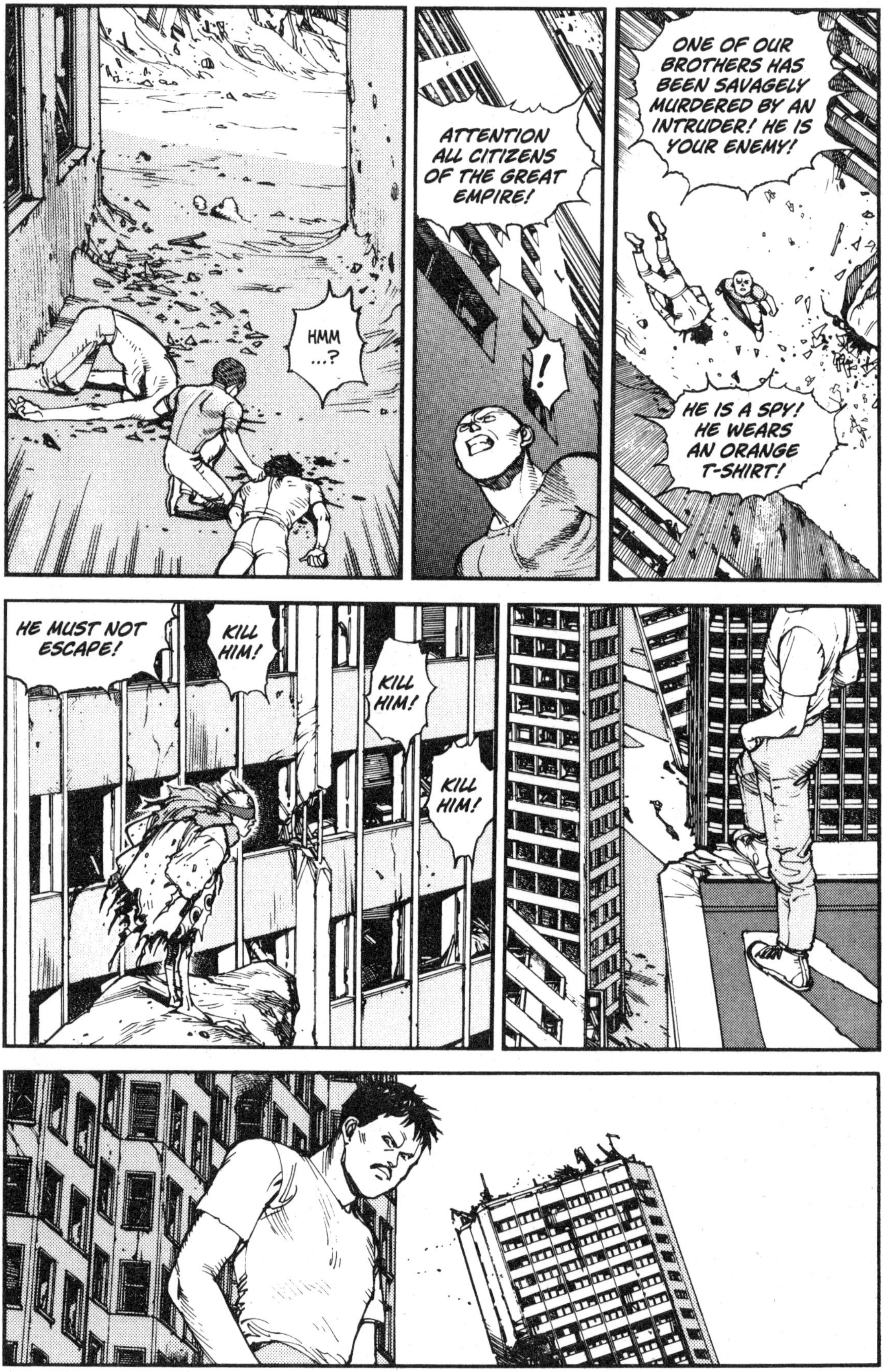
HMM ...?
ATTENTION ALL CITIZENS OF THE GREAT EMPIRE!
!
ONE OF OUR BROTHERS HAS BEEN SAVAGELY MURDERED BY AN INTRUDER! HE IS YOUR ENEMY!
HE IS A SPY! HE WEARS AN ORANGE T-SHIRT!
HE MUST NOT ESCAPE!
KILL HIM!
KILL HIM!
KILL HIM!

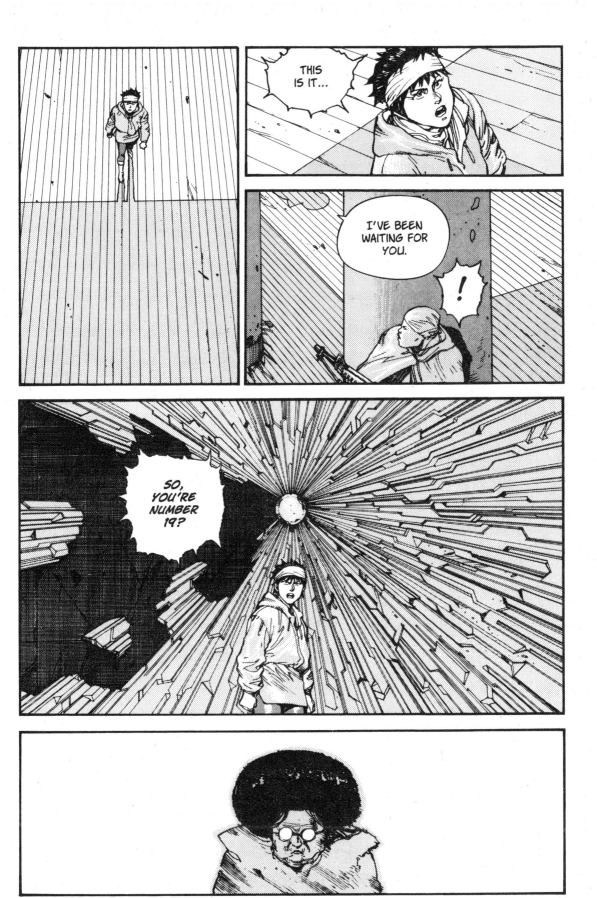

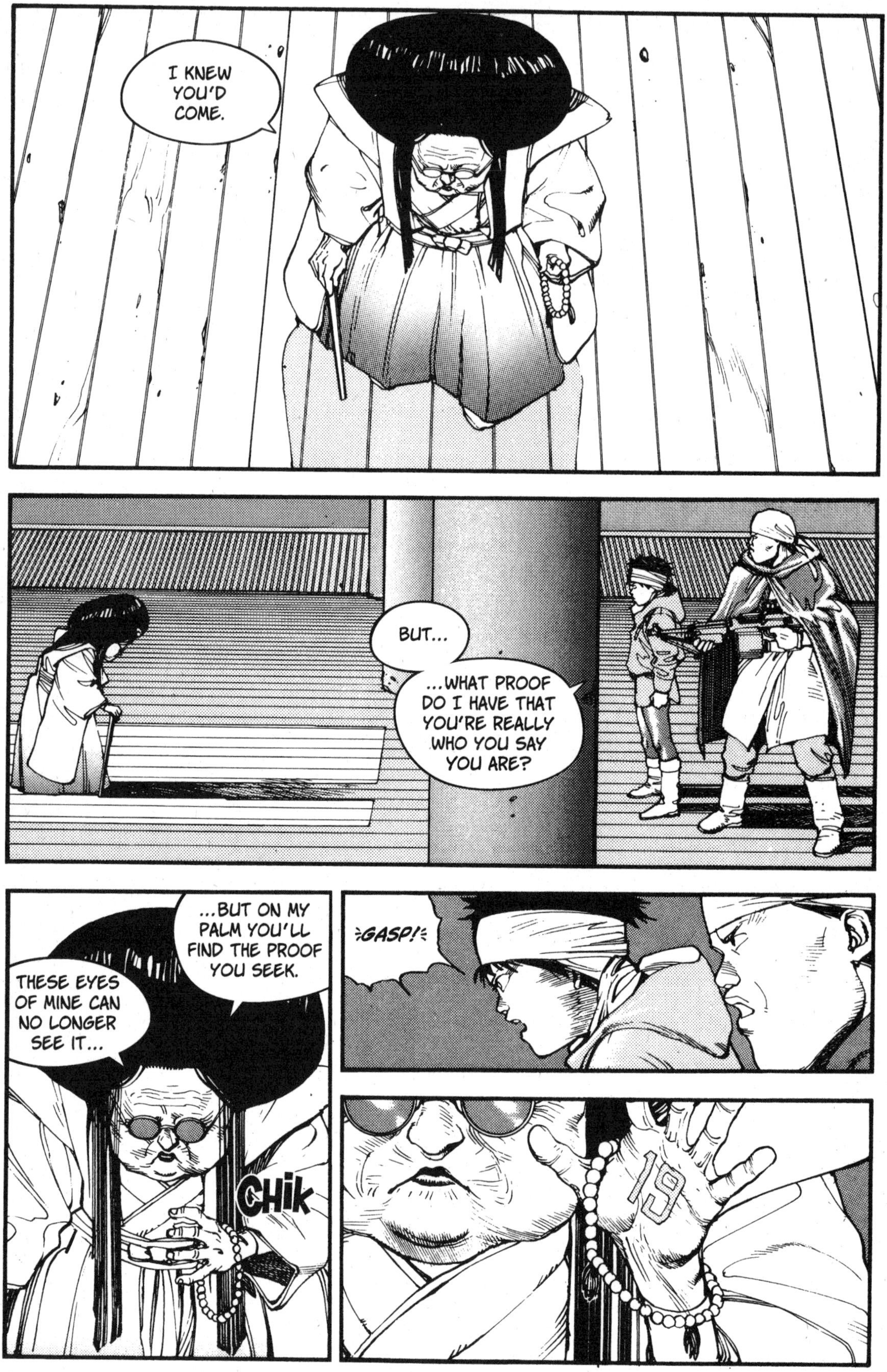

I KNEW YOU'D COME.
BUT...
...WHAT PROOF DO I HAVE THAT YOU'RE REALLY WHO YOU SAY YOU ARE?
THESE EYES OF MINE CAN NO LONGER SEE IT...
...BUT ON MY PALM YOU'LL FIND THE PROOF YOU SEEK.
CHIK
GASP!
19

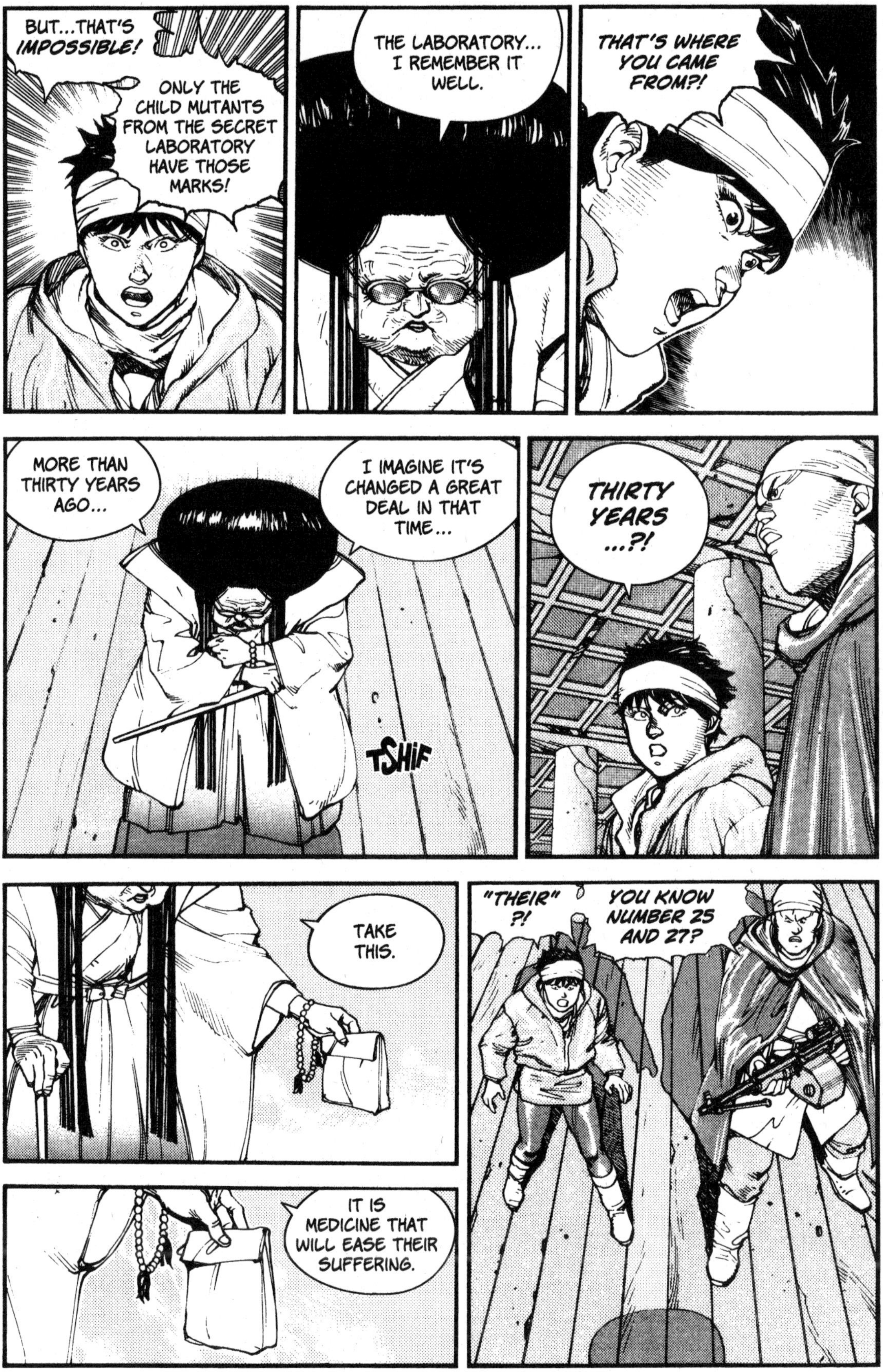
BUT...THAT'S IMPOSSIBLE!
ONLY THE CHILD MUTANTS FROM THE SECRET LABORATORY HAVE THOSE MARKS!
THE LABORATORY... I REMEMBER IT WELL.
THAT'S WHERE YOU CAME FROM?!
MORE THAN THIRTY YEARS AGO...
I IMAGINE IT'S CHANGED A GREAT DEAL IN THAT TIME...
TSHIF
THIRTY YEARS ...?!
TAKE THIS.
IT IS MEDICINE THAT WILL EASE THEIR SUFFERING.
"THEIR" ?!
YOU KNOW NUMBER 25 AND 27?

OUR ACQUAINTANCE WAS VERY BRIEF.

AFTER A SHORT TIME, THEY WERE PUT IN ISOLATION, BEHIND A WALL OF GLASS.

IN A NURSERY THAT LOOKED LIKE A BIG GREENHOUSE?

WHEN THEY ARE FEELING BETTER, YOU MUST BRING THEM TO SEE ME.

BUT, WHY?!

AT LEAST TELL ME--

EXPLANATIONS CAN WAIT!

IT IS URGENT THAT THEY TAKE THAT MEDICINE! GO NOW!

...

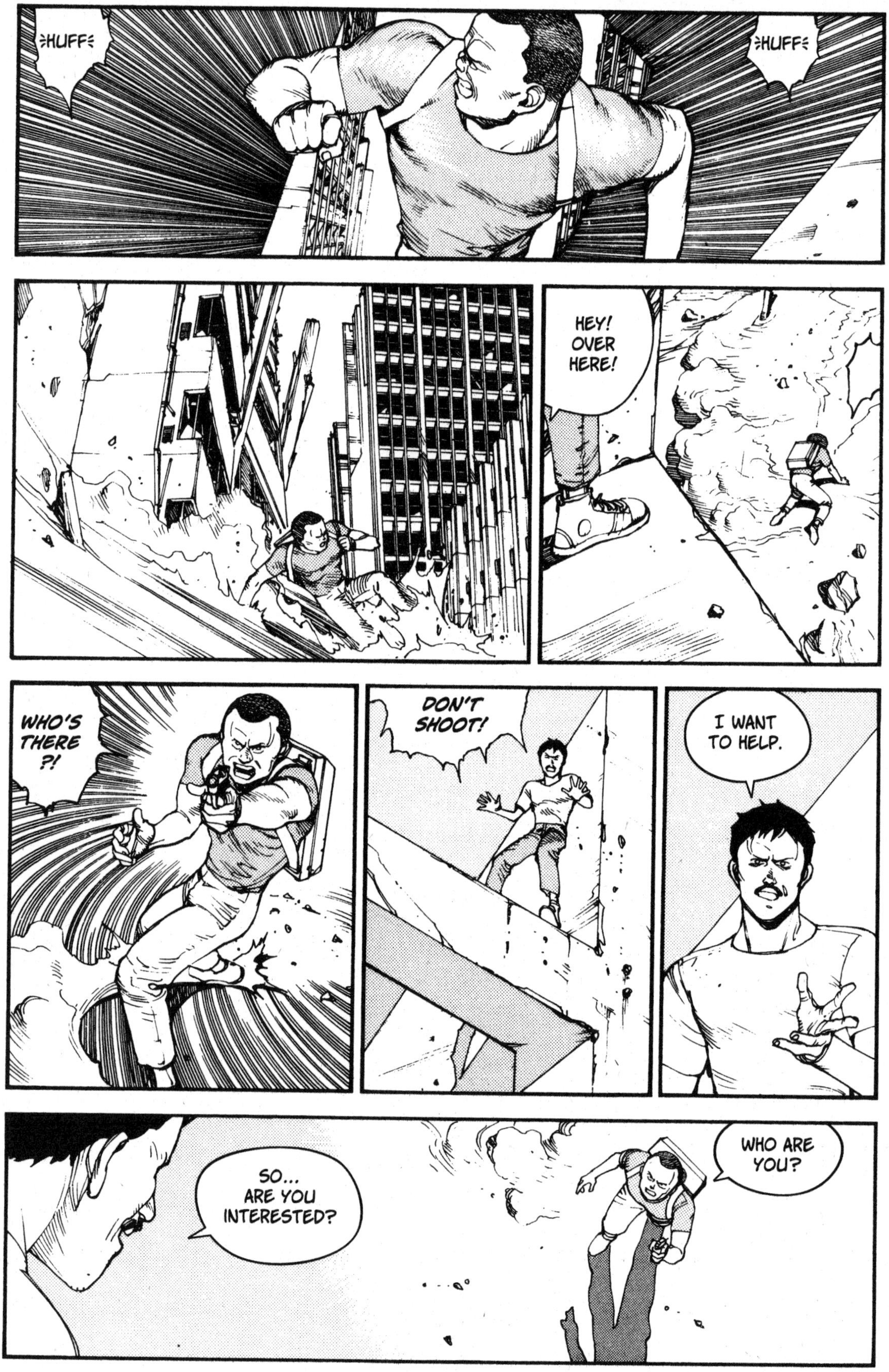
HUFF
HUFF
HEY! OVER HERE!
WHO'S THERE ?!
DON'T SHOOT!
I WANT TO HELP.
SO... ARE YOU INTERESTED?
WHO ARE YOU?

...I SEE A NEW UNKNOWN...

--ANOTHER INTRUDER HAS BECOME HIS GUIDE...!

...THEY HAVE PASSED BEYOND THE RANGE OF MY SIGHT...

ANY OF THE SPY'S OTHER FRIENDS STILL AROUND?

I CAN'T BE CERTAIN... BUT I FELT SOMETHING... THE SPY IS WARY OF HIS NEW COMPANION...

"THEY DO NOT KNOW EACH OTHER'S INTEN- TIONS... THEY ARE NOT ALLIES..."

FLISH FLISH

"WHICH CAN ONLY MEAN..."

...THAT THERE'S *ANOTHER* GROUP OPPOSING OUR LORD AKIRA!

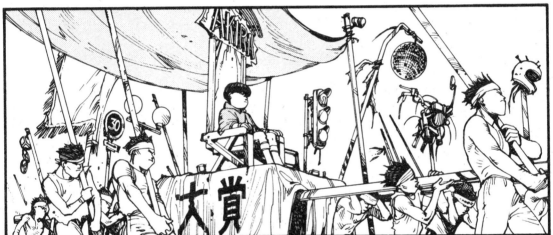

LORD AKIRA, IN HIS INFINITE MERCY, HAS DECREED THAT WE DISTRIBUTE FOOD TO YOU!

THANK YOU, LORD!

HURRAY FOR THE NOBLE AKIRA!

HURRAY!

FILTHY PIGS.

FROSH

HA HA! IN THE NAME OF OUR GREAT LORD AKIRA...

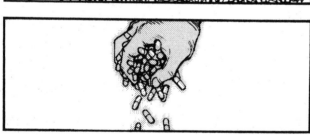

IT'S HERE! PLEASE!

LINE UP!

AIEE!

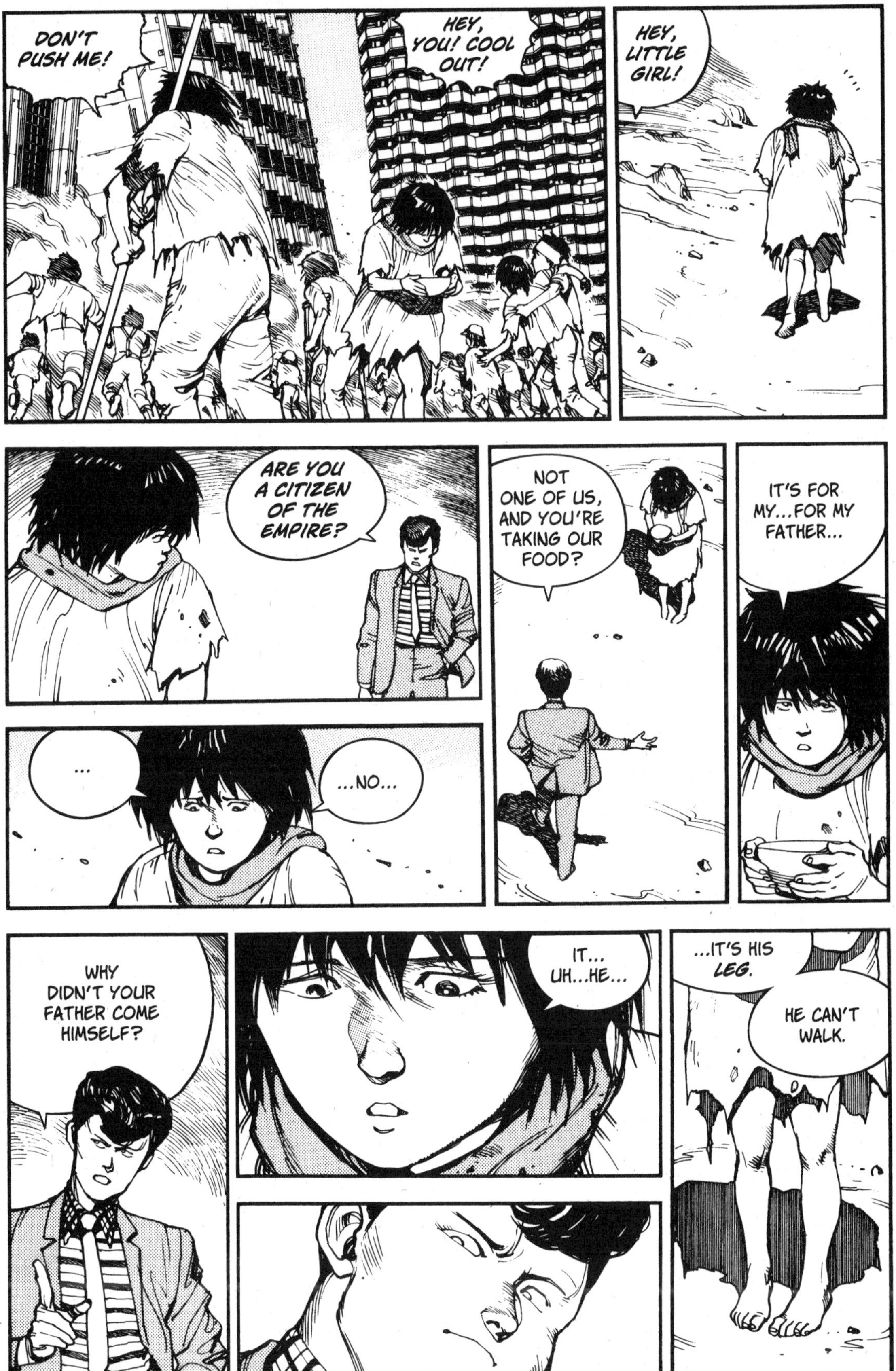
DON'T PUSH ME!
HEY, YOU! COOL OUT!
HEY, LITTLE GIRL!
ARE YOU A CITIZEN OF THE EMPIRE?
NOT ONE OF US, AND YOU'RE TAKING OUR FOOD?
IT'S FOR MY...FOR MY FATHER...
...
...NO...
WHY DIDN'T YOUR FATHER COME HIMSELF?
IT... UH...HE...
...IT'S HIS LEG.
HE CAN'T WALK.

AH, BUT WHEN YOU BECOME A CITIZEN OF THE EMPIRE, MASTER TETSUO WILL SEE TO IT YOUR FATHER'S LEG IS HEALED...

YES, BUT...

NO!

A PRETTY LITTLE GIRL LIKE YOU SHOULDN'T HAVE TO WAIT IN LINE FOR SLOP LIKE THIS.

I'LL TAKE YOUR FATHER SOMETHING NOURISHING.

BUT, I JUST...

PLOK

YOU CAN SERVE OUR EMPIRE...YOU CAN SERVE LORD AKIRA... AND MASTER TETSUO. YOU'LL BE A *LOYAL* CITIZEN, RIGHT? WHATTAYA SAY...?

TSHOK

THERE'S
SOMEONE
THERE!

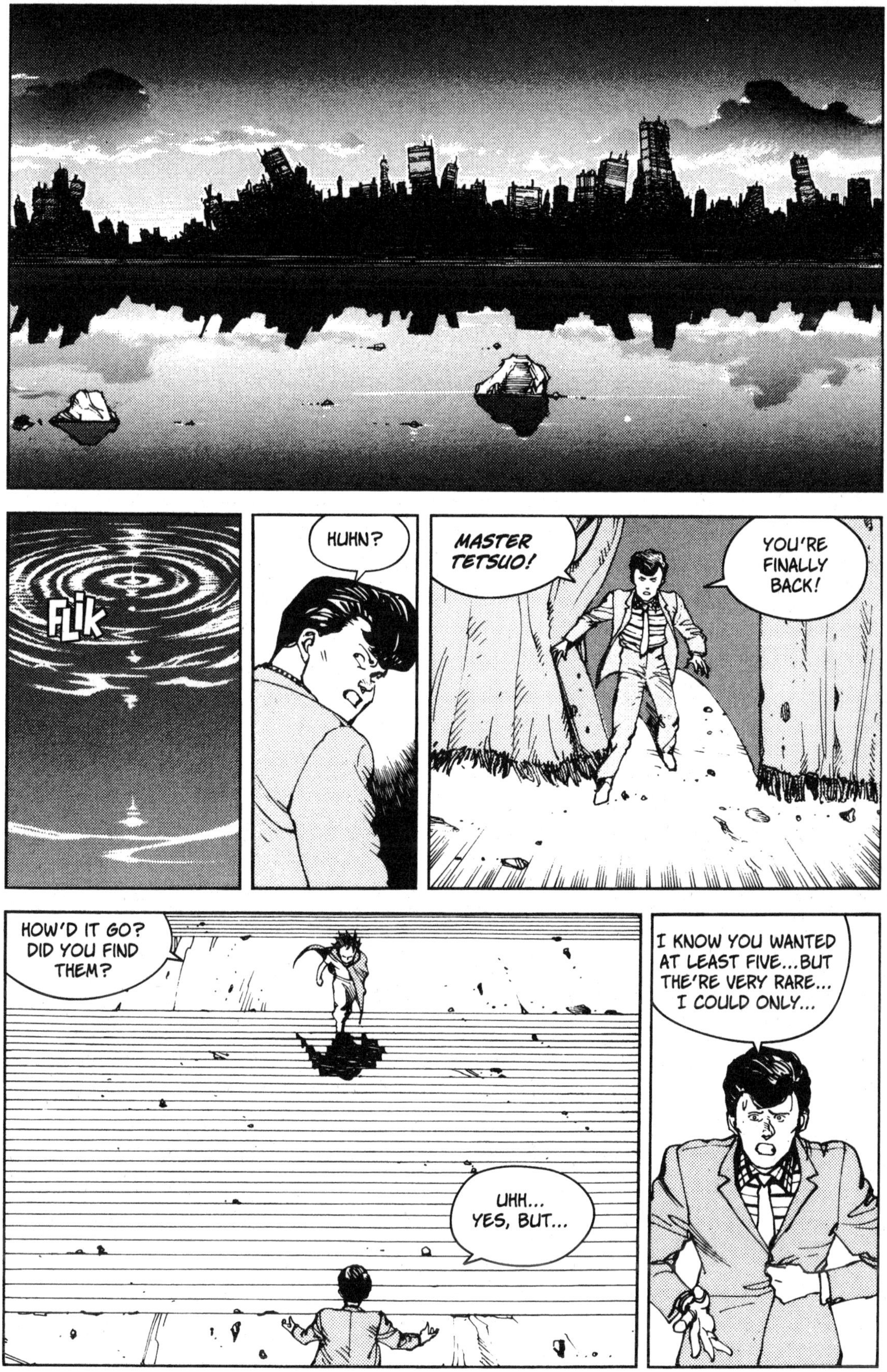
FLIK
HUHN?
MASTER TETSUO!
YOU'RE FINALLY BACK!
HOW'D IT GO? DID YOU FIND THEM?
UHH... YES, BUT...
I KNOW YOU WANTED AT LEAST FIVE...BUT THE'RE VERY RARE... I COULD ONLY...

HOW MANY?

TH...THREE OF THEM.

INSIDE, LORD.

WHERE?

SOME...SOME OF THEM STILL HAVE FAMILIES... SO, IF YOU COULD MAYBE GO *EASY* ON THEM...

IN FACT...

...TRY NOT TO *KILL* THEM, PLEASE...

SLAM

OH!

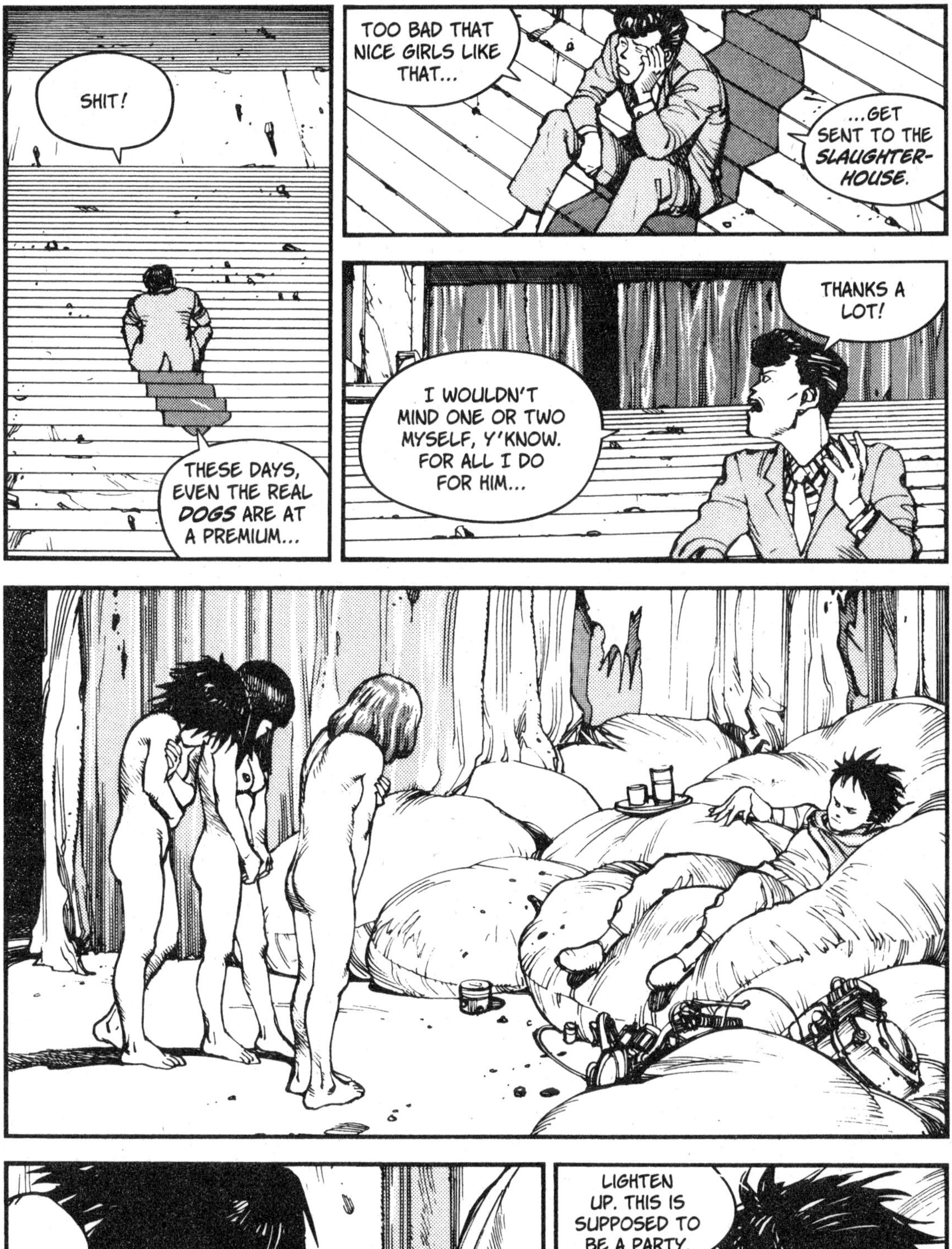
SHIT!
THESE DAYS, EVEN THE REAL DOGS ARE AT A PREMIUM...
TOO BAD THAT NICE GIRLS LIKE THAT...
...GET SENT TO THE SLAUGHTER-HOUSE.
I WOULDN'T MIND ONE OR TWO MYSELF, Y'KNOW. FOR ALL I DO FOR HIM...
THANKS A LOT!
LIGHTEN UP. THIS IS SUPPOSED TO BE A PARTY.

...AND I BROUGHT THE FAVORS!

DON'T WORRY... THEY AREN'T FULL STRENGTH. JUST ENOUGH TO MAKE YOU RELAX.

SLiF

OH!

...

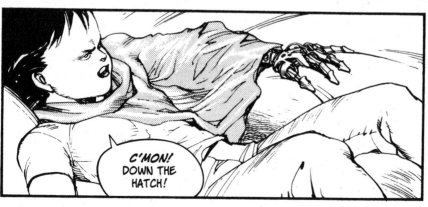

C'MON! DOWN THE HATCH!

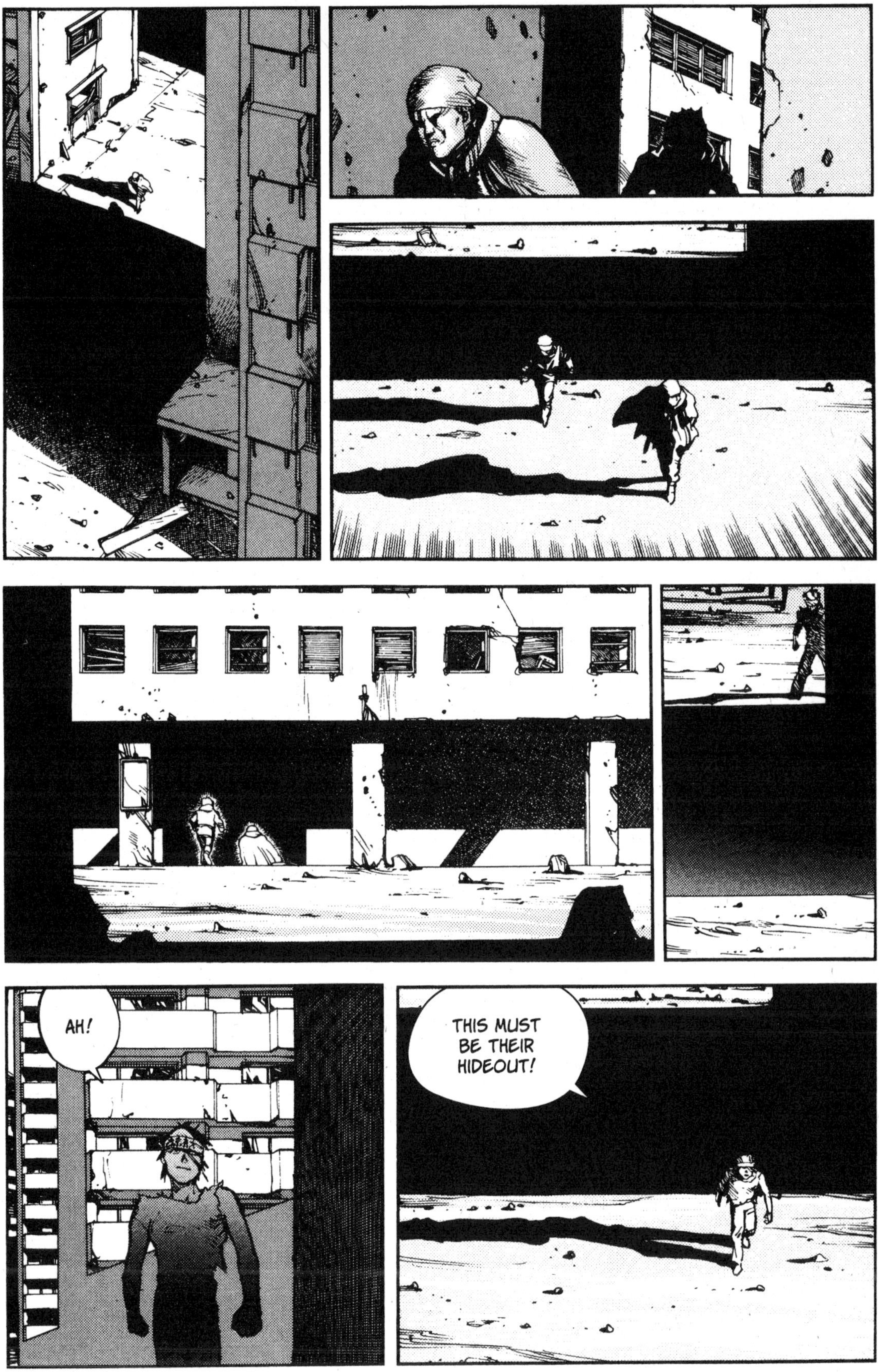
AH!
THIS MUST BE THEIR HIDEOUT!

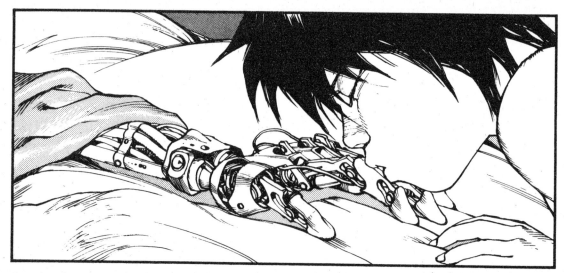

KLIC

OH!

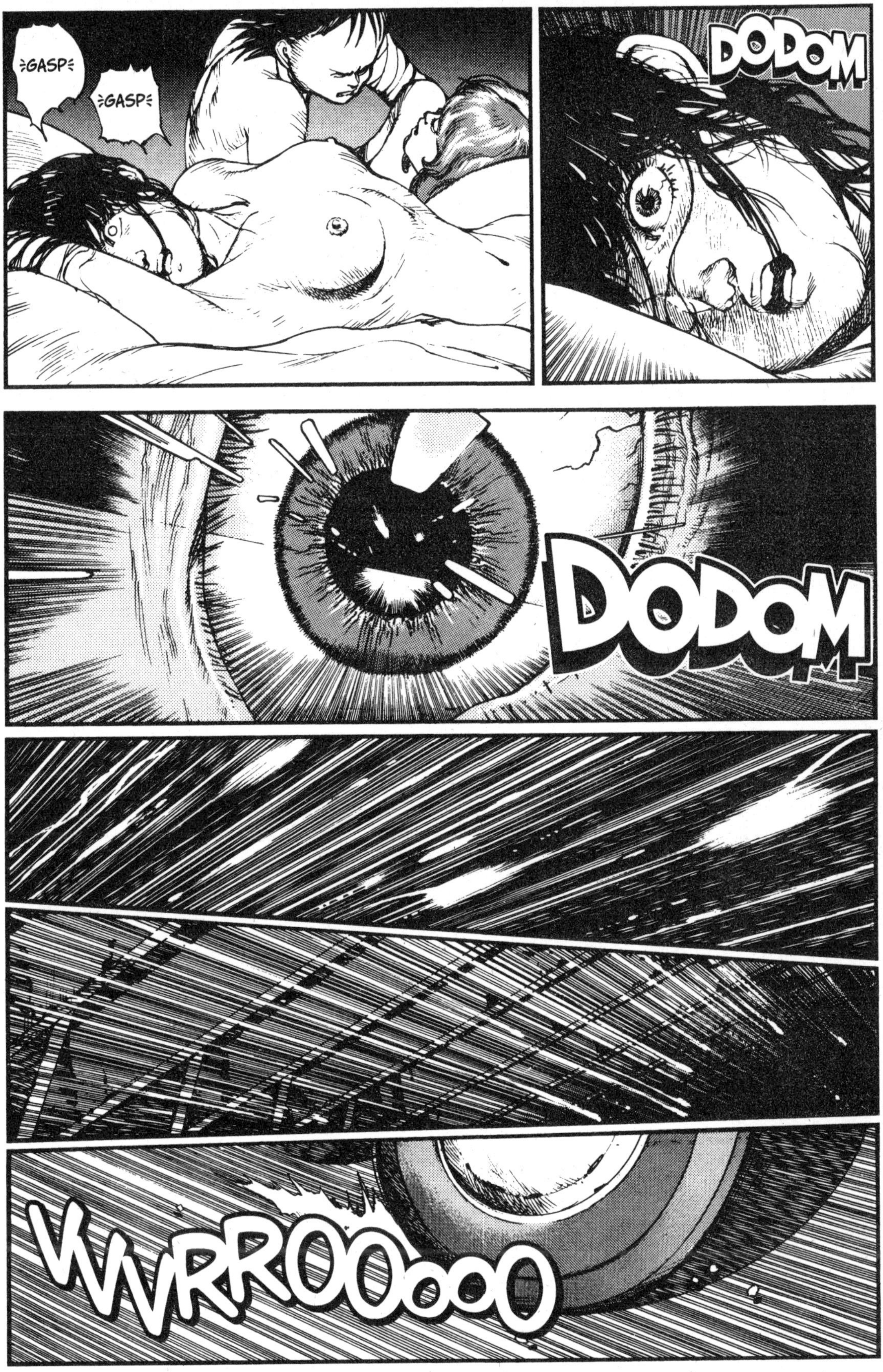

GASP
GASP
DODOM
DODOM
WVRROOooooO

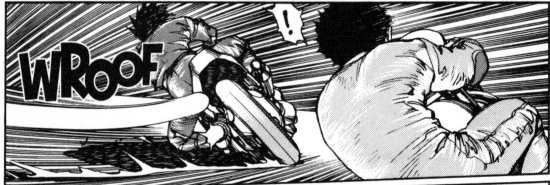

111

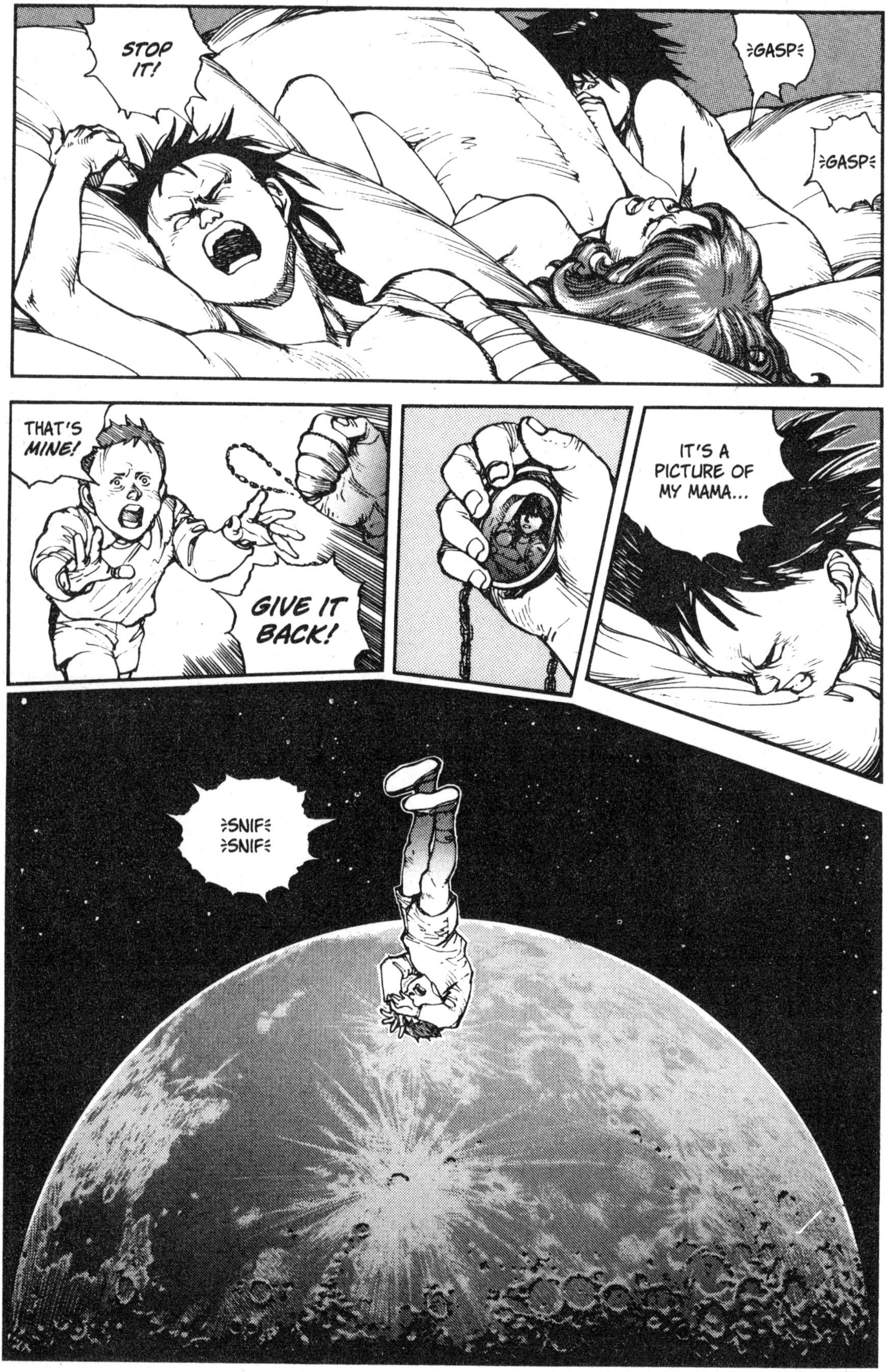
STOP IT!
≷GASP≶
≷GASP≶
THAT'S MINE!
GIVE IT BACK!
IT'S A PICTURE OF MY MAMA...
≷SNIF≶ ≷SNIF≶

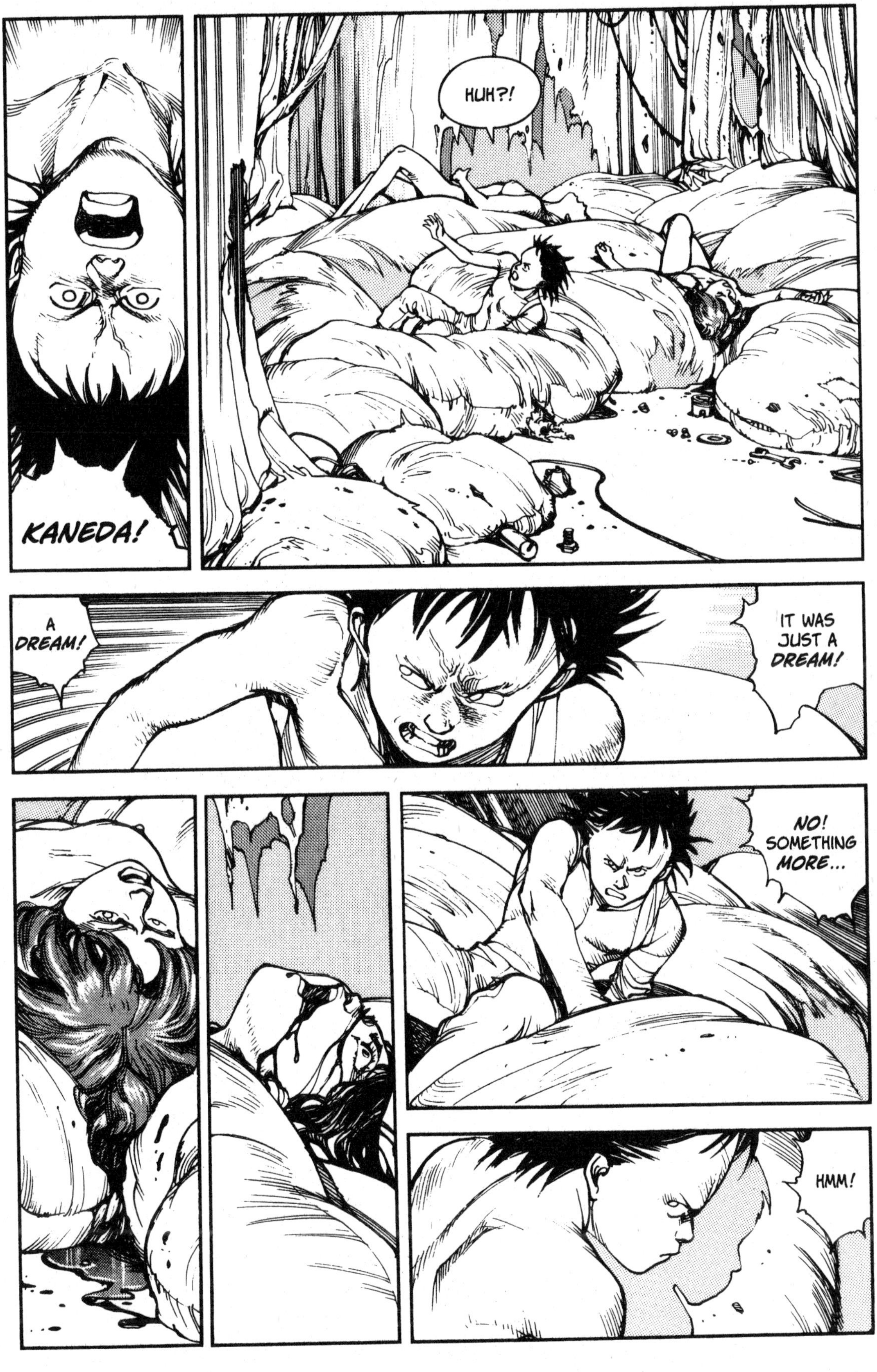
KANEDA!
HUH?!
A DREAM!
IT WAS JUST A DREAM!
NO! SOMETHING MORE...
HMM!

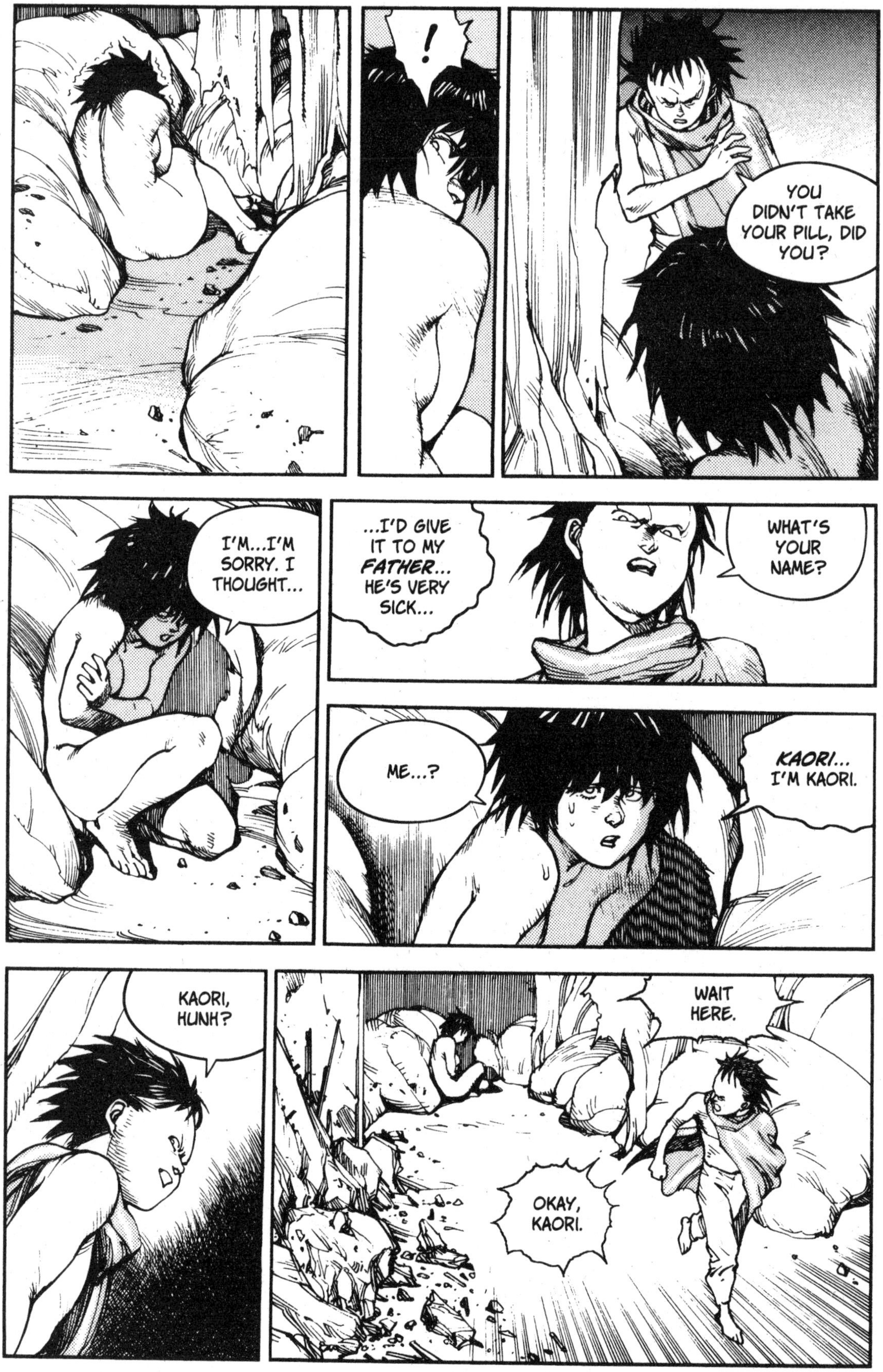
!
YOU DIDN'T TAKE YOUR PILL, DID YOU?
I'M...I'M SORRY. I THOUGHT...
...I'D GIVE IT TO MY FATHER... HE'S VERY SICK...
WHAT'S YOUR NAME?
ME...?
KAORI... I'M KAORI.
KAORI, HUNH?
WAIT HERE.
OKAY, KAORI.

117

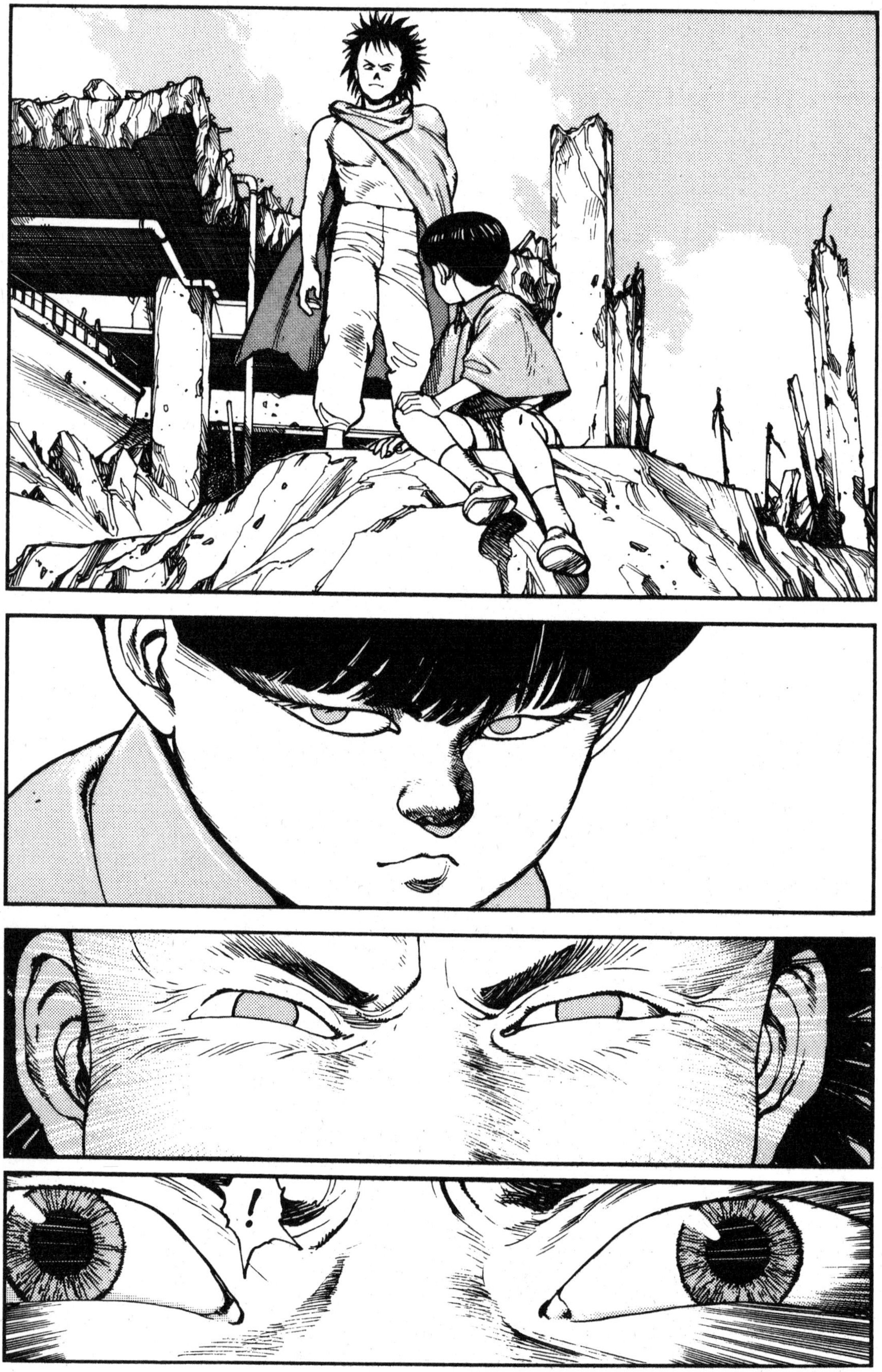
!

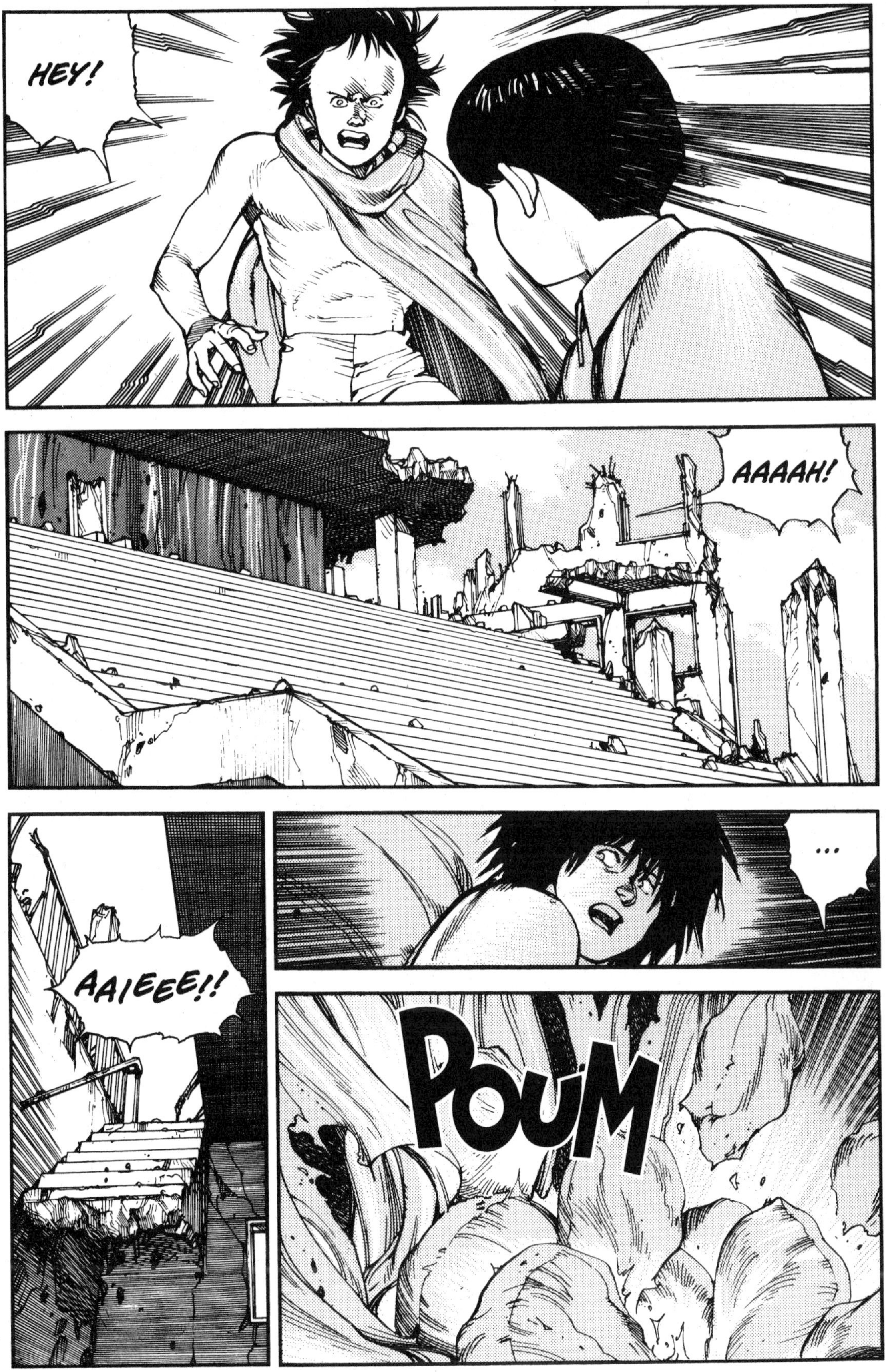
HEY!
AAAAH!
AAIEEE!!
...
POUM

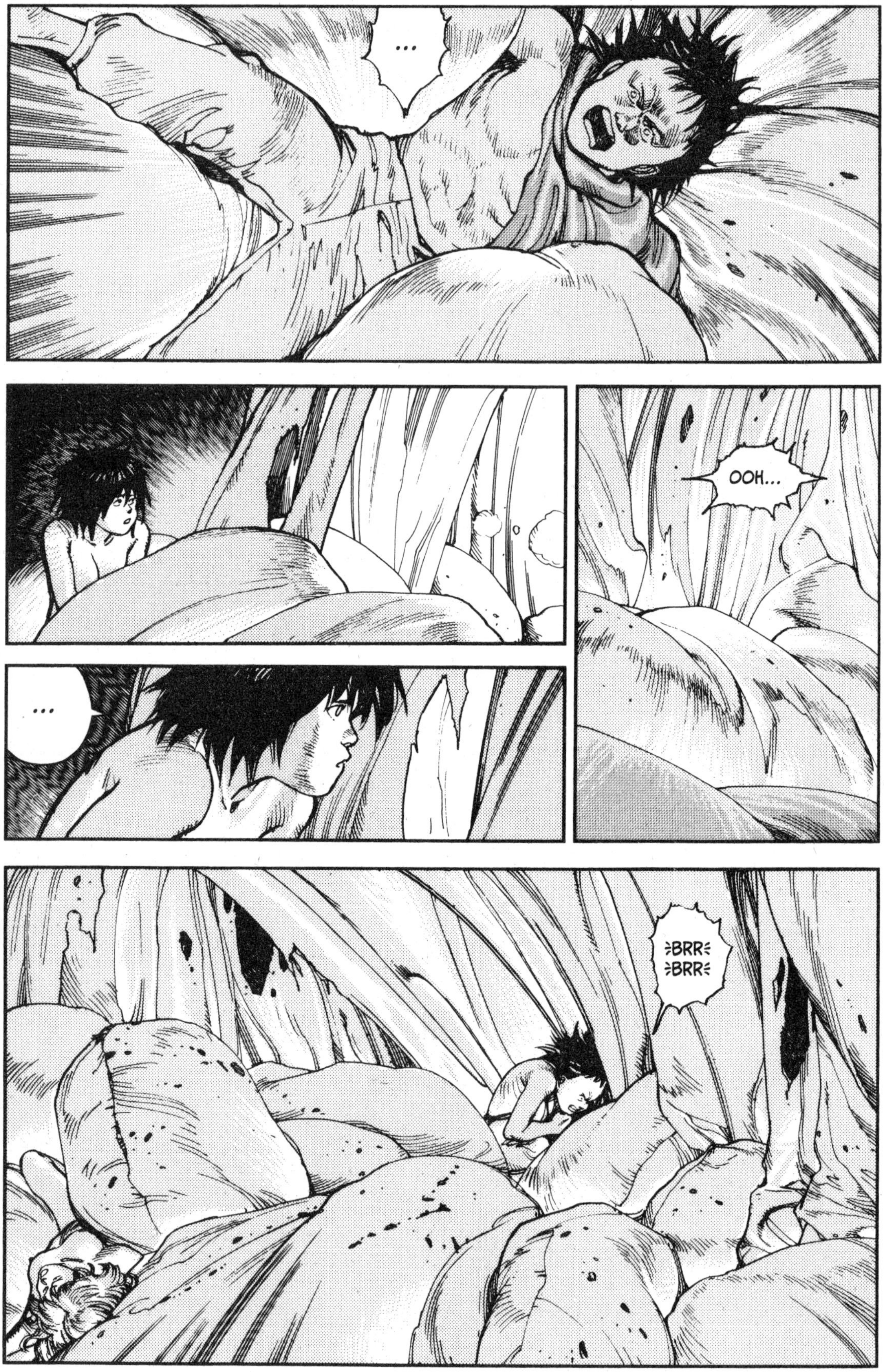
...
...
OOH...
BRR
BRR

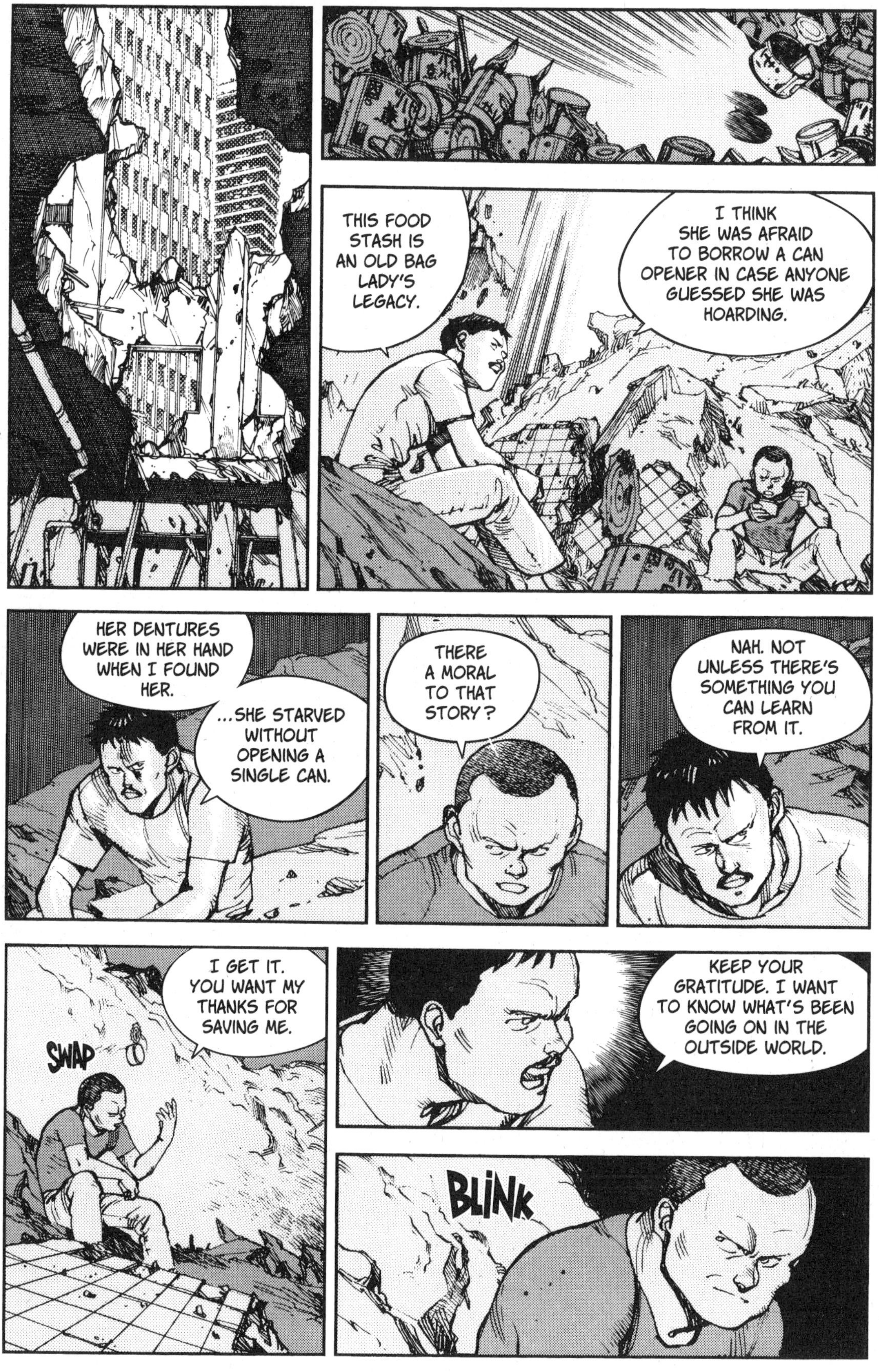
THIS FOOD STASH IS AN OLD BAG LADY'S LEGACY.
I THINK SHE WAS AFRAID TO BORROW A CAN OPENER IN CASE ANYONE GUESSED SHE WAS HOARDING.
HER DENTURES WERE IN HER HAND WHEN I FOUND HER.
...SHE STARVED WITHOUT OPENING A SINGLE CAN.
THERE A MORAL TO THAT STORY?
NAH. NOT UNLESS THERE'S SOMETHING YOU CAN LEARN FROM IT.
I GET IT. YOU WANT MY THANKS FOR SAVING ME.
SWAP
KEEP YOUR GRATITUDE. I WANT TO KNOW WHAT'S BEEN GOING ON IN THE OUTSIDE WORLD.
BLINK

LAST WEEK...

BLONK

THE RUSSIANS TOOK CONTROL OF NORTHERN JAPAN.

THERE WAS A FACE-OFF BETWEEN THE RUSSIAN AND JAPANESE NAVEL FLEETS IN THE STRAITS OF TSUGARU.

A MONTH AGO, A PROVISIONAL GOVERNMENT WAS APPOINTED, BUT IT'S STRICTLY FOR SHOW... IT HAS NO REAL POWER.

WHAT ABOUT...THE AMERICANS?

THEIR FLEET'S IN THE AREA...

...BUT THEY'RE KEEPING THEIR DISTANCE.

BUT THEY HAVE TO INTERVENE! WHAT ABOUT OUR TREATY?!

THEY ARE AFRAID OF AKIRA.

SEEMS THEY'D GATHERED SOME INTELLIGENCE ABOUT THE PROJECT, BUT THEY WEREN'T TAKING IT SERIOUSLY...

...UNTIL THEY SAW WHAT HAPPENED TO NEO-TOKYO. THEY'RE SCARED, AND I DON'T BLAME THEM.

YOU MEAN...

...NEO-TOKYO HAS BEEN COMPLETELY ABANDONED?!

EXCEPT FOR AKIRA...!

SO WHAT DO YOU PLAN TO DO ABOUT HIM?

WHAT'S IT TO YOU?

REMEMBER THE STORY OF THE BAG LADY...?

YOU'LL END UP *DEAD* IF YOU DON'T LEARN TO TRUST SOMEONE.

I USED TO BE PART OF A GROUP A LOT LIKE THE ONE YOU'RE IN.

WHERE ARE THEY NOW?

YOU'RE NO *CIVILIAN*...

WHO ARE YOU?

I'M THE ONLY ONE LEFT.

COME ON, LET ME HELP YOU...

VERY EFFICIENT. WHERE SHOULD I SEND MY RESUME?

SORRY. I'M NOT IN THE HABIT OF RECRUITING ON THE SPOT.

WASHINGTON?

YOU'LL NEVER MAKE IT ON YOUR OWN...

CAN'T YOU SEE THAT?

WHAT'S YOUR NAME, ANYWAY?

RYU.

KRRR
KRR

WHAT THE HELL'S GOING ON IN THERE ...?

MASTER TETSUO'S COMPLETELY LOST IT. HE'S CRINGING IN A CORNER.

AND EVERY TIME I TRY TO TALK TO HIM, HE SAYS "GET THE FUCK OUT"...!

SLOP

HEY!

SHIT! STUFF IT BACK IN!

...

UH...I HAVE SOMETHING IMPORTANT TO TELL YOU.

I'M LISTENING...

TWO PEOPLE ARMED WITH A PISTOL AND A MACHINE GUN? NOT FAR FROM HERE...?

PROBABLY MORE SPIES FROM WHO-KNOWS WHERE...

THEY SEEM TO BE WELL-TRAINED.

...AND HAD A COUPLE OF WEIRD KIDS AT THEIR HIDEOUT.

"WELL... I WASN'T CLOSE AND IT WAS DARK, SO I COULDN'T SEE TOO WELL..."

DEFINE WEIRD.

"...BUT I LOOKED IN WHEN ONE OF THEM WAS GIVING THE KIDS SOME KIND OF INJECTION..."

THEIR FACES ARE ALL WRINKLED AND THEIR HAIR IS WHITE, LIKE THEY WERE REAL OLD...

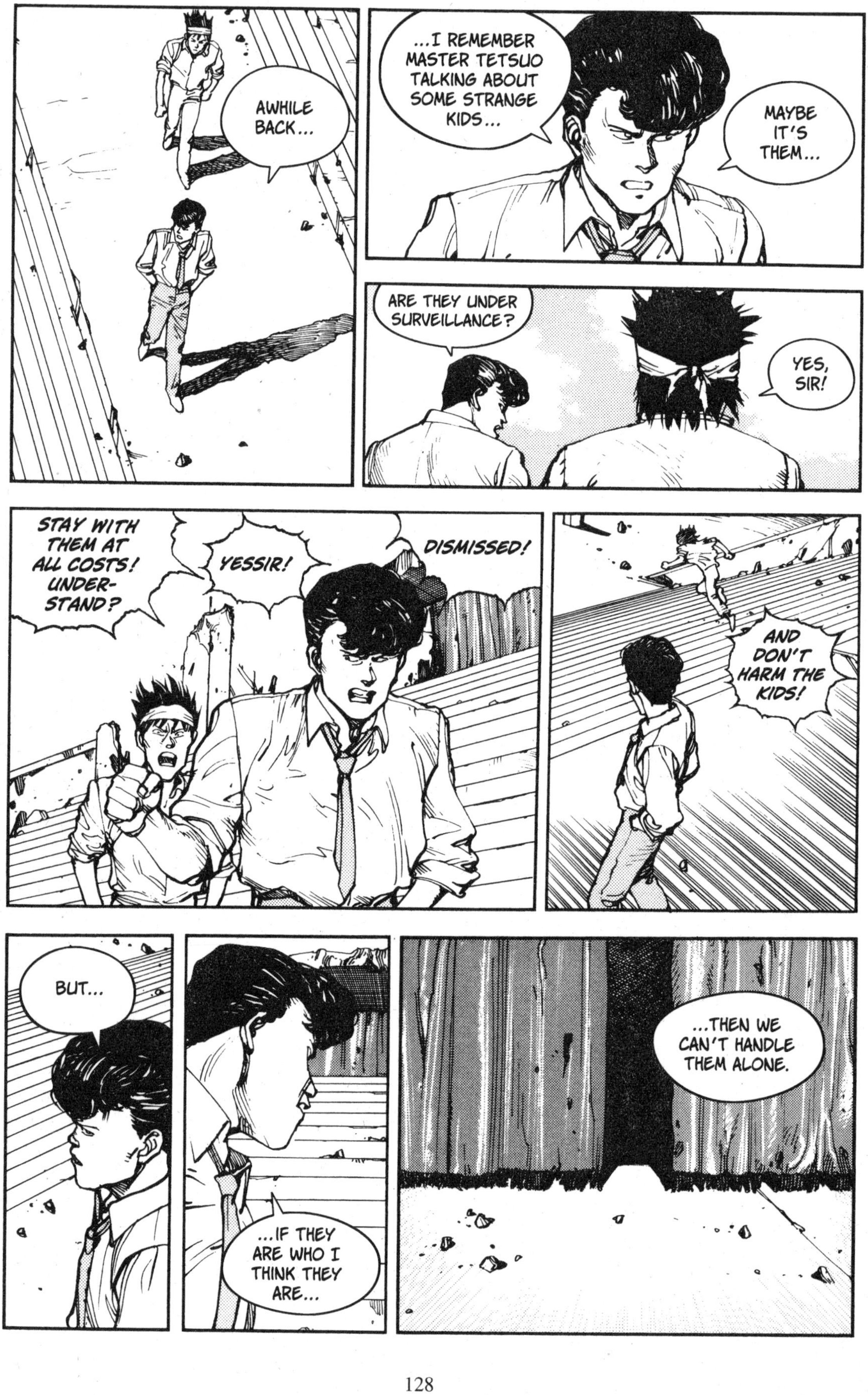
AWHILE BACK...
...I REMEMBER MASTER TETSUO TALKING ABOUT SOME STRANGE KIDS...
MAYBE IT'S THEM...
ARE THEY UNDER SURVEILLANCE?
YES, SIR!
STAY WITH THEM AT ALL COSTS! UNDER-STAND?
YESSIR!
DISMISSED!
AND DON'T HARM THE KIDS!
BUT...
...IF THEY ARE WHO I THINK THEY ARE...
...THEN WE CAN'T HANDLE THEM ALONE.

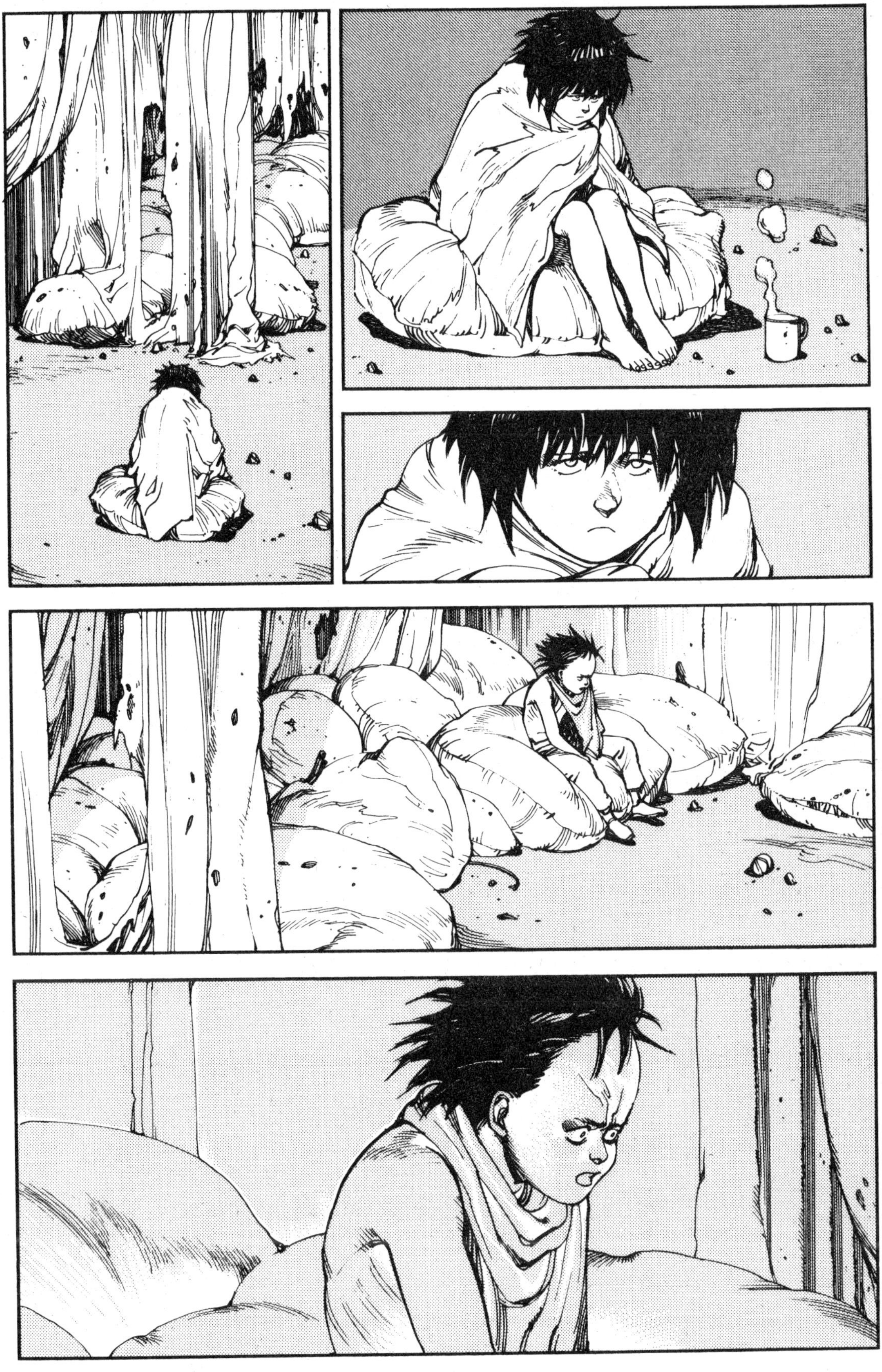

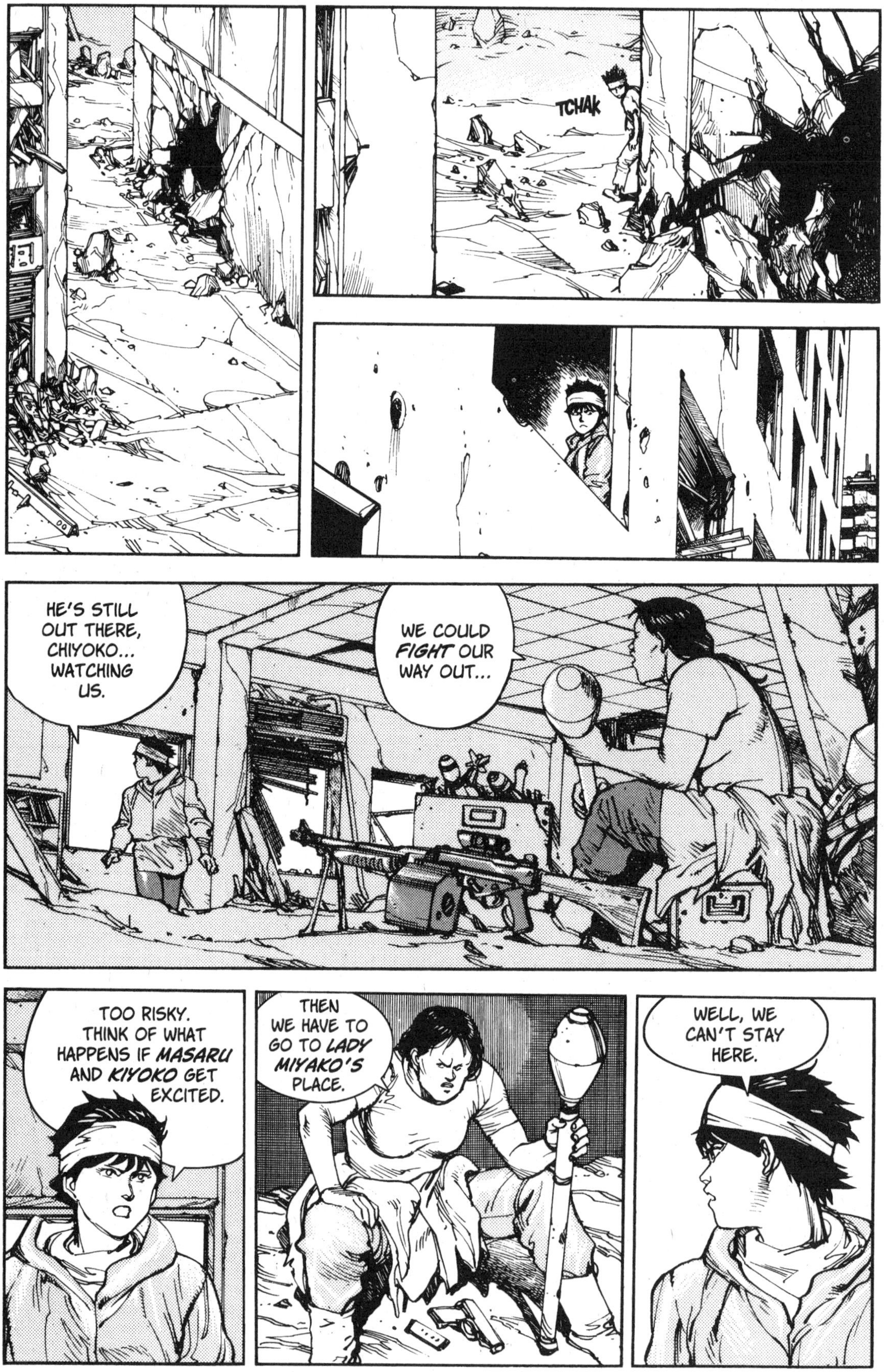
TCHAK
HE'S STILL OUT THERE, CHIYOKO... WATCHING US.
WE COULD *FIGHT* OUR WAY OUT...
TOO RISKY. THINK OF WHAT HAPPENS IF *MASARU* AND *KIYOKO* GET EXCITED.
THEN WE HAVE TO GO TO *LADY MIYAKO'S* PLACE.
WELL, WE CAN'T STAY HERE.

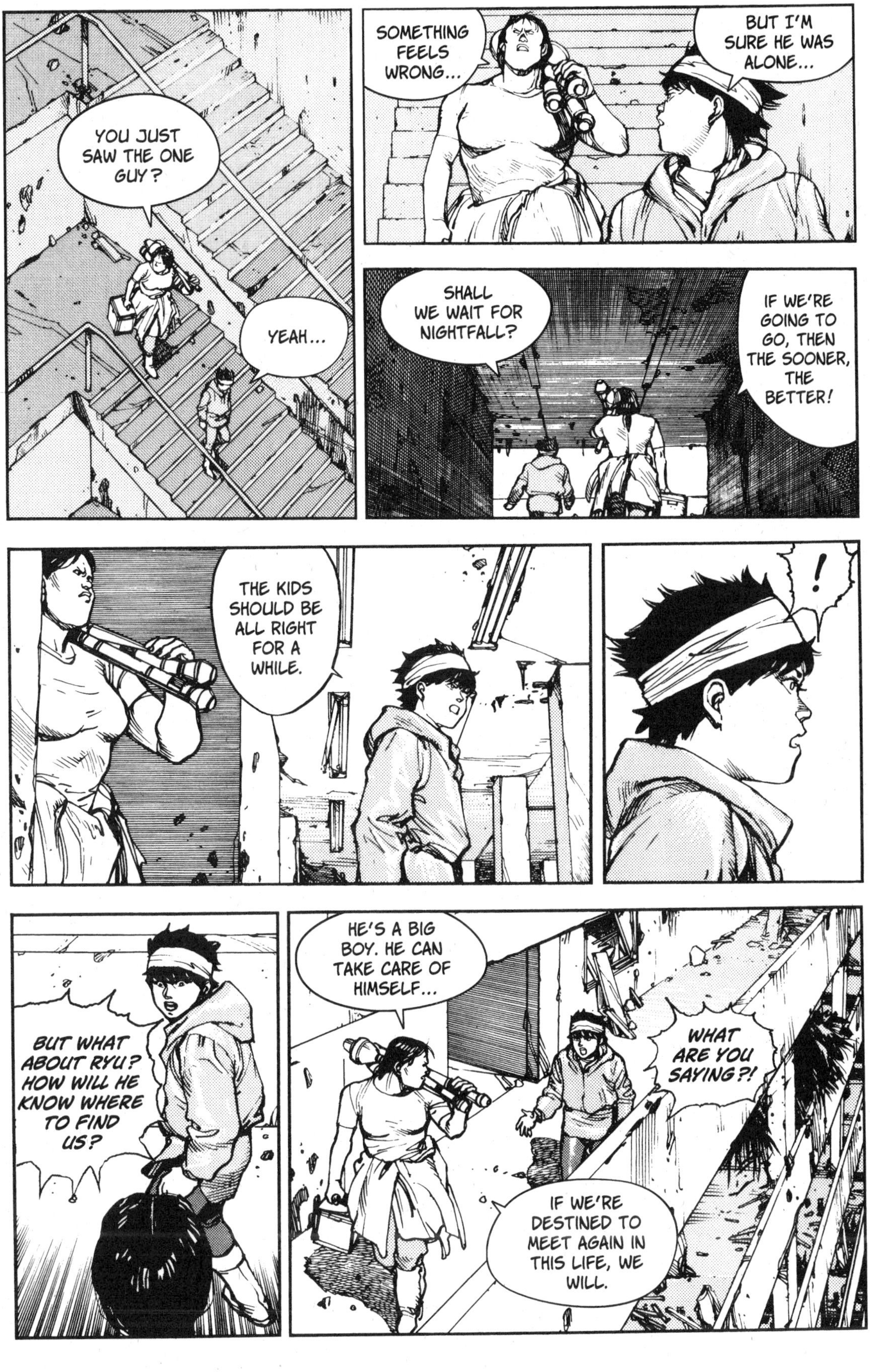
YOU JUST SAW THE ONE GUY?
YEAH...
SOMETHING FEELS WRONG...
BUT I'M SURE HE WAS ALONE...
SHALL WE WAIT FOR NIGHTFALL?
IF WE'RE GOING TO GO, THEN THE SOONER, THE BETTER!
THE KIDS SHOULD BE ALL RIGHT FOR A WHILE.
!
BUT WHAT ABOUT RYU? HOW WILL HE KNOW WHERE TO FIND US?
HE'S A BIG BOY. HE CAN TAKE CARE OF HIMSELF...
WHAT ARE YOU SAYING?!
IF WE'RE DESTINED TO MEET AGAIN IN THIS LIFE, WE WILL.

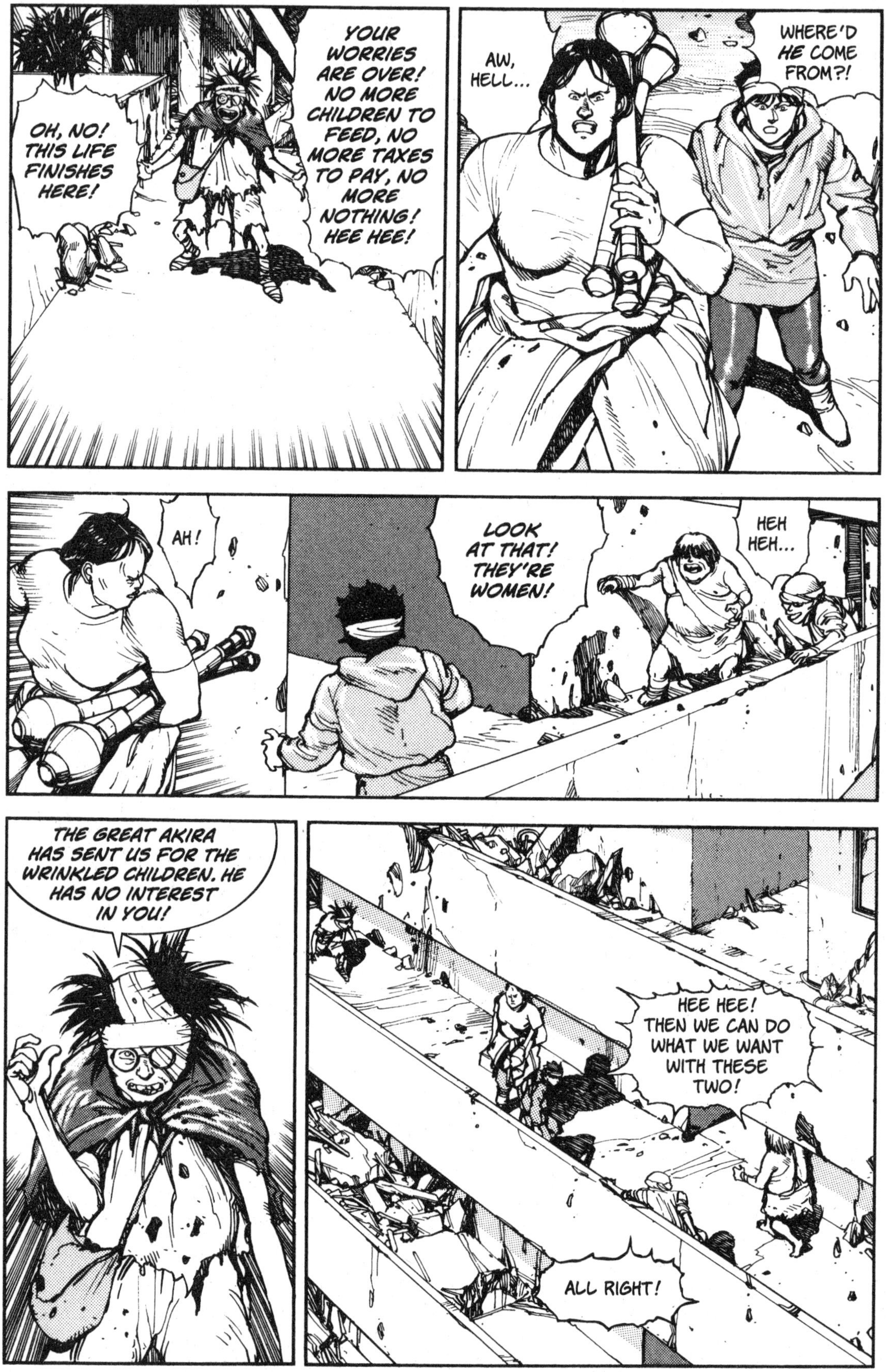
OH, NO! THIS LIFE FINISHES HERE!
YOUR WORRIES ARE OVER! NO MORE CHILDREN TO FEED, NO MORE TAXES TO PAY, NO MORE NOTHING! HEE HEE!
AW, HELL...
WHERE'D HE COME FROM?!
AH!
LOOK AT THAT! THEY'RE WOMEN!
HEH HEH...
THE GREAT AKIRA HAS SENT US FOR THE WRINKLED CHILDREN. HE HAS NO INTEREST IN YOU!
HEE HEE! THEN WE CAN DO WHAT WE WANT WITH THESE TWO!
ALL RIGHT!

YOU MUSTN'T DO ANYTHING TO UPSET THOSE CHILDREN...

IF THEY APPROACH AKIRA IT COULD--

IT'S TOO LATE FOR ADVICE...

THE CHILDREN ARE ALREADY IN OUR HANDS!

WHAT?!

WELL...

...LOOKS LIKE NEGOTIATIONS ARE OUT OF THE QUESTION...

READY WHENEVER YOU ARE...

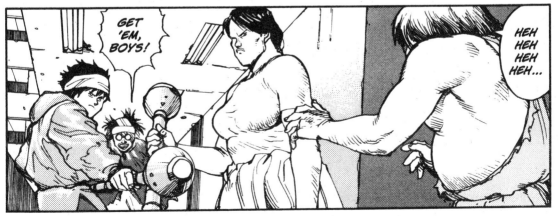

GET 'EM, BOYS!

HEH HEH HEH HEH...

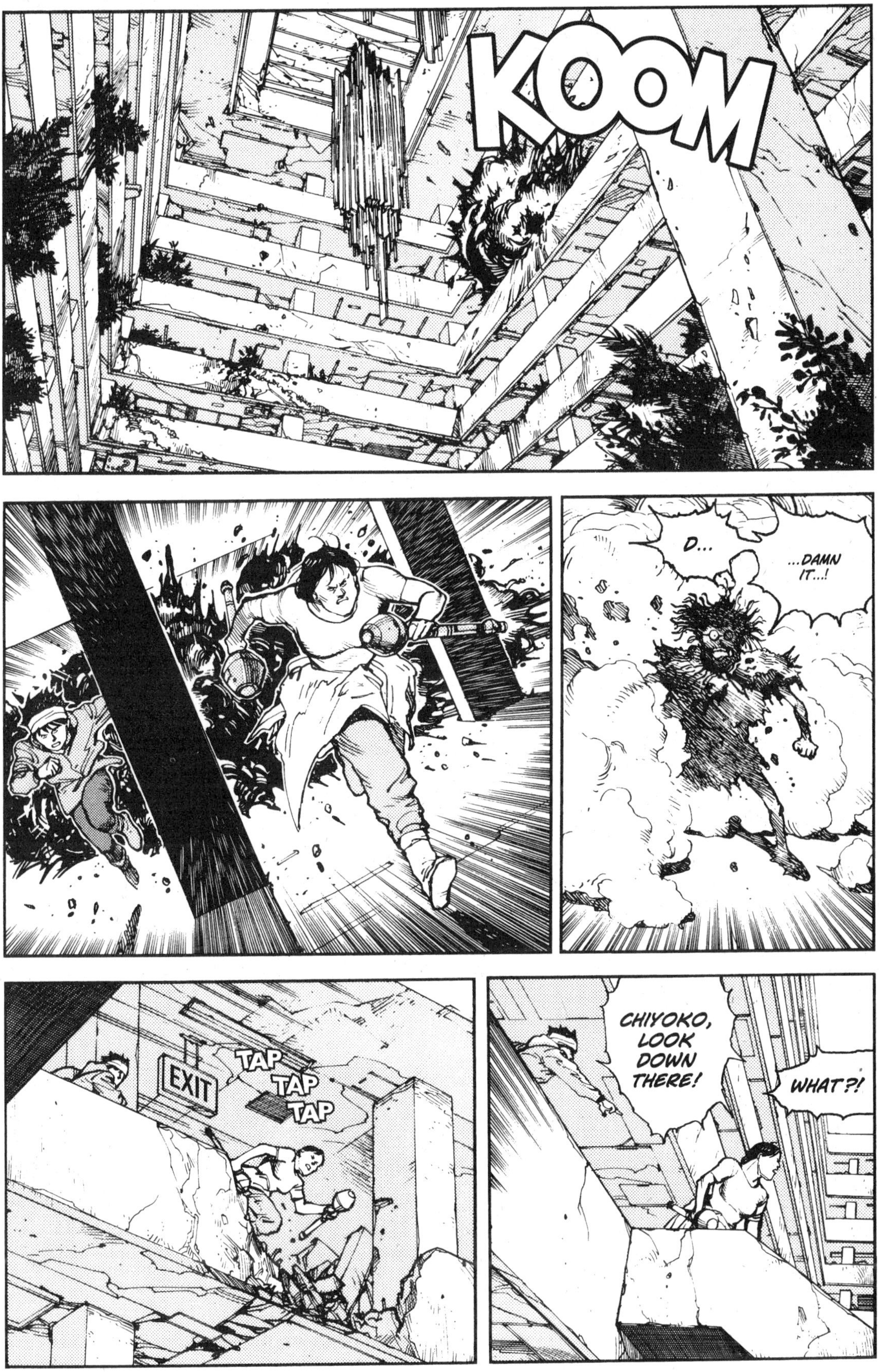
KOOM
D...
...DAMN IT...!
EXIT
TAP
TAP
TAP
CHIYOKO, LOOK DOWN THERE!
WHAT?!

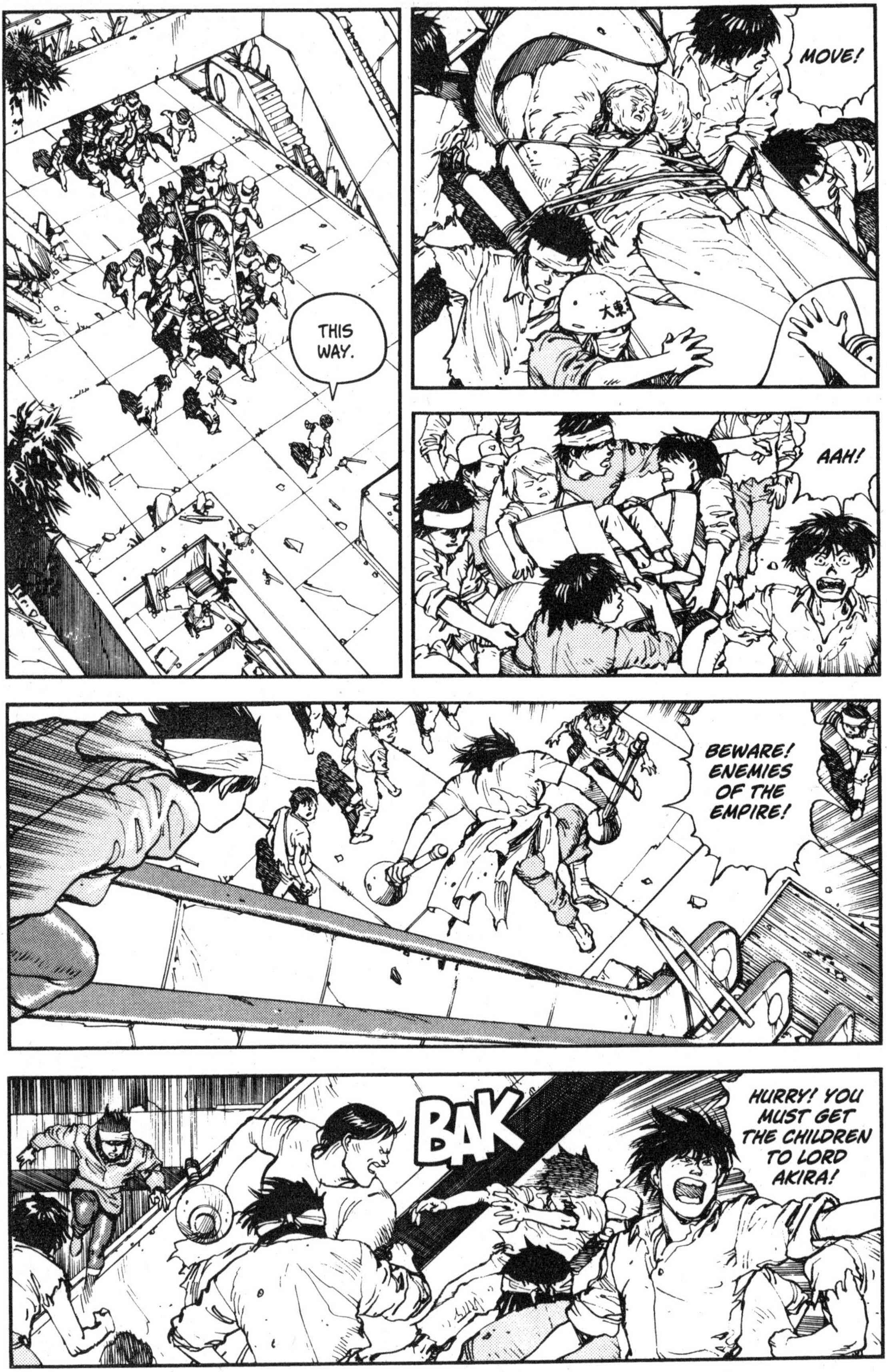
THIS WAY.
MOVE!
AAH!
BEWARE! ENEMIES OF THE EMPIRE!
BAK
HURRY! YOU MUST GET THE CHILDREN TO LORD AKIRA!

BRROM

≈UHN!≈

KEI!!

SMAK

GOT HER!

PAOF

! SLAP

SUR-PRISE...

138

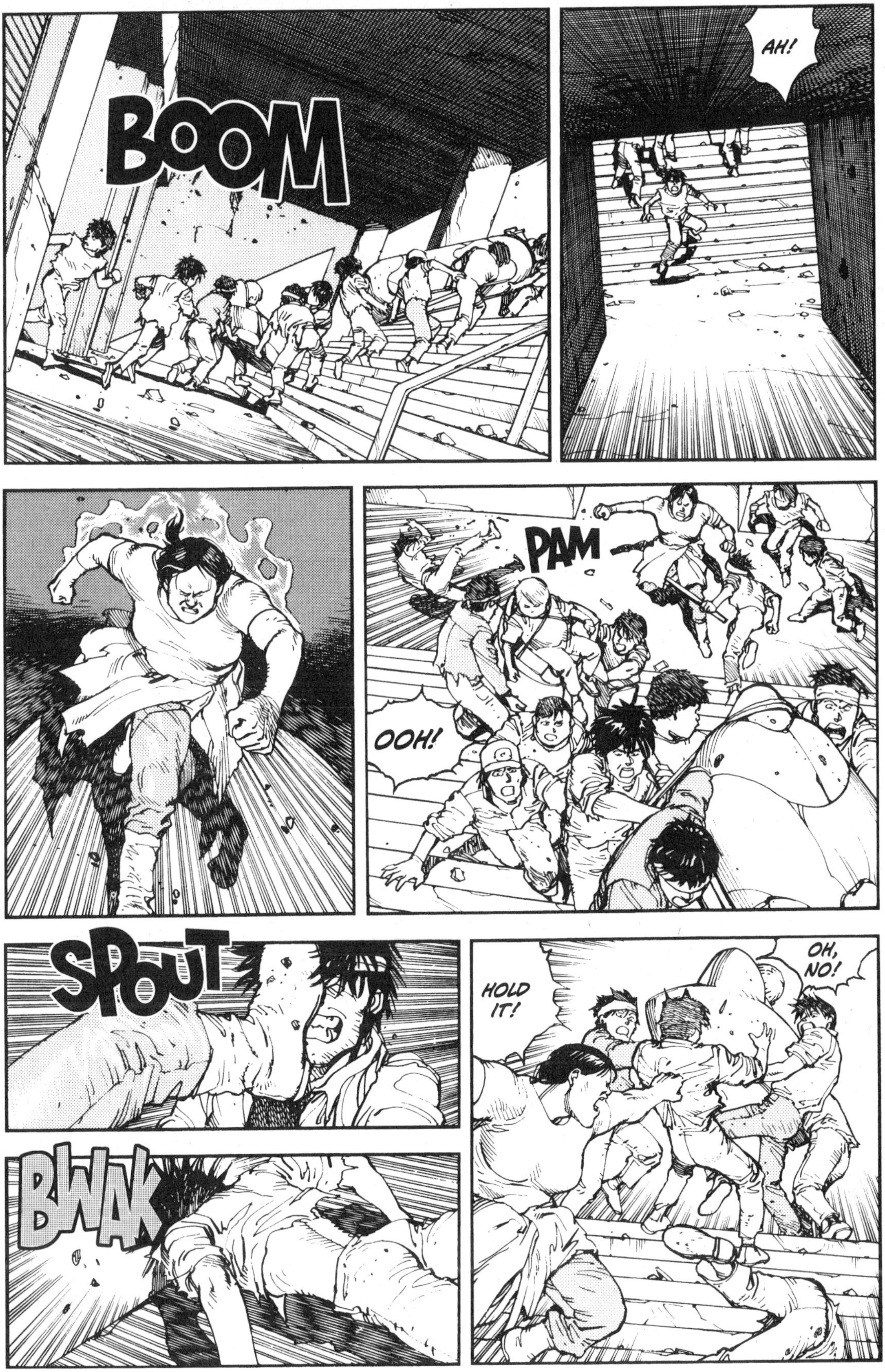

BOOM
AH!
PAM
OOH!
SPOUT
BWAK
HOLD IT!
OH, NO!

TIME FOR US TO GO.

KISS YOUR ASS GOODBYE, BITCH!

TSHIK

IT'LL WORK BETTER...

...IF YOU TAKE THE *SAFETY* OFF.

SAFETY...?

STAK

≒UHH!≒

GARF

DUMB-ASS...

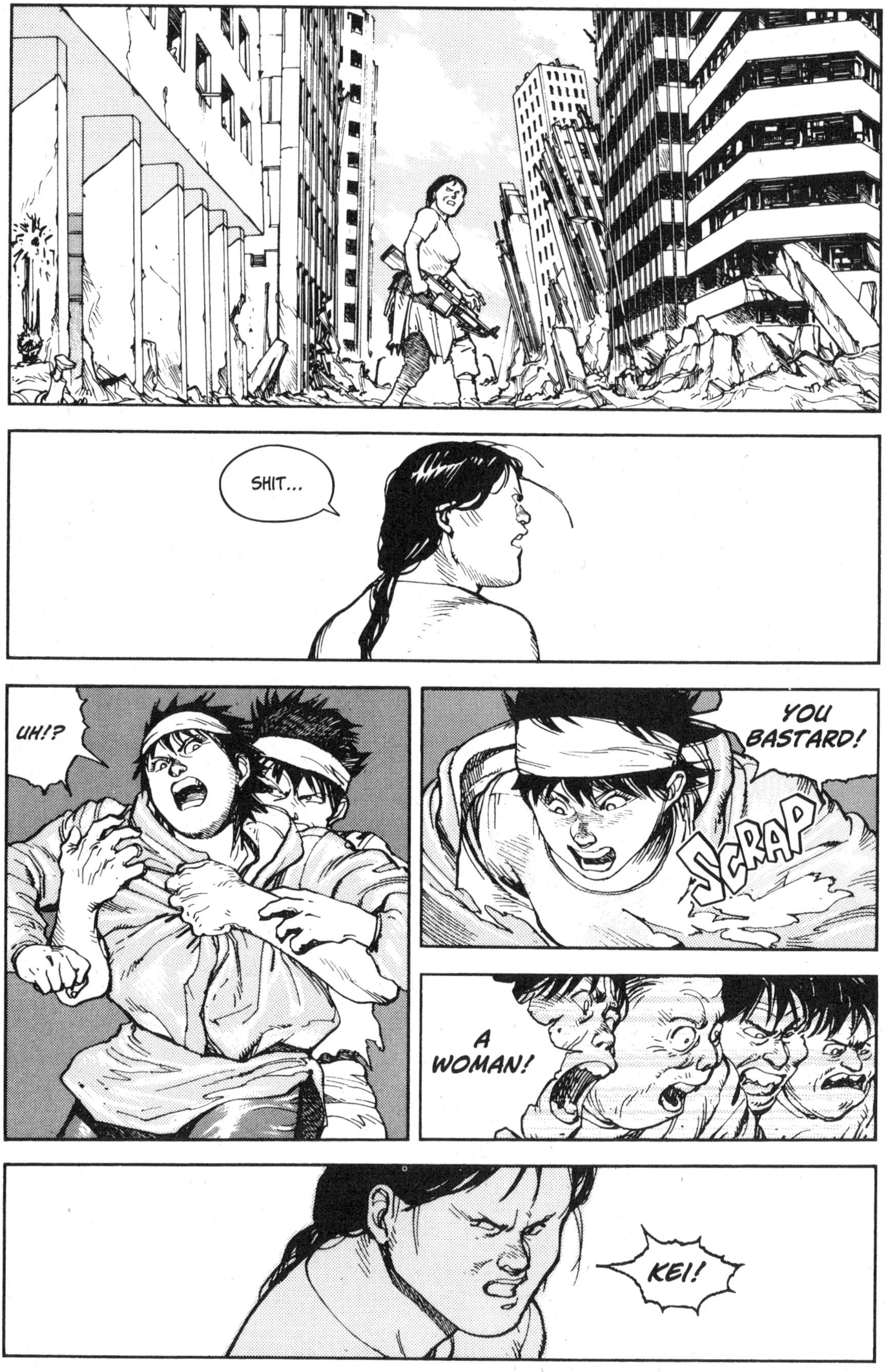
SHIT...
UH!?
YOU BASTARD!
SCRAP
A WOMAN!
KEI!

TAK
!
SSH!
GET DOWN, KEI!

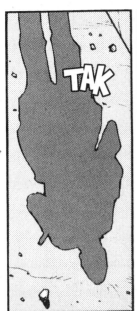

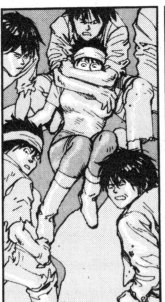

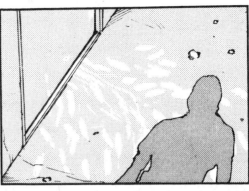

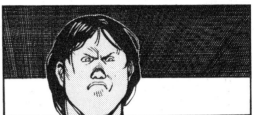

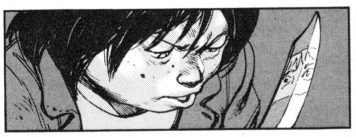

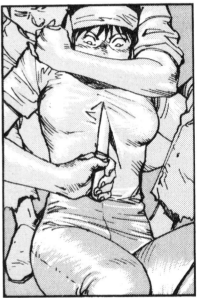

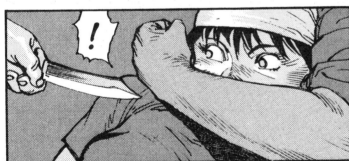

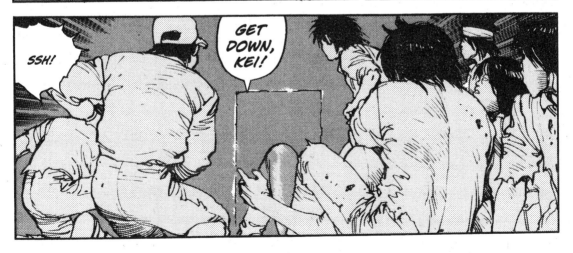

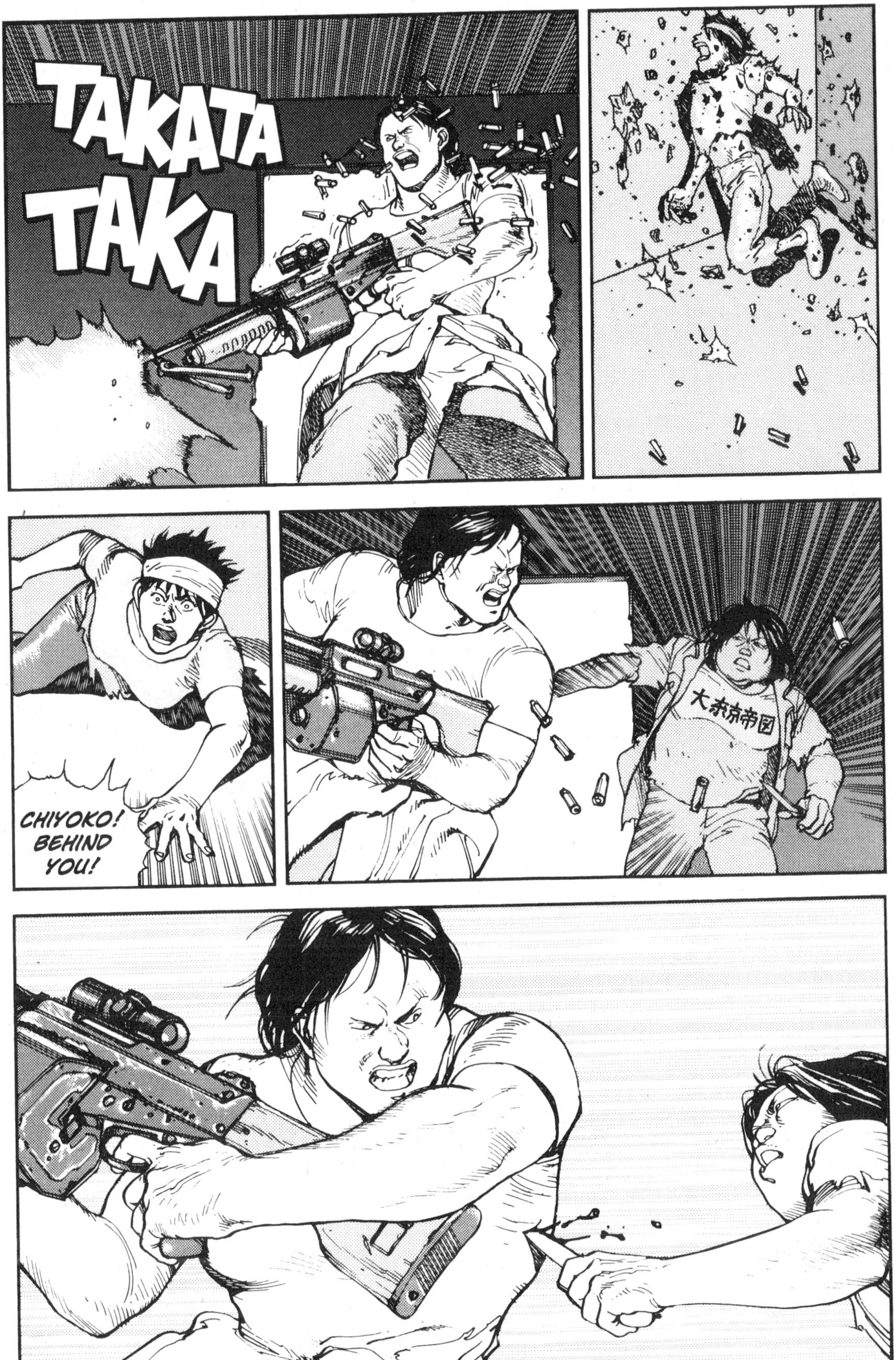
TAKATA TAKA
CHIYOKO! BEHIND YOU!
大東京帝国

KSHAKAKA KAKAKA

SHUIIN

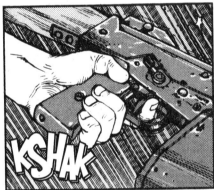

KSHAK

DID THEY... DO ANYTHING TO YOU?

CHIYOKO! YOU'RE WOUNDED!

...CHIYOKO!

TAKE HIM TO *LADY MIYAKO.*

I'LL GO GET THE *OTHER* ONE.

NO, YOU'RE HURT! YOU CAN'T GO ALONE! THEY'LL KILL YOU!

YOU KNOW WE CAN'T JUST LEAVE HIM HERE.

THINK ABOUT WHAT'S GONNA HAPPEN ONCE THAT DRUG WEARS OFF.

...AND THE SAME THING WILL HAPPEN TO THE GIRL.

WE'VE RUN OUT OF OPTIONS.

TOP TOP

WAIT FOR ME AT LADY MIYAKO'S TEMPLE!

I'LL BRING THE GIRL, ONE WAY OR ANOTHER!

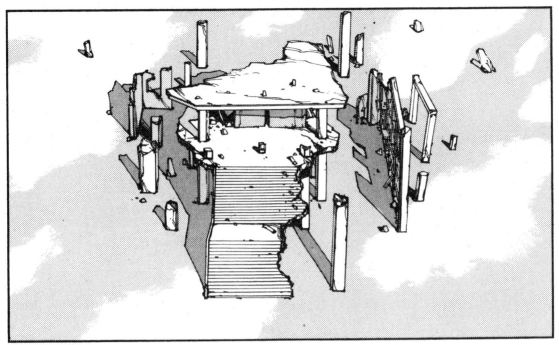

LONG LIVE LORD AKIRA!

NOBLE AKIRA!

YAY!

ALL HAIL THE MASTER!

POPULAR, ISN'T HE?

BUT THERE'S NOTHING *HAPPENING* OVER THERE...

RUMOR HAS IT HE APPEARS BEFORE THE FAITHFUL TWICE A DAY.

THEN I INTEND TO STICK AROUND AND GET A GOOD LOOK AT HIS EXHALTED PRESENCE...

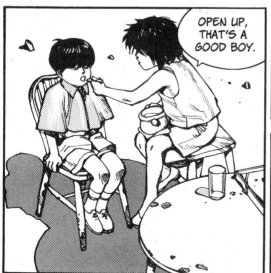

OPEN UP, THAT'S A GOOD BOY.

COME ON... IT'S NOT SO BAD. COULDN'T YOU SMILE JUST A LITTLE?

HOW'S HE DOING?

NOT GOOD. I WISH I COULD FIGURE IT OUT.

IF HE DOESN'T HOLD AN AUDIENCE SOON, THE FAITHFUL ARE GOING TO GET UGLY. WHATTA WE DO?

JUST IN CASE, DISTRIBUTE EXTRA RATIONS. THAT SHOULD KEEP 'EM BUSY.

HMM?

CLING

WHAT DOES THE MASTER WANT? WHY DID YOU LEAVE HIM?

HE FELL ASLEEP.

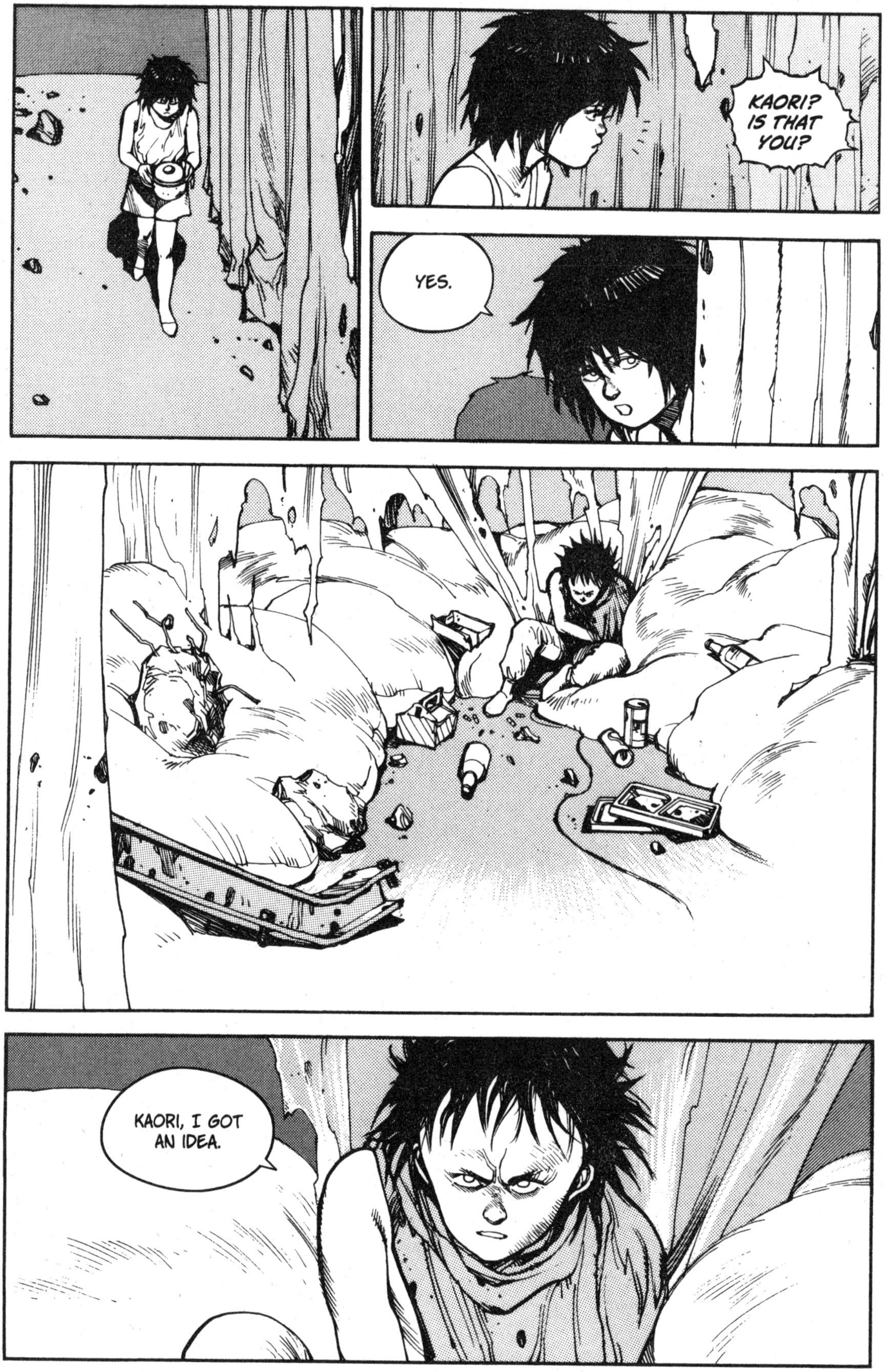
KAORI? IS THAT YOU?
YES.
KAORI, I GOT AN IDEA.

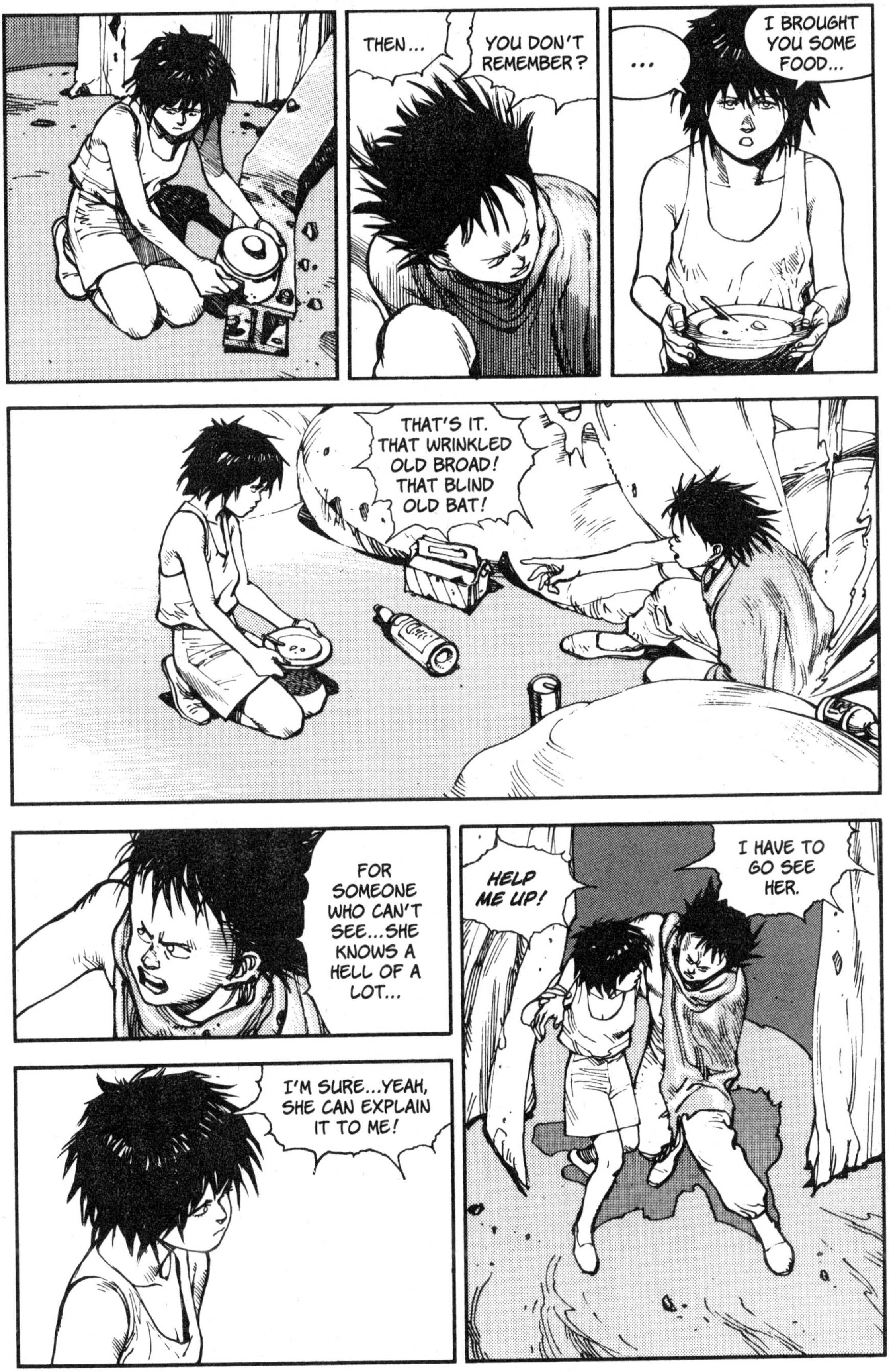
THEN...
YOU DON'T REMEMBER?
...
I BROUGHT YOU SOME FOOD...
THAT'S IT. THAT WRINKLED OLD BROAD! THAT BLIND OLD BAT!
FOR SOMEONE WHO CAN'T SEE...SHE KNOWS A HELL OF A LOT...
I'M SURE...YEAH, SHE CAN EXPLAIN IT TO ME!
HELP ME UP!
I HAVE TO GO SEE HER.

MOVE YOUR ASSES!
SHAAAA
HEY-- WHAT'S THAT?
SHIIIIIIZ
WOW !!

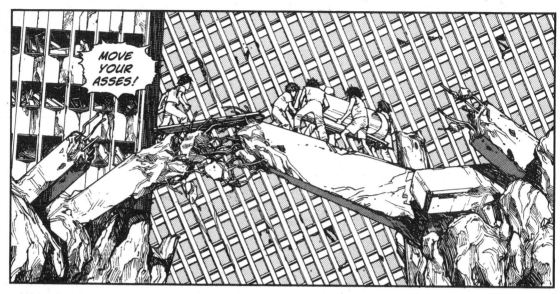

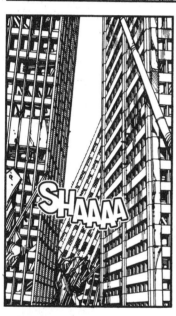

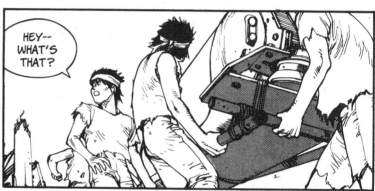

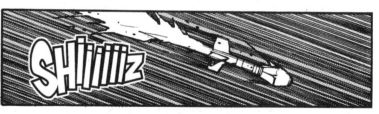

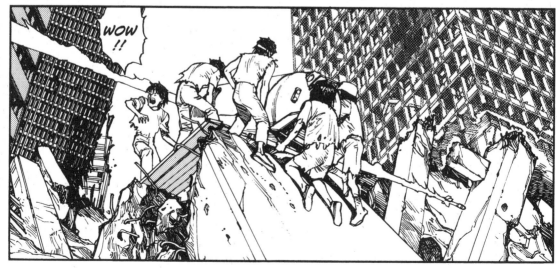

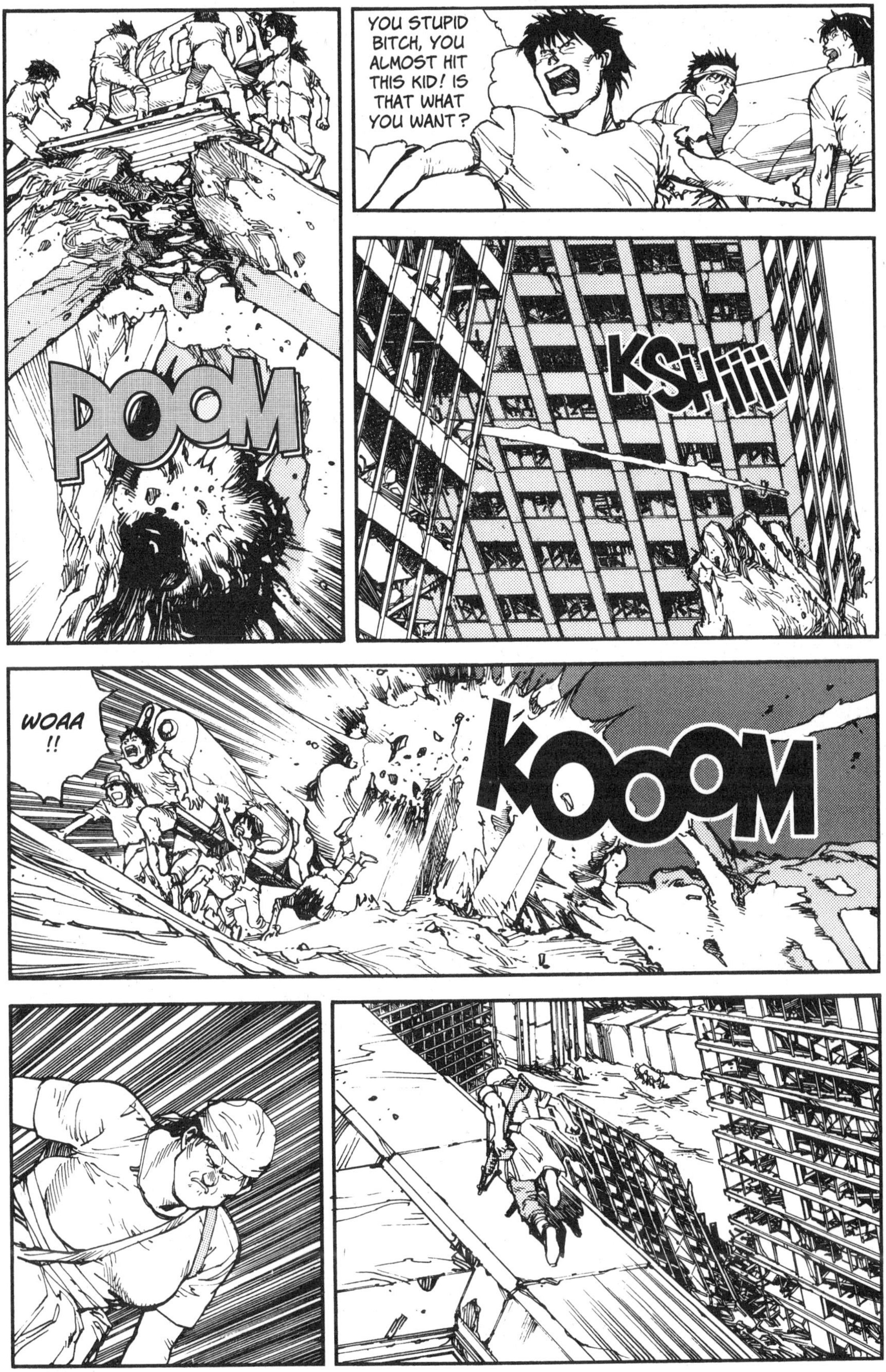
YOU STUPID BITCH, YOU ALMOST HIT THIS KID! IS THAT WHAT YOU WANT?
POOM
KSHiii
WOAA !!
KOOOM

AAH...

MOVE!

HAUL ASS!

ONCE WE CROSS THE EMPIRE'S BORDERS, WE'RE HOME FREE!

COME ON YOU PUSSIES! ACT LIKE CITIZENS OF THE EMPIRE! COME ON!

HE'S RIGHT! LET'S DO IT!

≷HFF≷

≷HFF≷

≷HUFF≷

≷HFF≷

SHIT! TURN BACK! IT'S THE COW!

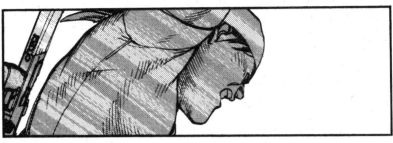

161

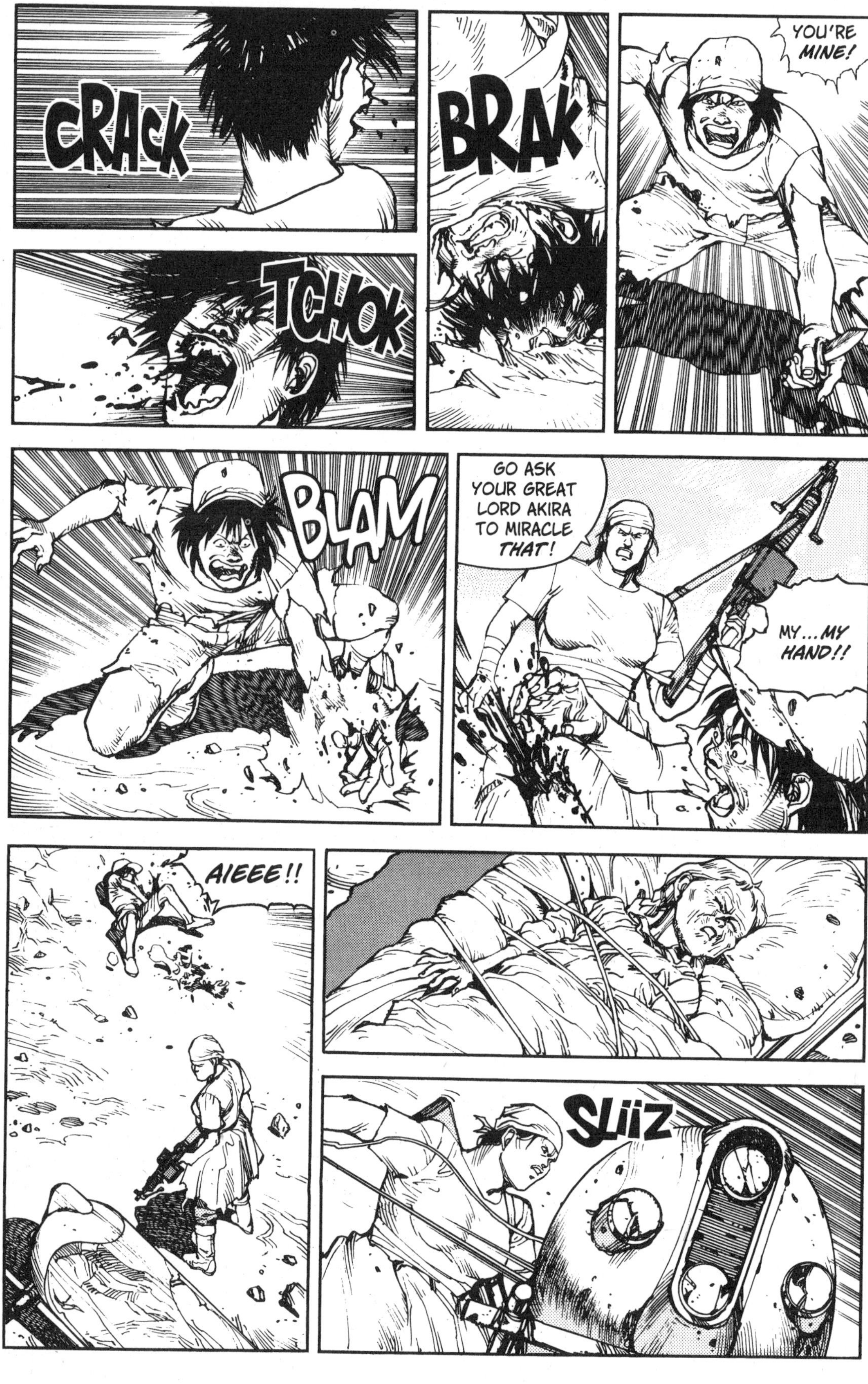
CRACK
TCHOK
BRAK
YOU'RE *MINE!*
BLAM
GO ASK YOUR GREAT LORD AKIRA TO MIRACLE *THAT!*
MY... *MY HAND!!*
AIEEE!!
SLIIZ

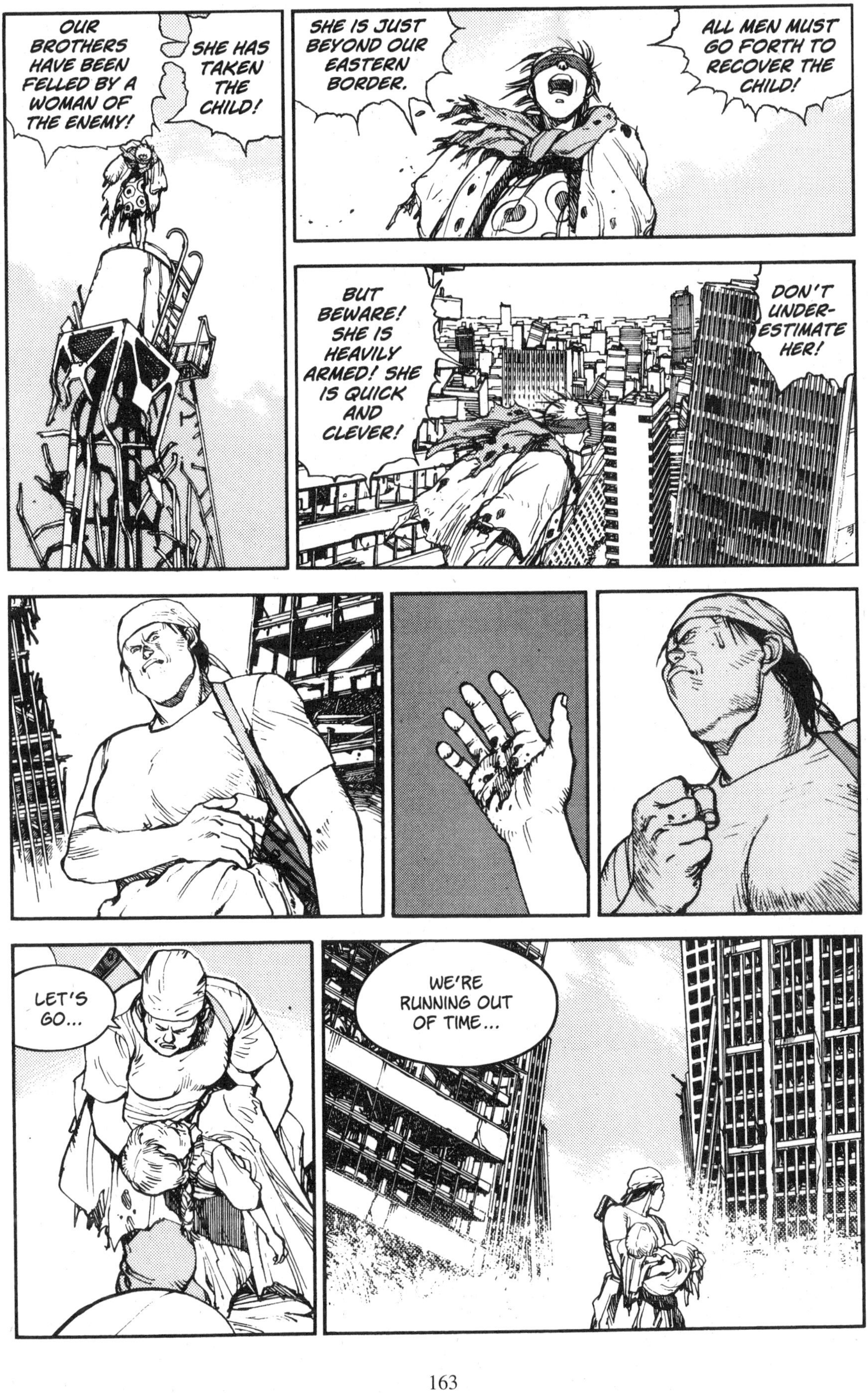
OUR BROTHERS HAVE BEEN FELLED BY A WOMAN OF THE ENEMY!
SHE HAS TAKEN THE CHILD!
SHE IS JUST BEYOND OUR EASTERN BORDER.
ALL MEN MUST GO FORTH TO RECOVER THE CHILD!
BUT BEWARE! SHE IS HEAVILY ARMED! SHE IS QUICK AND CLEVER!
DON'T UNDER-ESTIMATE HER!
LET'S GO...
WE'RE RUNNING OUT OF TIME...

YOU KNOW, MASARU...

EVER CONSIDER... MAYBE *WORKING OUT* A LITTLE?

...YOU WEIGH A TON.

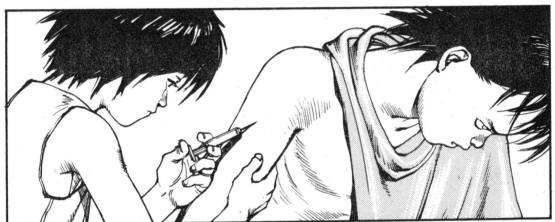

ARE YOU FEELING BETTER?

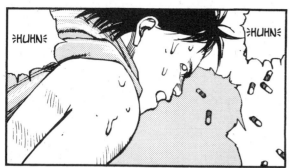

166

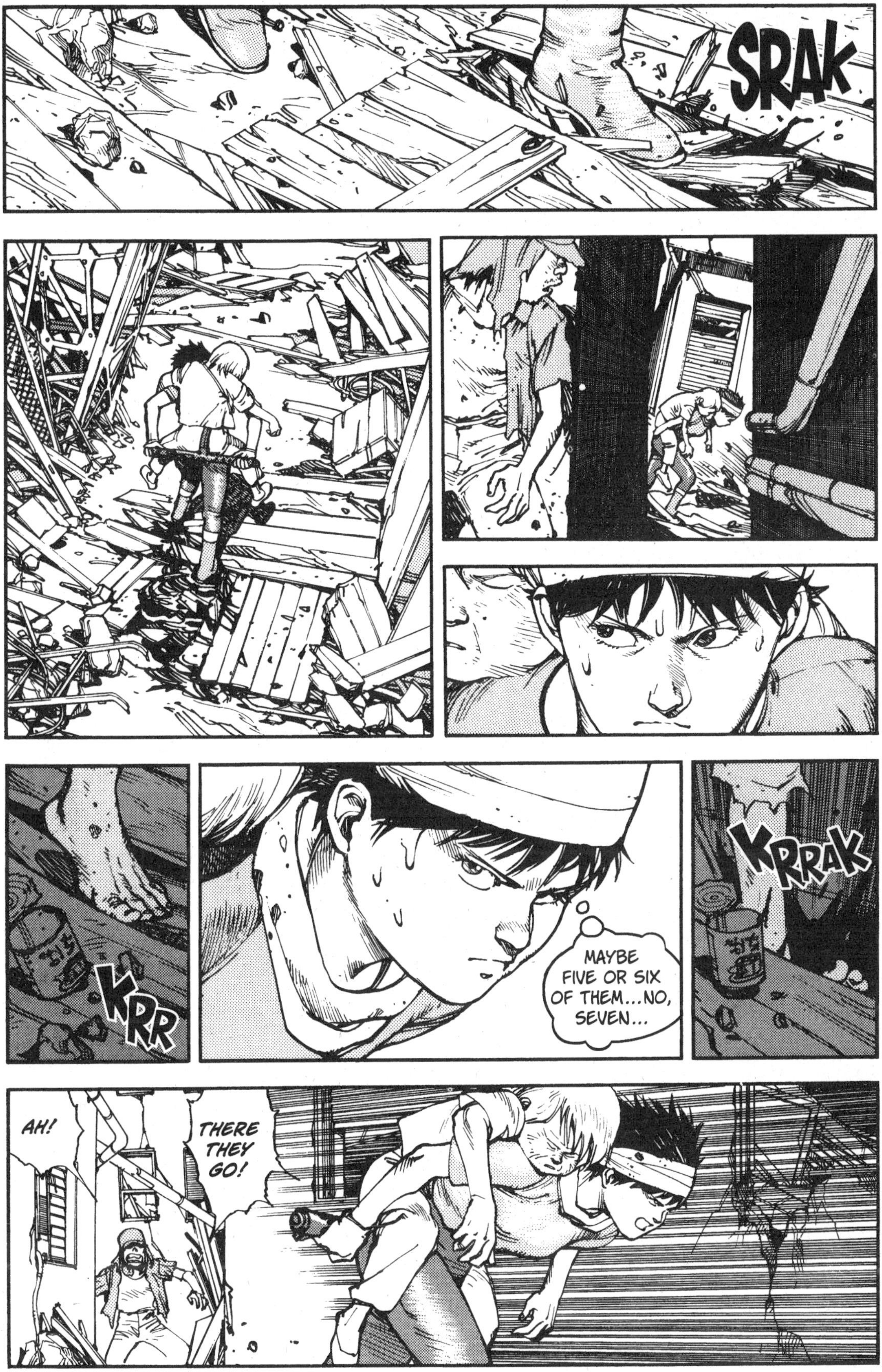
SRAK
KRR
MAYBE FIVE OR SIX OF THEM...NO, SEVEN...
KRRAK
AH!
THERE THEY GO!

I SEE HER!

WAA!

TAKATATAKA

THESE GUYS...

...AREN'T FROM TETSUO'S GROUP!

THEN, WHO ARE THEY?!

PRAK

SPRIINK

FWOP

OUPH!

GAK

PIECE OF--

--OH, SHIT...

TALK FAST. WHO ARE YOU GUYS AND WHAT DO YOU WANT?

IF Y-YOU HAVE ANYTHING TO GIVE US IN TRADE... W-WE'LL SPARE YOUR LIFE.

COMMON THIEVES...!

!

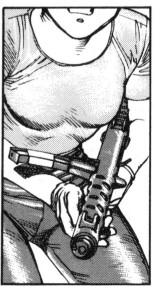

LEMME GO, OKAY? I'M NOT SUCH A BAD GUY. WE COULD BE FRIENDS, RIGHT?

STAY WHERE YOU ARE!

BLAK

SLAP

OKAY! I'M STAYIN,' I'M STAYIN!

LOOK, TELL ME WHAT YOU WANT. I'LL HELP YOU...

YOU HUNGRY? NEED MEDICINE? DON'T HESITATE TO ASK...WE CAN WORK SOMETHING OUT.

I DON'T UNDER-STAND...

YOU KNOW WHAT I MEAN... I WOULDN'T SAY NOTHIN' TO THE OTHERS. WE MAKE A DEAL, HAVE A LITTLE QUALITY TIME, JUST YOU AND ME...

TCHOP

THINK OF ME AS YOUR GIGOLO. IT'LL BE FUN!

HEY...WHAT'S WITH THE ROCK?

BLOP

LET'S GET GOING.

BROM

THAT'S ALL SHE WROTE. HIS SKULL'S CAVED IN.

THIN SKULL...

HE'S READY FOR MORE, THE BASTARD!

IT'S THE WAY HE WOULD HAVE WANTED TO GO...

I FOUND 'EM! OVER THERE!

...

YOU, HONORED LADY, ARE *KEI*, ARE YOU NOT?

HOW DO YOU KNOW MY NAME?!

THERE SHE IS!

SHIT! THEY'RE HERE!

≈GASP≈

STOP!

DON'T SHOOT THEM!

WHY NOT?!

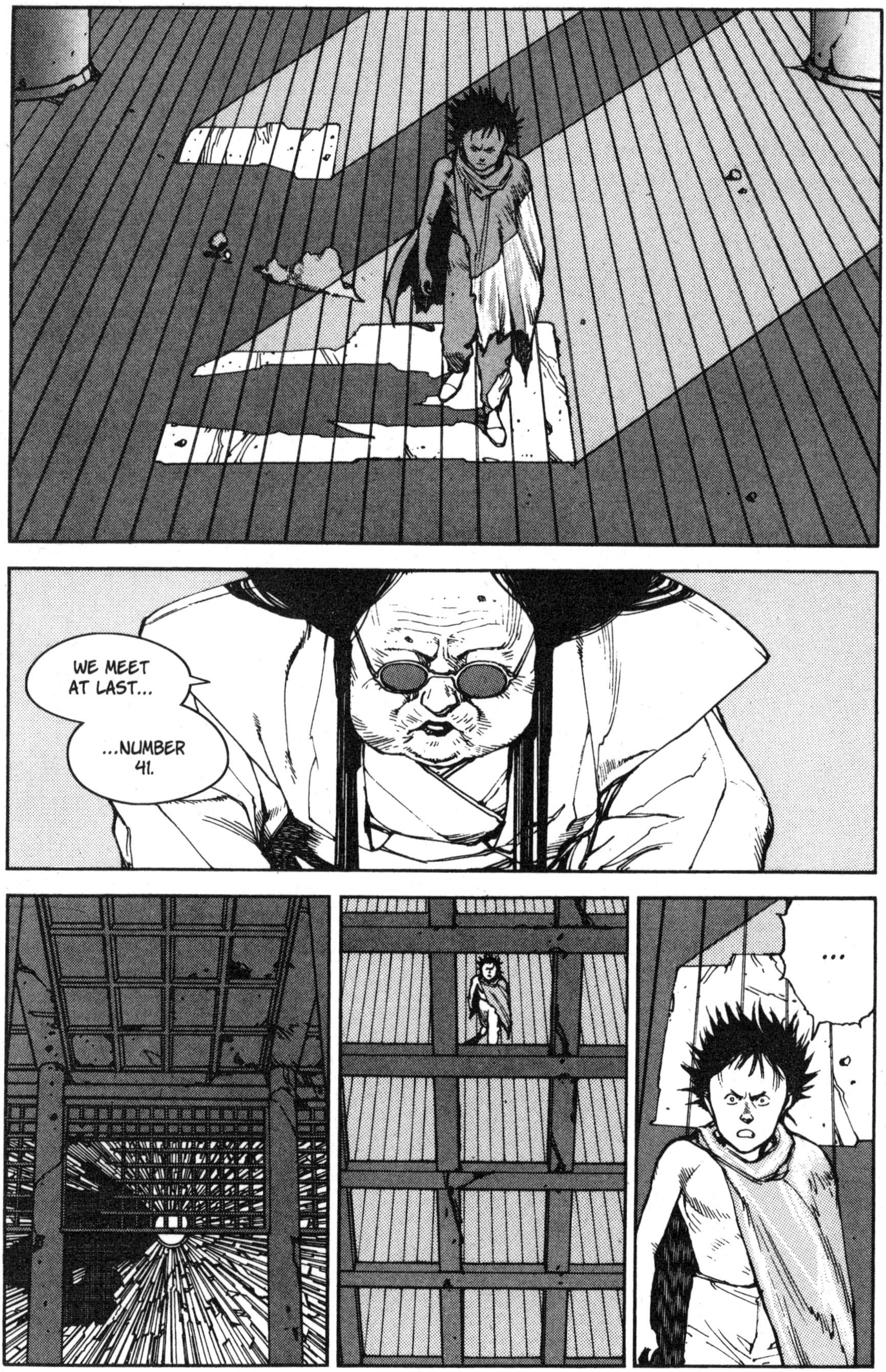
WE MEET AT LAST...
...NUMBER 41.
...

THIS PLACE... IT LOOKS EXACTLY LIKE...

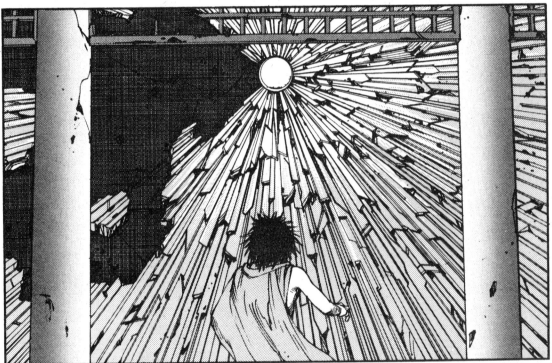

OH...IT IS FAMILIAR?

YEAH...

THAT DESIGN BEHIND YOU. I *KNOW* IT...

THEN, THE BAS-RELIEF REMINDS YOU OF SOMETHING YOU'VE SEEN BEFORE?

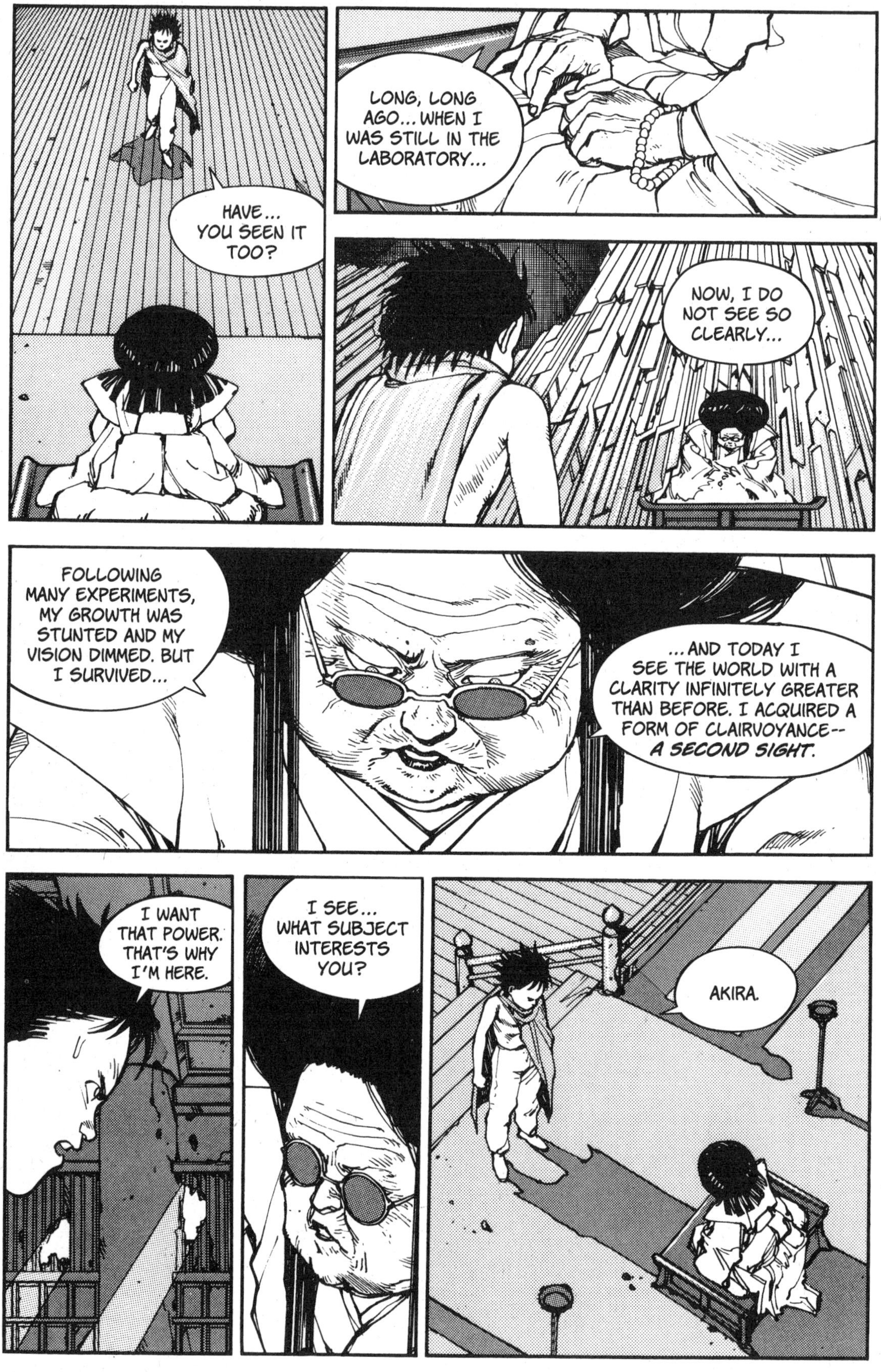
HAVE... YOU SEEN IT TOO?
LONG, LONG AGO... WHEN I WAS STILL IN THE LABORATORY...
NOW, I DO NOT SEE SO CLEARLY...
FOLLOWING MANY EXPERIMENTS, MY GROWTH WAS STUNTED AND MY VISION DIMMED. BUT I SURVIVED...
...AND TODAY I SEE THE WORLD WITH A CLARITY INFINITELY GREATER THAN BEFORE. I ACQUIRED A FORM OF CLAIRVOYANCE-- *A SECOND SIGHT*.
I WANT THAT POWER. THAT'S WHY I'M HERE.
I SEE... WHAT SUBJECT INTERESTS YOU?
AKIRA.

VRAKAKA TAKA

HEAVE!

KRRR KRR

!

DIIIE!

THAT'S ENOUGH. GO DOWN AND FINISH HER.

BUT WHATEVER YOU DO, DON'T HURT THE CHILD. I DON'T WANT HER GETTING SO MUCH AS A *SCRATCH*.

THE COW'S AMMO CAN'T LAST FOREVER...

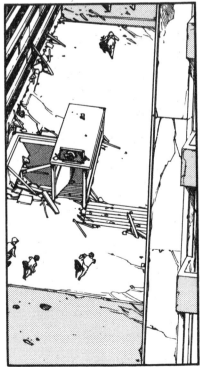

IT BEGAN IN THE 1960'S...A SMALL PROJECT WITHOUT EVEN A CODE NAME....JUST "THE PROJECT."

AT FIRST, JUST A HANDFUL OF PEOPLE IN THE MINISTRY OF DEFENSE, COLLATING DATA AND ANALYZING IT...

BY THE 1970'S, BASED ON THEIR FINDINGS, A GROUP OF PEOPLE THOUGHT TO HAVE PARTICULAR TRAITS WERE BROUGHT TOGETHER.

THE SCIENTISTS PERFORMED ALL MANNER OF EXPERIMENTS ON THEIR SUBJECTS AND DEVELOPED NEW TRAINING TECHNIQUES...

A CERTAIN HIGHLY CONTROVERSIAL SCHOLAR JOINED THE PROJECT.

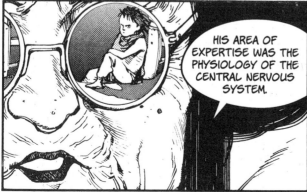

HIS AREA OF EXPERTISE WAS THE PHYSIOLOGY OF THE CENTRAL NERVOUS SYSTEM.

SPECIALISTS FROM OTHER DISCIPLINES CONSIDERED HIM AN ECCENTRIC...AND HIS COLLEAGUES TOOK A DIM VIEW OF HIS FINDINGS...

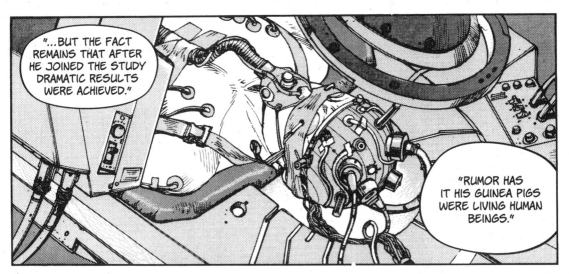

"...BUT THE FACT REMAINS THAT AFTER HE JOINED THE STUDY DRAMATIC RESULTS WERE ACHIEVED."

"RUMOR HAS IT HIS GUINEA PIGS WERE LIVING HUMAN BEINGS."

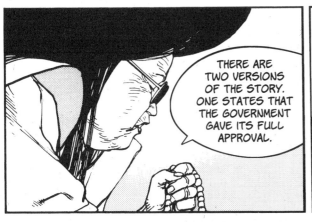

THERE ARE TWO VERSIONS OF THE STORY. ONE STATES THAT THE GOVERNMENT GAVE ITS FULL APPROVAL.

THE OTHER IS THAT THE SCHOLAR WAS SOLELY RESPONSIBLE. AS NO ONE KNOWS THE TRUTH, YOU MAY BELIEVE WHICHEVER SATISFIES YOU.

THESE EXPERIMENTS... WHAT DID THEY USE? SURGERY? NEW DRUGS?

HMM... HOW BEST TO EXPLAIN...?

USING A GLASS-LIKE MATERIAL, THEY MANUFACTUR-ED TUBES, FINER THAN THE DIAMETER OF THE SMALLEST BLOOD VESSEL...

...AND FILLED THESE TUBES WITH A SALT WATER SOLUTION.

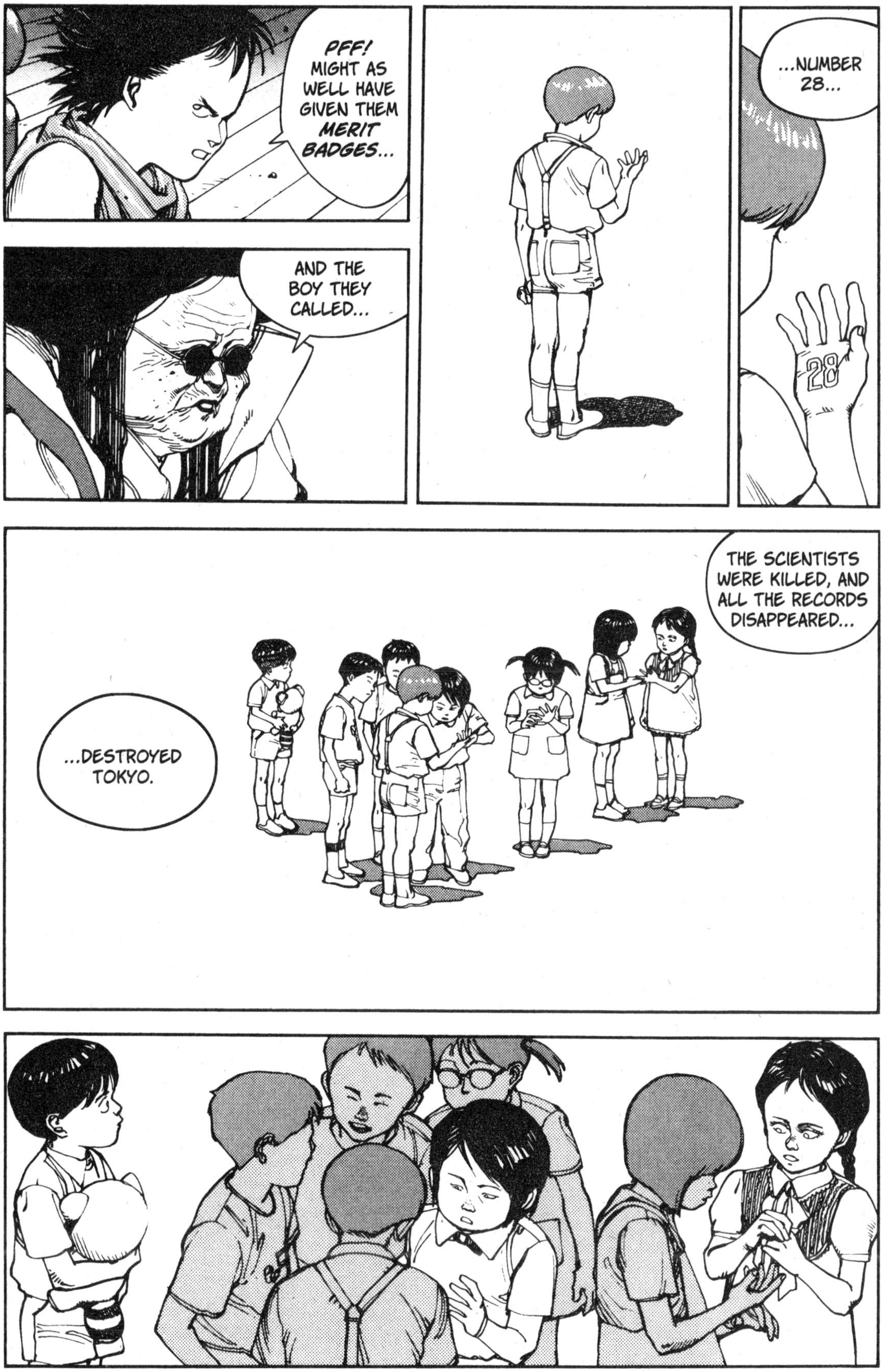
PFF! MIGHT AS WELL HAVE GIVEN THEM MERIT BADGES...
AND THE BOY THEY CALLED...
...NUMBER 28...
28
THE SCIENTISTS WERE KILLED, AND ALL THE RECORDS DISAPPEARED...
...DESTROYED TOKYO.

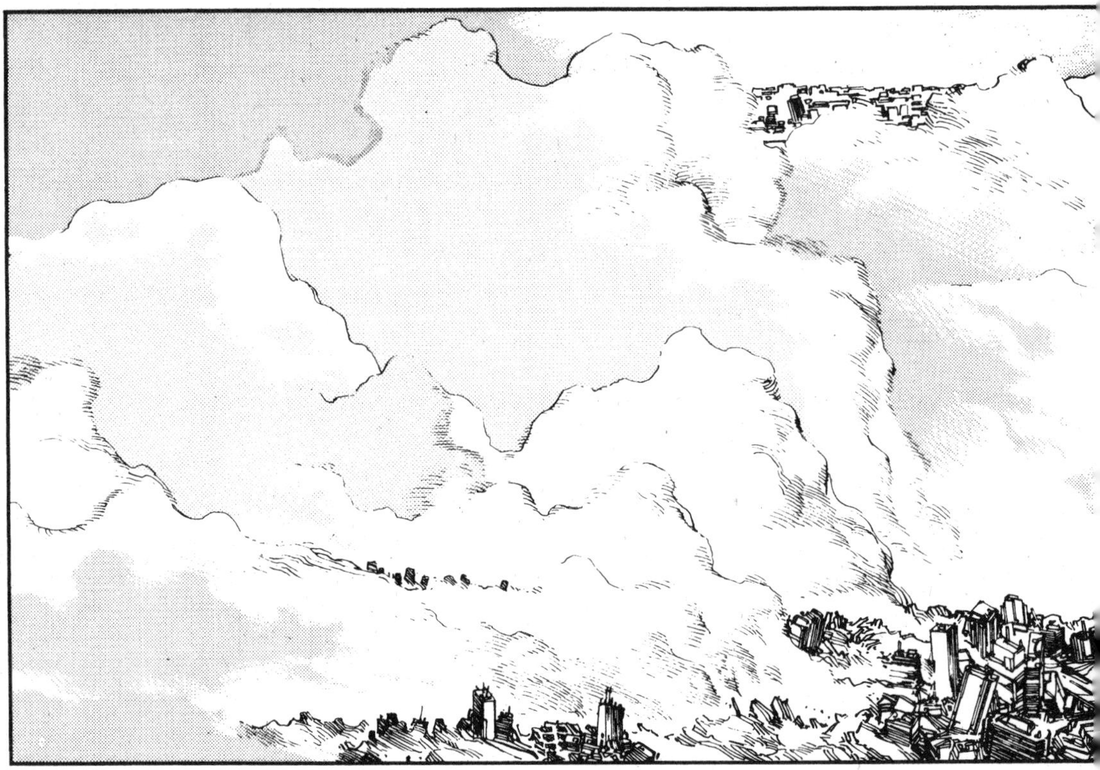

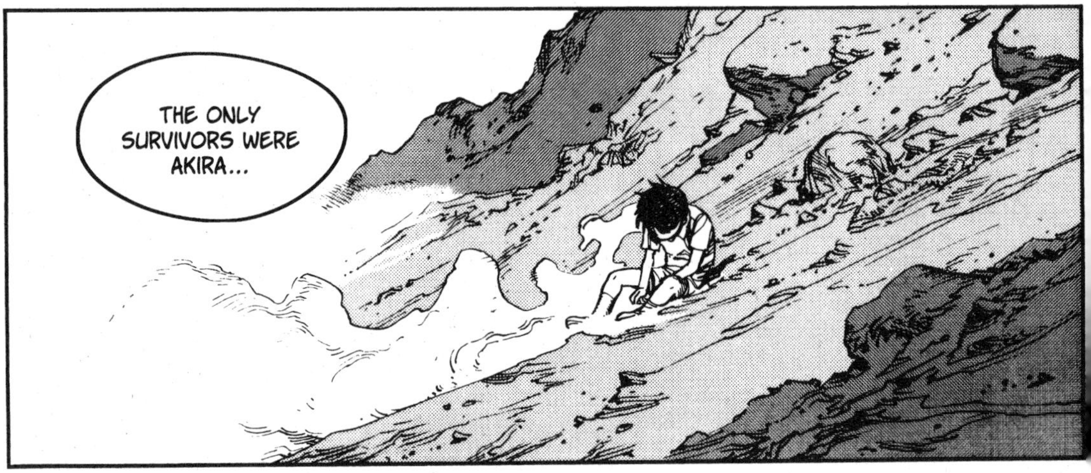
THE ONLY SURVIVORS WERE AKIRA...

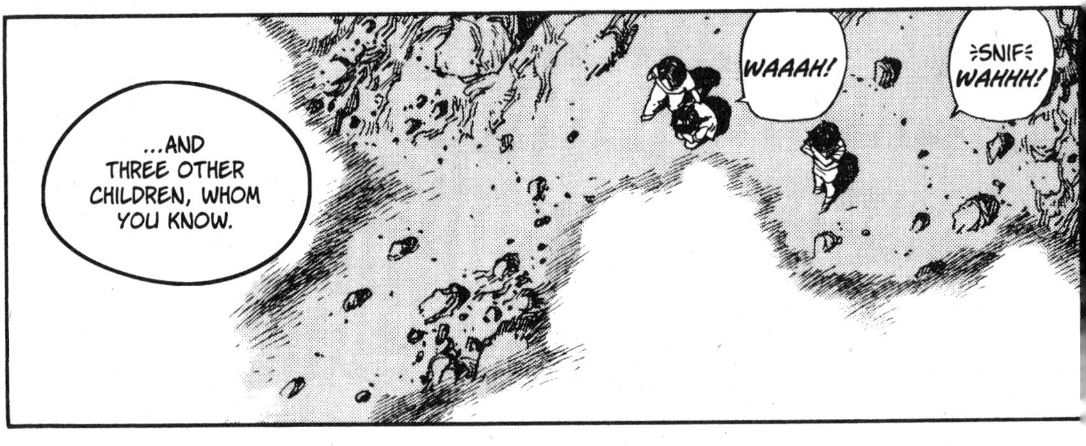
...AND THREE OTHER CHILDREN, WHOM YOU KNOW.
WAAAH!
SNIF
WAHHH!

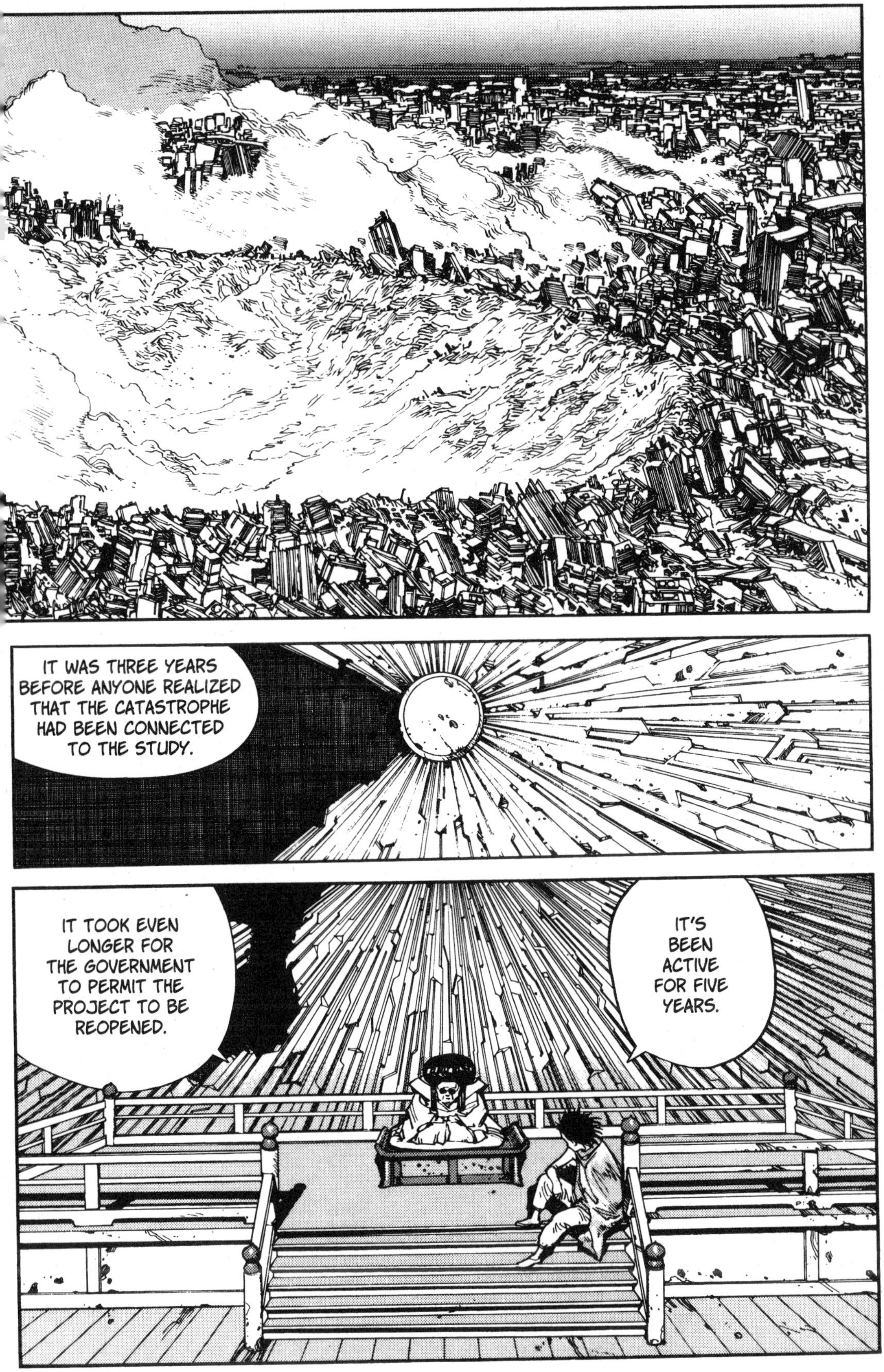
IT WAS THREE YEARS BEFORE ANYONE REALIZED THAT THE CATASTROPHE HAD BEEN CONNECTED TO THE STUDY.
IT TOOK EVEN LONGER FOR THE GOVERNMENT TO PERMIT THE PROJECT TO BE REOPENED.
IT'S BEEN ACTIVE FOR FIVE YEARS.

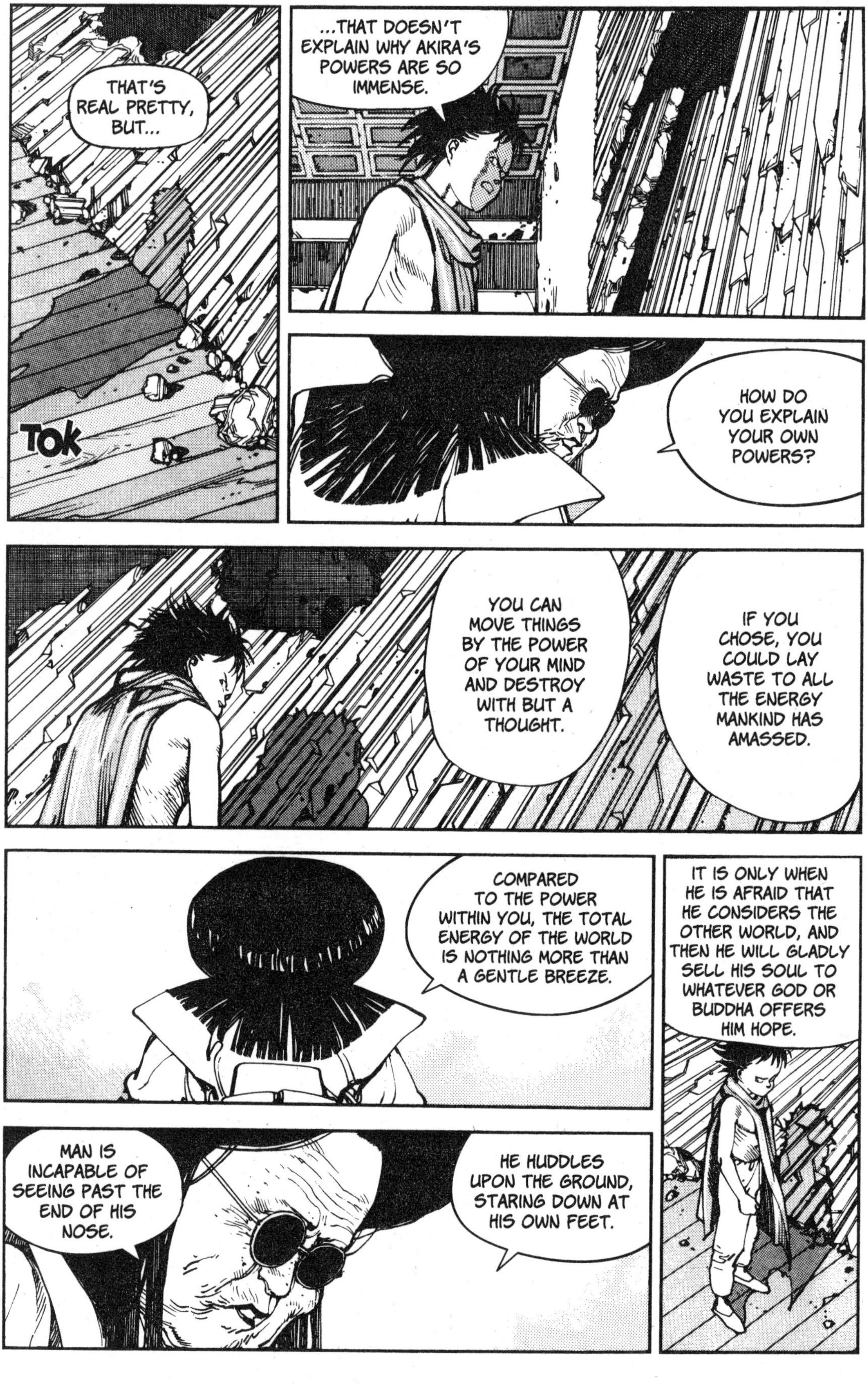
THAT'S REAL PRETTY, BUT...
TOK
...THAT DOESN'T EXPLAIN WHY AKIRA'S POWERS ARE SO IMMENSE.
HOW DO YOU EXPLAIN YOUR OWN POWERS?
YOU CAN MOVE THINGS BY THE POWER OF YOUR MIND AND DESTROY WITH BUT A THOUGHT.
IF YOU CHOSE, YOU COULD LAY WASTE TO ALL THE ENERGY MANKIND HAS AMASSED.
COMPARED TO THE POWER WITHIN YOU, THE TOTAL ENERGY OF THE WORLD IS NOTHING MORE THAN A GENTLE BREEZE.
MAN IS INCAPABLE OF SEEING PAST THE END OF HIS NOSE.
HE HUDDLES UPON THE GROUND, STARING DOWN AT HIS OWN FEET.
IT IS ONLY WHEN HE IS AFRAID THAT HE CONSIDERS THE OTHER WORLD, AND THEN HE WILL GLADLY SELL HIS SOUL TO WHATEVER GOD OR BUDDHA OFFERS HIM HOPE.

IN REALITY, WE ARE ALL PART OF THE FLOW OF THE SAME COSMIC STREAM.

EVEN SCIENTISTS DON'T GRASP WHAT THEIR CALCULATIONS TRULY SHOW THEM...

...INFINITY... TIME WITHOUT SPACE... ETERNITY...SPACE WITHOUT BOUNDS...ENERGY BEYOND IMAGINATION...AND WHAT DO THEY DO WITH THEIR FINDINGS?

ANNOUNCE THEM AT SOCIETY DINNERS FOR PLAQUES AND THE RECORDING OF THEIR NAMES IN THE ANNALS OF HISTORY. NO MORE THAN THAT!

BUT EVEN SO...

THE STREAM FLOWS ON BEYOND OUR AWARENESS.

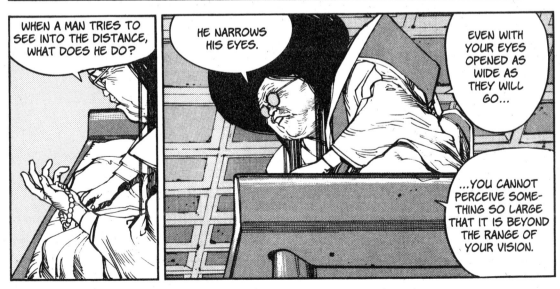

WHEN A MAN TRIES TO SEE INTO THE DISTANCE, WHAT DOES HE DO?

HE NARROWS HIS EYES.

EVEN WITH YOUR EYES OPENED AS WIDE AS THEY WILL GO...

...YOU CANNOT PERCEIVE SOMETHING SO LARGE THAT IT IS BEYOND THE RANGE OF YOUR VISION.

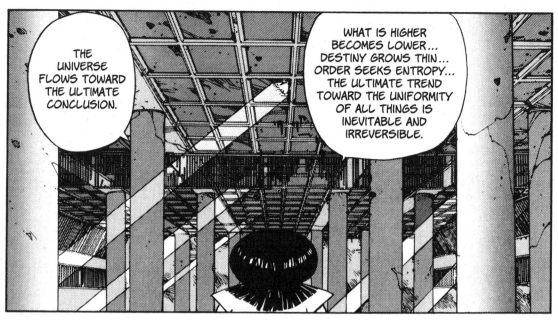

THE UNIVERSE FLOWS TOWARD THE ULTIMATE CONCLUSION.

WHAT IS HIGHER BECOMES LOWER... DESTINY GROWS THIN... ORDER SEEKS ENTROPY... THE ULTIMATE TREND TOWARD THE UNIFORMITY OF ALL THINGS IS INEVITABLE AND IRREVERSIBLE.

MEN GATHER TOGETHER AS THOUGH THEY WOULD REVERSE THE COSMIC STREAM, BUT IN TRUTH THEY ARE ONLY DRIFTWOOD.

YET, EVEN AS THE STREAM SWEEPS THEM ALONG...

...THEY POSSESS ONE POWER CAPABLE OF STOPPING THE STREAM.

WHEN THIS POWER IS USED, THE STREAM WILL STOP FOR AN INSTANT... AND THEN RESUME ITS COURSE WITH REDOUBLED INTENSITY.

WHEN IT IS BEFORE THEM, PEOPLE RECOGNIZE THE STREAM FOR WHAT IT IS AND FEAR ITS POWER...

...AS YOU'VE ALREADY SEEN.

191

YOU MUST LEARN THAT FOR YOURSELF, NUMBER 41.

YOU HEARD ME. ONLY YOU CAN FIND THE ANSWERS. TO DO SO IS YOUR DESTINY.

WHAT?!

BUT...

I DON'T WANT THE JOB! I CAN'T DO IT!

...WHY ME?

ONE LOOK INSIDE HIS MIND WAS PLENTY! I ALMOST GOT BLOWN AWAY!

HO HO HO... WHY, NUMBER 41, THIS DOESN'T SOUND LIKE YOU AT ALL.

ARE YOU AFRAID?

CALL IT WHATEVER YOU LIKE, BUT THAT WAS THE LAST LOOK I'LL EVER TAKE INSIDE HIS HEAD! I'LL NEVER DO IT AGAIN!

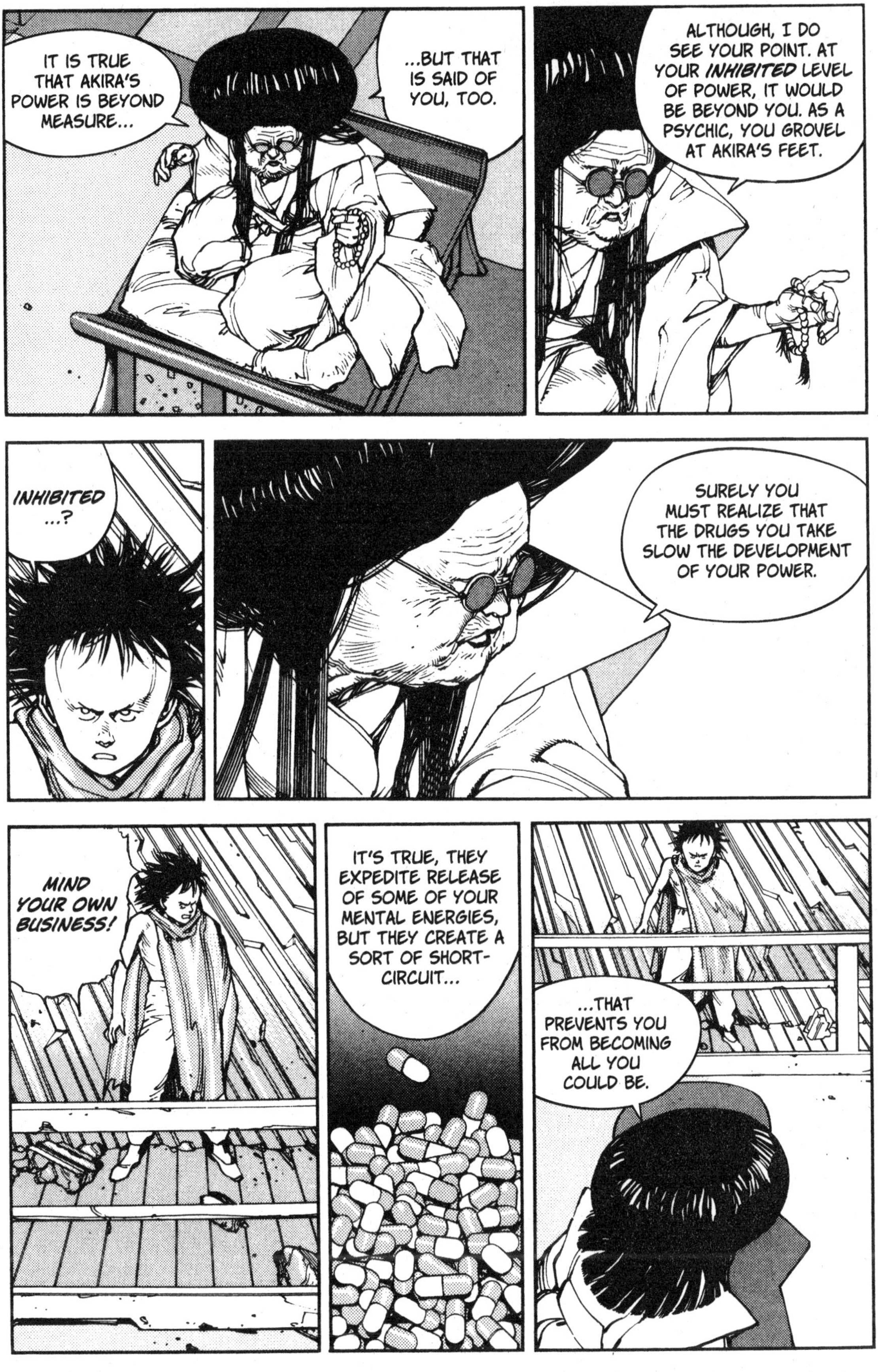
IT IS TRUE THAT AKIRA'S POWER IS BEYOND MEASURE...
...BUT THAT IS SAID OF YOU, TOO.
ALTHOUGH, I DO SEE YOUR POINT. AT YOUR INHIBITED LEVEL OF POWER, IT WOULD BE BEYOND YOU. AS A PSYCHIC, YOU GROVEL AT AKIRA'S FEET.
INHIBITED ...?
SURELY YOU MUST REALIZE THAT THE DRUGS YOU TAKE SLOW THE DEVELOPMENT OF YOUR POWER.
MIND YOUR OWN BUSINESS!
IT'S TRUE, THEY EXPEDITE RELEASE OF SOME OF YOUR MENTAL ENERGIES, BUT THEY CREATE A SORT OF SHORT-CIRCUIT...
...THAT PREVENTS YOU FROM BECOMING ALL YOU COULD BE.

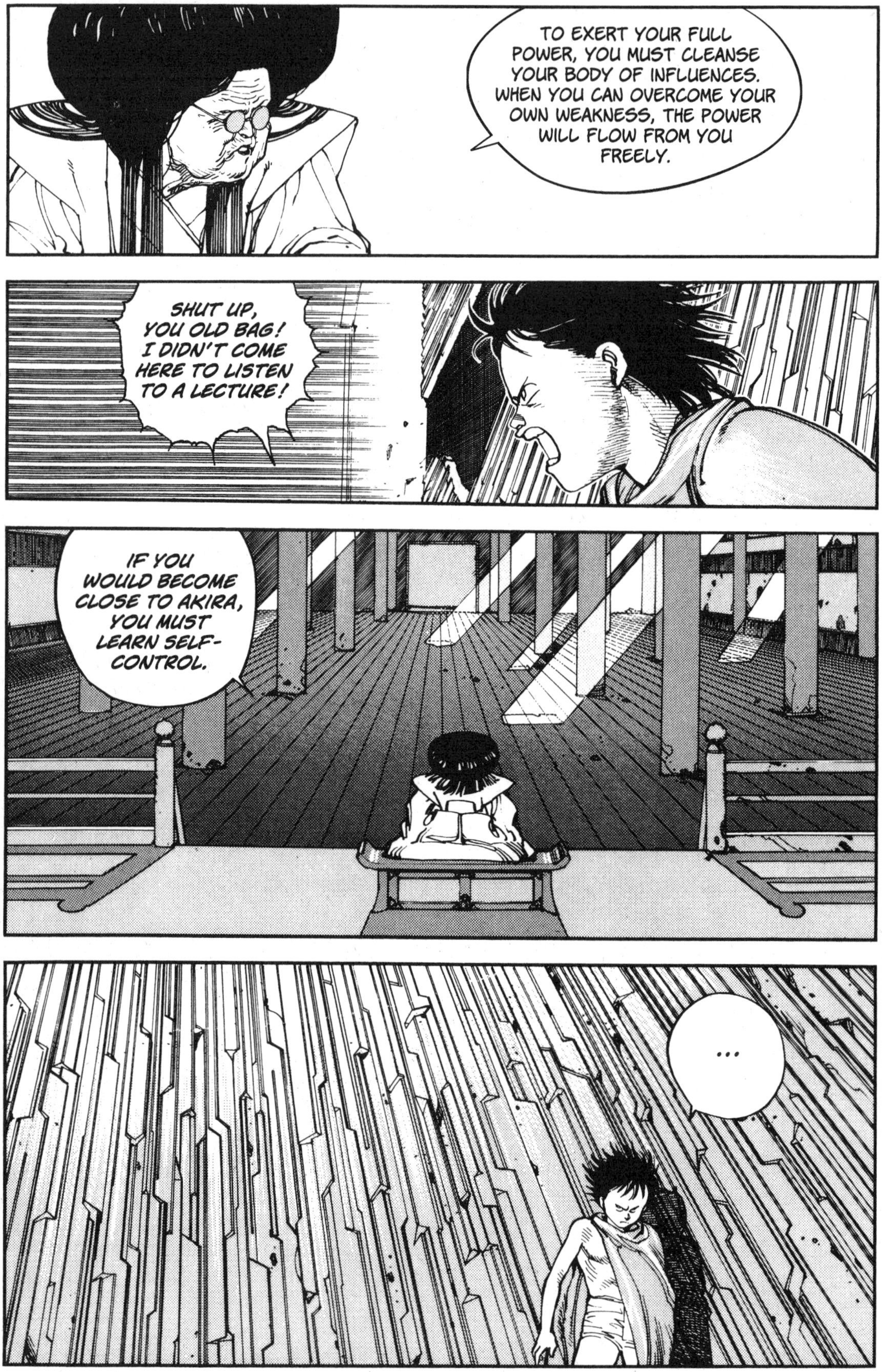
TO EXERT YOUR FULL POWER, YOU MUST CLEANSE YOUR BODY OF INFLUENCES. WHEN YOU CAN OVERCOME YOUR OWN WEAKNESS, THE POWER WILL FLOW FROM YOU FREELY.
SHUT UP, YOU OLD BAG! I DIDN'T COME HERE TO LISTEN TO A LECTURE!
IF YOU WOULD BECOME CLOSE TO AKIRA, YOU MUST LEARN SELF-CONTROL.
...

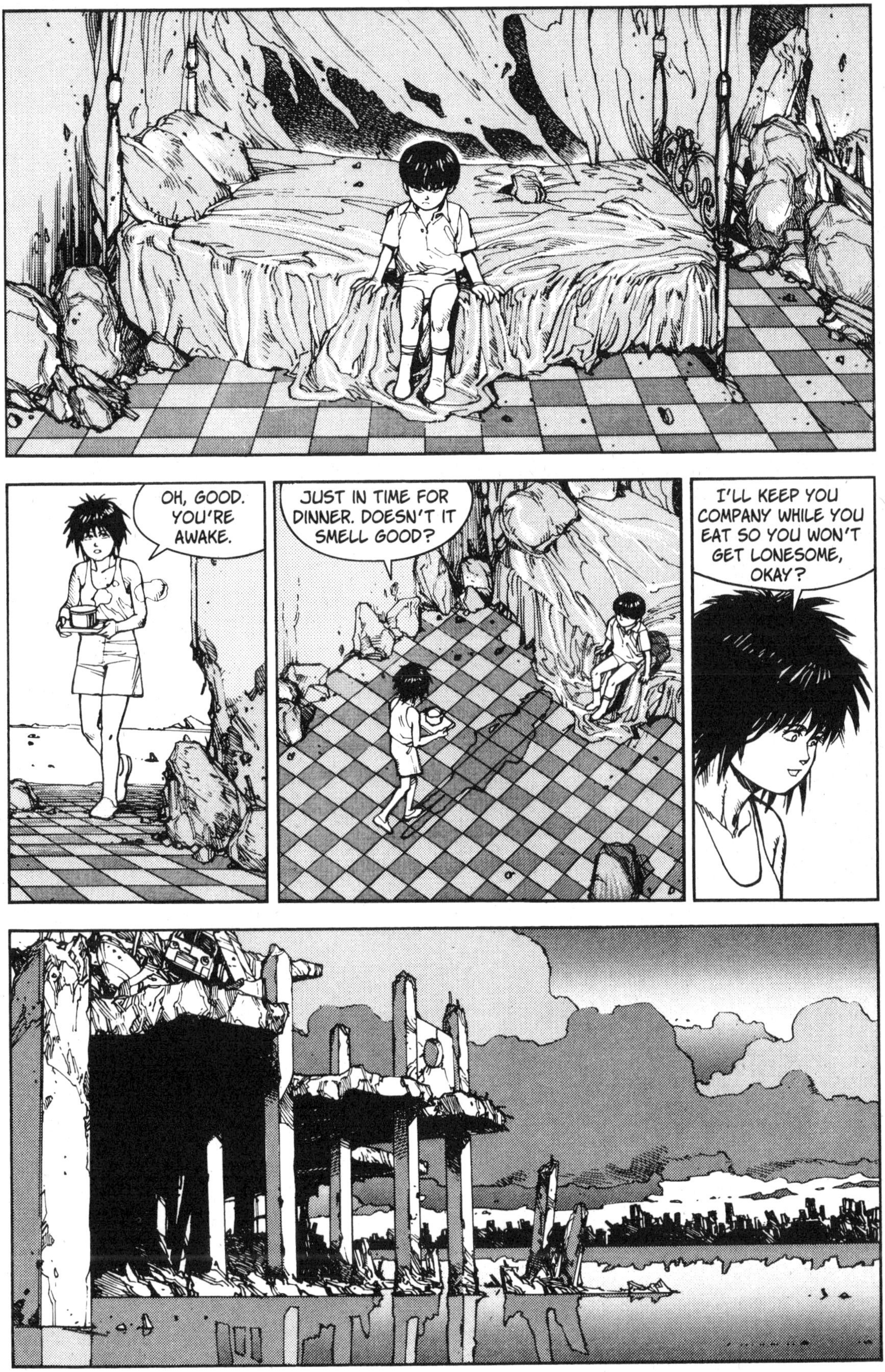

OH, GOOD. YOU'RE AWAKE.
JUST IN TIME FOR DINNER. DOESN'T IT SMELL GOOD?
I'LL KEEP YOU COMPANY WHILE YOU EAT SO YOU WON'T GET LONESOME, OKAY?

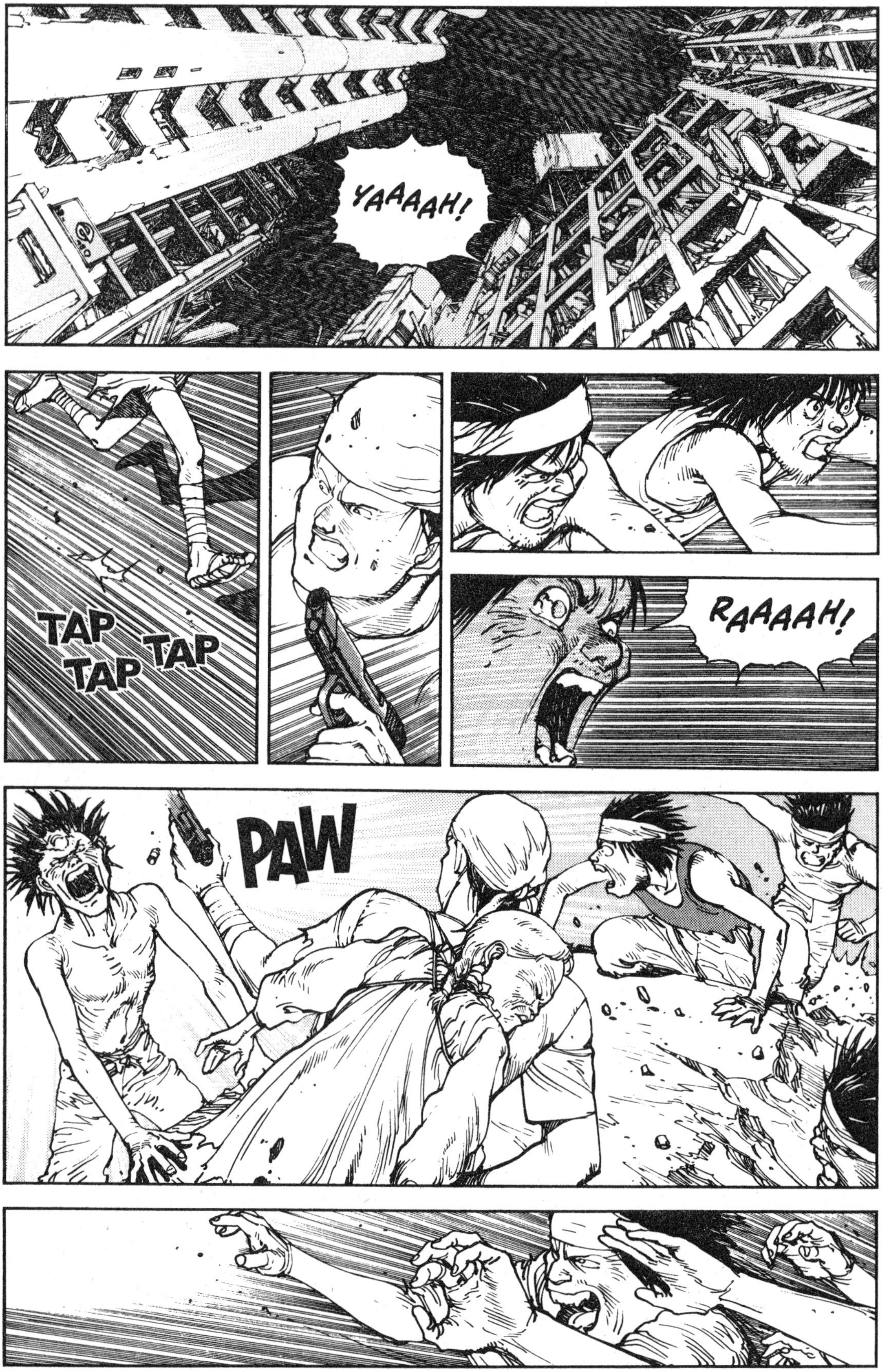
YAAAAH!
TAP TAP TAP
RAAAAH!
PAW

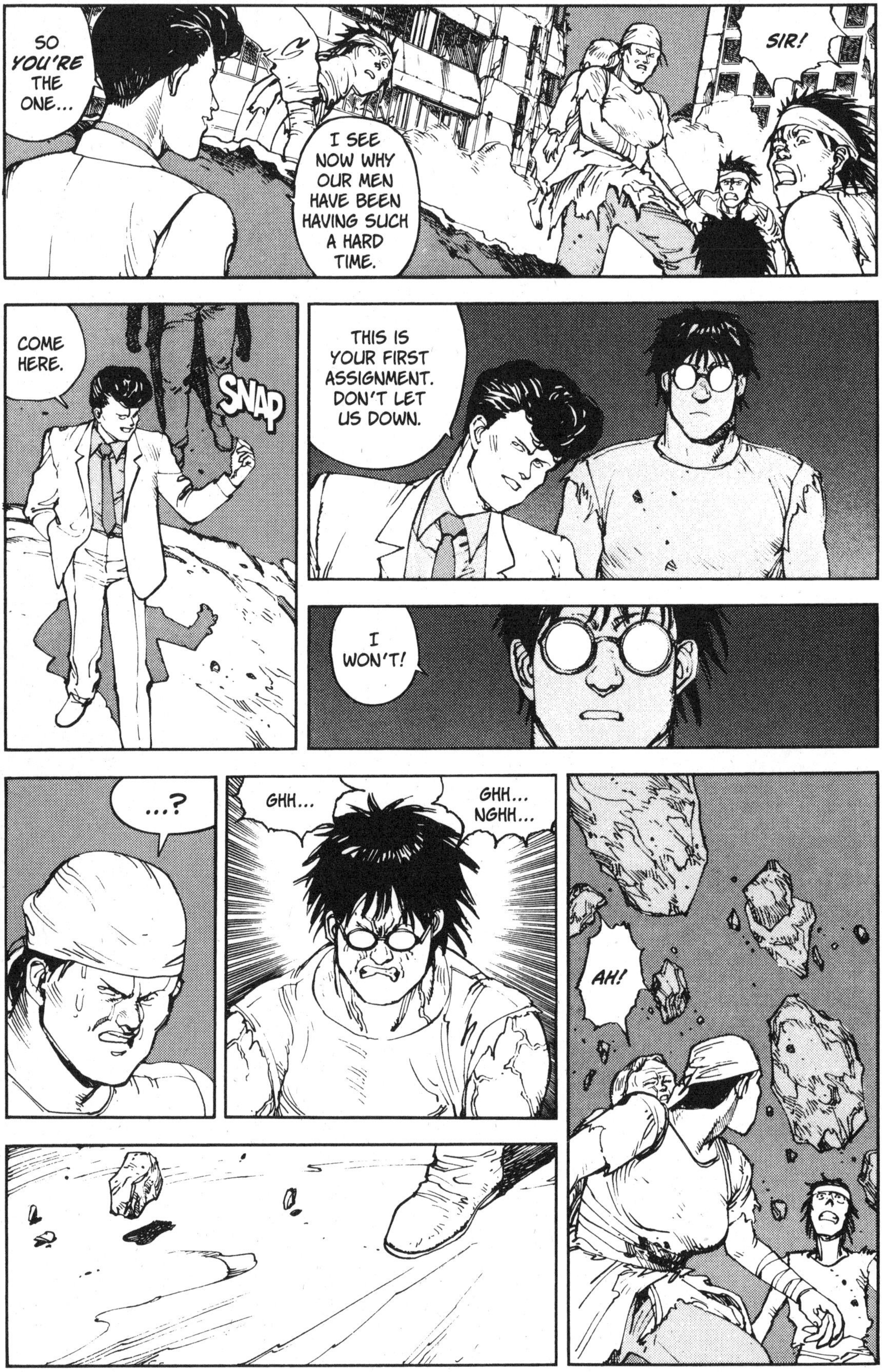
SO YOU'RE THE ONE...
I SEE NOW WHY OUR MEN HAVE BEEN HAVING SUCH A HARD TIME.
SIR!
COME HERE.
SNAP
THIS IS YOUR FIRST ASSIGNMENT. DON'T LET US DOWN.
I WON'T!
...?
GHH...
GHH... NGHH...
AH!

GWAAR!

GROM

YOUR AIM SUCKS, PAL!

BE CAREFUL, YOU IDIOT! REMEMBER THE KID!

OKAY, OKAY ...!

KROMF

GYAAAH!

AFTER THEM!

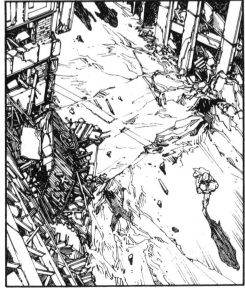

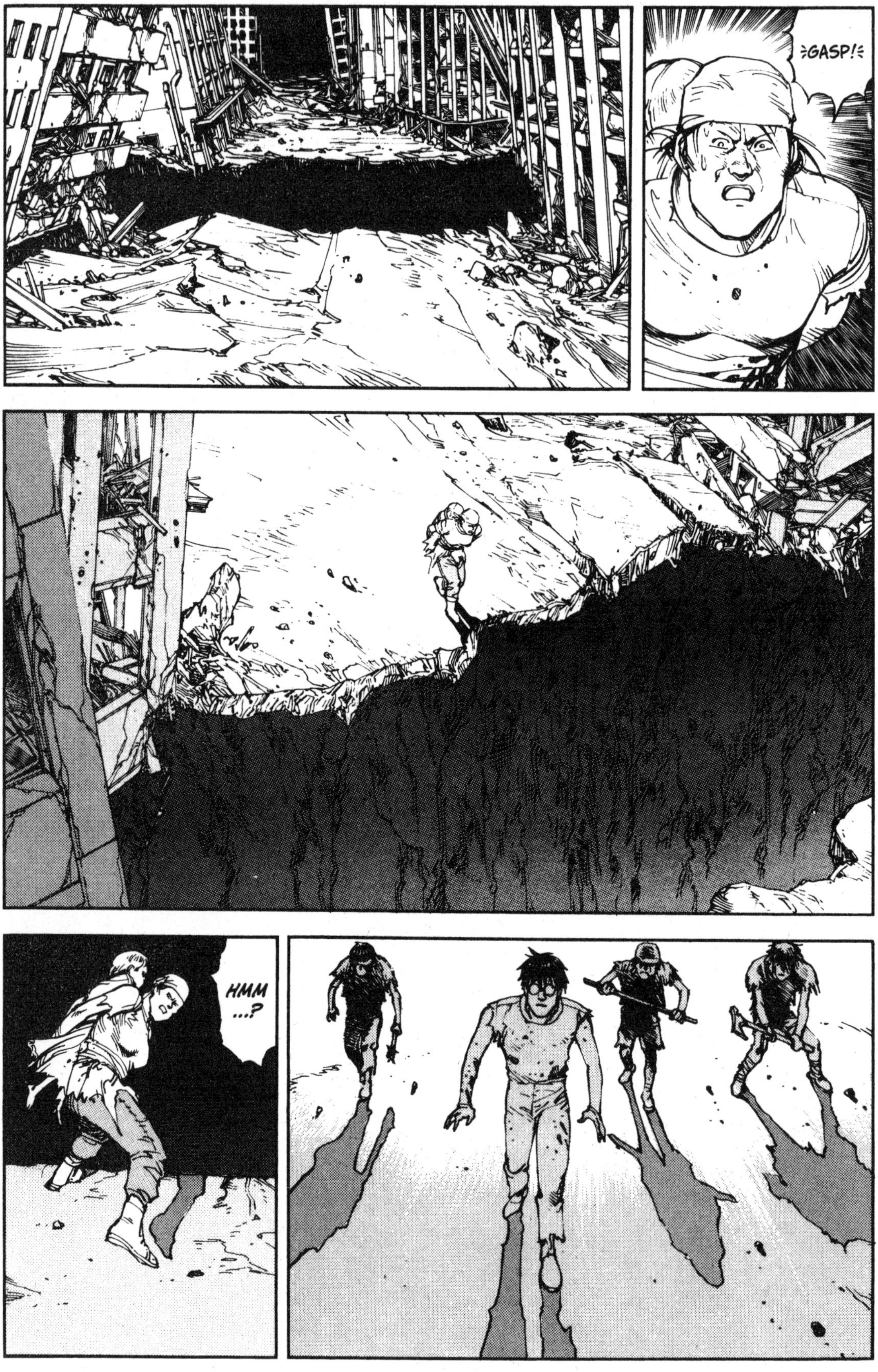
GASP!
HMM ...?

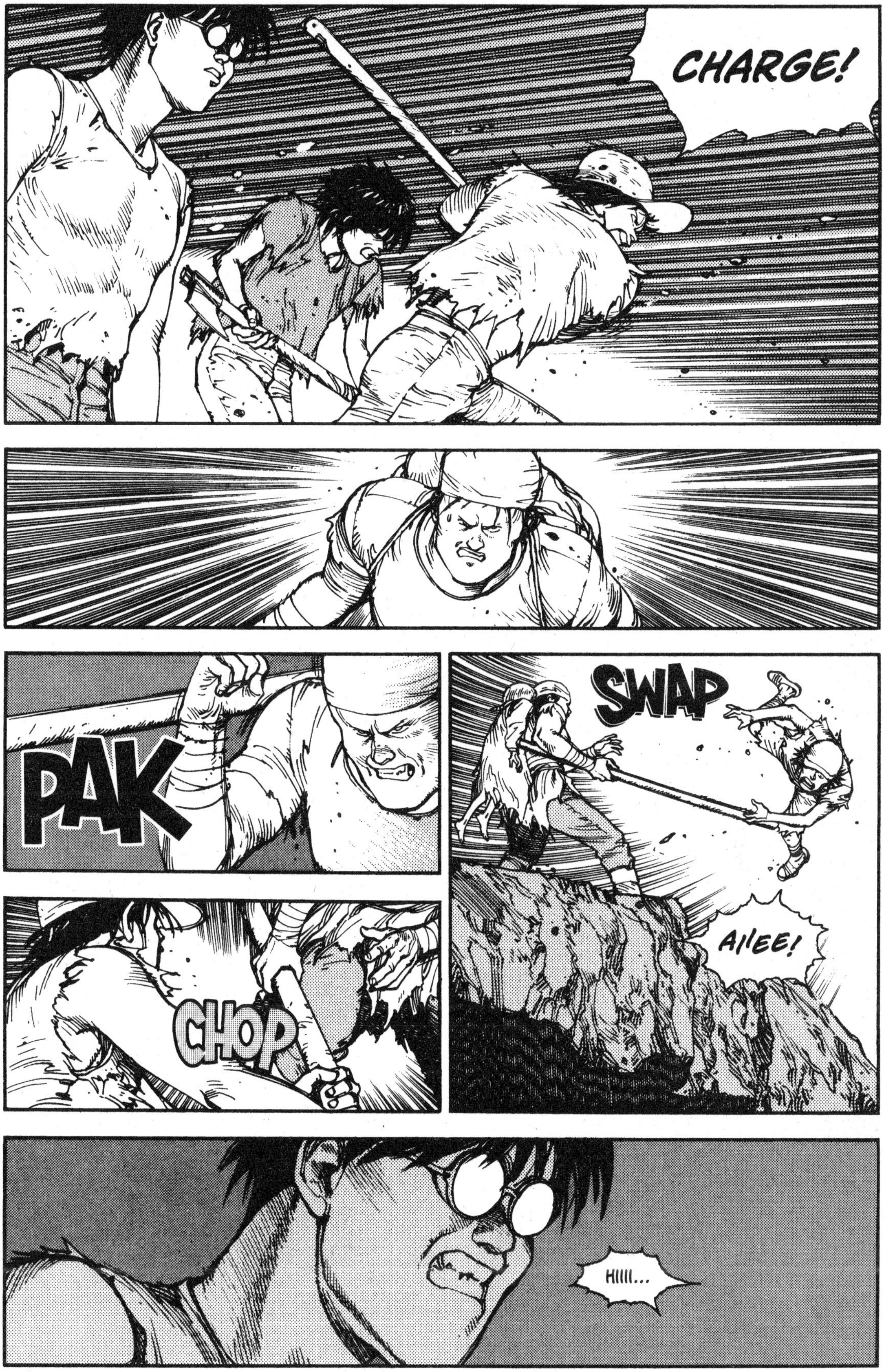
CHARGE!
PAK
SWAP
AIIEE!
CHOP
HIIII...

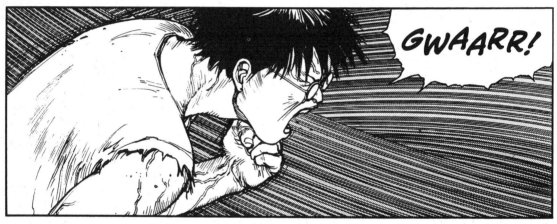

203

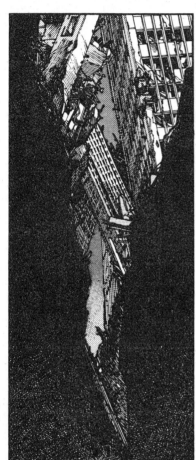

POTSH

!

OH, NO! IT CAN'T BE--!!

BLOP
BLUP

BLOP
BLUP

OW!

Kiii

?!

RATS!

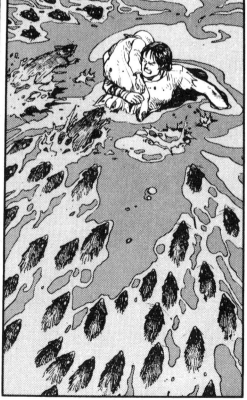

SQUEEE!

TSHiii

HUH ...?!

CHTOK

CRiiii
CRiiii

COME ON, IF YOU GOT THE GUTS!

?!

I'M DREAM-ING...! YOU'RE...

...THE COLONEL!

WE MEET AGAIN.

HUHN?

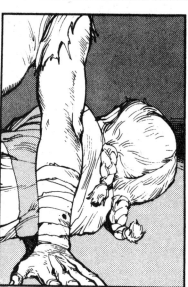

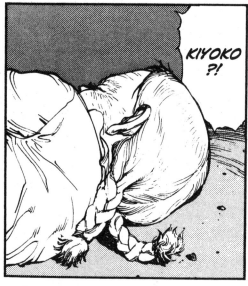

KIYOKO ?!

WHERE ARE YOU TAKING HER?

FLISH FLOSH

NONE OF YOUR BUSINESS.

THEY MADE IT DOWN HERE.

WHO ARE THEY?

LET'S GO. YOU CAN EXPLAIN LATER. FOLLOW ME!

HURRY! THIS WAY!

FLAP

WHAT IS THIS CRAP?

OWW! SOMETHING BIT MY LEG!!

THERE'S RATS DOWN HERE!

THEY'RE EVERYWHERE! YAAA!!

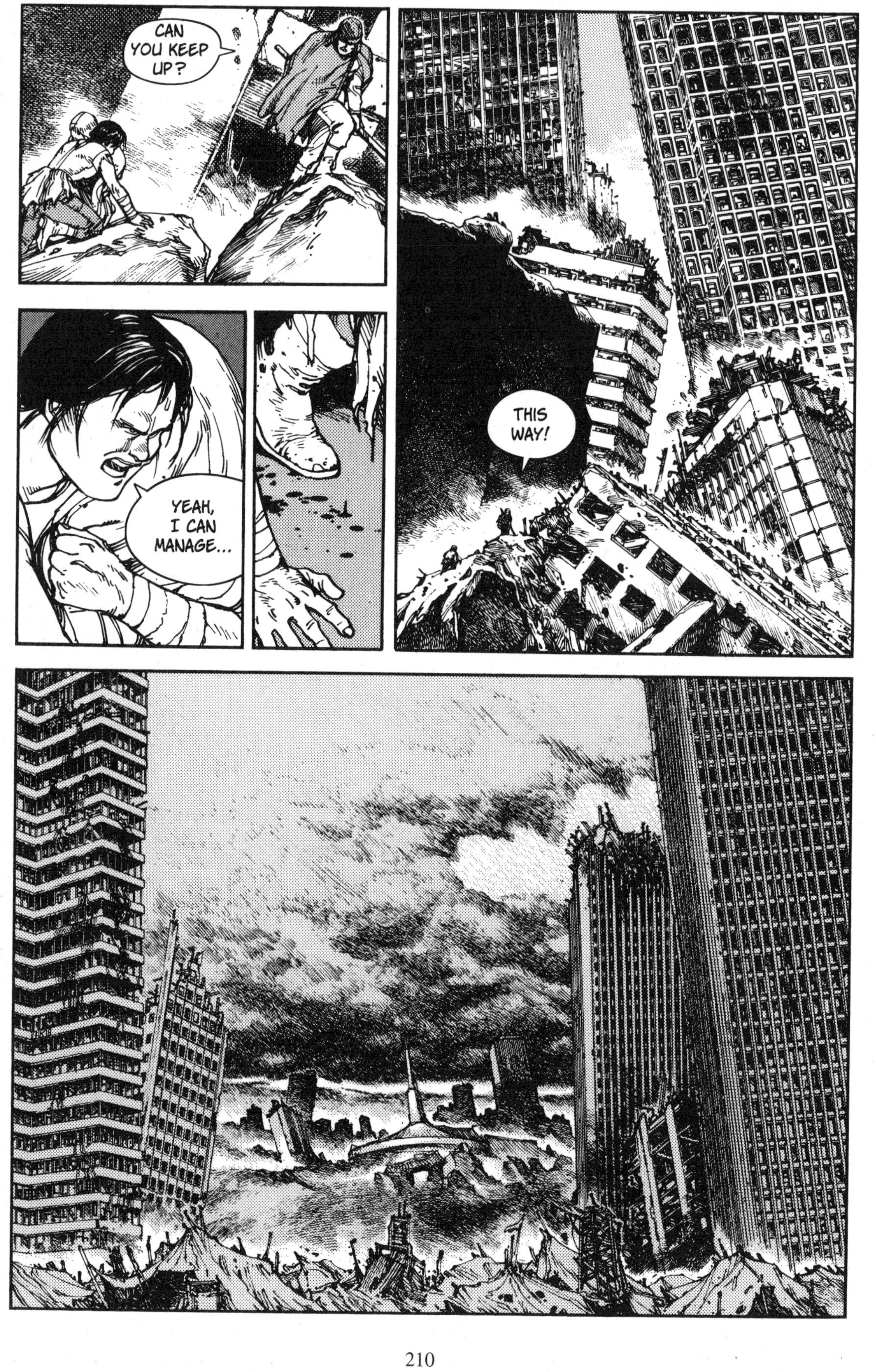
CAN YOU KEEP UP?
YEAH, I CAN MANAGE...
THIS WAY!

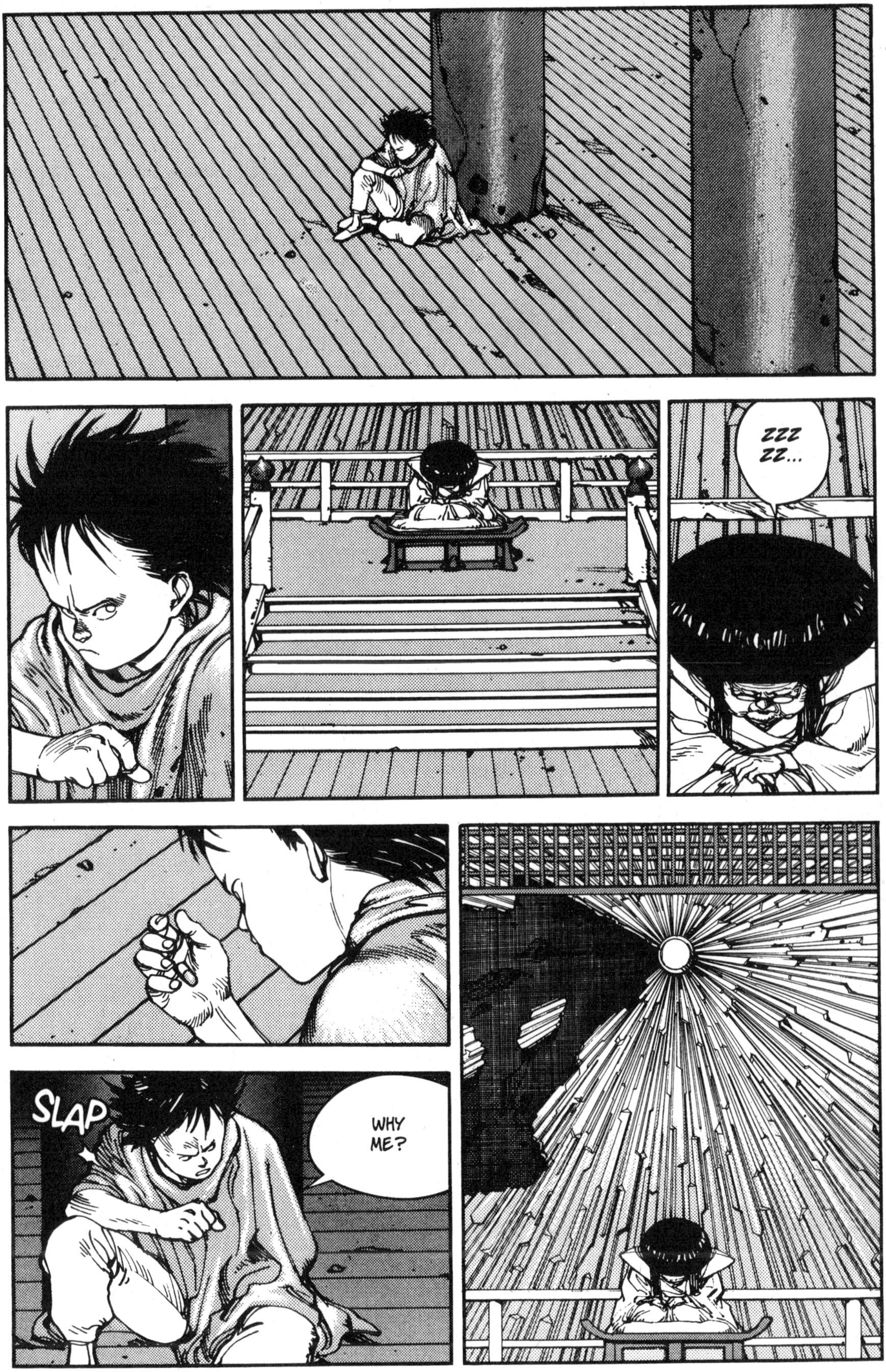
ZZZ
ZZ...
SLAP
WHY ME?

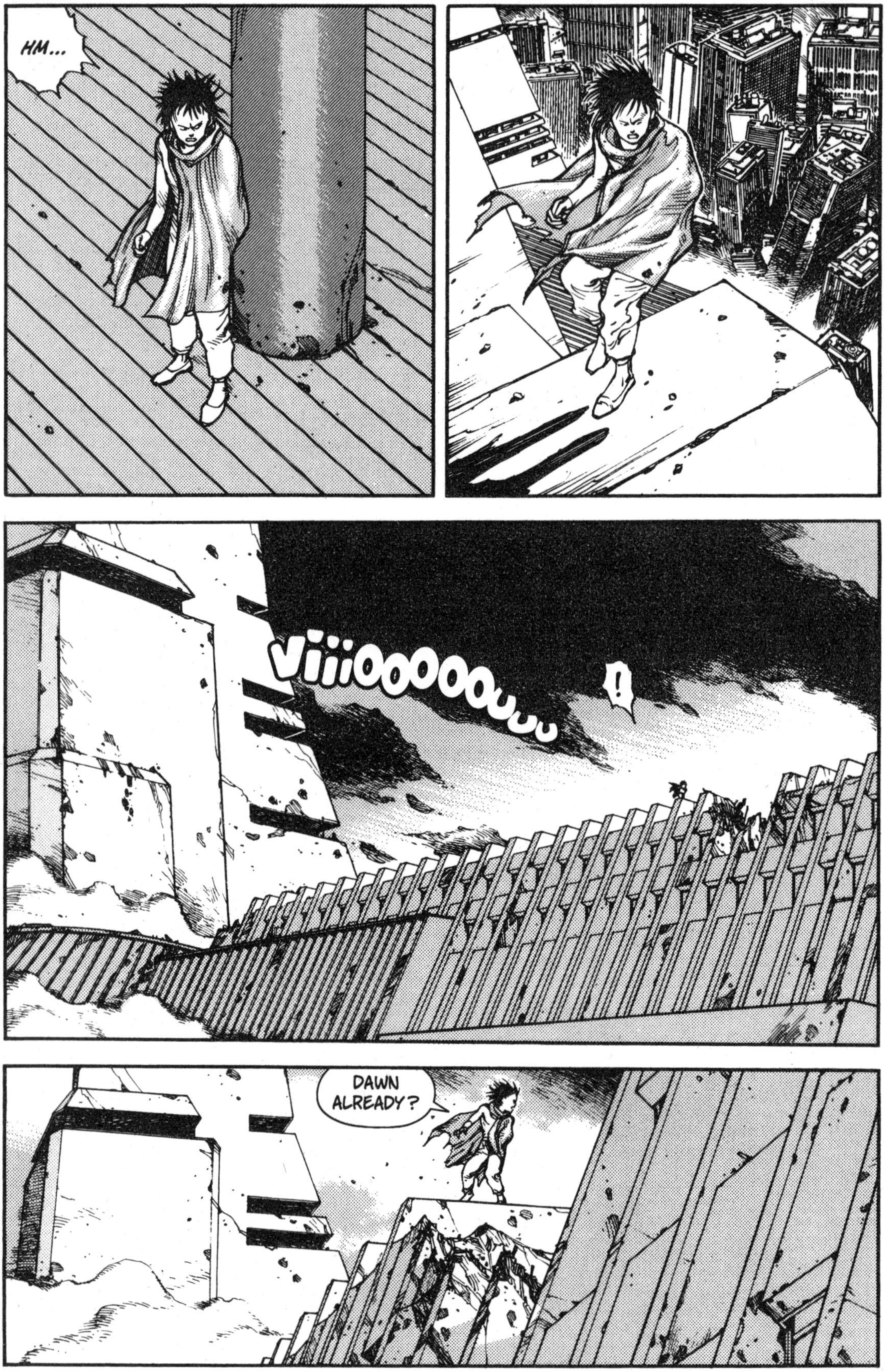
HM...
ViiiOOOOOuuu
!
DAWN ALREADY?

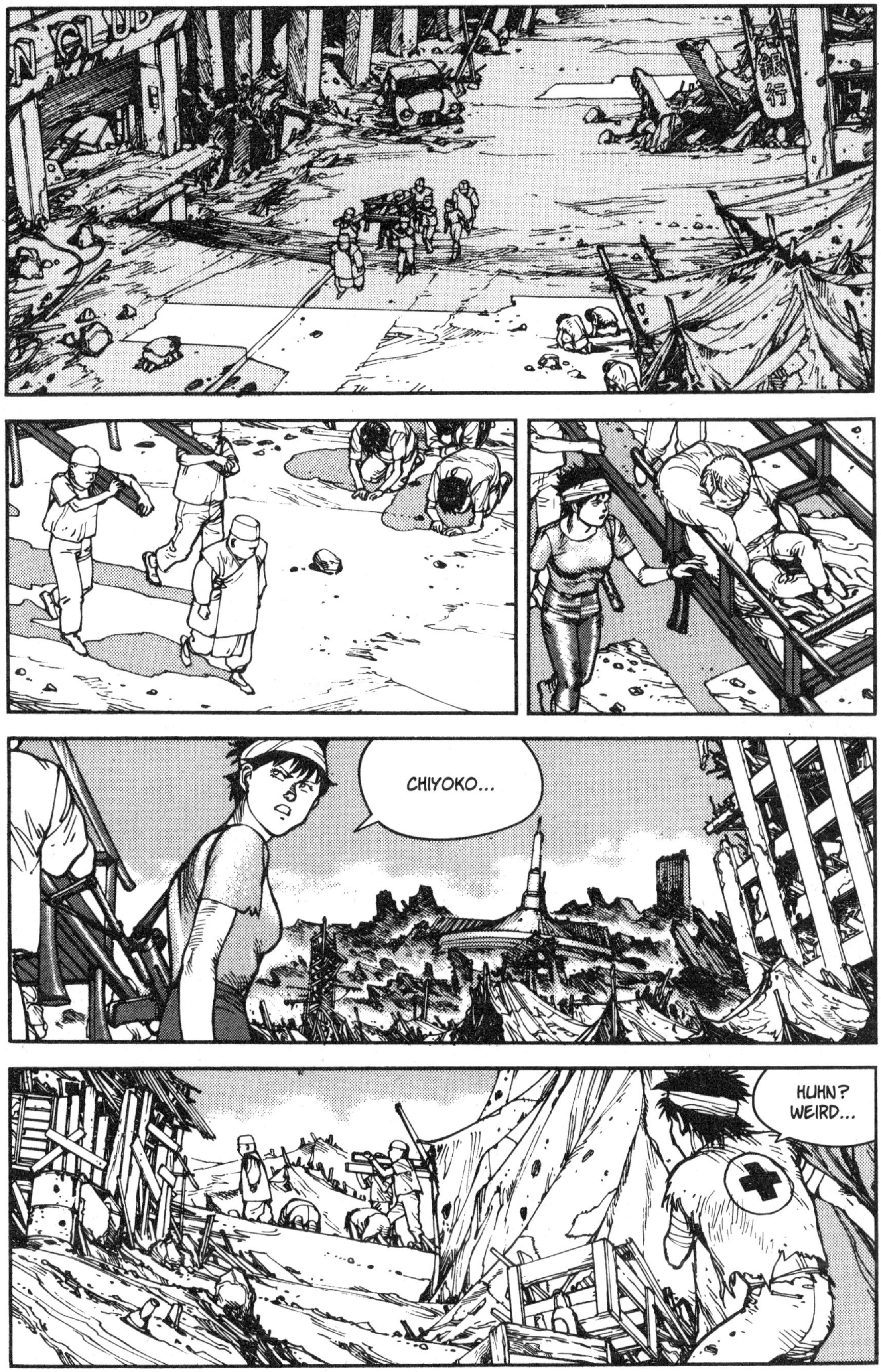
銀行
CHIYOKO...
HUHN?
WEIRD...

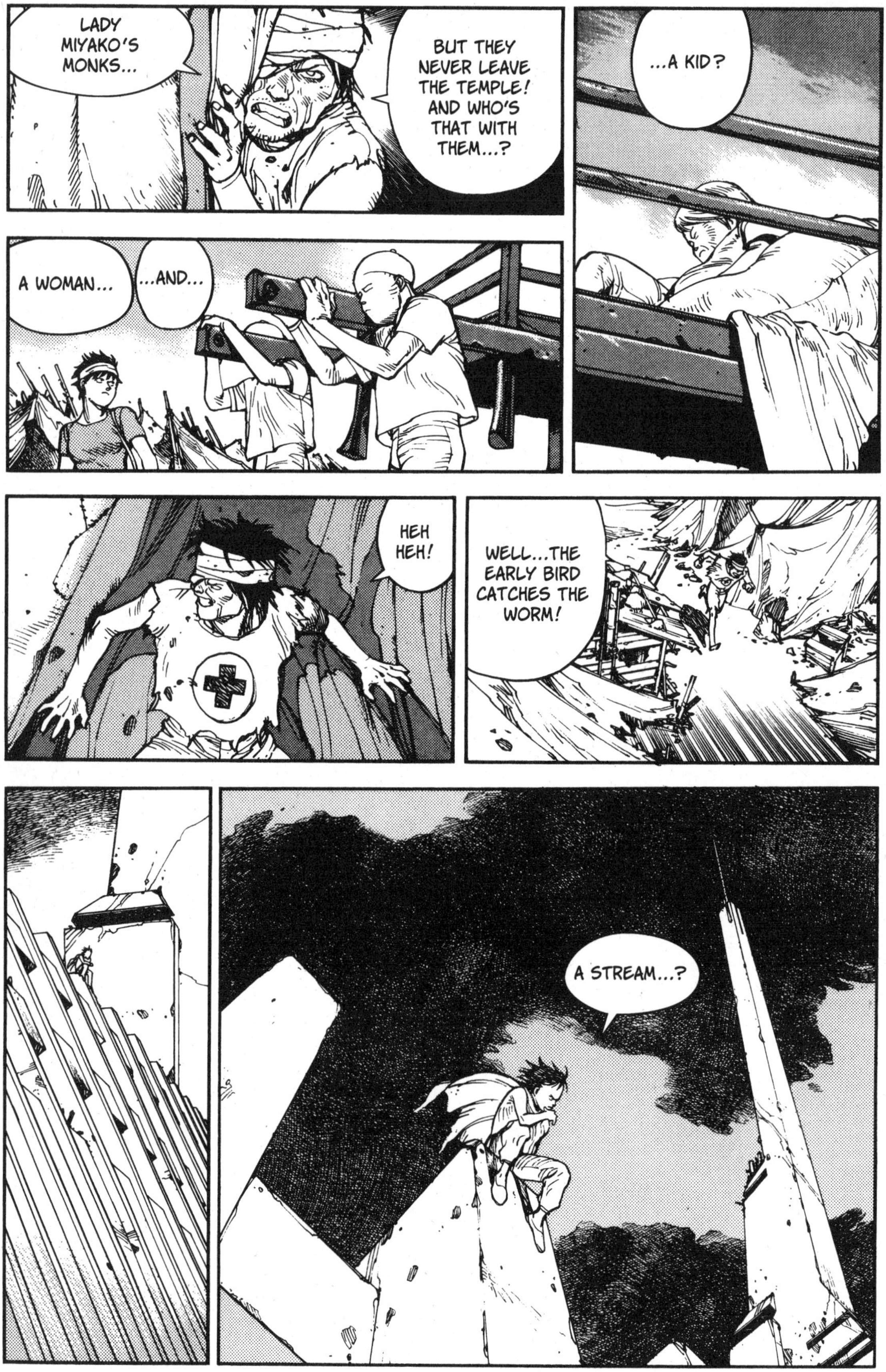
LADY MIYAKO'S MONKS...
BUT THEY NEVER LEAVE THE TEMPLE! AND WHO'S THAT WITH THEM...?
...A KID?
A WOMAN...
...AND...
HEH HEH!
WELL...THE EARLY BIRD CATCHES THE WORM!
A STREAM...?

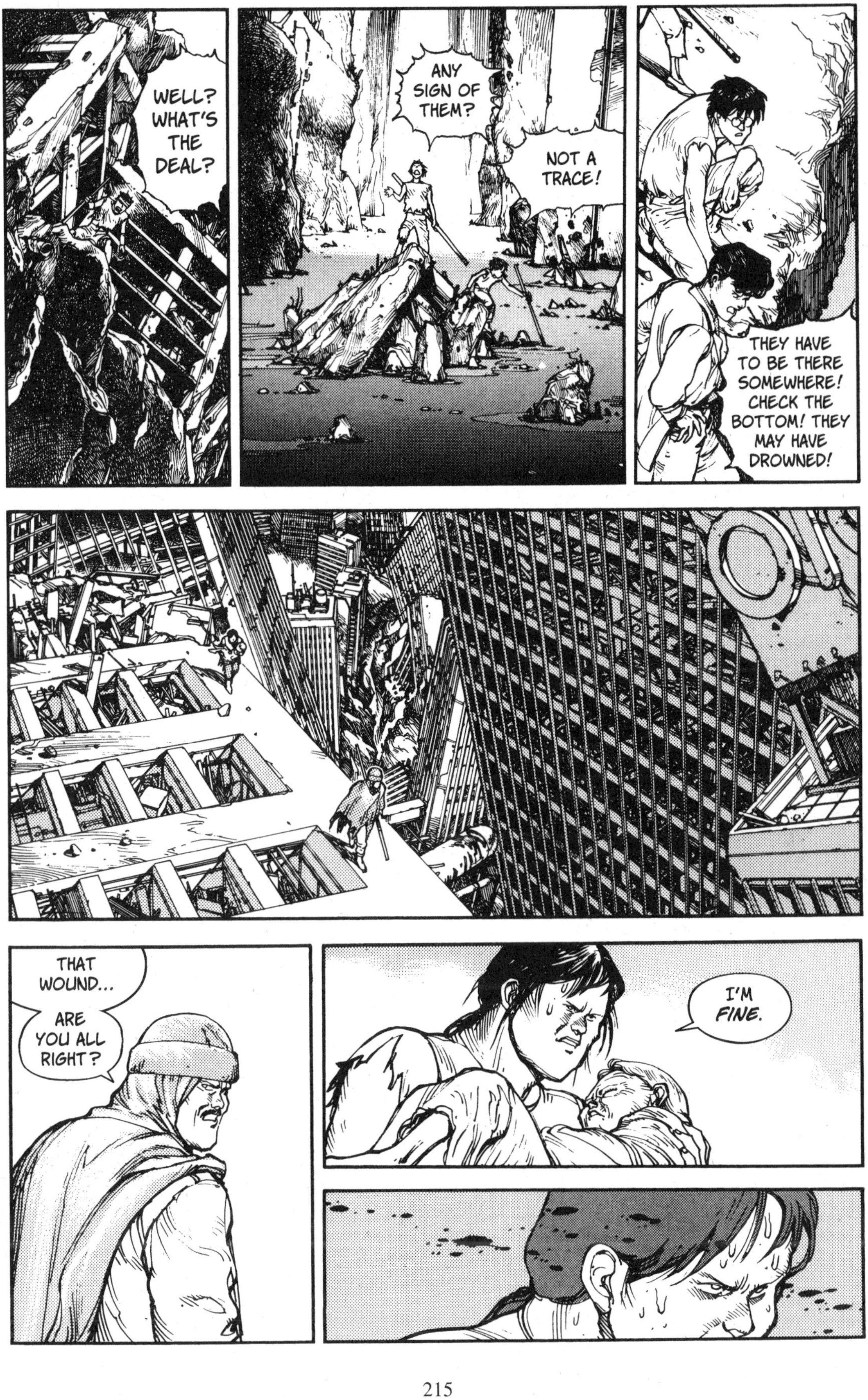
WELL? WHAT'S THE DEAL?
ANY SIGN OF THEM?
NOT A TRACE!
THEY HAVE TO BE THERE SOMEWHERE! CHECK THE BOTTOM! THEY MAY HAVE DROWNED!
THAT WOUND...
ARE YOU ALL RIGHT?
I'M *FINE*.

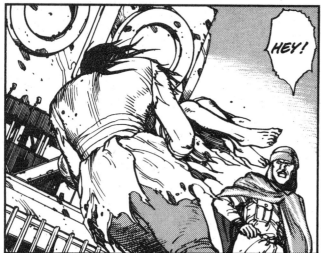

HEY!

THIS ISN'T THE TIME TO QUIT! GET UP!

STAC

NOW!!

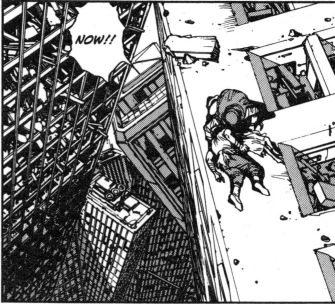

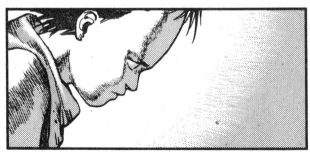

MASTER TETSUO ...?

!

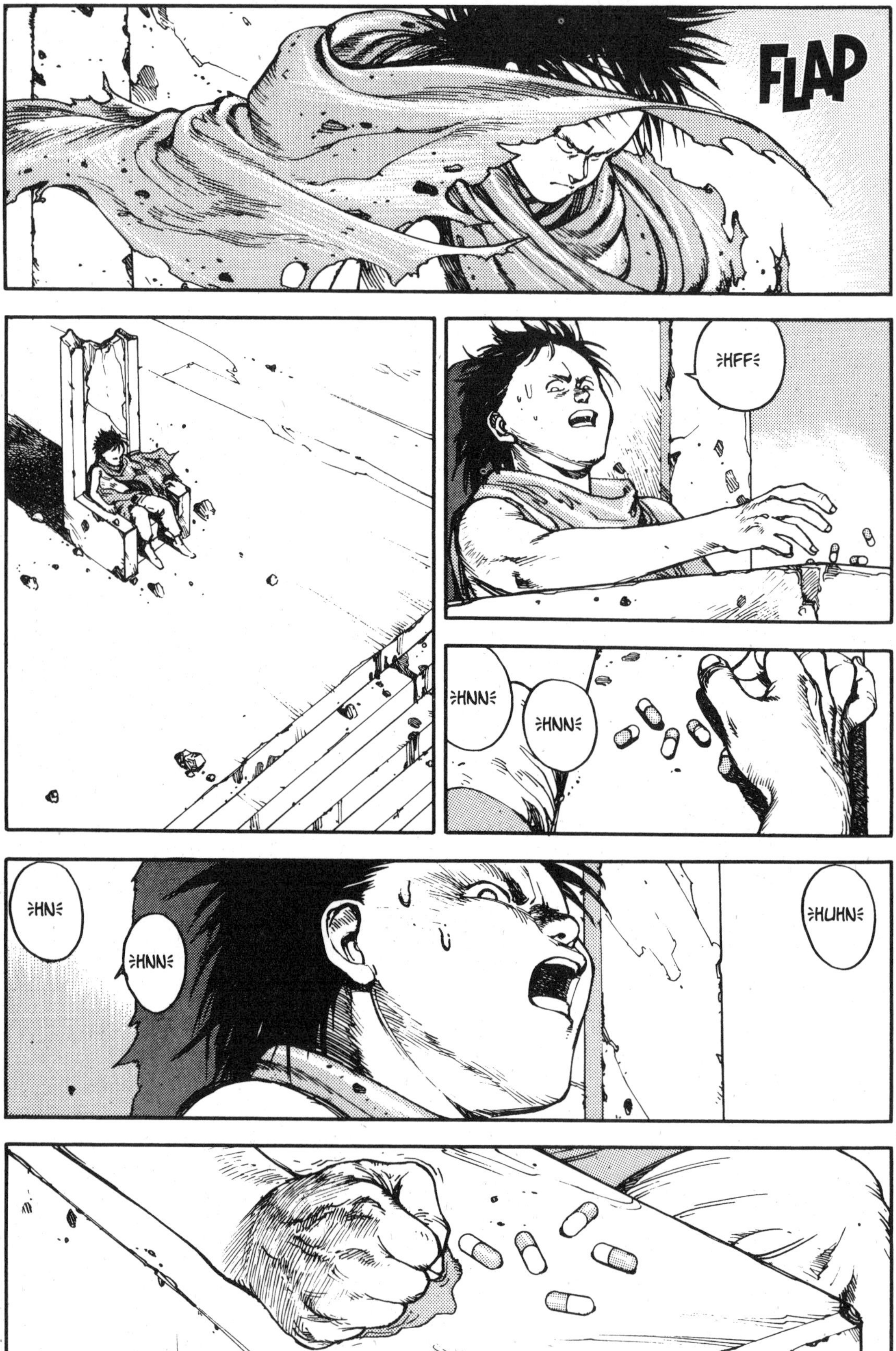
FLAP
HFF
HNN
HNN
HN
HNN
HUHN

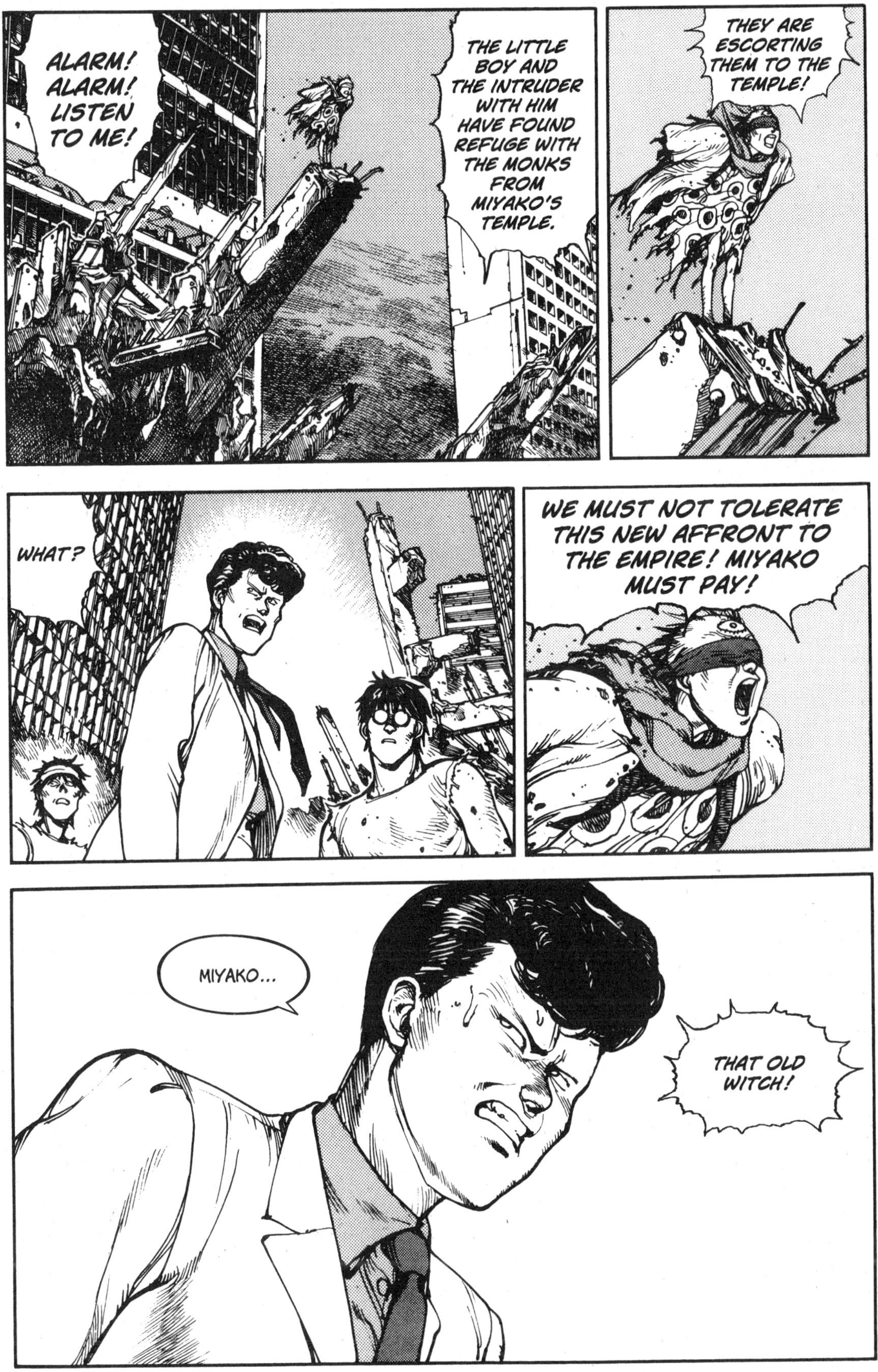
ALARM! ALARM! LISTEN TO ME!
THE LITTLE BOY AND THE INTRUDER WITH HIM HAVE FOUND REFUGE WITH THE MONKS FROM MIYAKO'S TEMPLE.
THEY ARE ESCORTING THEM TO THE TEMPLE!
WHAT?
WE MUST NOT TOLERATE THIS NEW AFFRONT TO THE EMPIRE! MIYAKO MUST PAY!
MIYAKO...
THAT OLD WITCH!

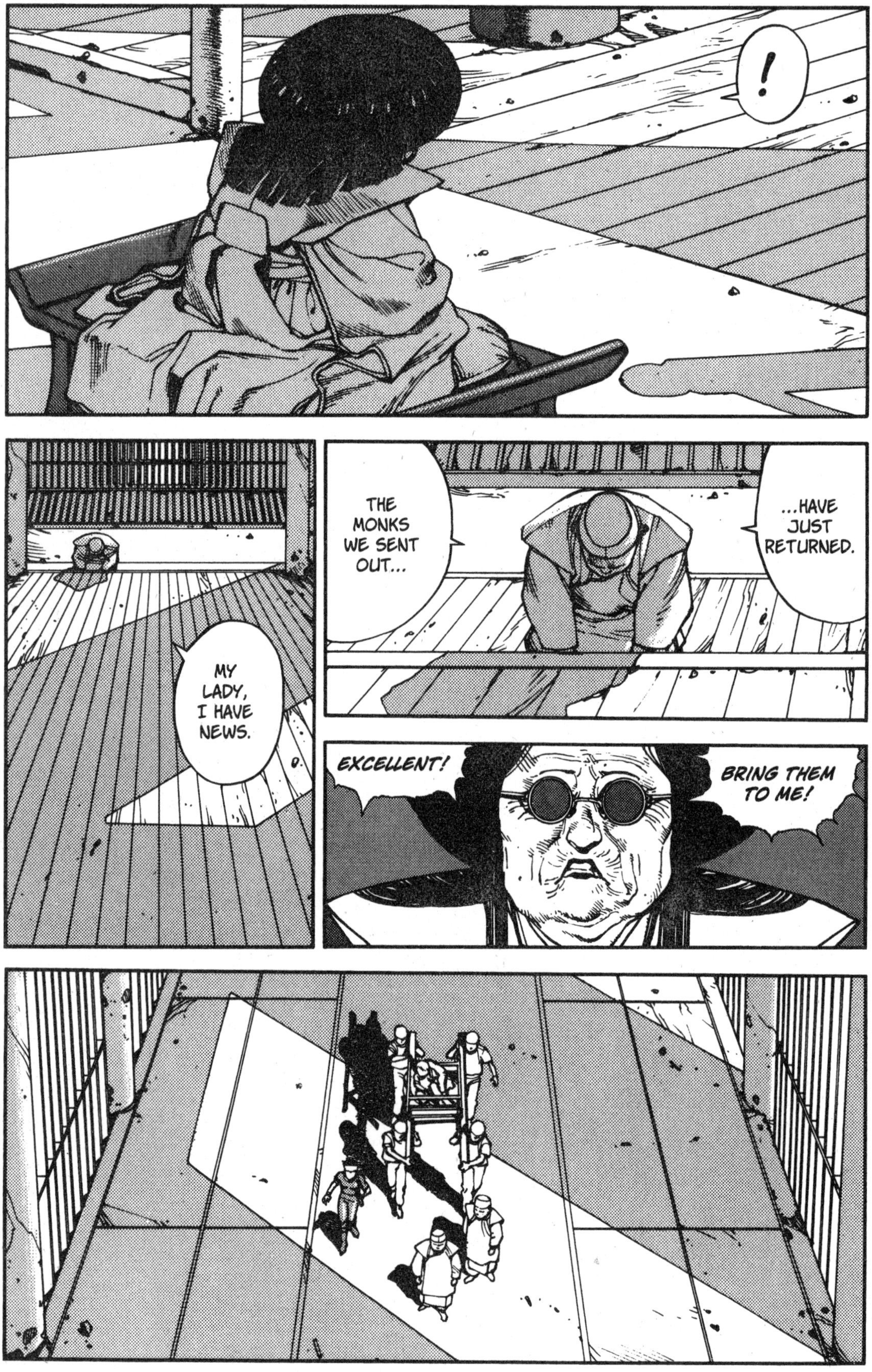
!
MY LADY, I HAVE NEWS.
THE MONKS WE SENT OUT...
...HAVE JUST RETURNED.
EXCELLENT!
BRING THEM TO ME!

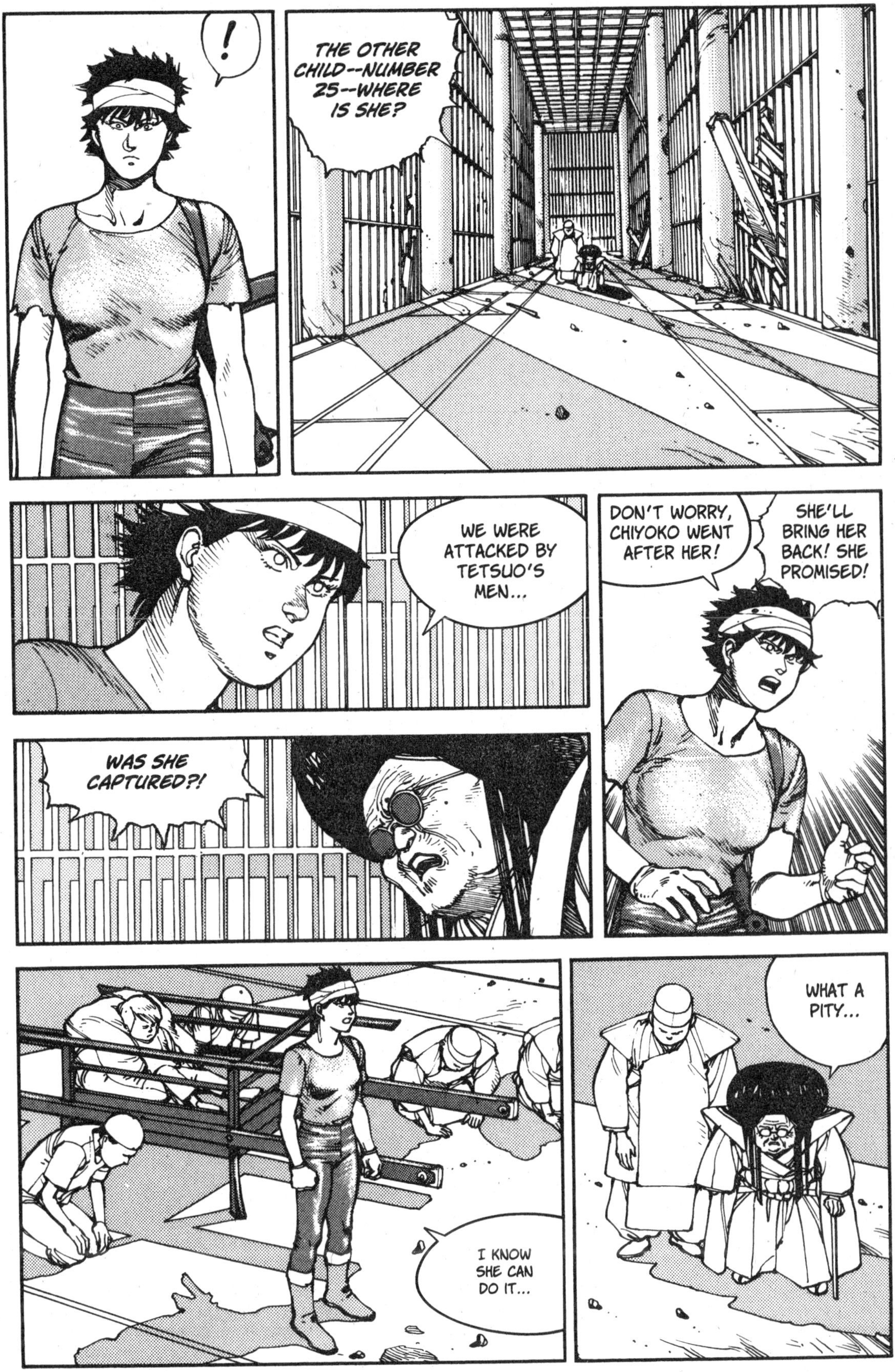
!
THE OTHER CHILD--NUMBER 25--WHERE IS SHE?
WE WERE ATTACKED BY TETSUO'S MEN...
WAS SHE CAPTURED?!
DON'T WORRY, CHIYOKO WENT AFTER HER!
SHE'LL BRING HER BACK! SHE PROMISED!
I KNOW SHE CAN DO IT...
WHAT A PITY...

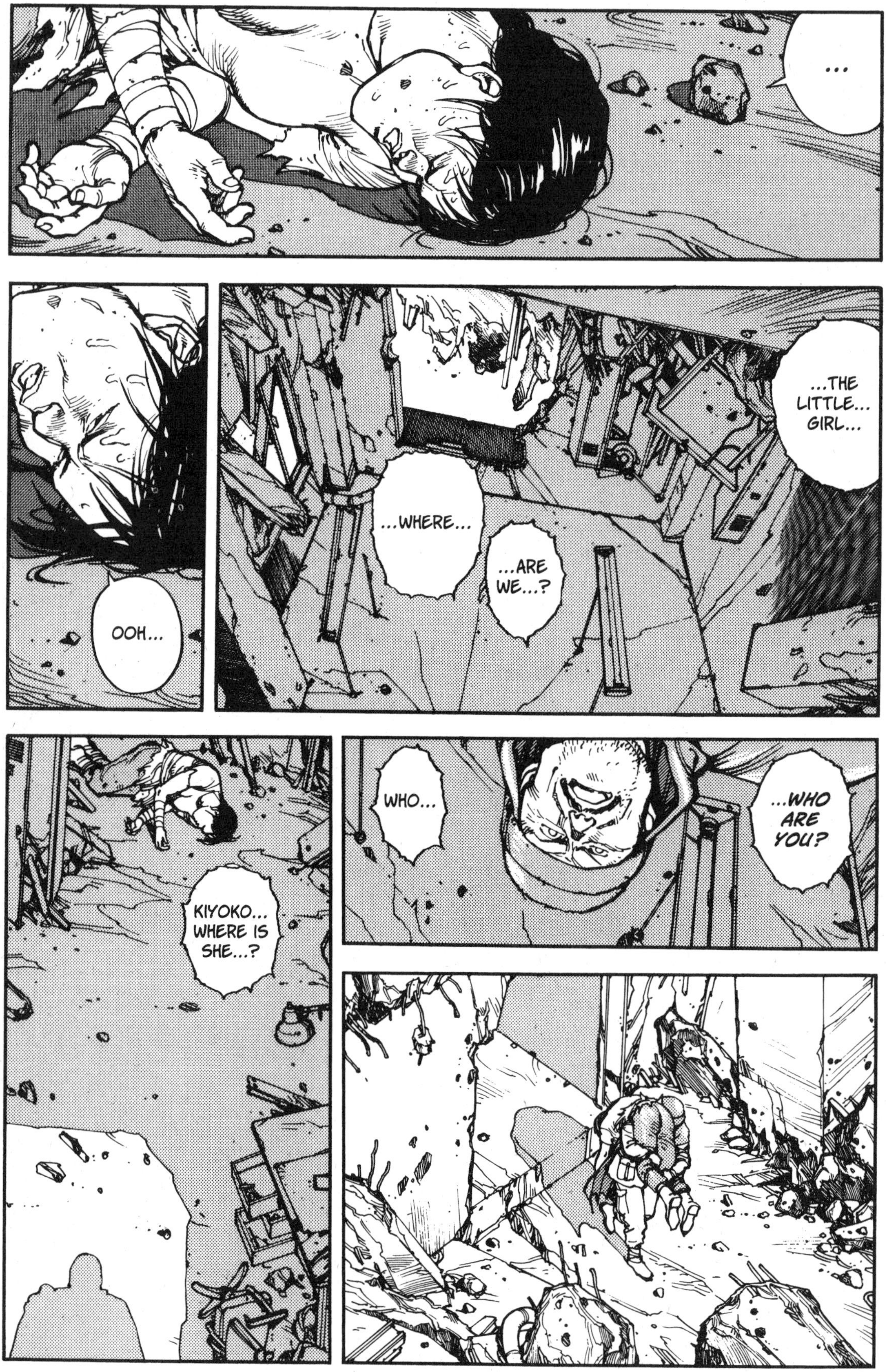
...
OOH...
...WHERE...
...ARE WE...?
...THE LITTLE... GIRL...
KIYOKO... WHERE IS SHE...?
WHO...
...WHO ARE YOU?

...PL...

...PLEASE...

SHUT UP!

KI... KIYOKO... TAKE HER...

...TO NUMBER 19...

NUMBER 19?!

WHAT OTHER CHILD?

MASARU?! ARE YOU TALKING ABOUT MASARU?!

WAKE UP!

...OTHER CHILD... WAITING... AT THE SHRINE...

ANSWER ME!

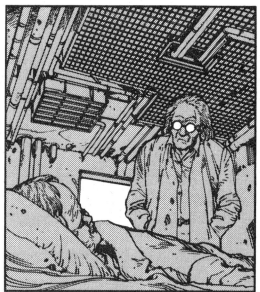

TCHAK

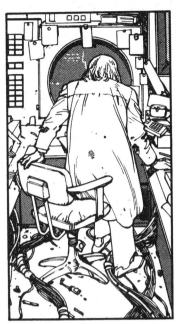
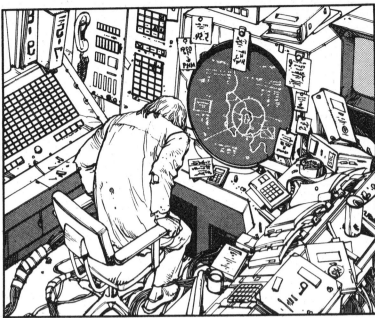

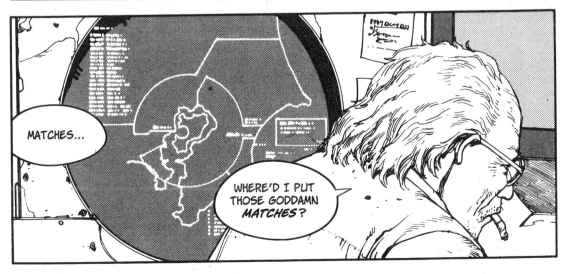

225

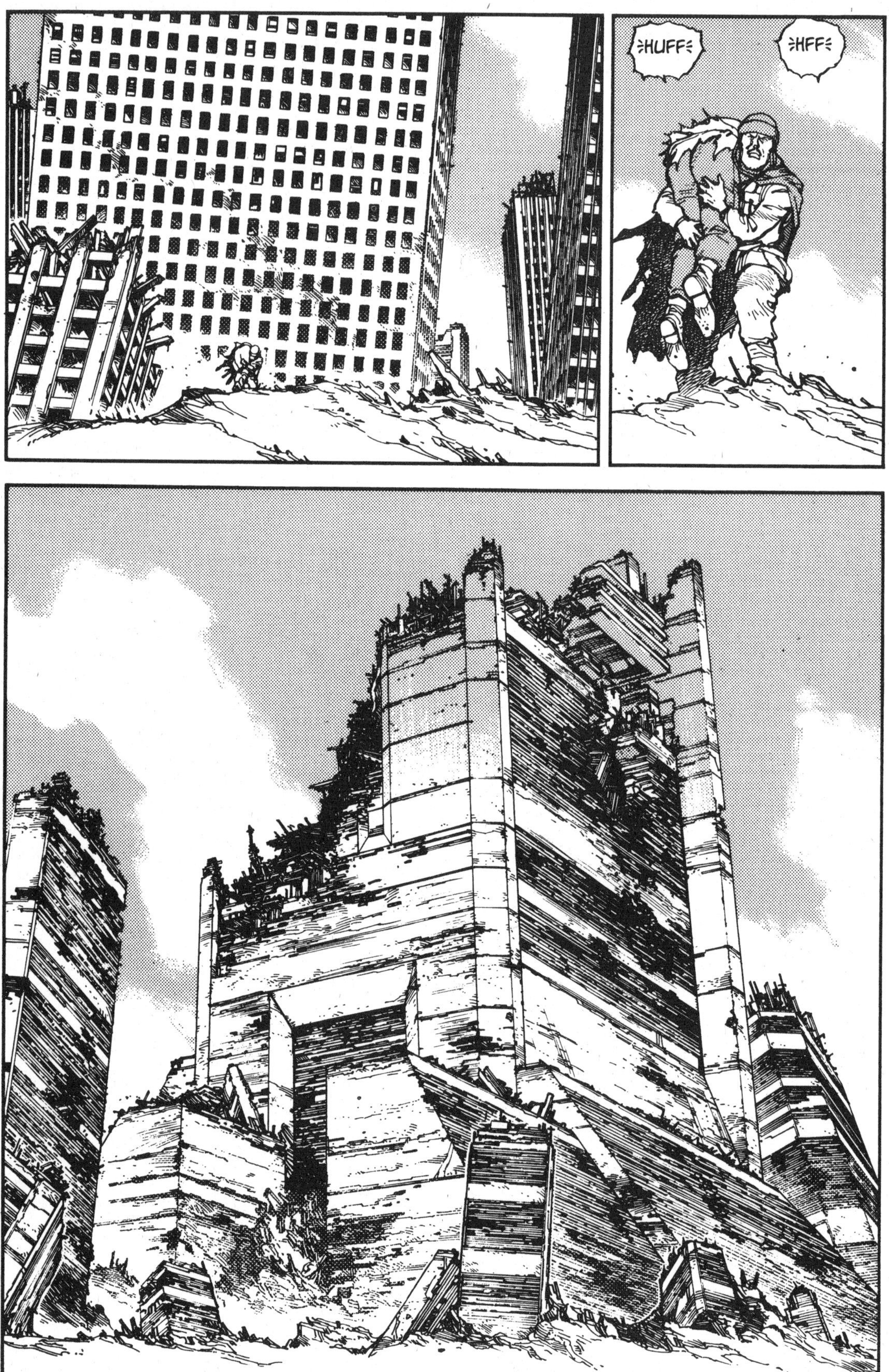
HUFF
HFF

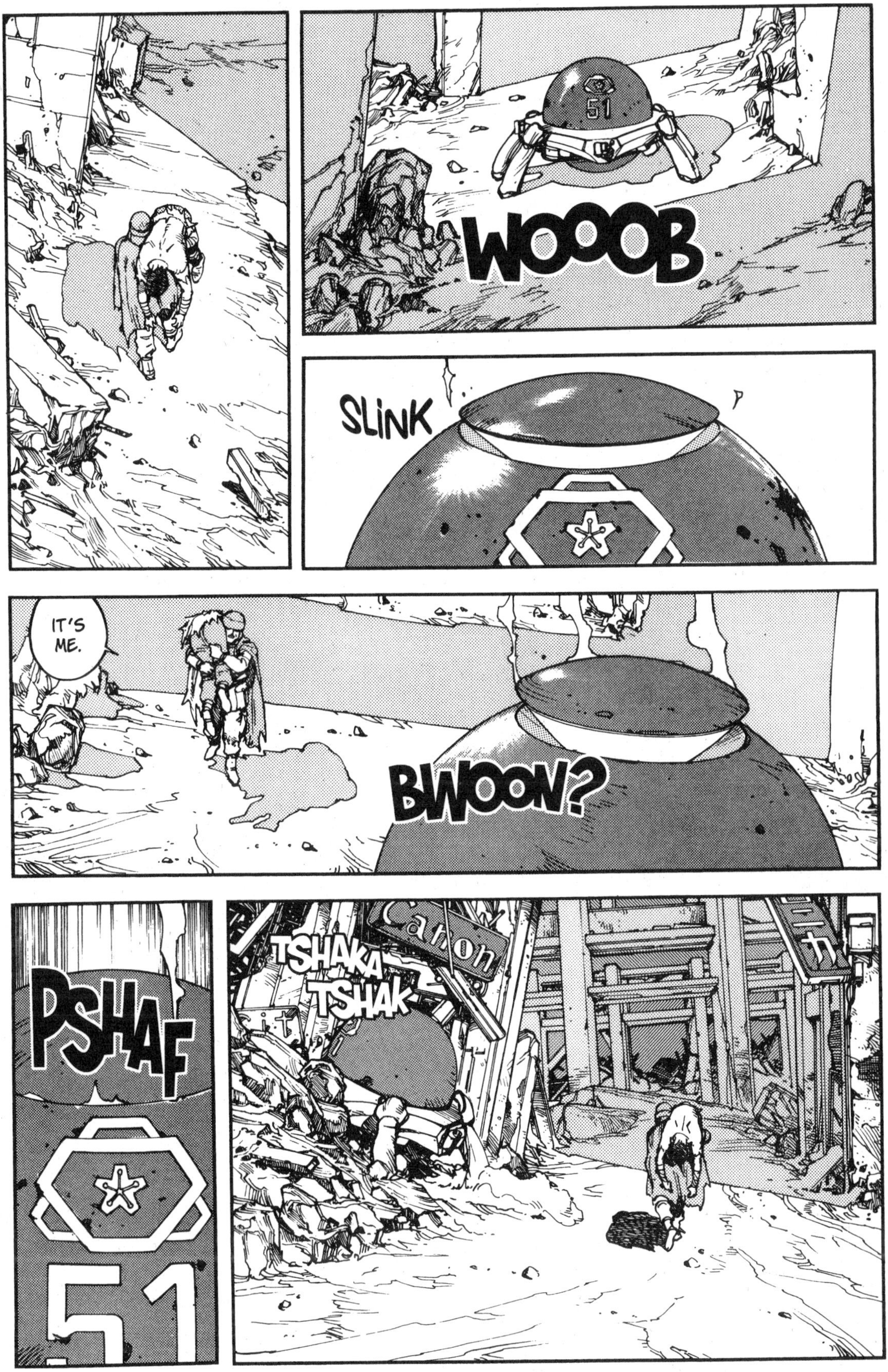
51
WOOOB
SLINK
IT'S ME.
BWOON?
PSHAF
51
Canon
TSHAKA TSHAK

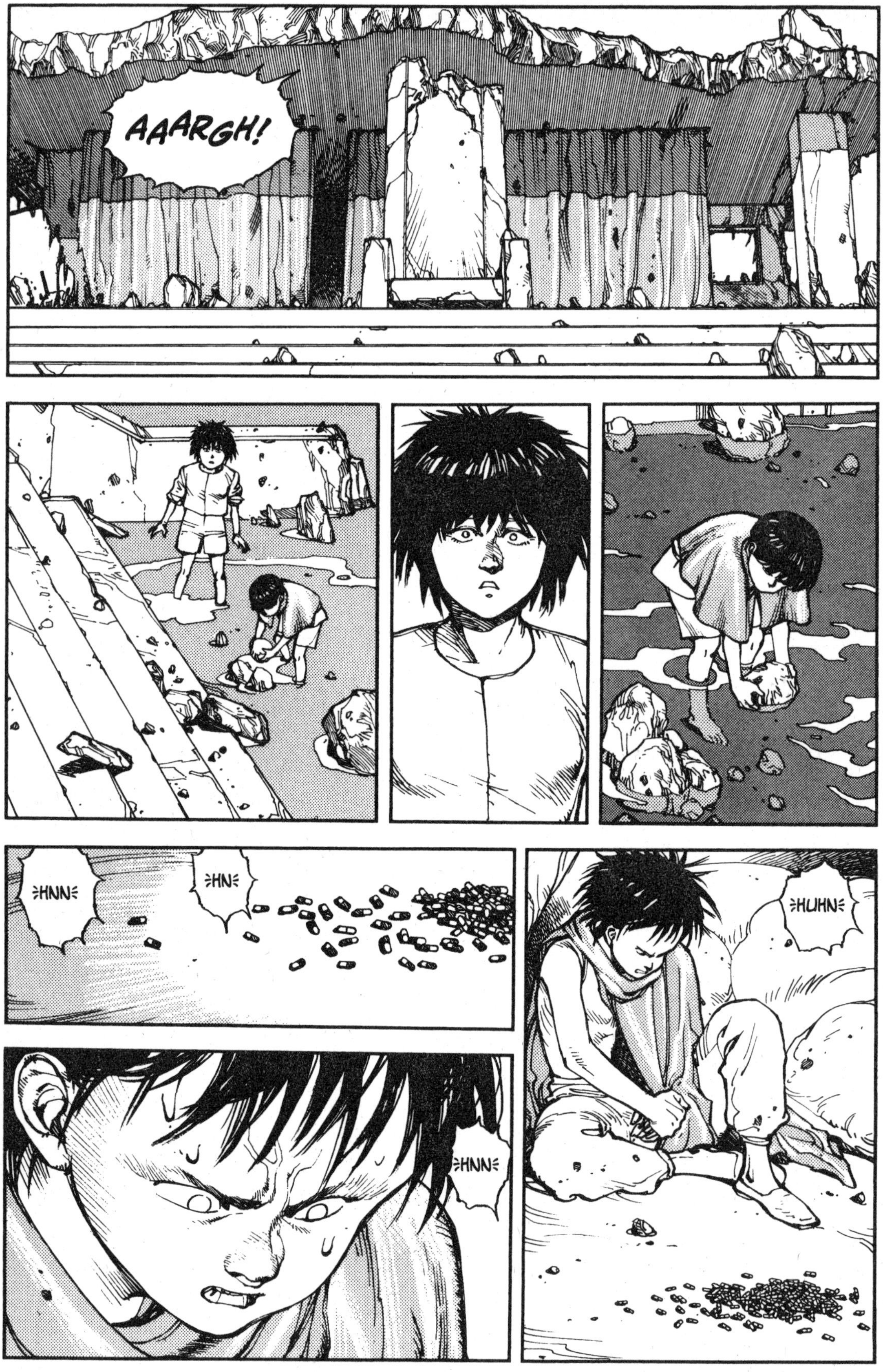
AAARGH!
HNN
HN
HUHN
HNN

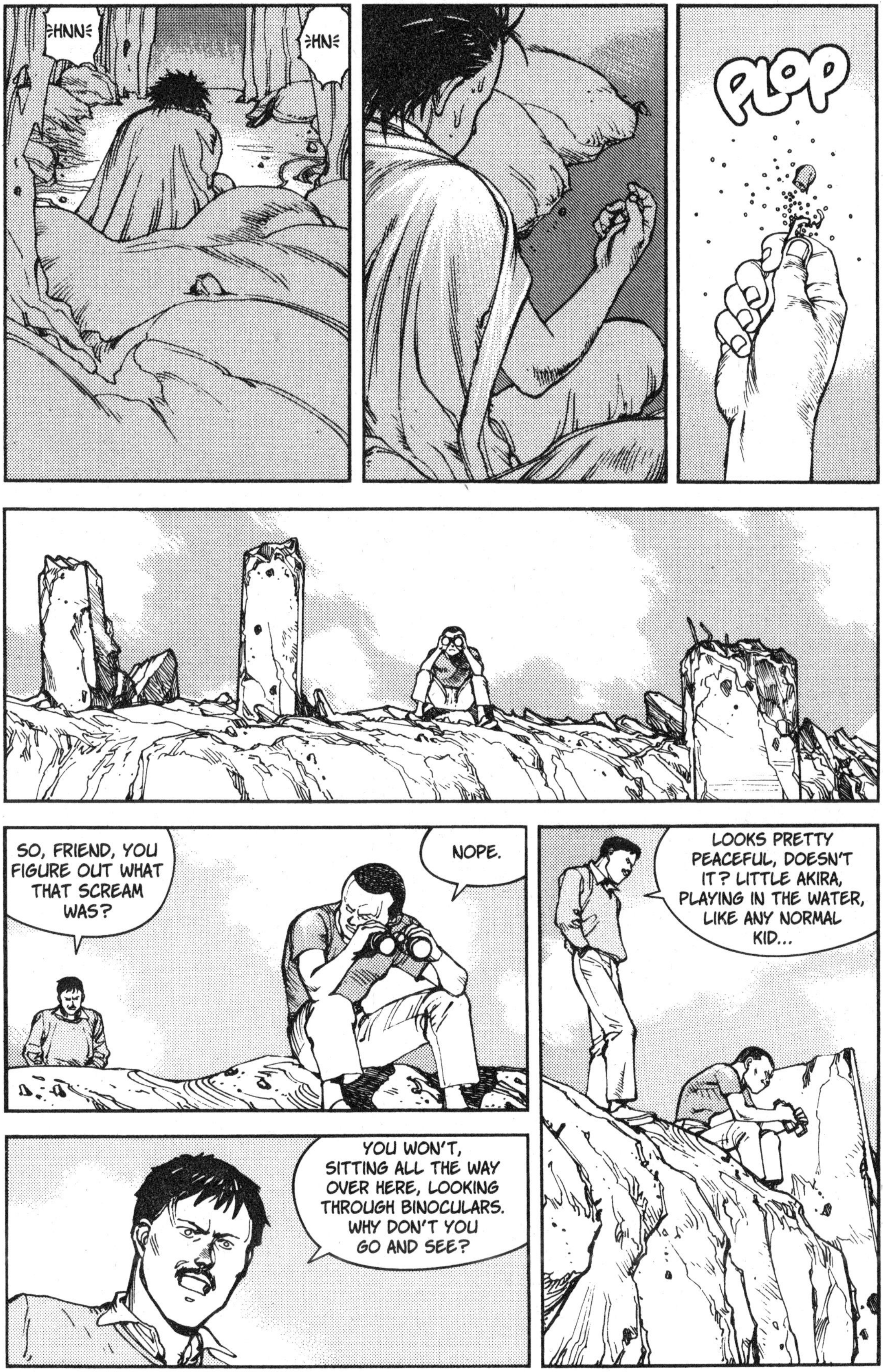
HNN
HN
PLOP
SO, FRIEND, YOU FIGURE OUT WHAT THAT SCREAM WAS?
NOPE.
YOU WON'T, SITTING ALL THE WAY OVER HERE, LOOKING THROUGH BINOCULARS. WHY DON'T YOU GO AND SEE?
LOOKS PRETTY PEACEFUL, DOESN'T IT? LITTLE AKIRA, PLAYING IN THE WATER, LIKE ANY NORMAL KID...

HMM?

HEY!

LET'S SEE WHO'S VISITING...

KAORI! HAS MASTER TETSUO RETURNED YET?

GOOD!!

HE'S IN HIS ROOM.

AAH...

GNN...

A-AAGH...

AAAH...

...

DODOM

GNN...
GNNNN...

AAUGH!

TCHOOF

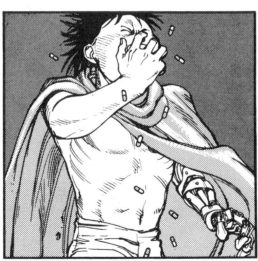

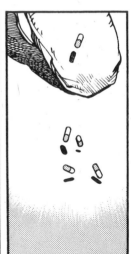

231

WHAT DO YOU WANT?!

IT...IT'S ABOUT THOSE KIDS WE WERE AFTER...

GET LOST.

BUT, MASTER TETSUO, ONE OF THEM...

...IS IN THE HANDS OF MIYAKO'S MONKS.

GET YOUR ASS OUT OF HERE!

Y-YESSIR!

LEAVE ME...

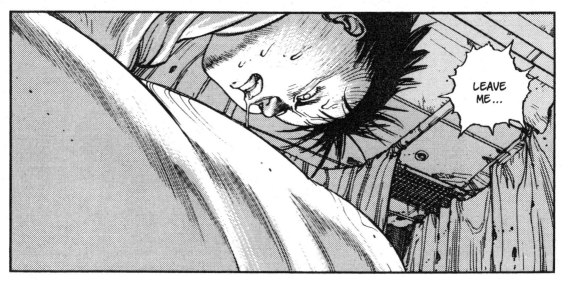

DO I HAVE TO DO EVERYTHING *ALONE?*

DAMN IT TO HELL! I CAN'T TAKE THIS SHIT!

SHOF

...

IF YOU WANT SOMETHING DONE RIGHT, DO IT YOUR-SELF!

LISTEN UP!

I'M ASSUMING COMMAND OF THE EMPIRE'S ARMY!

ROUND UP ALL THE FIGHTING MEN!

DID YOU REMEMBER MY CIGARETTES?

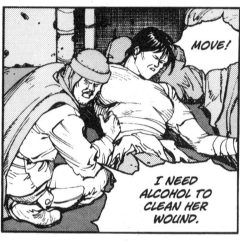

MOVE!

I NEED ALCOHOL TO CLEAN HER WOUND.

A FEW CIGARETTES ISN'T SO MUCH TO ASK FOR...

SRiiiC

...YOU ALWAYS FORGET MY CIGARETTES...AND YOU PROMISED!

AH ....!

234

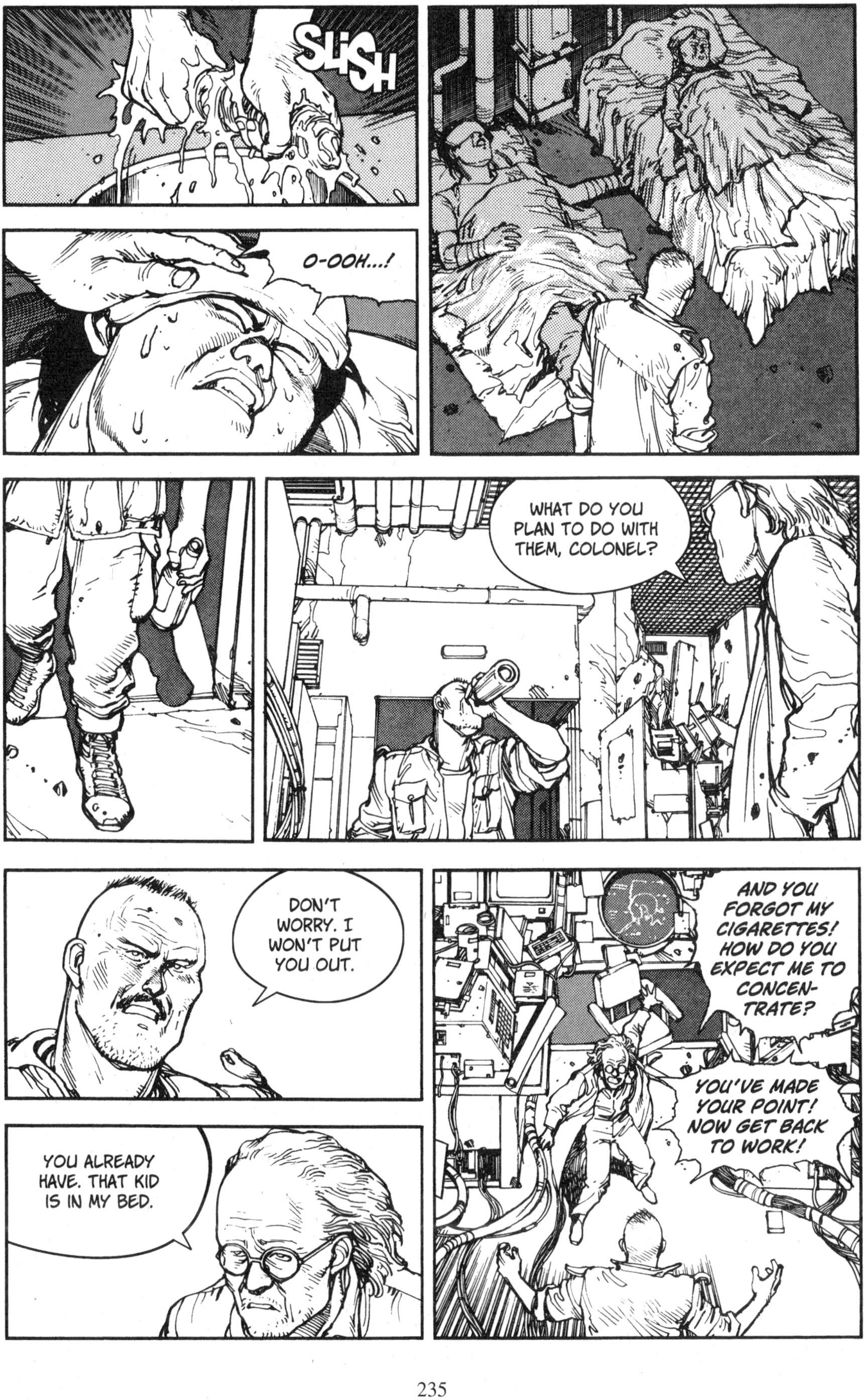

SLISH
O-OOH...!
WHAT DO YOU PLAN TO DO WITH THEM, COLONEL?
DON'T WORRY. I WON'T PUT YOU OUT.
YOU ALREADY HAVE. THAT KID IS IN MY BED.
AND YOU FORGOT MY CIGARETTES! HOW DO YOU EXPECT ME TO CONCEN-TRATE?
YOU'VE MADE YOUR POINT! NOW GET BACK TO WORK!

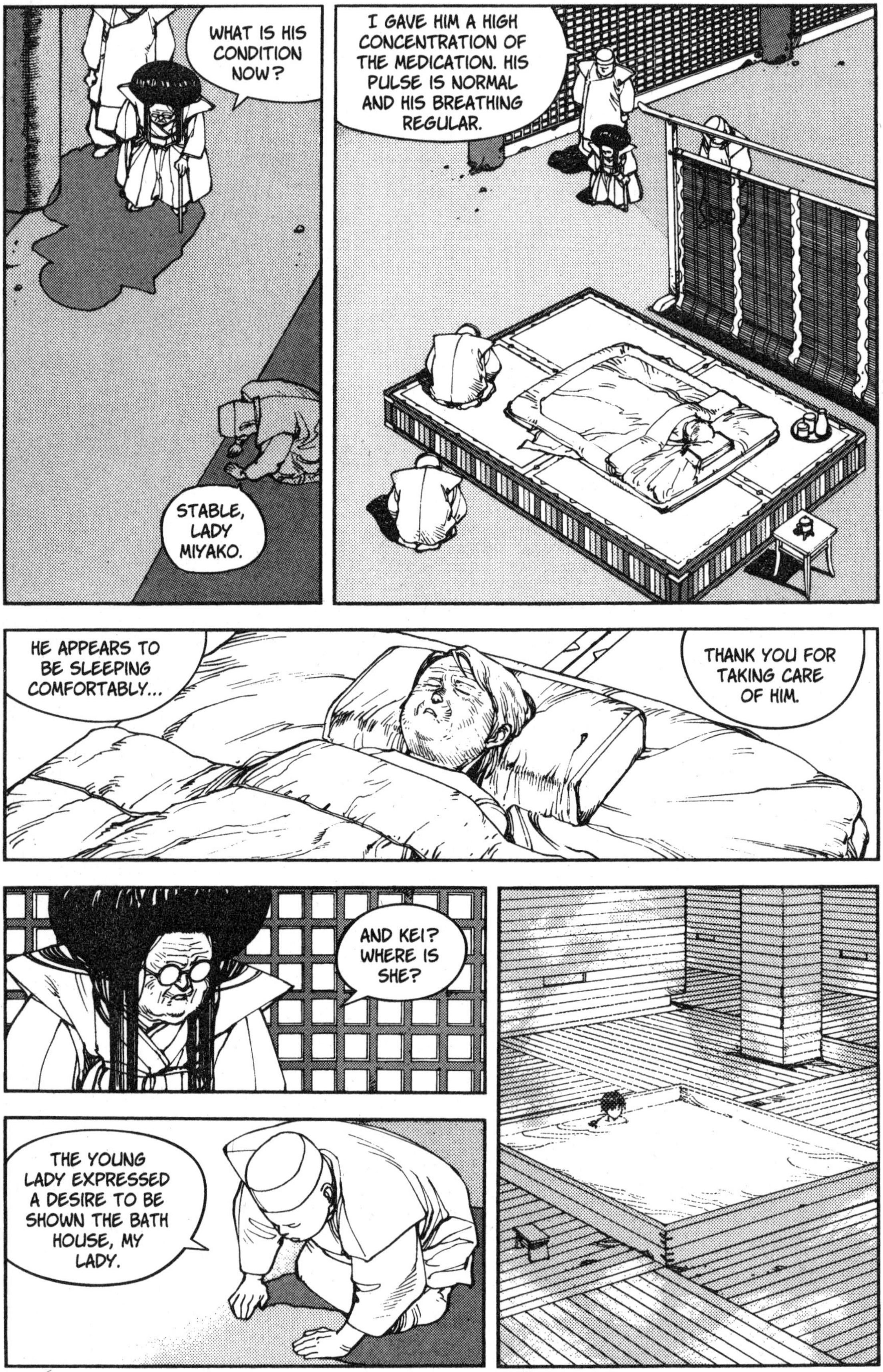
WHAT IS HIS CONDITION NOW?
STABLE, LADY MIYAKO.
I GAVE HIM A HIGH CONCENTRATION OF THE MEDICATION. HIS PULSE IS NORMAL AND HIS BREATHING REGULAR.
HE APPEARS TO BE SLEEPING COMFORTABLY...
THANK YOU FOR TAKING CARE OF HIM.
AND KEI? WHERE IS SHE?
THE YOUNG LADY EXPRESSED A DESIRE TO BE SHOWN THE BATH HOUSE, MY LADY.

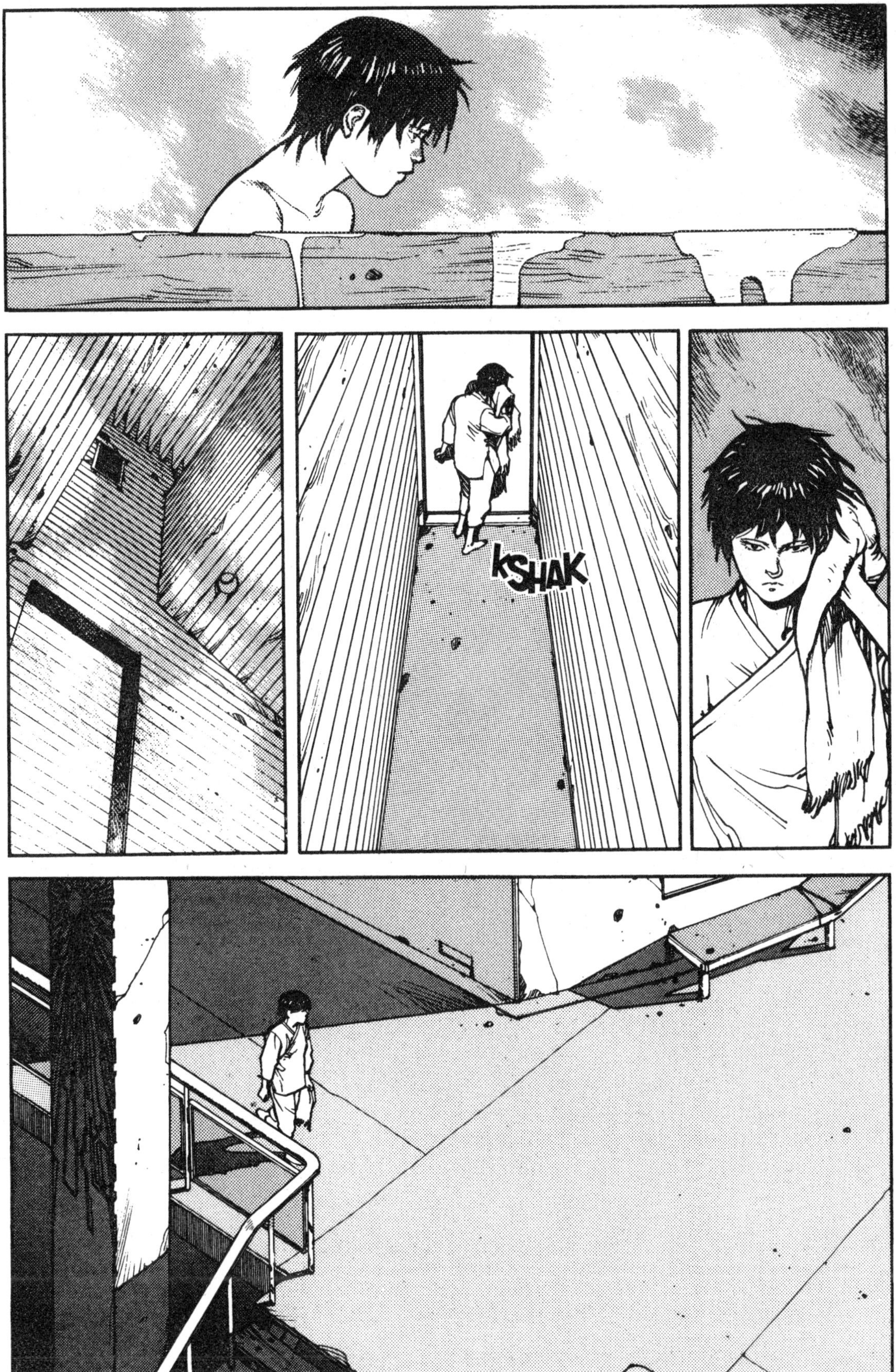
KSHAK

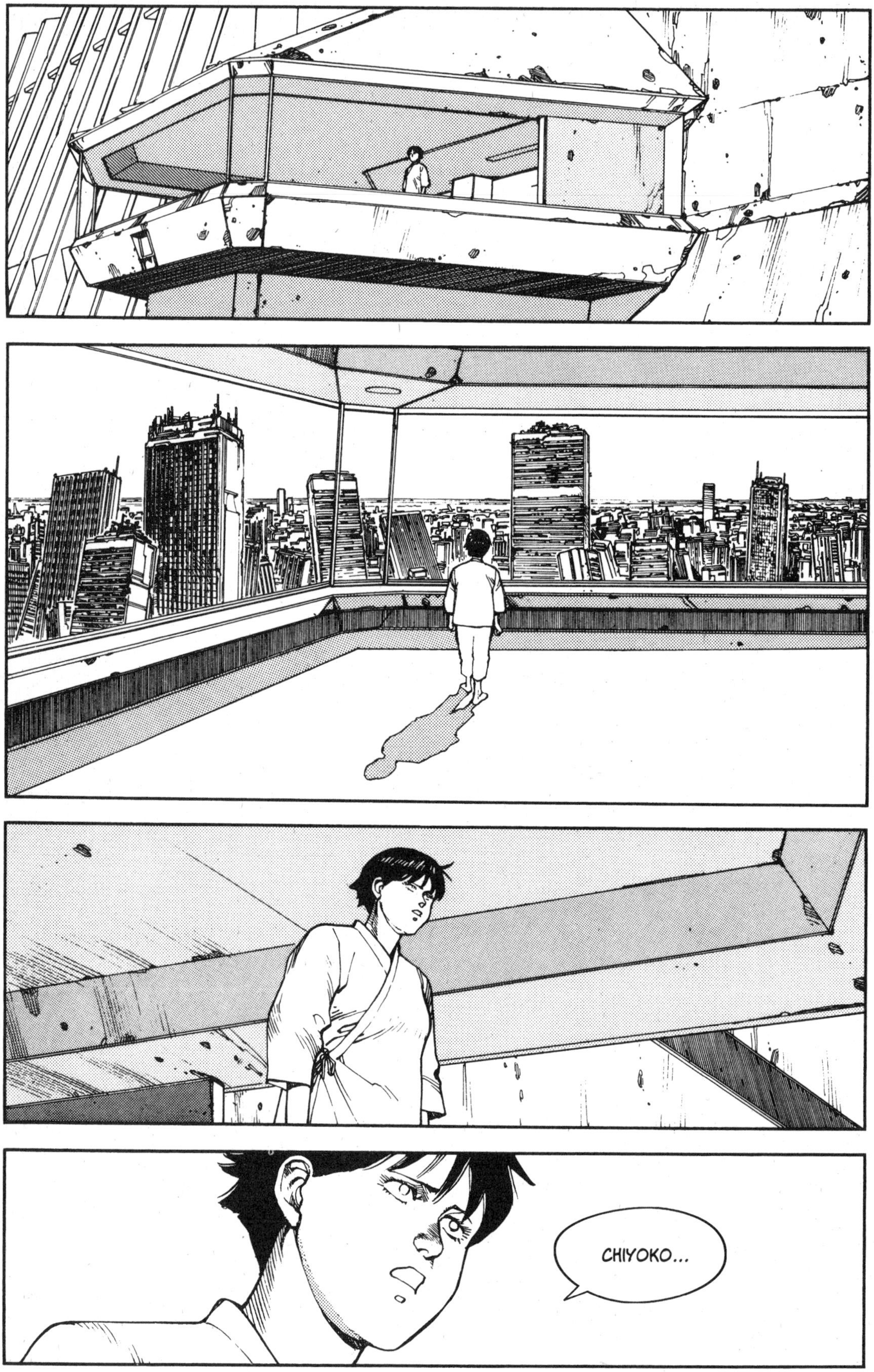
CHIYOKO...

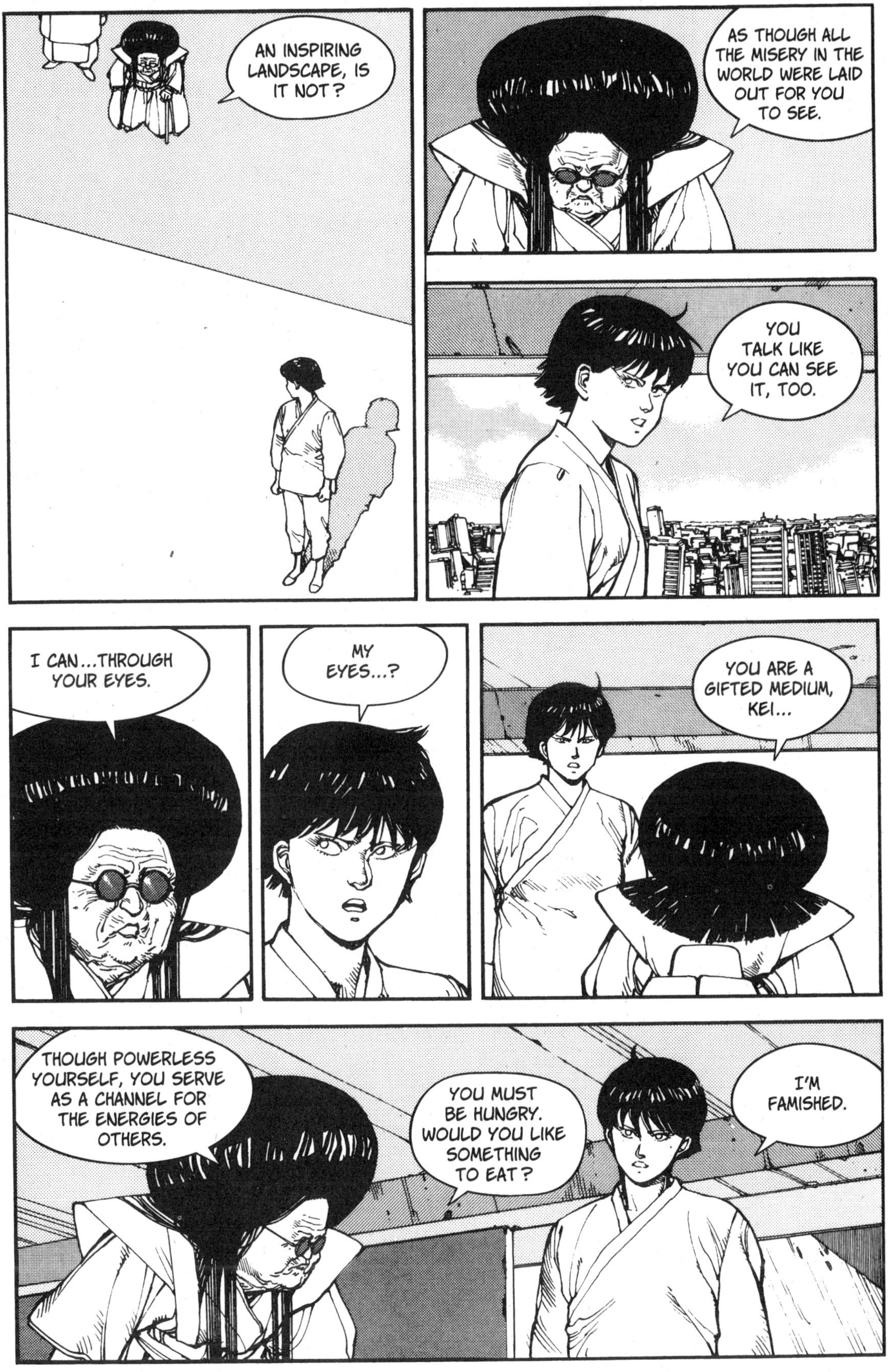
AN INSPIRING LANDSCAPE, IS IT NOT?
AS THOUGH ALL THE MISERY IN THE WORLD WERE LAID OUT FOR YOU TO SEE.
YOU TALK LIKE YOU CAN SEE IT, TOO.
I CAN...THROUGH YOUR EYES.
MY EYES...?
YOU ARE A GIFTED MEDIUM, KEI...
THOUGH POWERLESS YOURSELF, YOU SERVE AS A CHANNEL FOR THE ENERGIES OF OTHERS.
YOU MUST BE HUNGRY. WOULD YOU LIKE SOMETHING TO EAT?
I'M FAMISHED.

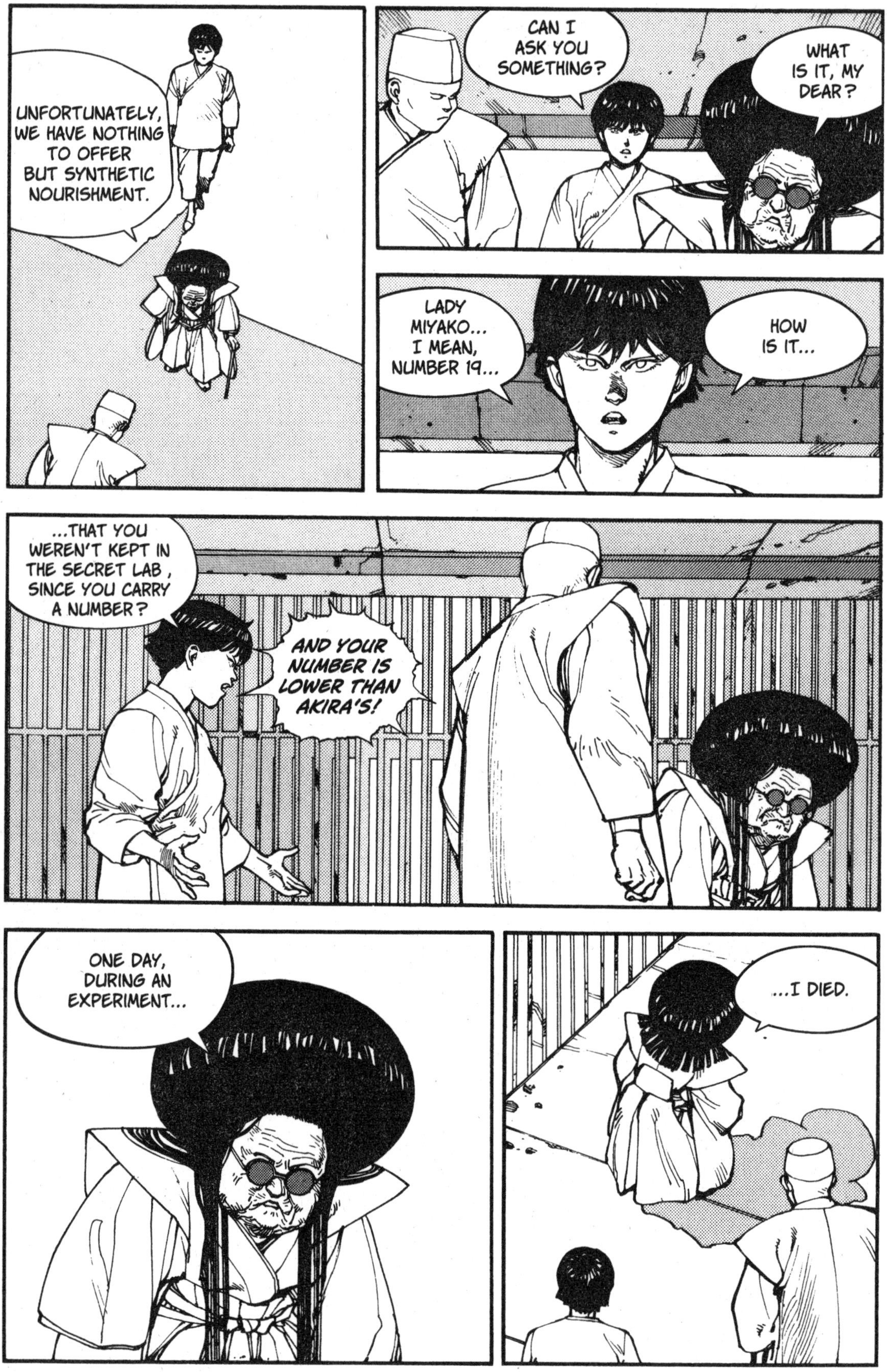
UNFORTUNATELY, WE HAVE NOTHING TO OFFER BUT SYNTHETIC NOURISHMENT.
CAN I ASK YOU SOMETHING?
WHAT IS IT, MY DEAR?
LADY MIYAKO... I MEAN, NUMBER 19...
HOW IS IT...
...THAT YOU WEREN'T KEPT IN THE SECRET LAB, SINCE YOU CARRY A NUMBER?
AND YOUR NUMBER IS LOWER THAN AKIRA'S!
ONE DAY, DURING AN EXPERIMENT...
...I DIED.

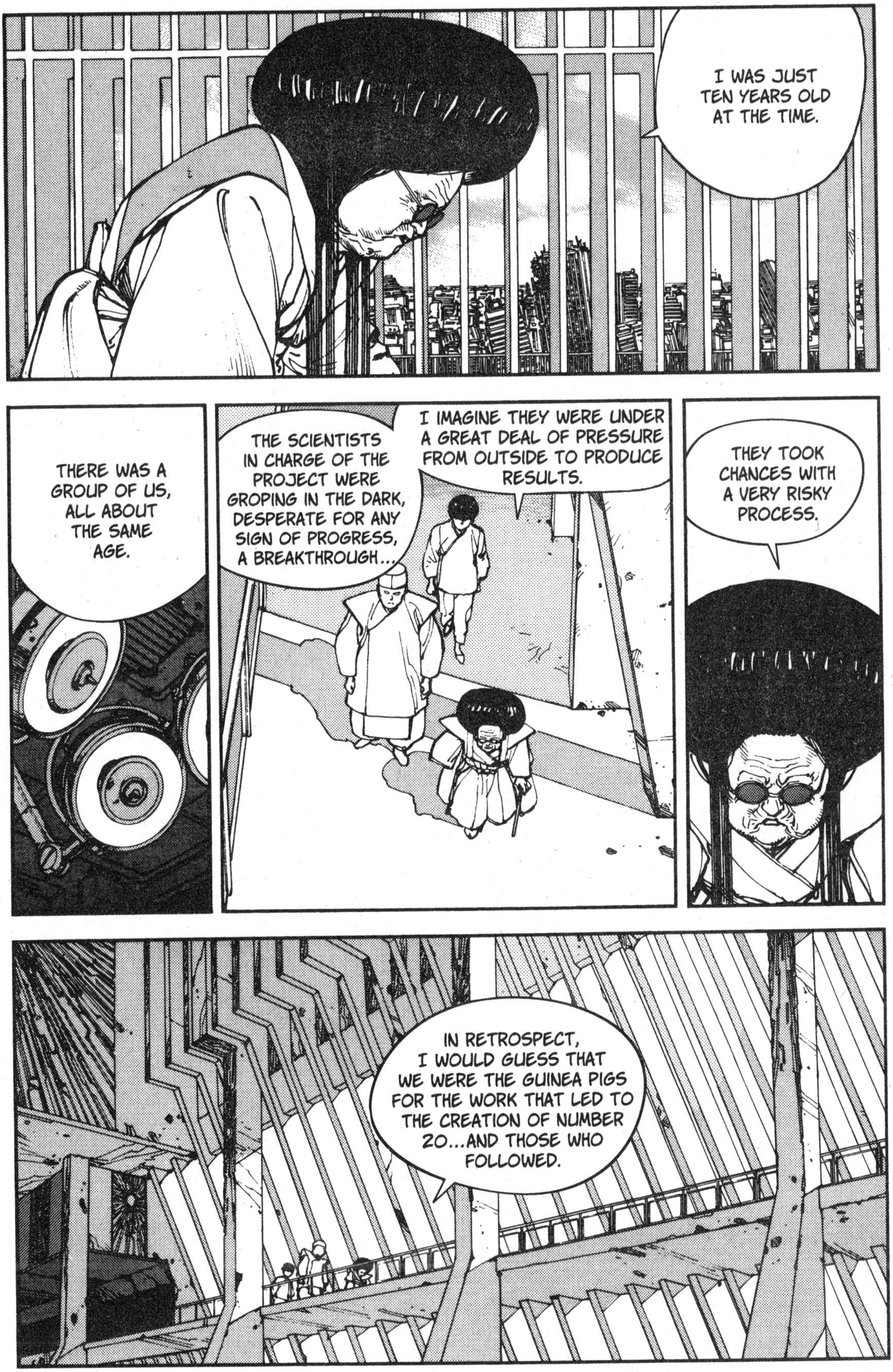
I WAS JUST TEN YEARS OLD AT THE TIME.
THERE WAS A GROUP OF US, ALL ABOUT THE SAME AGE.
THE SCIENTISTS IN CHARGE OF THE PROJECT WERE GROPING IN THE DARK, DESPERATE FOR ANY SIGN OF PROGRESS, A BREAKTHROUGH...
I IMAGINE THEY WERE UNDER A GREAT DEAL OF PRESSURE FROM OUTSIDE TO PRODUCE RESULTS.
THEY TOOK CHANCES WITH A VERY RISKY PROCESS.
IN RETROSPECT, I WOULD GUESS THAT WE WERE THE GUINEA PIGS FOR THE WORK THAT LED TO THE CREATION OF NUMBER 20...AND THOSE WHO FOLLOWED.

DURING THE COURSE OF THE EXPERIMENT, I LOST CONSCIOUSNESS AND FELL INTO A COMA. THEY REMOVED ME FROM THE PROJECT--AND PROJECT RECORDS--AND PLACED ME IN A STATE OF SUSPENDED ANIMATION...

...WHICH LASTED THIRTEEN YEARS.

THIRTEEN YEARS?

LADY MIYAKO...

THIS IS AN HONOR!

GLORY TO LADY MIYAKO!

MY LADY!

BY THE TIME I AWOKE, NEO-TOKYO WAS UNDER CONSTRUCTION AND EVERYONE HAD LONG SINCE FORGOTTEN MY EXISTENCE.

THOSE WHO KNEW MY SECRET VANISHED WHEN TOKYO WAS DESTROYED!

DURING MY LONG SLEEP, I HAD A DREAM...

A DREAM?

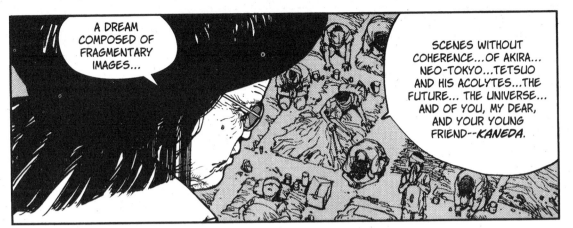

A DREAM COMPOSED OF FRAGMENTARY IMAGES...

SCENES WITHOUT COHERENCE...OF AKIRA... NEO-TOKYO...TETSUO AND HIS ACOLYTES...THE FUTURE... THE UNIVERSE... AND OF YOU, MY DEAR, AND YOUR YOUNG FRIEND--*KANEDA.*

KA... KANEDA?!

WHAT DO YOU KNOW ABOUT HIM?

DO YOU WHAT HAPPENED TO HIM?

HE'S BEYOND THE BOUNDARIES OF THIS WORLD!

TAP TAP

...FOR THE MOMENT...

GLORY TO YOU!

LADY MIYAKO!

245

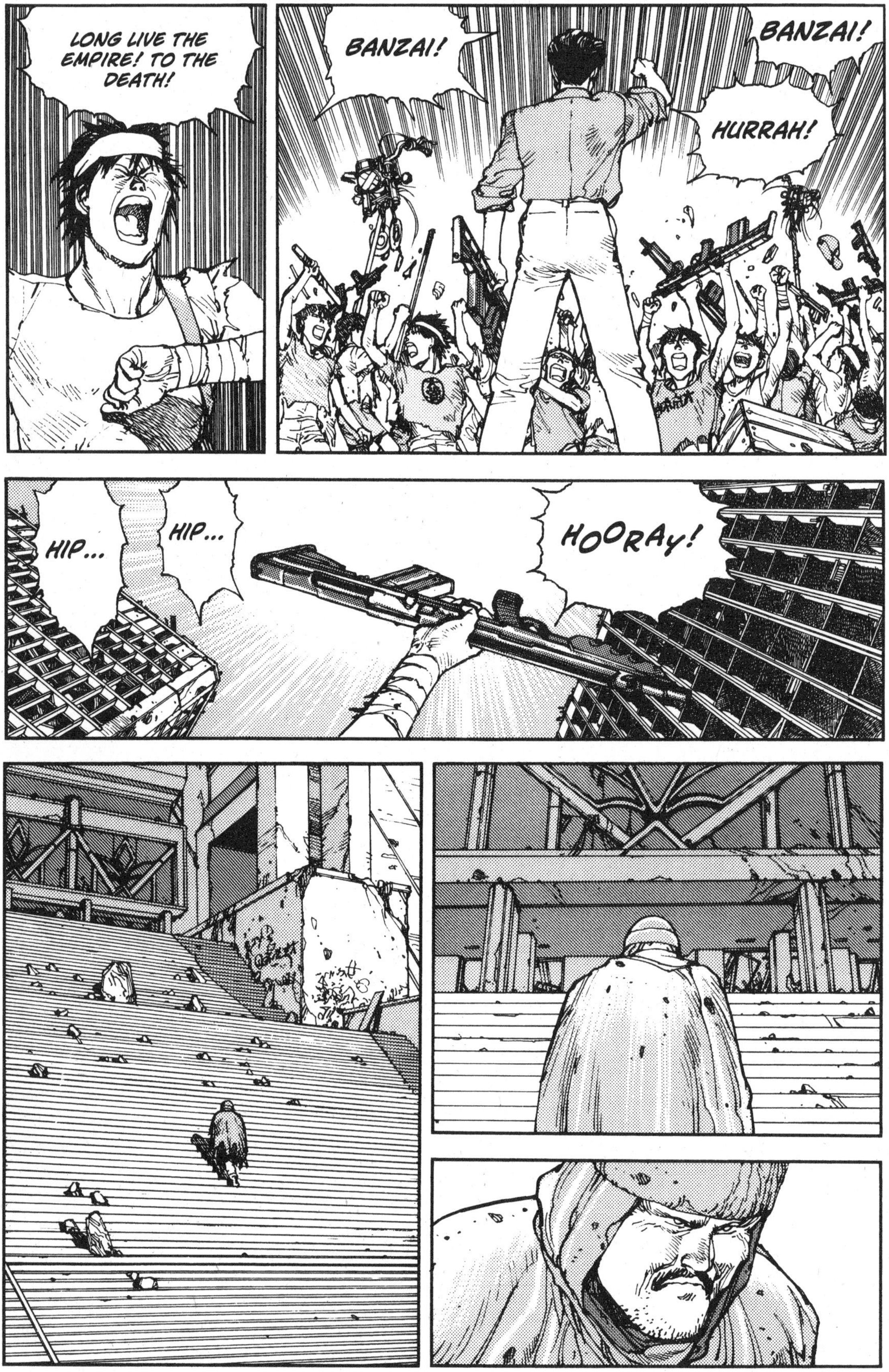
LONG LIVE THE EMPIRE! TO THE DEATH!
BANZAI!
BANZAI!
HURRAH!
HIP...
HIP...
HOORAY!

GWiiP
GWiiiP
GWiiiP
GWiiP
GWiiP

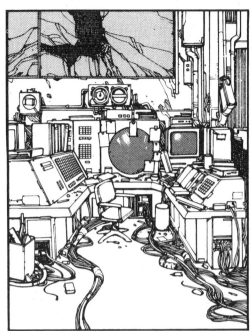

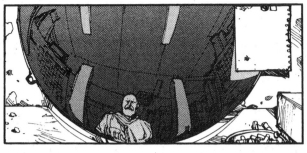

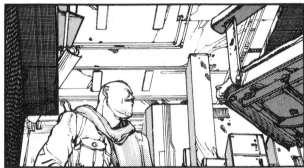

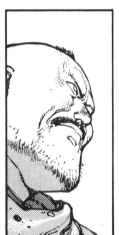

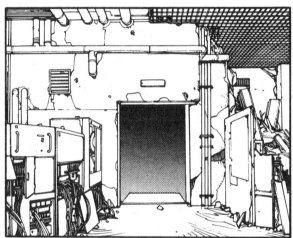

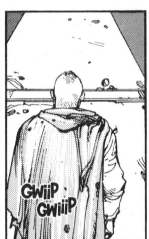

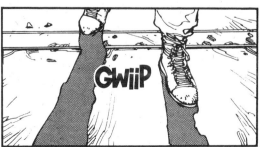

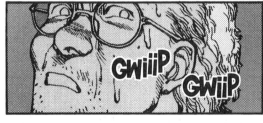

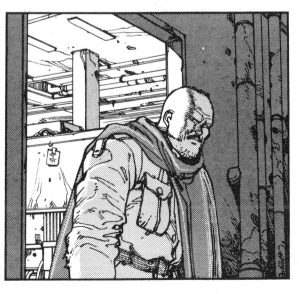

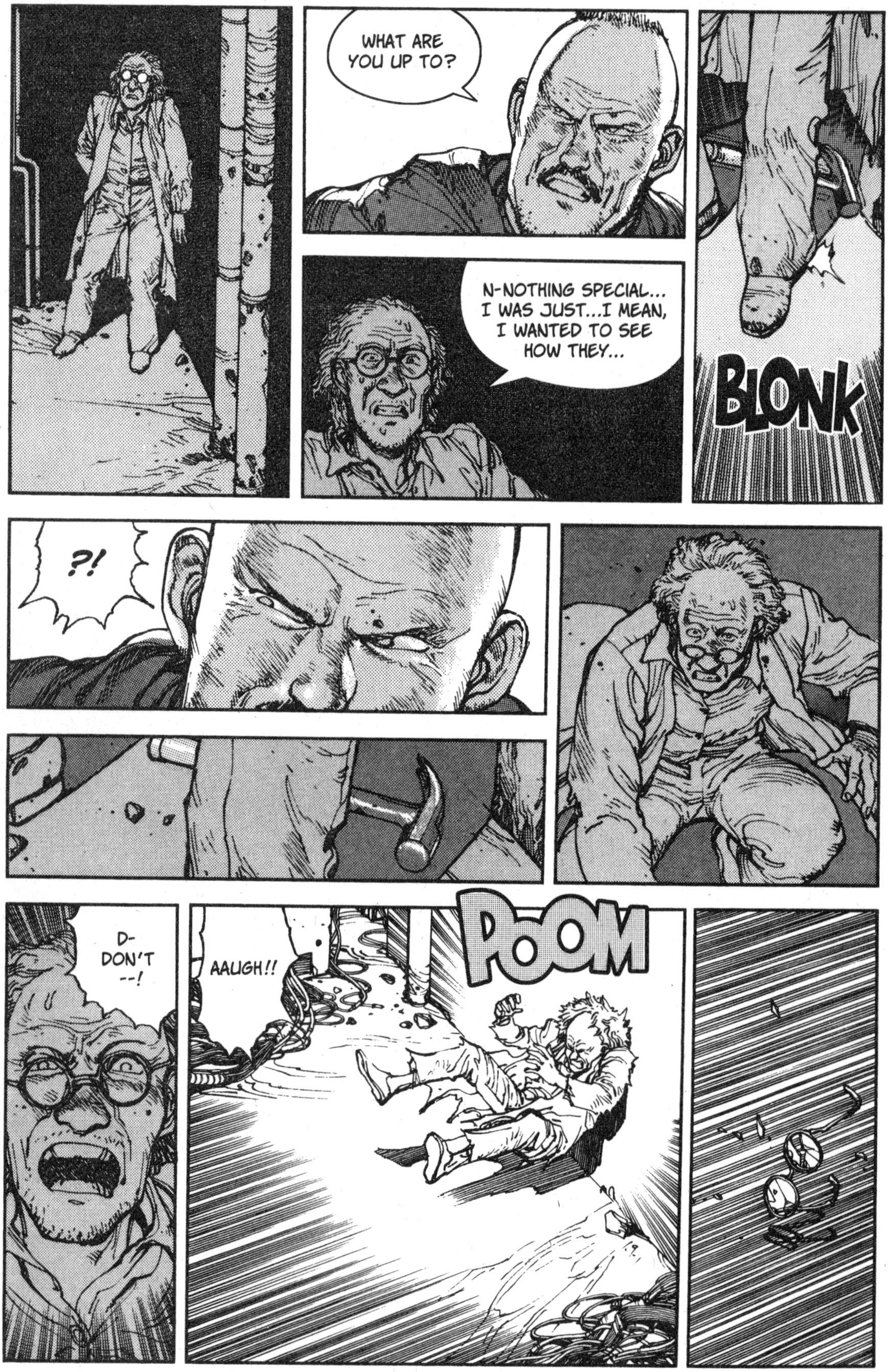
WHAT ARE YOU UP TO?
N-NOTHING SPECIAL... I WAS JUST...I MEAN, I WANTED TO SEE HOW THEY...
BLONK
?!
D-DON'T --!
AAUGH!!
POOM

...O-OHH...

WHAT WERE YOU PLANNING TO DO WITH THIS?

TO KILL THAT ABOMINABLE CHILD!

WHY?!

SHE AND OTHERS LIKE HER CAUSED THIS SHIT!

KILL HER RIGHT NOW!

THE TRAUMA HER DEATH WOULD CAUSE COULD TRIGGER ANOTHER MASSIVE REACTION IN AKIRA!

FOOL! DON'T YOU UNDERSTAND ANYTHING?

AND IF IT DOES...?

I HAVE NOTHING LEFT TO LOSE!

BOK

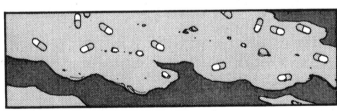

WHAT'S THAT FLOATING IN THE WATER?

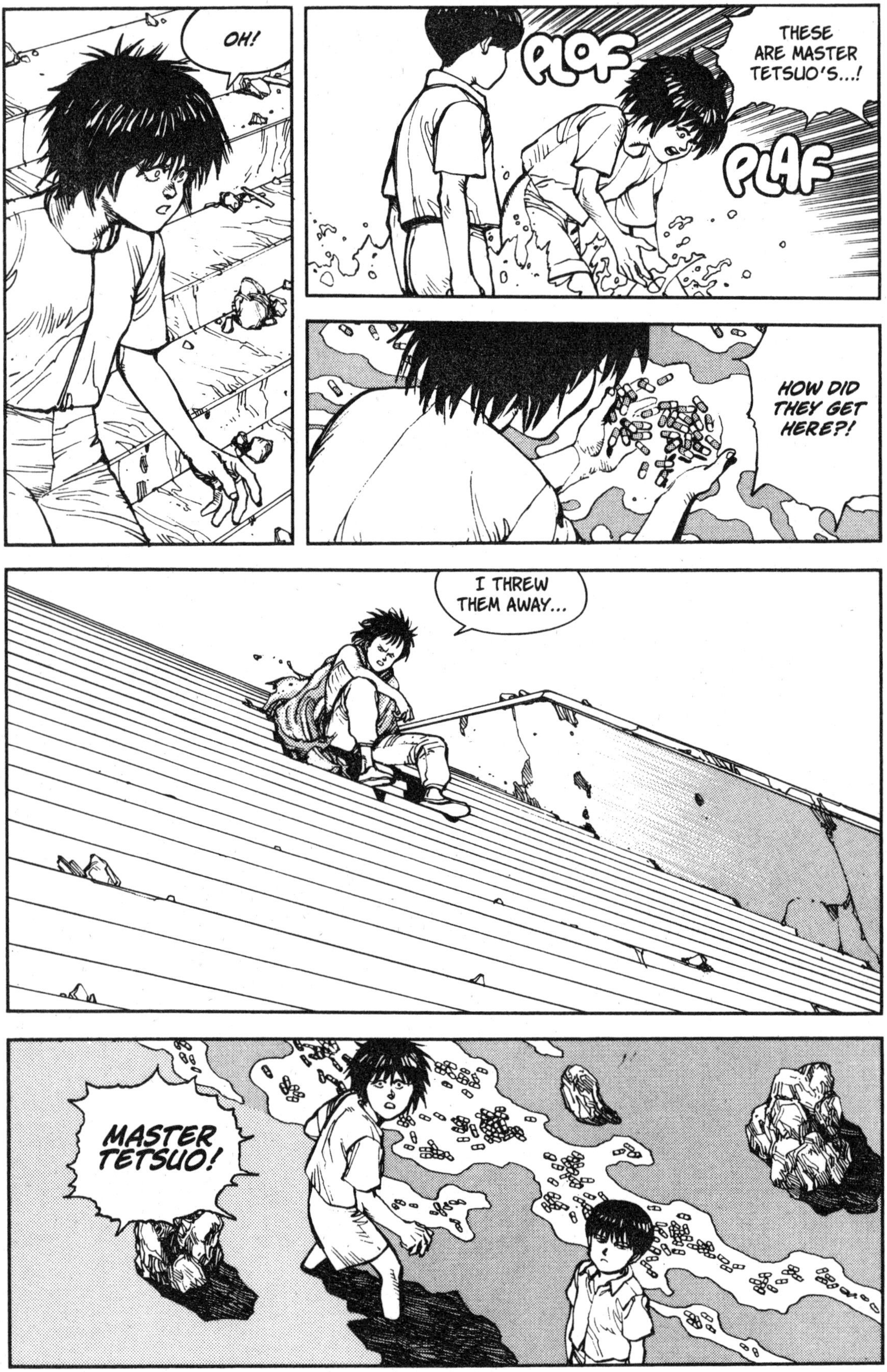
OH!
PLOF
THESE ARE MASTER TETSUO'S...!
PLAF
HOW DID THEY GET HERE?!
I THREW THEM AWAY...
MASTER TETSUO!

253

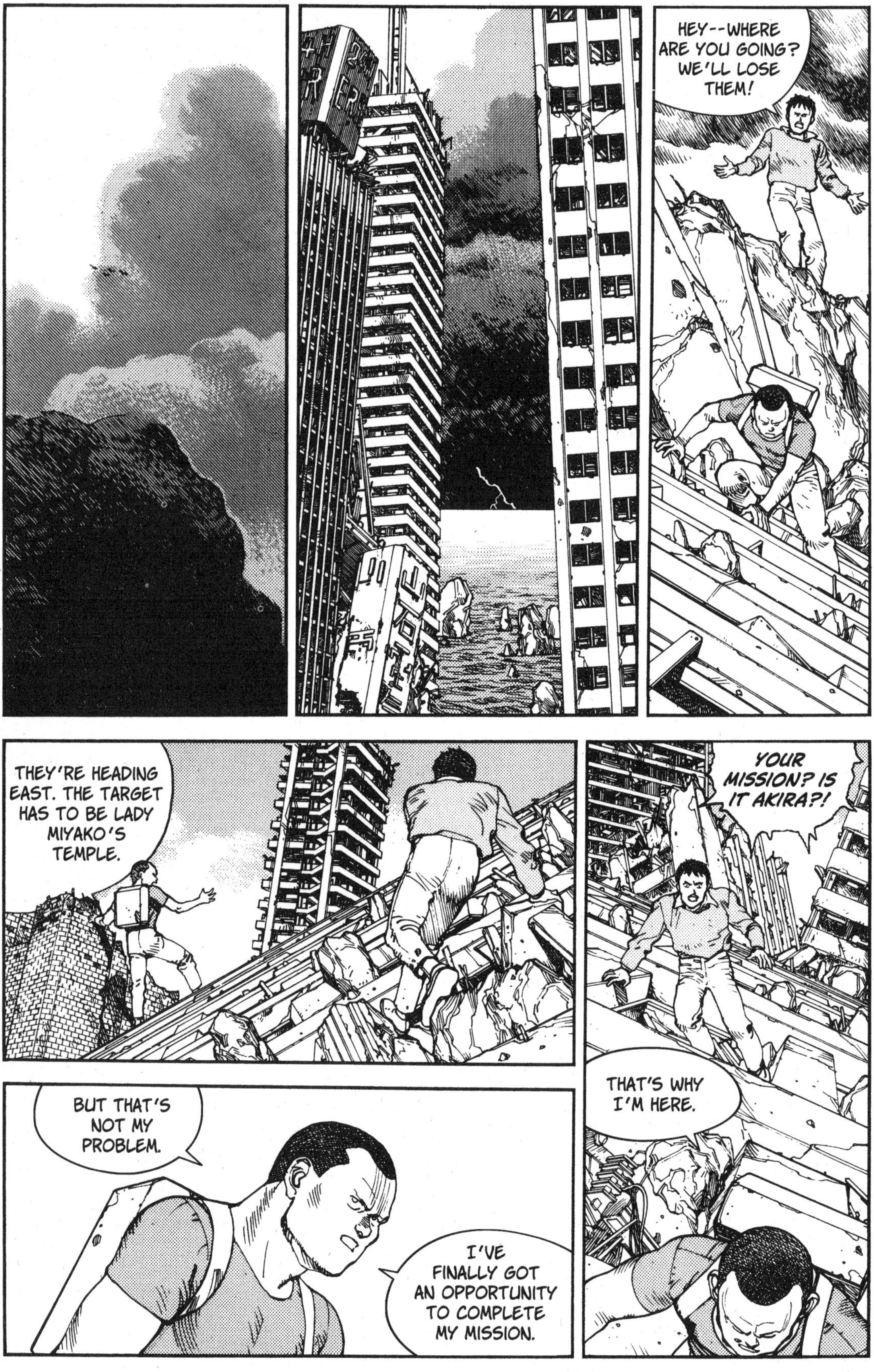
HEY--WHERE ARE YOU GOING? WE'LL LOSE THEM!
THEY'RE HEADING EAST. THE TARGET HAS TO BE LADY MIYAKO'S TEMPLE.
YOUR MISSION? IS IT AKIRA?!
THAT'S WHY I'M HERE.
BUT THAT'S NOT MY PROBLEM.
I'VE FINALLY GOT AN OPPORTUNITY TO COMPLETE MY MISSION.

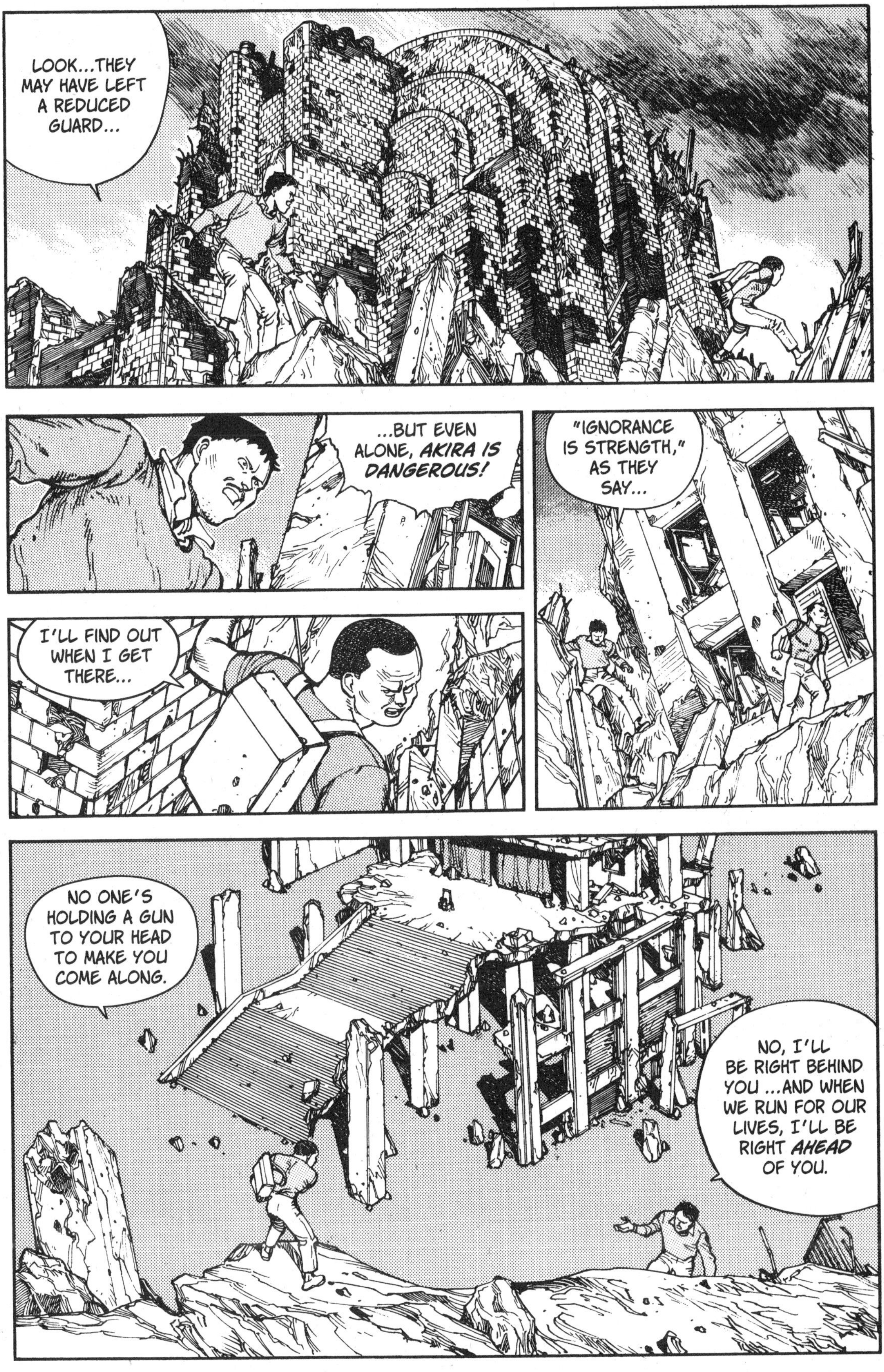
LOOK...THEY MAY HAVE LEFT A REDUCED GUARD...
...BUT EVEN ALONE, *AKIRA IS DANGEROUS!*
"IGNORANCE IS STRENGTH," AS THEY SAY...
I'LL FIND OUT WHEN I GET THERE...
NO ONE'S HOLDING A GUN TO YOUR HEAD TO MAKE YOU COME ALONG.
NO, I'LL BE RIGHT BEHIND YOU ...AND WHEN WE RUN FOR OUR LIVES, I'LL BE RIGHT *AHEAD* OF YOU.

...OH ...OOH...

...

THAT'S *TETSUO*, ISN'T IT?

YEP...HE'S AKIRA'S RIGHT-HAND MAN. RUNS THE SHOW.

DOES HE HAVE THE *POWER*?

SO I'VE HEARD, BUT I'VE NEVER SEEN HIM USE IT.

I'VE CROSSED PATHS WITH HIM BEFORE... A VERY STRANGE CUSTOMER.

I'D LIKE TO TALK TO HIM...

GNN...GNNNN...!!

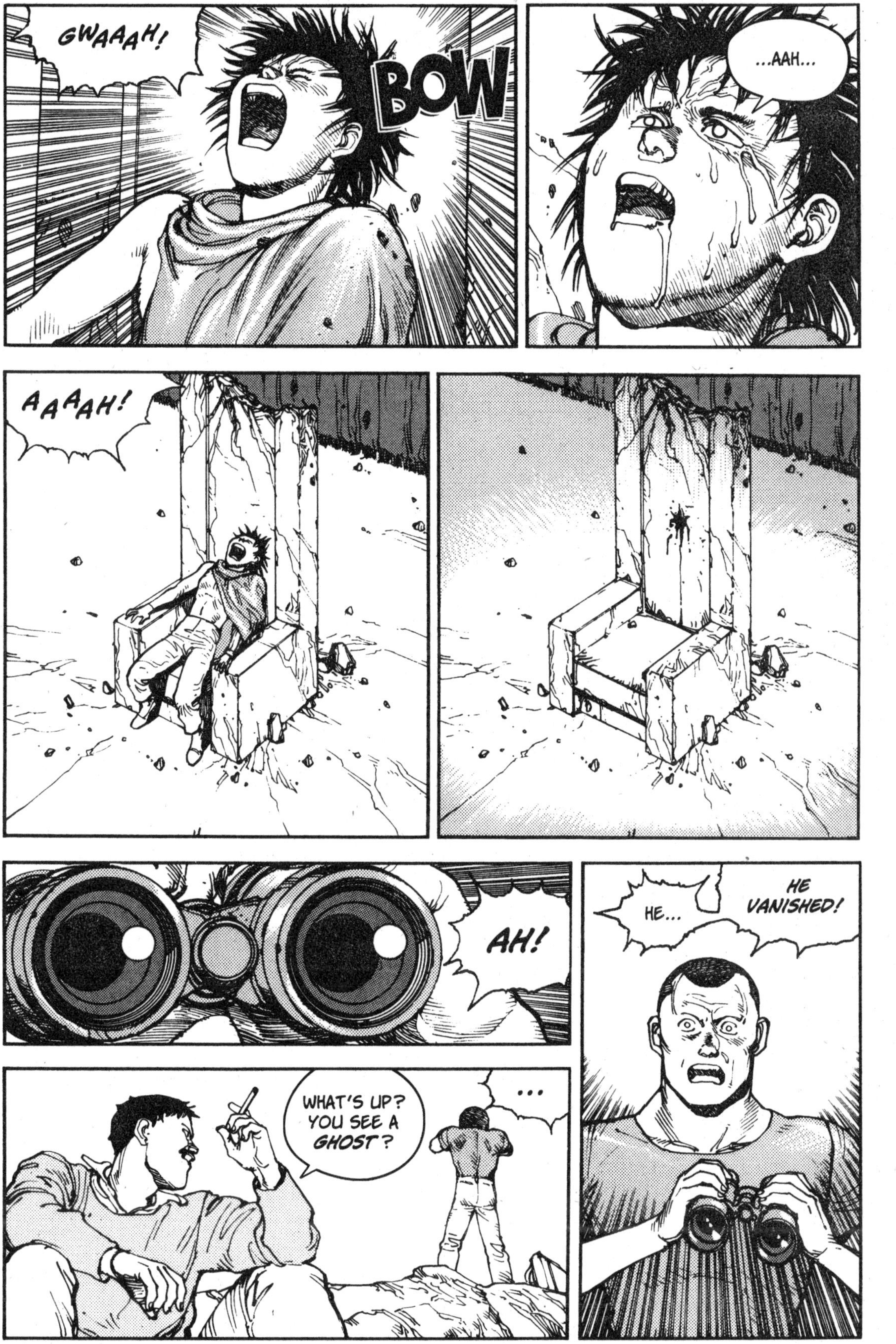
GWAAAH!
BOW
...AAH...
AAAAH!
AH!
HE...
HE VANISHED!
WHAT'S UP? YOU SEE A GHOST?
...

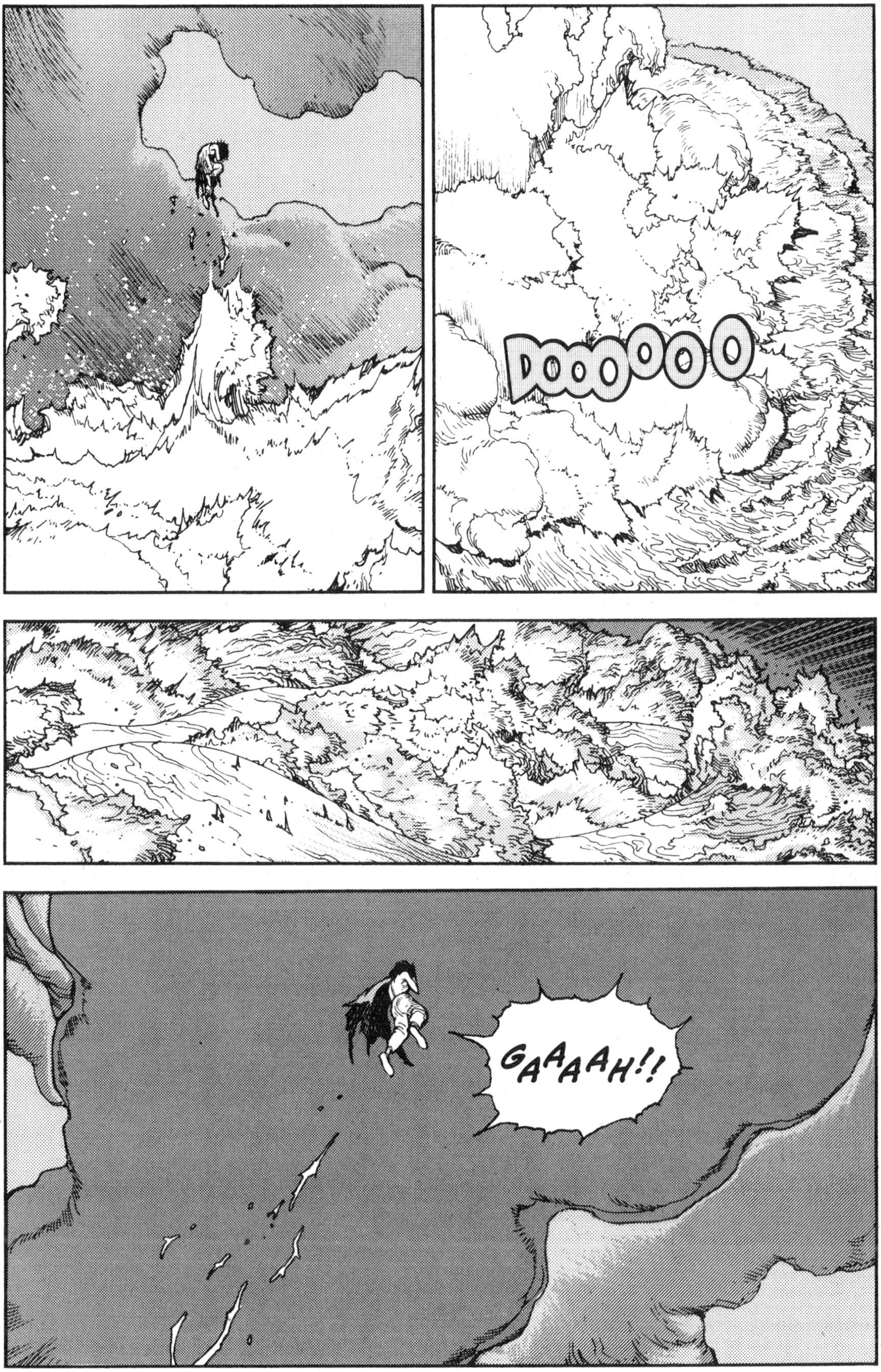
DOOOOOO
GAAAAH!!

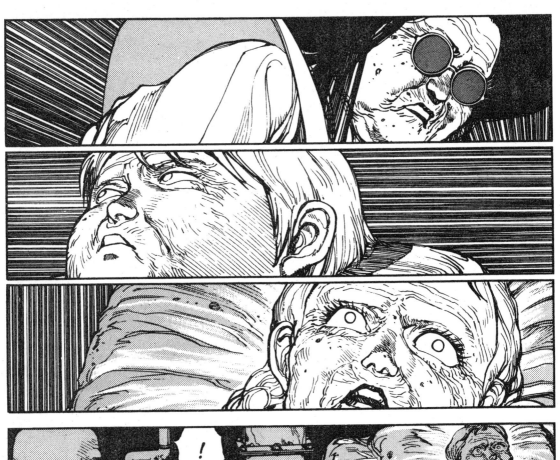

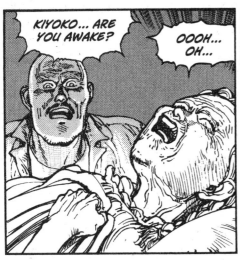

KIYOKO... ARE YOU AWAKE?

OOOH... OH...

...

KIYOKO, IT'S ME! DON'T YOU RECOGNIZE ME?!

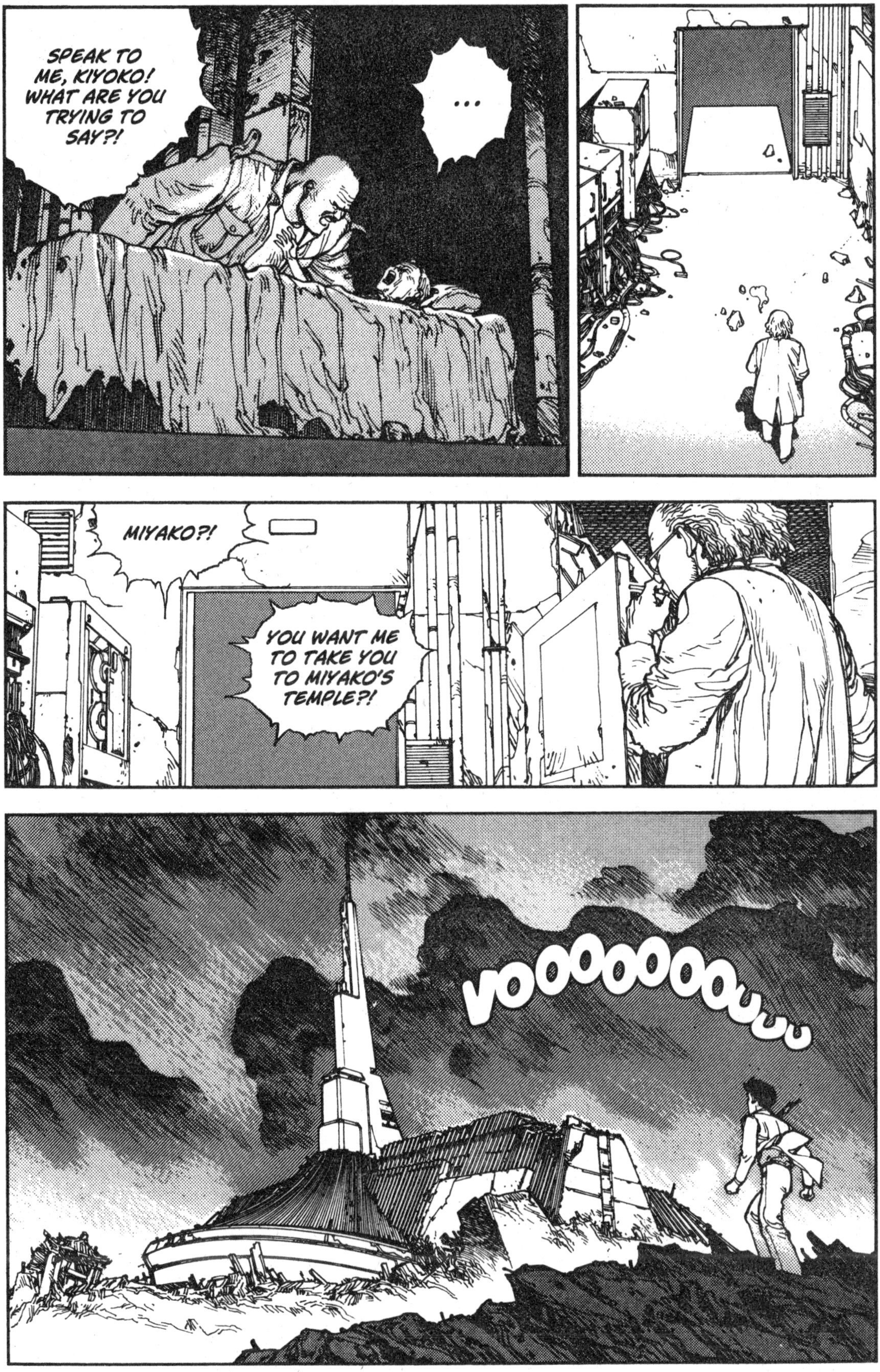

SPEAK TO ME, KIYOKO! WHAT ARE YOU TRYING TO SAY?!
...
MIYAKO?!
YOU WANT ME TO TAKE YOU TO MIYAKO'S TEMPLE?!
VOOOOOOOUUU

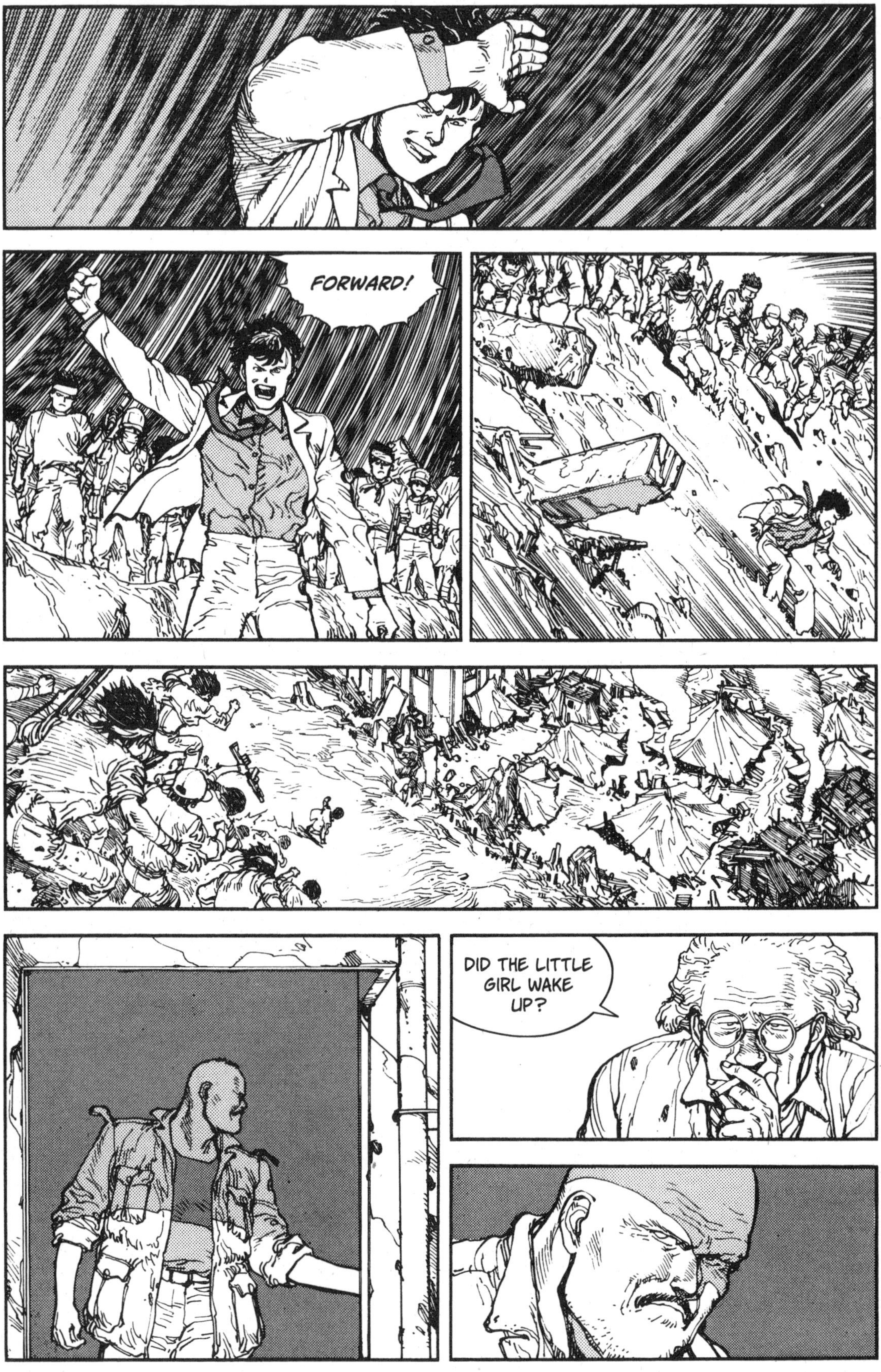
FORWARD!
DID THE LITTLE GIRL WAKE UP?

IS IT READY?

YES.

IS IT RELIABLE?

THE MARGIN FOR ERROR IS FIVE OR SIX METERS. TARGETING SOMETHING WITHIN A TEN METER RADIUS IS GOING TO BE HIGHLY DANGEROUS.

I TOLD YOU IT WAS TOO SMALL...

WITH SO MUCH MINIATURIZATION, PRECISION IS IMPOSSIBLE.

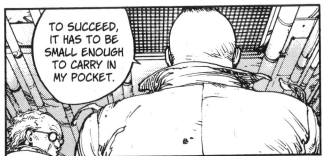

TO SUCCEED, IT HAS TO BE SMALL ENOUGH TO CARRY IN MY POCKET.

I TAKE IT...

...YOU EXPECT TO ACT SOON.

NO, FIRST I MUST MOVE KIYOKO TO SAFETY.

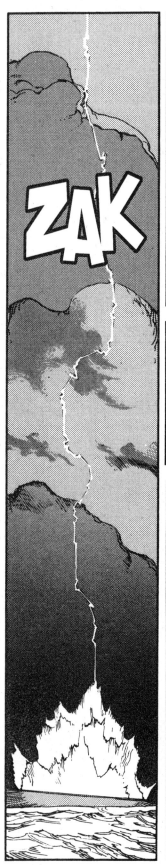

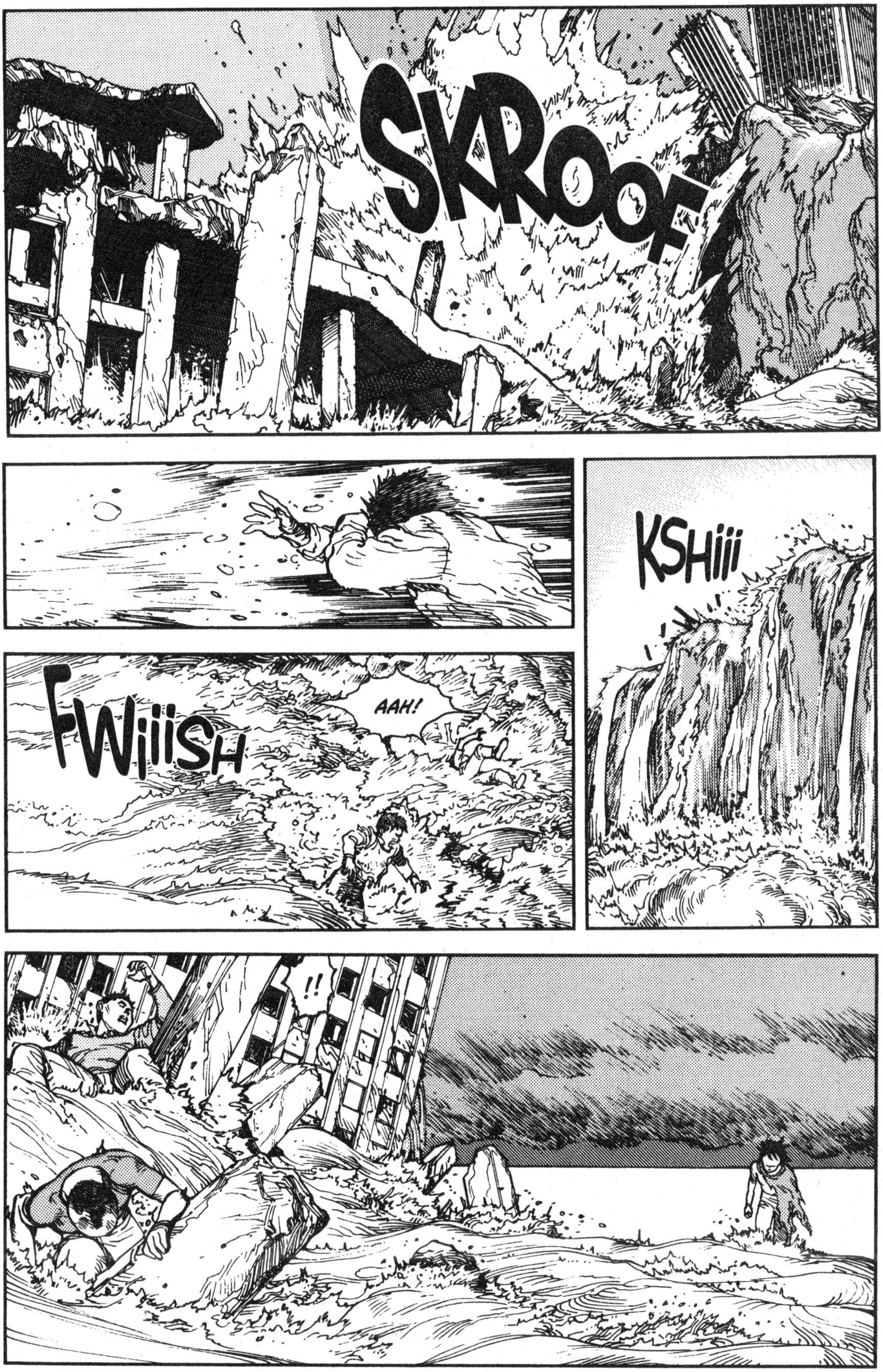
SKROOF
KSHiiii
FWiiiSH
AAH!
!!

SHIT!

TETSUO!

I SAW A LOT OF SHIPS OUT THERE. *BIG* ONES...

THEY'RE YOUR FRIENDS...

... *AREN'T* THEY?

THEIR CANNONS AND MISSILES ARE POINTED AT US...

SHIPS...?

FREAK! HOW DO *YOU* KNOW THAT?

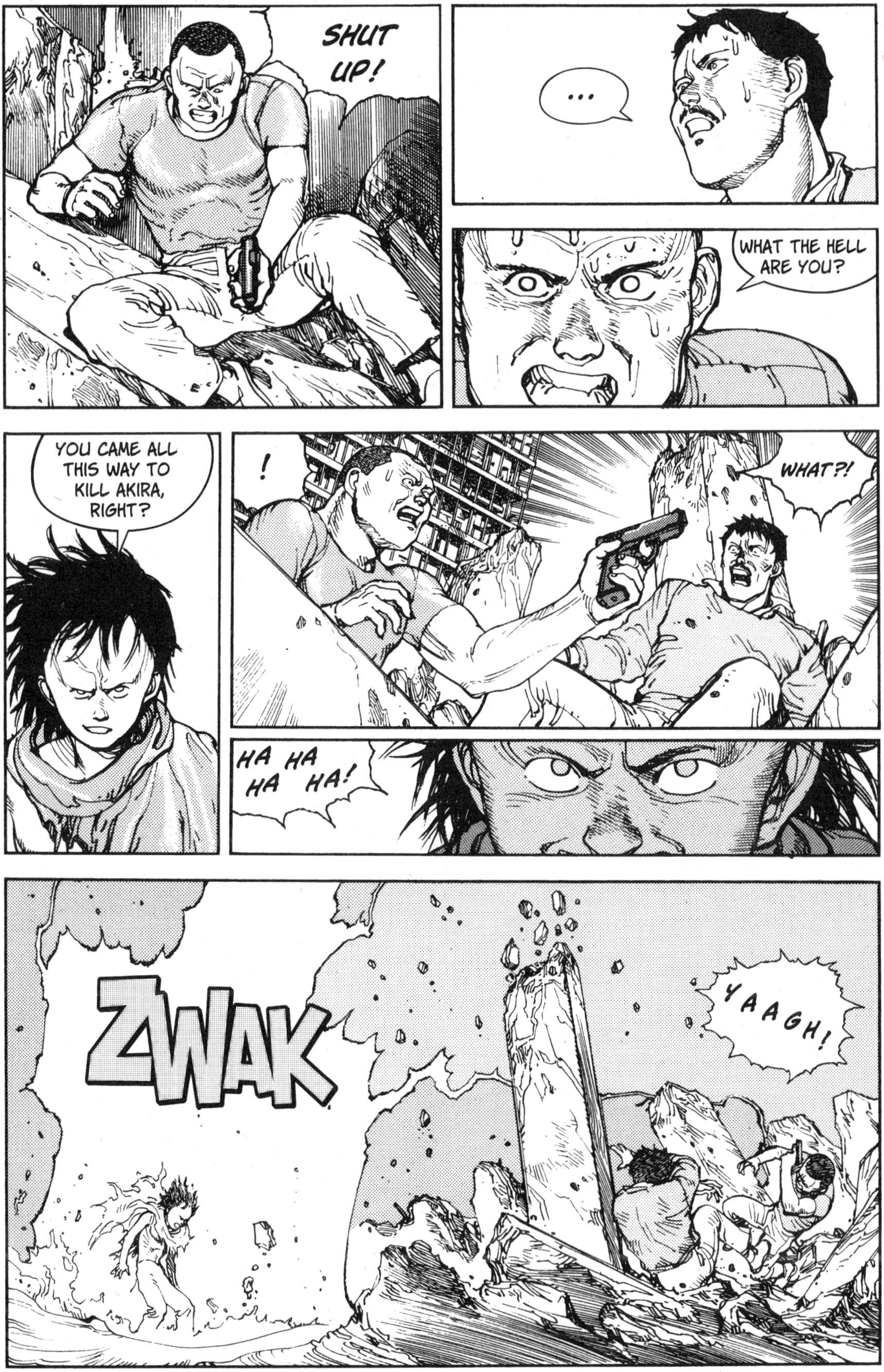
SHUT UP!
...
WHAT THE HELL ARE YOU?
YOU CAME ALL THIS WAY TO KILL AKIRA, RIGHT?
!
WHAT?!
HA HA HA HA!
ZWAK
YAAGH!

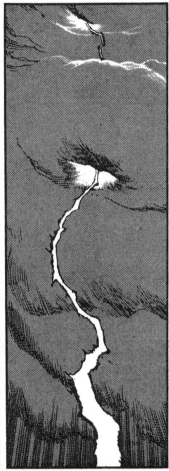

WAK

268

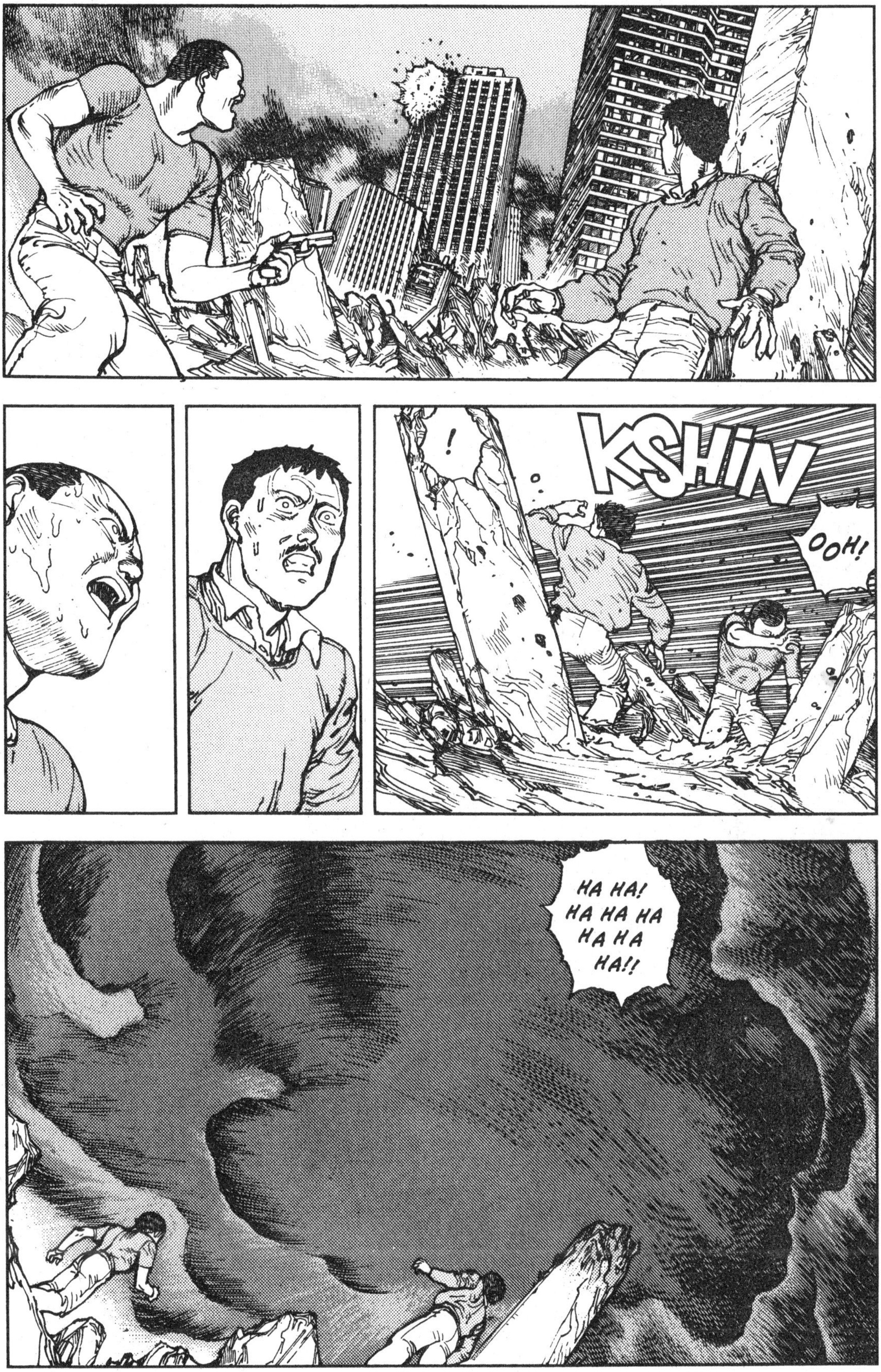
!
KSHIN
OOH!
HA HA!
HA HA HA
HA HA
HA!!

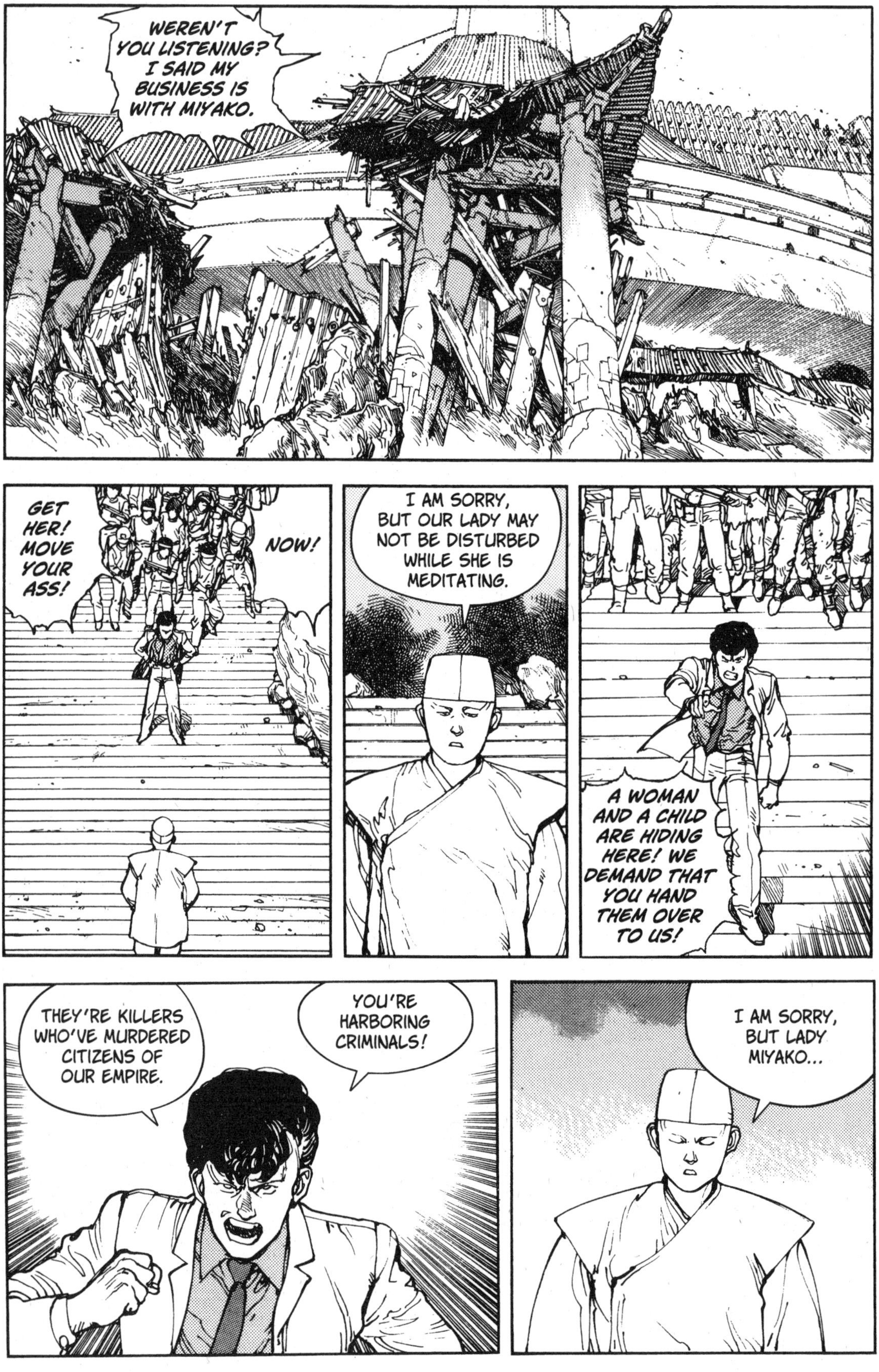

WEREN'T YOU LISTENING? I SAID MY BUSINESS IS WITH MIYAKO.
GET HER! MOVE YOUR ASS!
NOW!
I AM SORRY, BUT OUR LADY MAY NOT BE DISTURBED WHILE SHE IS MEDITATING.
A WOMAN AND A CHILD ARE HIDING HERE! WE DEMAND THAT YOU HAND THEM OVER TO US!
THEY'RE KILLERS WHO'VE MURDERED CITIZENS OF OUR EMPIRE.
YOU'RE HARBORING CRIMINALS!
I AM SORRY, BUT LADY MIYAKO...

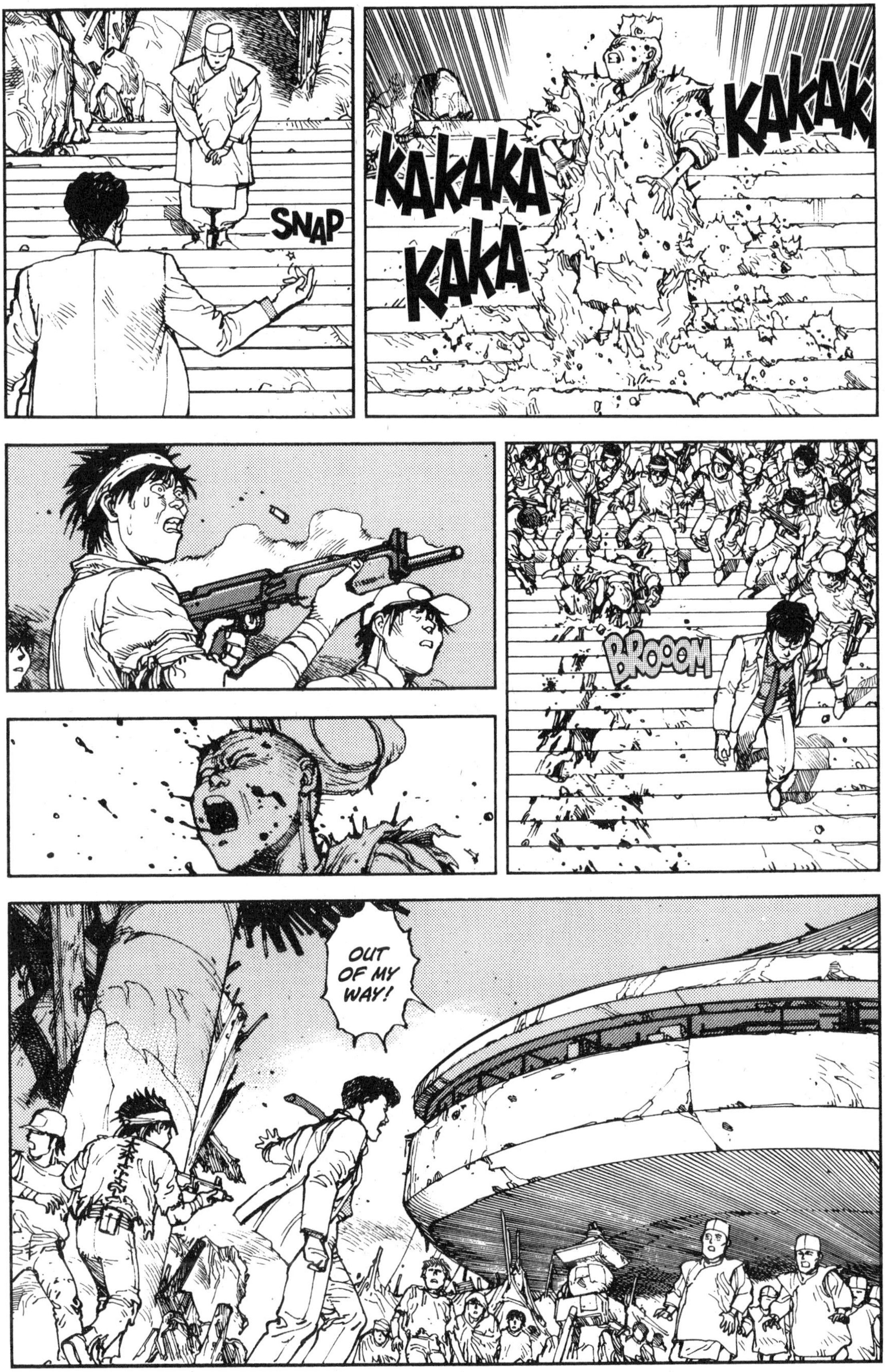
SNAP
KAKAKA
KAKA
KAKAK
BROOOM
OUT OF MY WAY!

WHAT IS THAT NOISE?!

MEN FROM THE GREAT TOKYO EMPIRE HAVE COME DEMANDING THAT WE SURRENDER THE YOUNG WOMAN AND THE CHILD.

SURELY THIS MATTER CAN BE SETTLED WITHOUT ME.

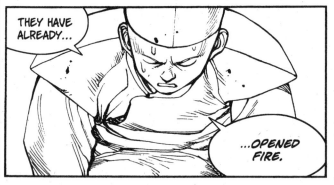

THEY HAVE ALREADY...

...OPENED FIRE.

WHAT?!

CHARGE!! YAAAAA!

KATAKA

TAKATA

HEAD FOR THE CENTRAL CHAMBER!

ADVANCE IN GROUPS OF TWO AND THREE.

YOU GO THAT WAY!

EVERY-ONE ELSE FOLLOW ME!

TAP TAP

REPORT AT ONCE IF YOU LOCATE THE WOMEN AND CHILD!

AND DON'T SHOOT THEM!

TAP

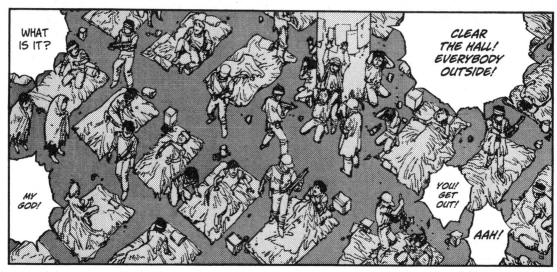

COME NO FURTHER! LAY DOWN YOUR WEAPONS!

C'MON, YOU GUYS!

TAKATA

KEEP MOVING!

WH-WHAT ARE YOU DOING? I... I FORBID...

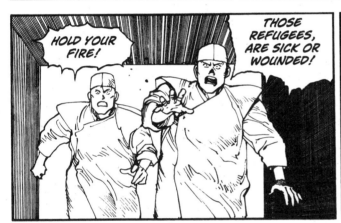

HOLD YOUR FIRE!

THOSE REFUGEES, ARE SICK OR WOUNDED!

...AND YOU'RE DEAD!

ISHIK

VRAKAKA

KAKKAKA

275

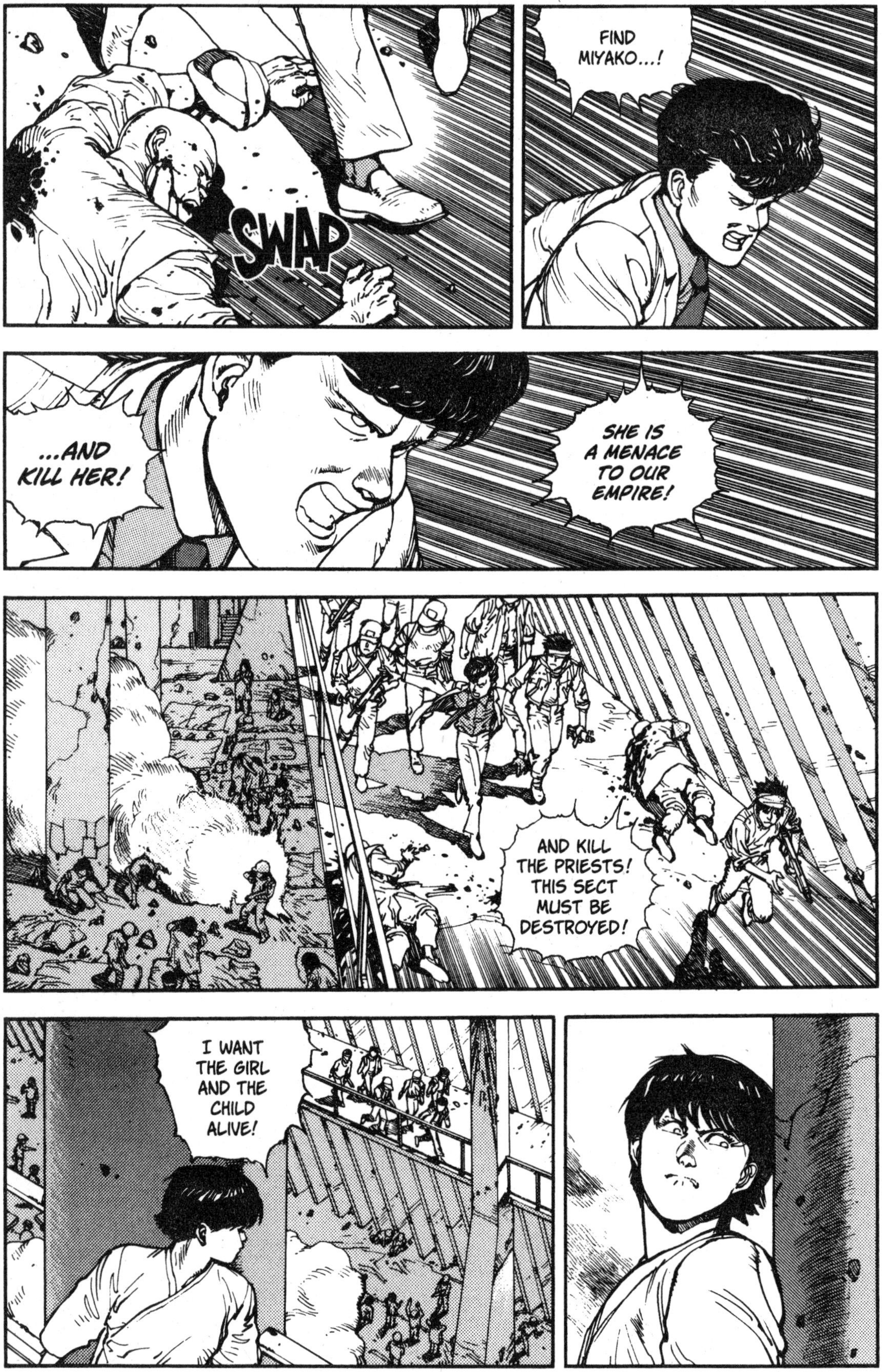
SWAP
FIND MIYAKO...!
...AND KILL HER!
SHE IS A MENACE TO OUR EMPIRE!
AND KILL THE PRIESTS! THIS SECT MUST BE DESTROYED!
I WANT THE GIRL AND THE CHILD ALIVE!

OH!

HERE SHE IS!

I FOUND THE GIRL!

TAP

?!

HE-EY!

STOP...!

TAP TAP

...OR I'LL SHOOT!

PLOK

TAKA

POUM

TAKATA TAKA

YOUR LEADER WANTS ME ALIVE!

YOU'RE DEAD, BITCH! HEAR ME?!

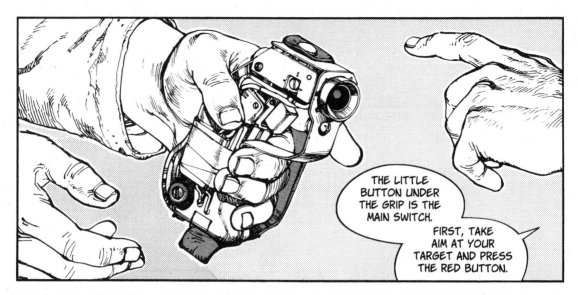

THE LITTLE BUTTON UNDER THE GRIP IS THE MAIN SWITCH.

FIRST, TAKE AIM AT YOUR TARGET AND PRESS THE RED BUTTON.

THE OPTICAL CELL EMITS A LASER BEAM THAT YOU POINT AT THE TARGET, AND THE PROCESSOR CALCULATES THE DISTANCE AND CONVERTS THE POSITION TO *GPS* COORDINATES...

...AND THEN SENDS THE DATA TO *SOL.*

THEN, YOU PULL THE TRIGGER.

HOW DO I CHANGE TARGETS?

TURN OFF THE MAIN SWITCH AND START AGAIN.

LET ME REPEAT, FOR YOUR OWN PROTECTION, DO NOT USE THE DEVICE...

...WITHIN A DISTANCE OF TEN METERS.

HAVE YOU CONFIRMED YOUR CALCULATIONS?

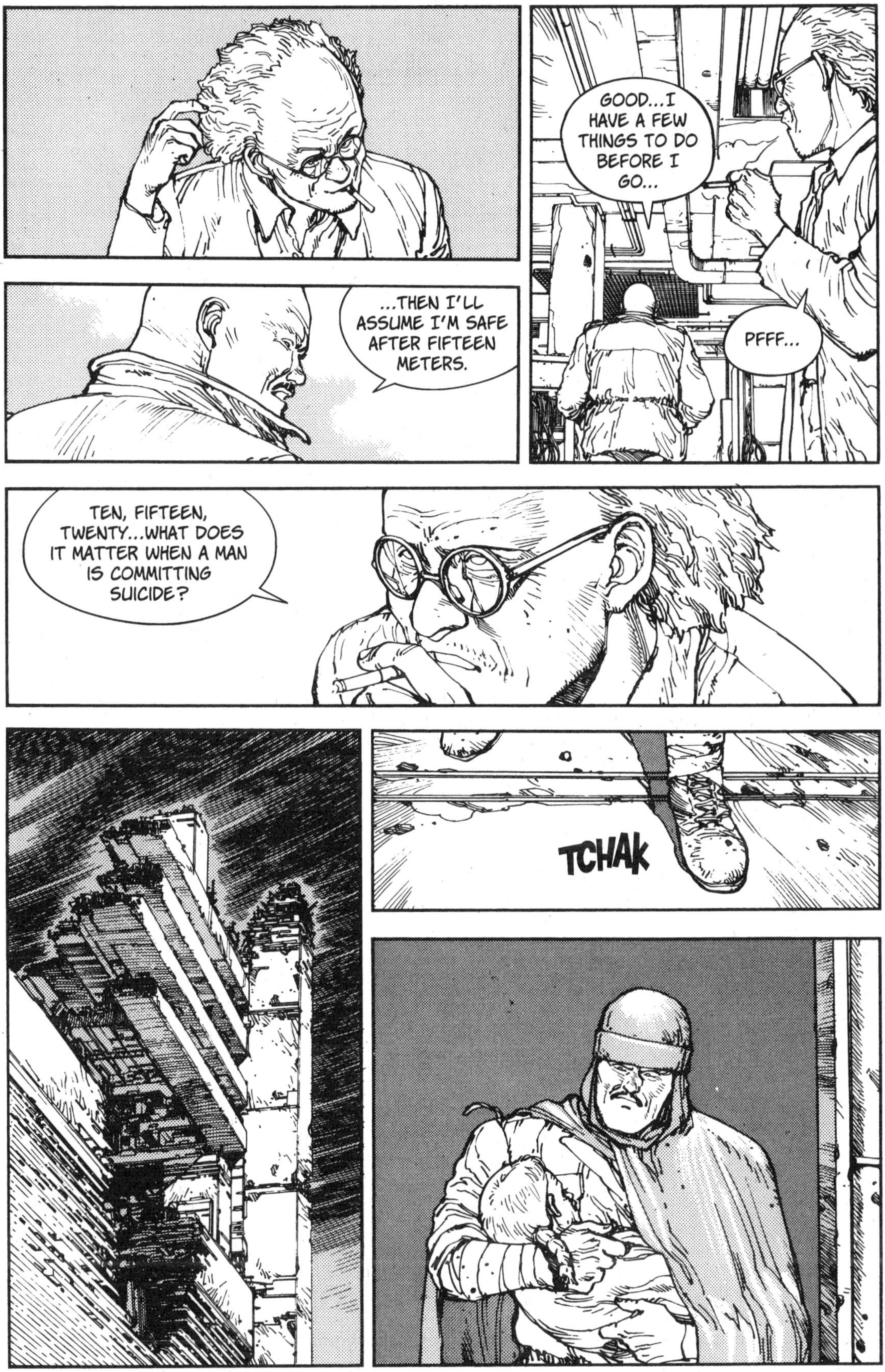
GOOD...I HAVE A FEW THINGS TO DO BEFORE I GO...
...THEN I'LL ASSUME I'M SAFE AFTER FIFTEEN METERS.
PFFF...
TEN, FIFTEEN, TWENTY...WHAT DOES IT MATTER WHEN A MAN IS COMMITTING SUICIDE?
TCHAK

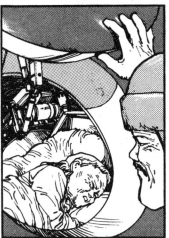

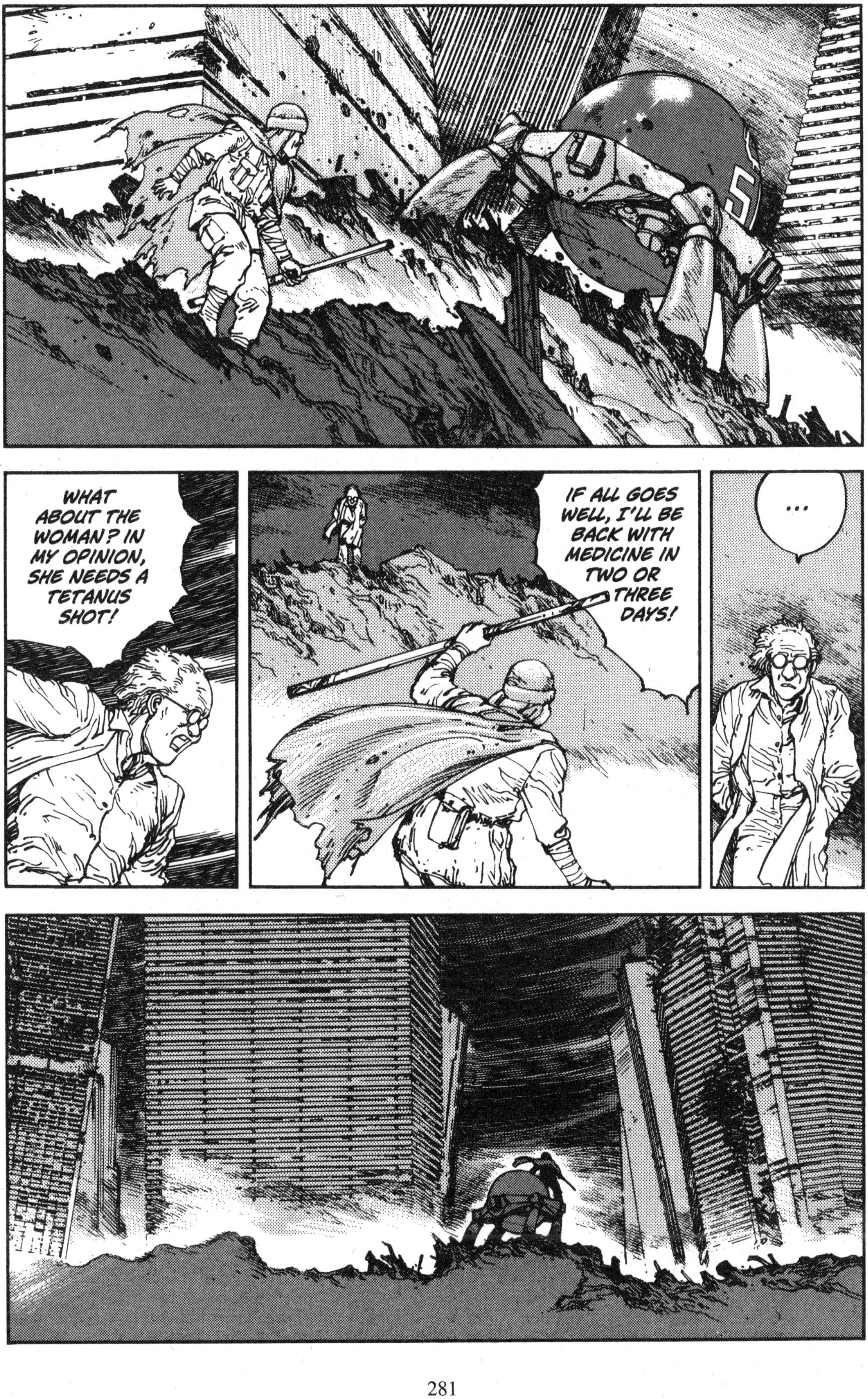
WHAT ABOUT THE WOMAN? IN MY OPINION, SHE NEEDS A TETANUS SHOT!
IF ALL GOES WELL, I'LL BE BACK WITH MEDICINE IN TWO OR THREE DAYS!
...

283

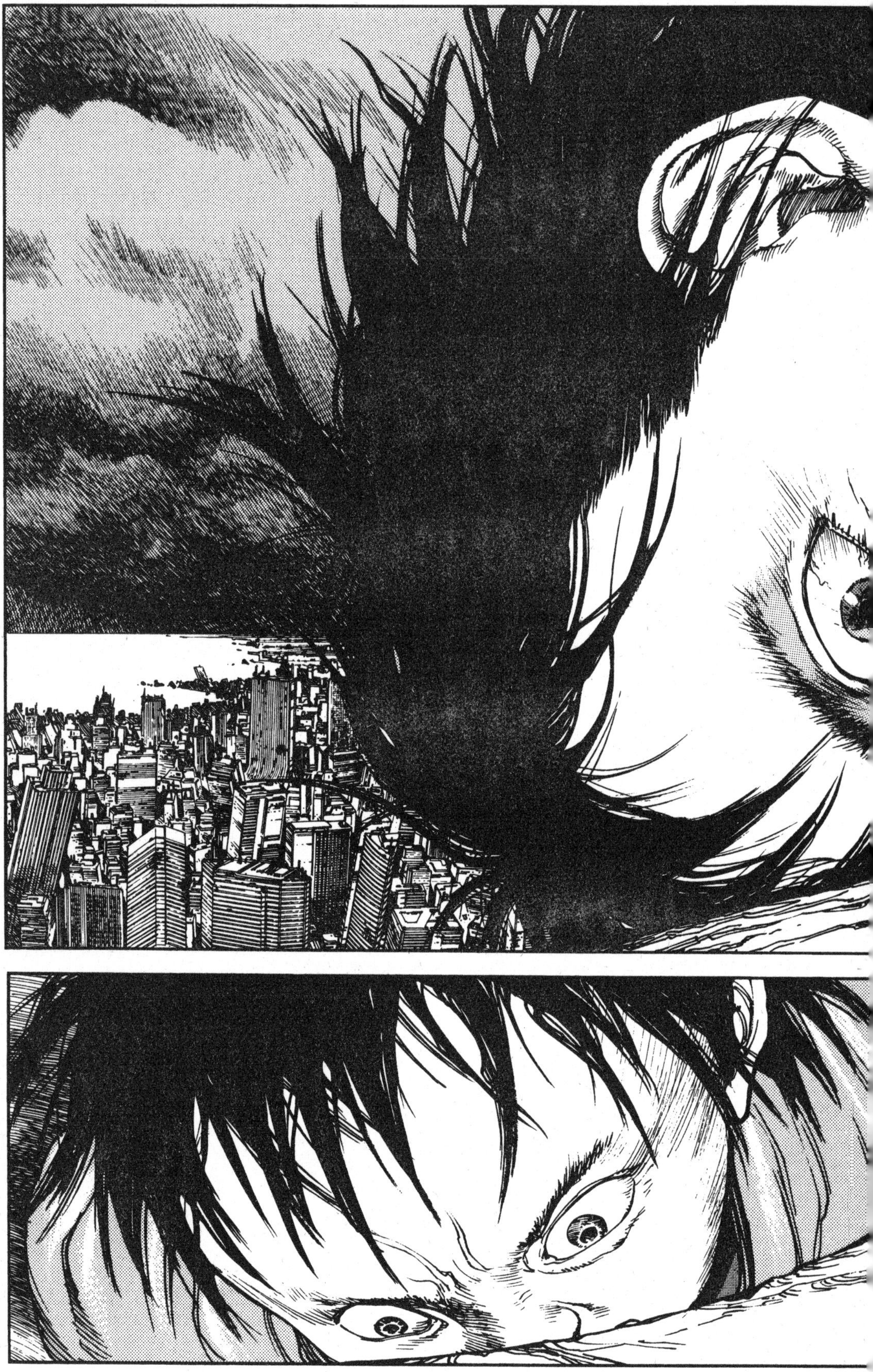

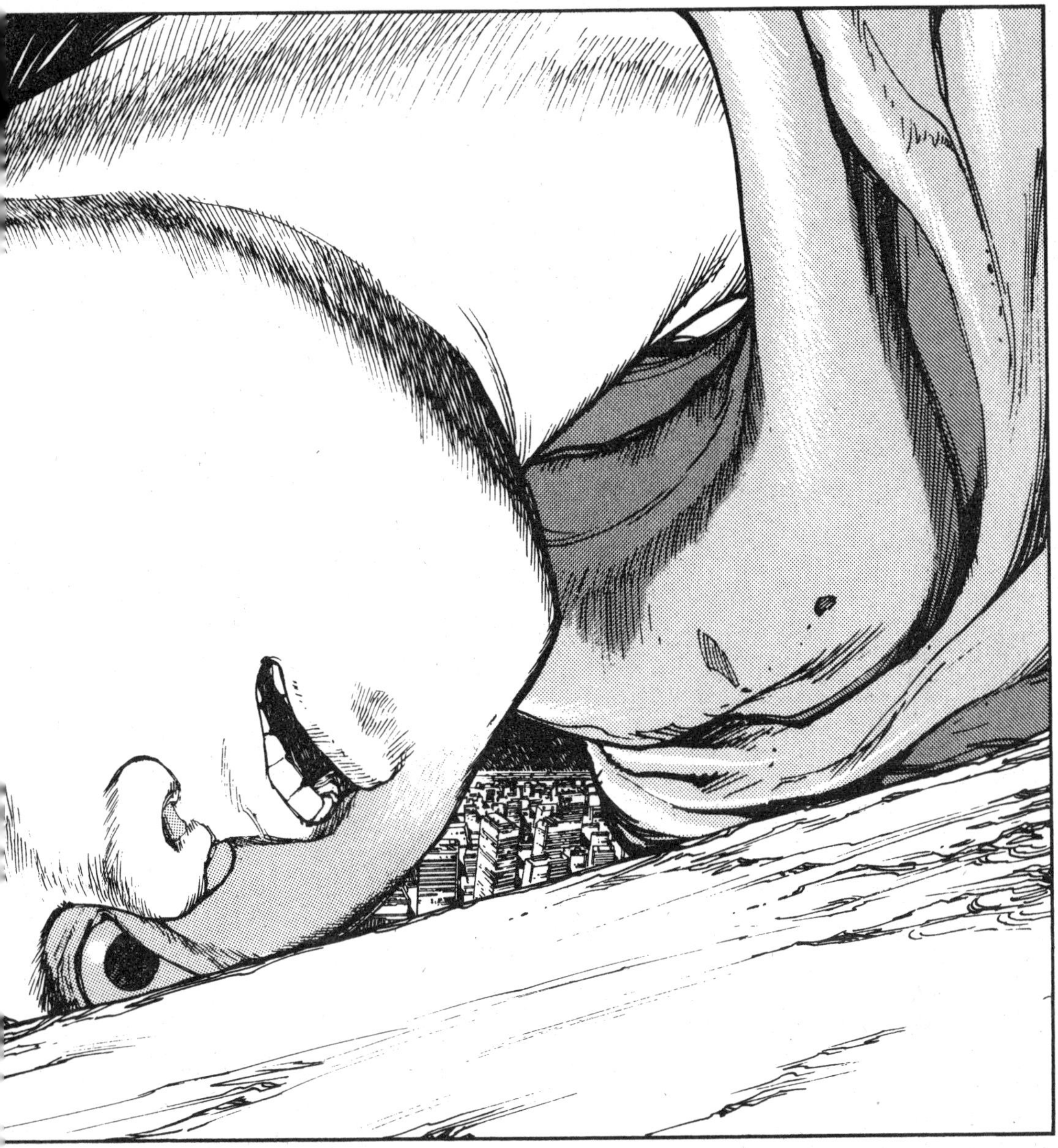

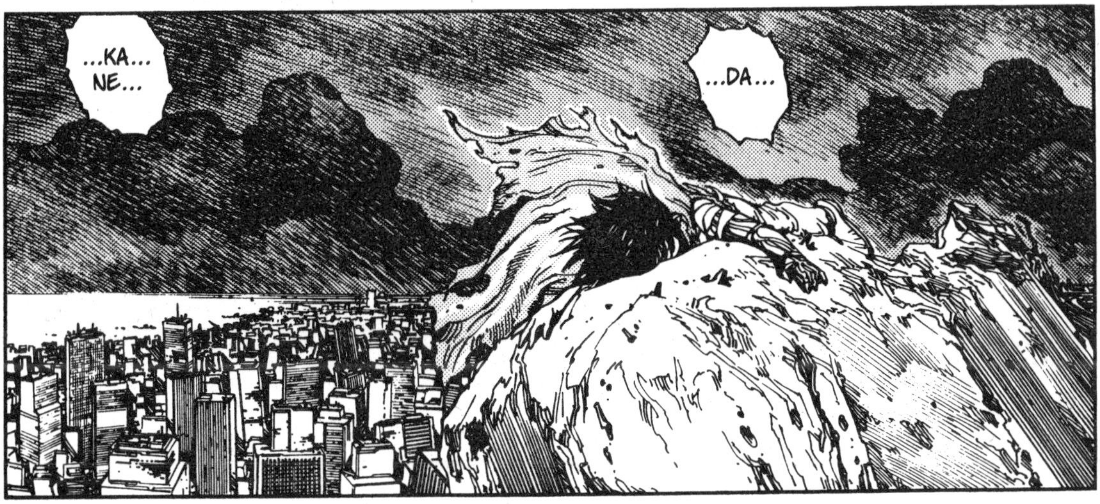
...KA... NE...
...DA...

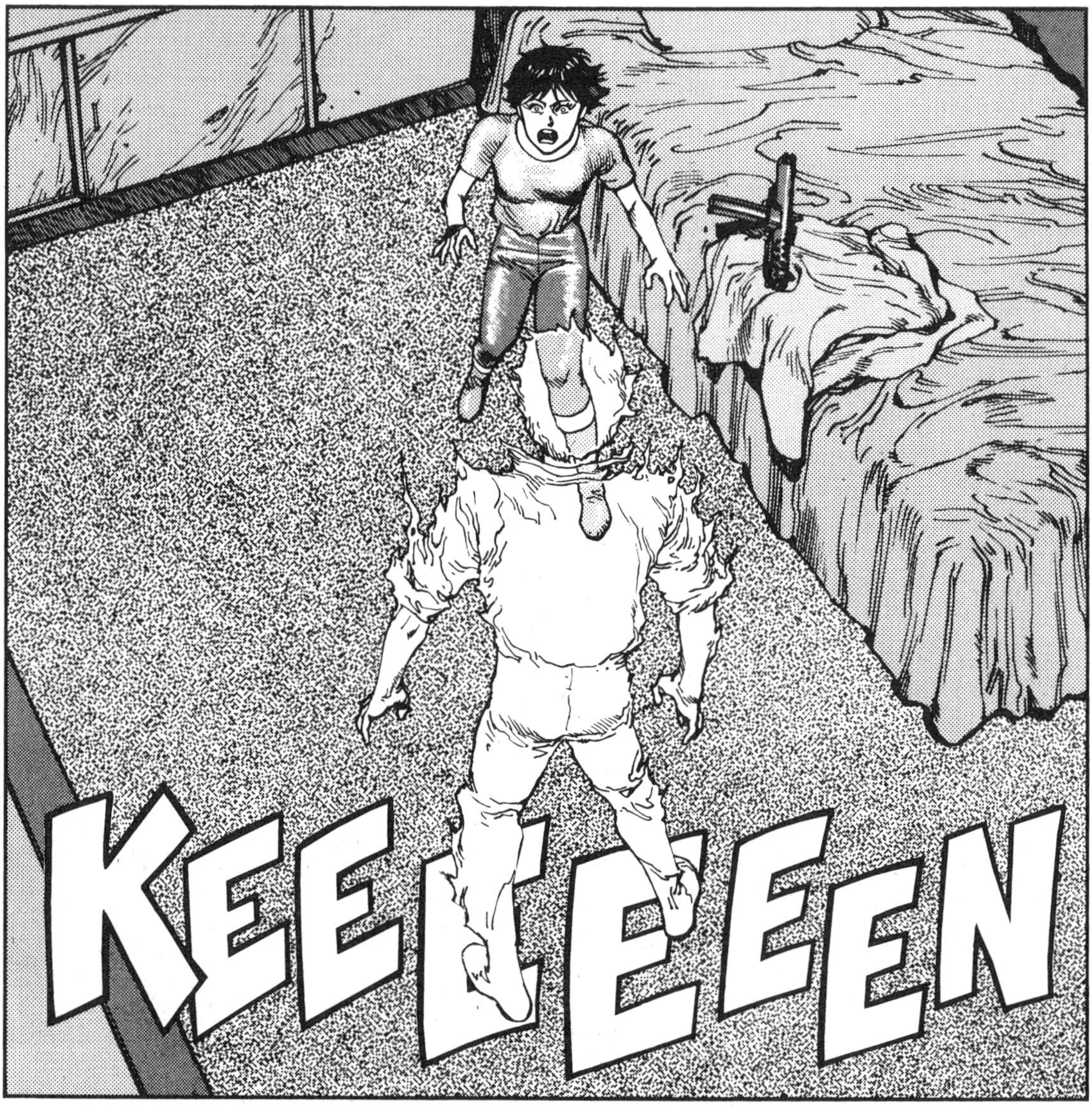
KEEEEEEN

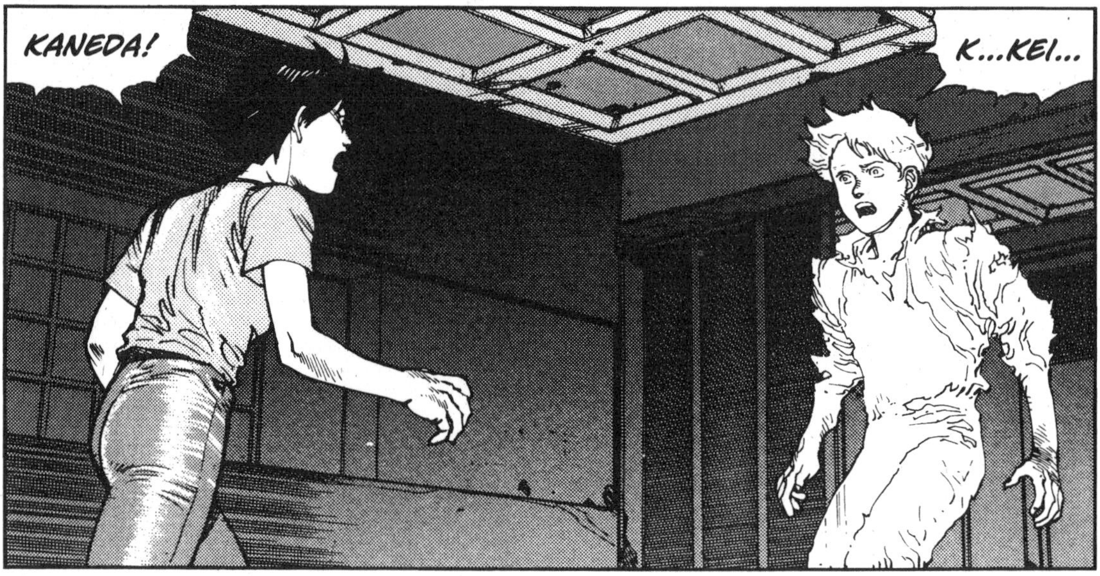
KANEDA!
K...KEI...

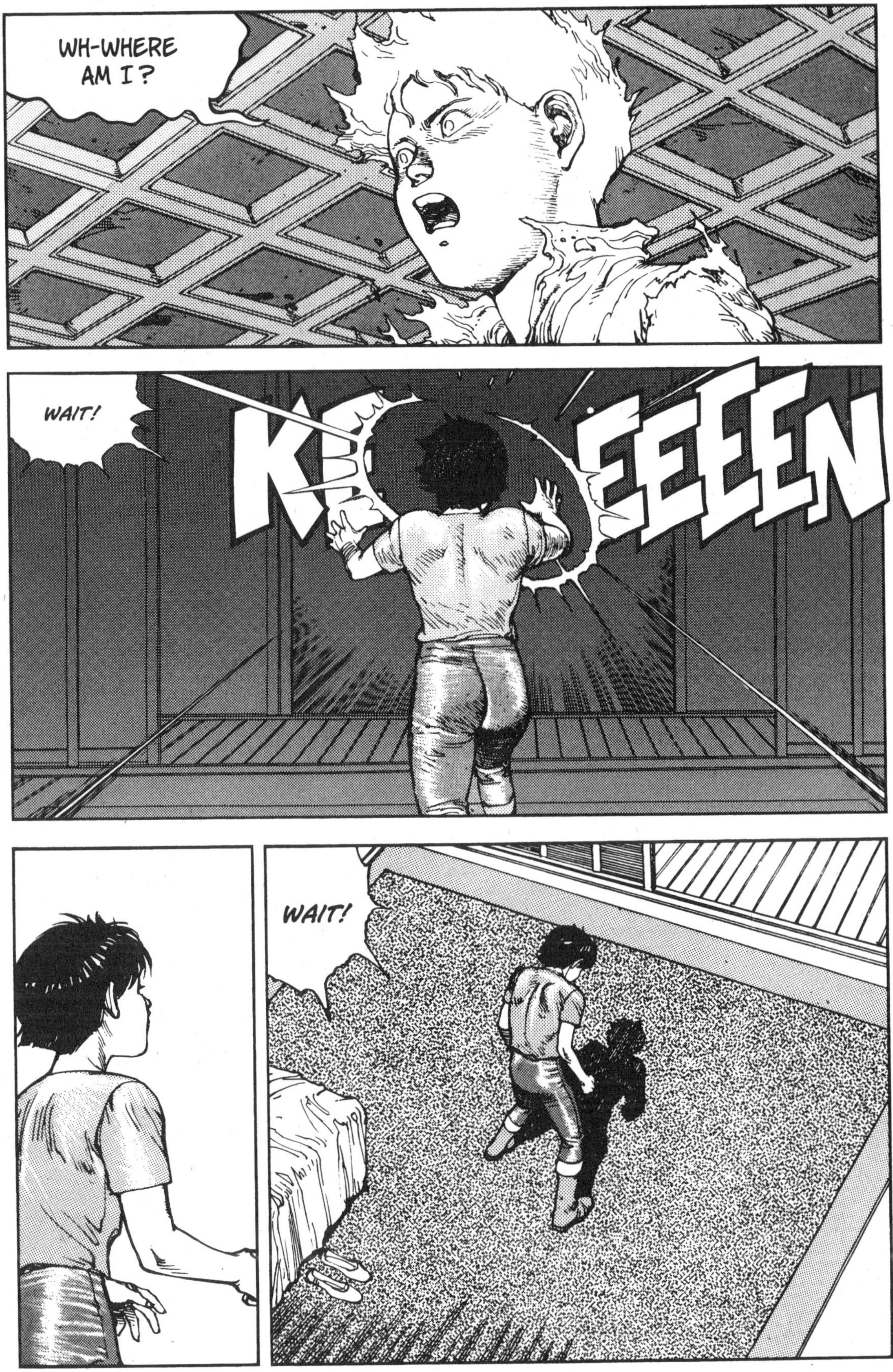
WH-WHERE AM I?
WAIT!
KI EEEEN
WAIT!

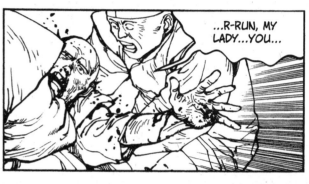

288

WHAT TO YOU HOPE TO ACHIEVE WITH THIS VIOLENCE?!

WELL, THE GREATER GLORY OF MY MASTER AKIRA AND OUR LORD TETSUO!

AND YOURS TOO, OF COURSE...

ENOUGH OF YOUR LIES! THE ONLY GLORY THAT INTERESTS YOU IS YOUR OWN! YOUR THIRST FOR BLOOD SPEAKS FOR YOU!

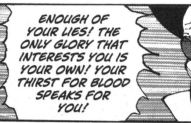

WHAT THE HELL WOULD YOU KNOW ABOUT IT, YOU SENILE FREAK?!

I'VE HAD ENOUGH! WASTE 'EM!

LOVE TO!

SLAK

WHAT TH--?!

WHAT'S WRONG WITH THE DAMN' GUNS?

SLAK

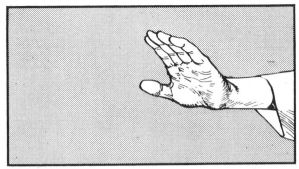

HUHN?!

THEY HAVE THE POWER...

BLAM

AAIEE!

IT BACKFIRED!

TAP

BLAM !

STAND YOUR GROUND!

USE YOUR BARE HANDS IF YOU HAVE TO!

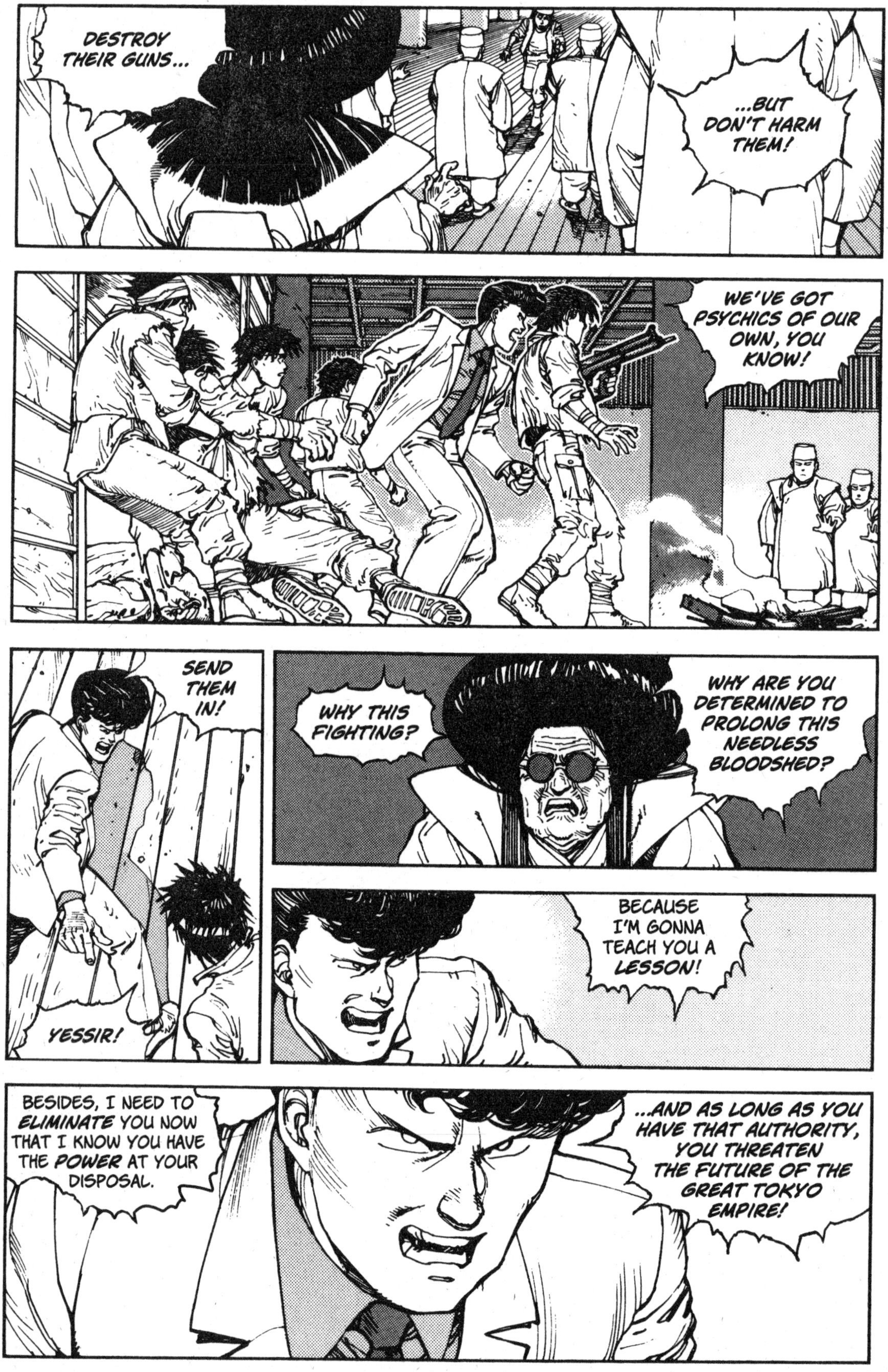
DESTROY THEIR GUNS...
...BUT DON'T HARM THEM!
WE'VE GOT PSYCHICS OF OUR OWN, YOU KNOW!
SEND THEM IN!
YESSIR!
WHY THIS FIGHTING?
WHY ARE YOU DETERMINED TO PROLONG THIS NEEDLESS BLOODSHED?
BECAUSE I'M GONNA TEACH YOU A LESSON!
BESIDES, I NEED TO ELIMINATE YOU NOW THAT I KNOW YOU HAVE THE POWER AT YOUR DISPOSAL.
...AND AS LONG AS YOU HAVE THAT AUTHORITY, YOU THREATEN THE FUTURE OF THE GREAT TOKYO EMPIRE!

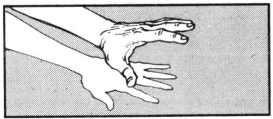

MY EYES!

WHO IN HELL--?

HEY!

...UH ...HN...

SO, NOT *DEAD* YET? I CAN *FIX* THAT...

TCHAC

NOW!

GET HIM!

TSK TSK

FIX *THIS*, ASSHOLE!

HELP ME! HURRY!

KILL 'IM!

BAM

PAY-BACK'S A BITCH, AIN'T IT?!

NO! DON'T DIE!

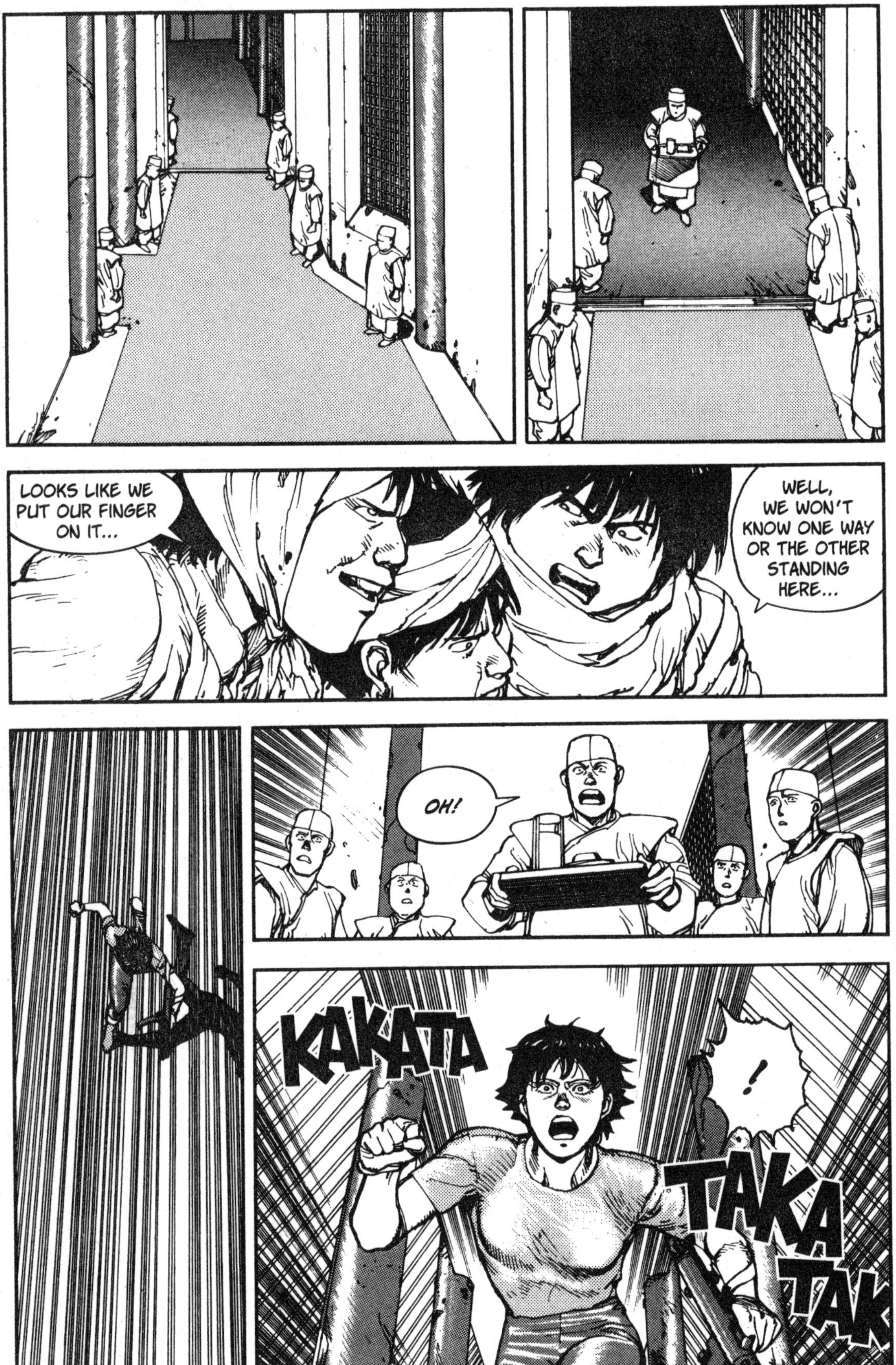
LOOKS LIKE WE PUT OUR FINGER ON IT...
WELL, WE WON'T KNOW ONE WAY OR THE OTHER STANDING HERE...
OH!
KAKATA
!
TAKA TAK

STAK

KLiNG

THERE'S GOTTA BE OTHERS INSIDE! TAKE A LOOK!

AH... AAH...

AH...BE QUIET!

!

VRAKAKA

ONE OF US?

SOMEONE'S COMING!

300

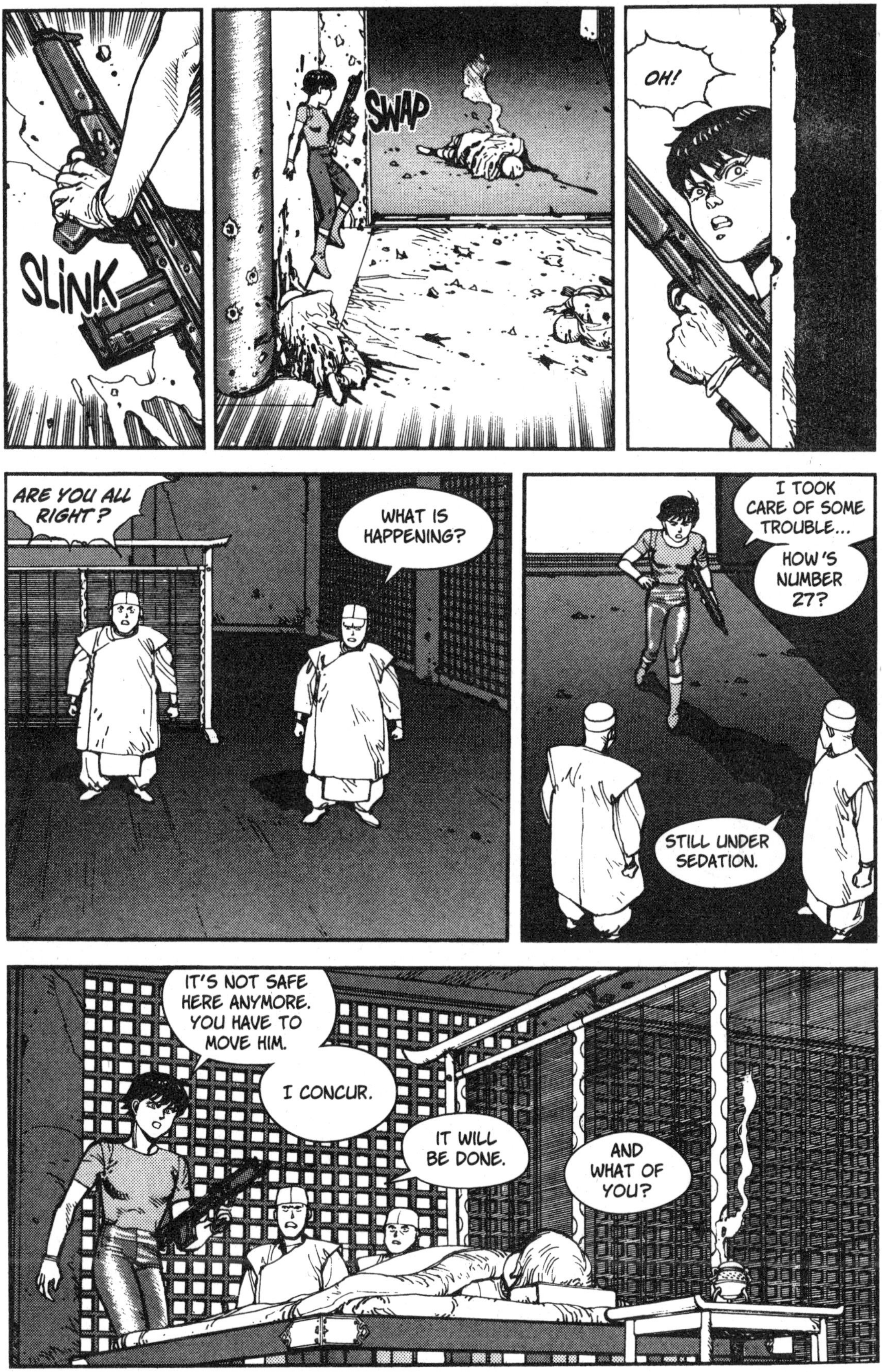
SLINK
SWAP
OH!
ARE YOU ALL RIGHT?
WHAT IS HAPPENING?
I TOOK CARE OF SOME TROUBLE...
HOW'S NUMBER 27?
STILL UNDER SEDATION.
IT'S NOT SAFE HERE ANYMORE. YOU HAVE TO MOVE HIM.
I CONCUR.
IT WILL BE DONE.
AND WHAT OF YOU?

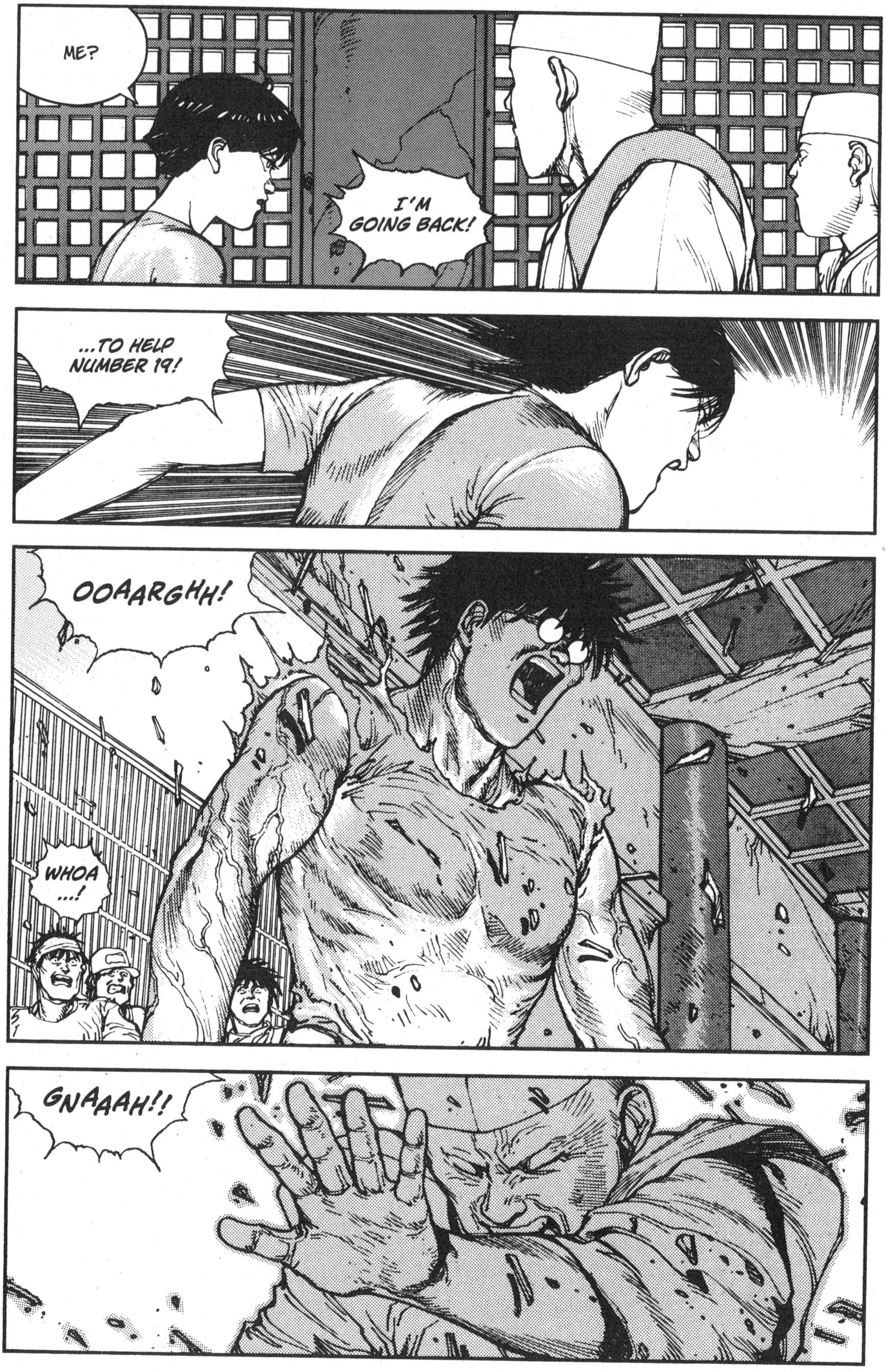
ME?
I'M GOING BACK!
...TO HELP NUMBER 19!
OOAARGHH!
WHOA ...!
GNAAAH!!

304

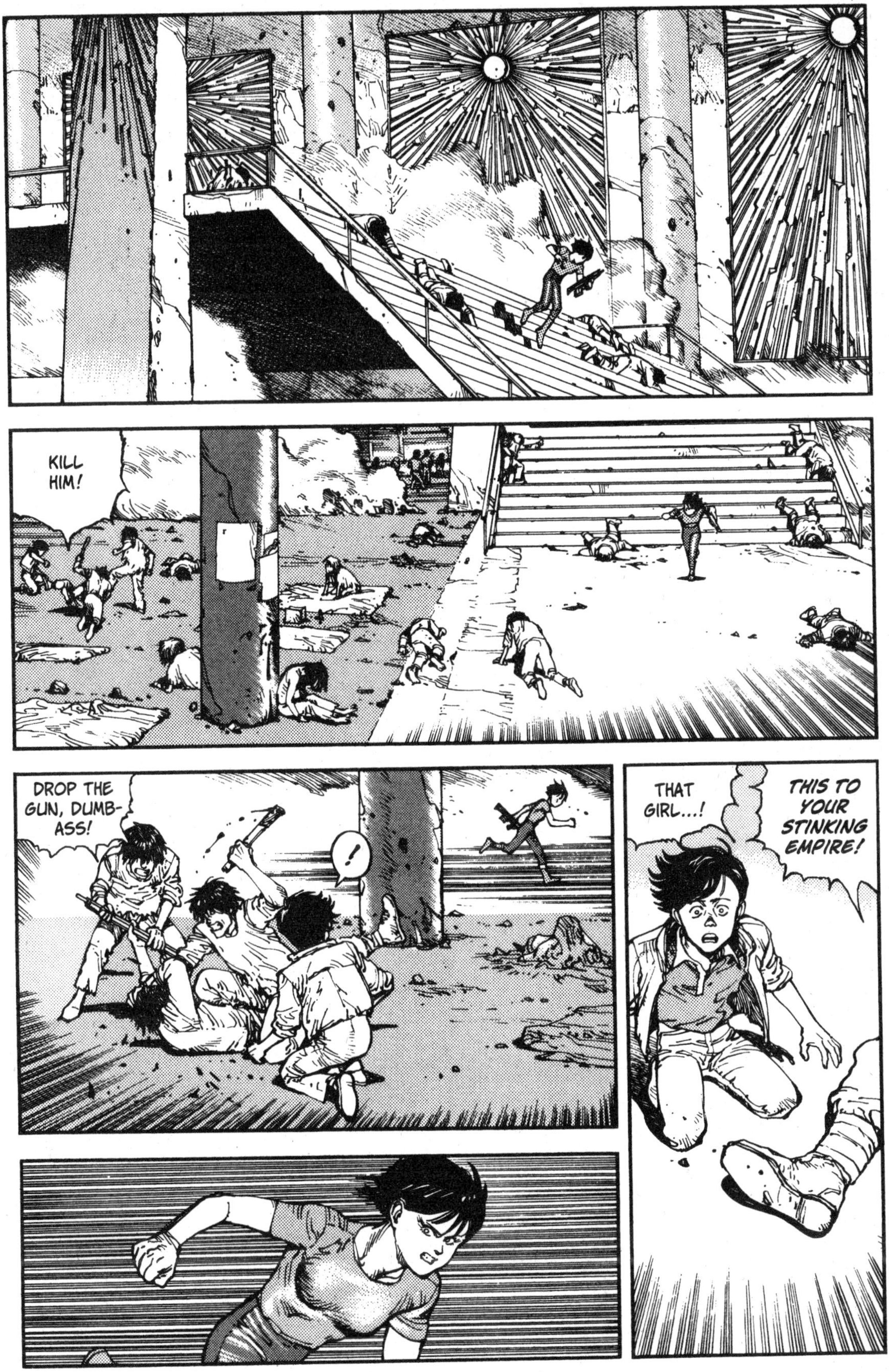
KILL HIM!
DROP THE GUN, DUMB-ASS!
!
THAT GIRL...!
THIS TO YOUR STINKING EMPIRE!

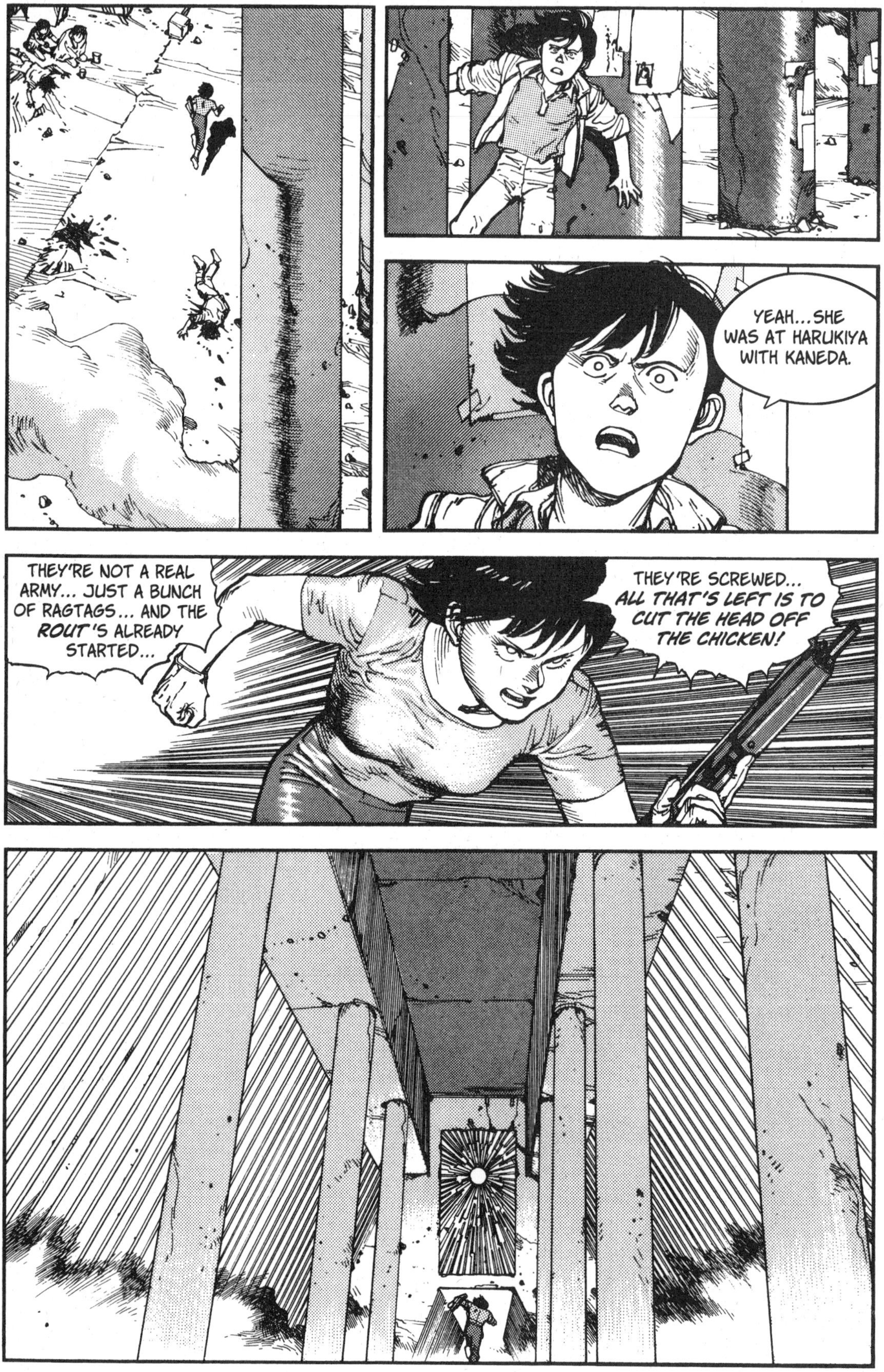
YEAH...SHE WAS AT HARUKIYA WITH KANEDA.
THEY'RE NOT A REAL ARMY... JUST A BUNCH OF RAGTAGS... AND THE *ROUT*'S ALREADY STARTED...
THEY'RE SCREWED... *ALL THAT'S LEFT IS TO CUT THE HEAD OFF THE CHICKEN!*

CATCH THIS!

TO HELL WITH IT! I'M OUTTA HERE!

WAAA

KOP

SHIT! IT'S GAS!

LOOK OUT!

SHIiiiiiz

KEEP MOVING!

IT WAS JUST A SMOKE BOMB!

BOOOM

=HFF=

=HUFF=

WHERE ARE THE OTHERS? WHERE'S THE COMMANDER?

SAME HERE! THE COMMANDER FOUND LADY MIYAKO, BUT HE'S HAVING PROBLEMS!

THE DEFENDERS ARE TOUGHER THAN WE THOUGHT! THEY TOOK OUR OUR BEST MEN!

IT WAS A MISTAKE TO DIVIDE OUR FORCES! WE HAVE TO REASSEMBLE...

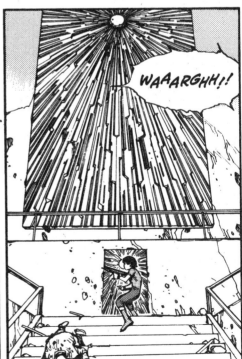

WAAARGHH!!

VOOF

O-OAA
...AH...

GOOD!
THAT'S MORE
LIKE IT!

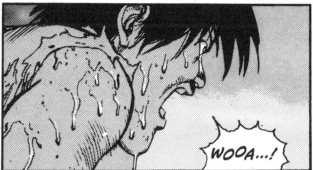

WOOA...!

BAD NEWS,
COMMAN-
DER!

?!

THE MONKS AND
THE REFUGEES
ARE AFTER
US!

HUFF

HUFF

WHAT
?!

WHAT'LL
WE DO?!

SHUT
UP!

WE'VE
FAILED. WE
HAVE TO
LEAVE...

WHAT?!

312

DON'T YOU KNOW WHEN YOU'RE BEATEN?!

...BEATEN...?

HAVE WE BEEN BEATEN?

I GUESS SO.

NOW DROP THOSE GUNS BEFORE WE KILL YOUR LEADER--

--AND KICK YOUR BUTTS AGAIN!

CLANG

CLANG

CLANG

WE'RE SORRY, SIR! THEY WERE TOO MUCH FOR US!

DON'T THINK THIS IS OVER! THE EMPIRE WILL LIQUIDATE ALL IT'S ENEMIES! WHEN YOUR TURN COMES, IT'LL BE A PLEASURE--

I'M TERRIFIED, CHICKENSHIT...

NEXT TIME TELL TETSUO TO COME IN PERSON!

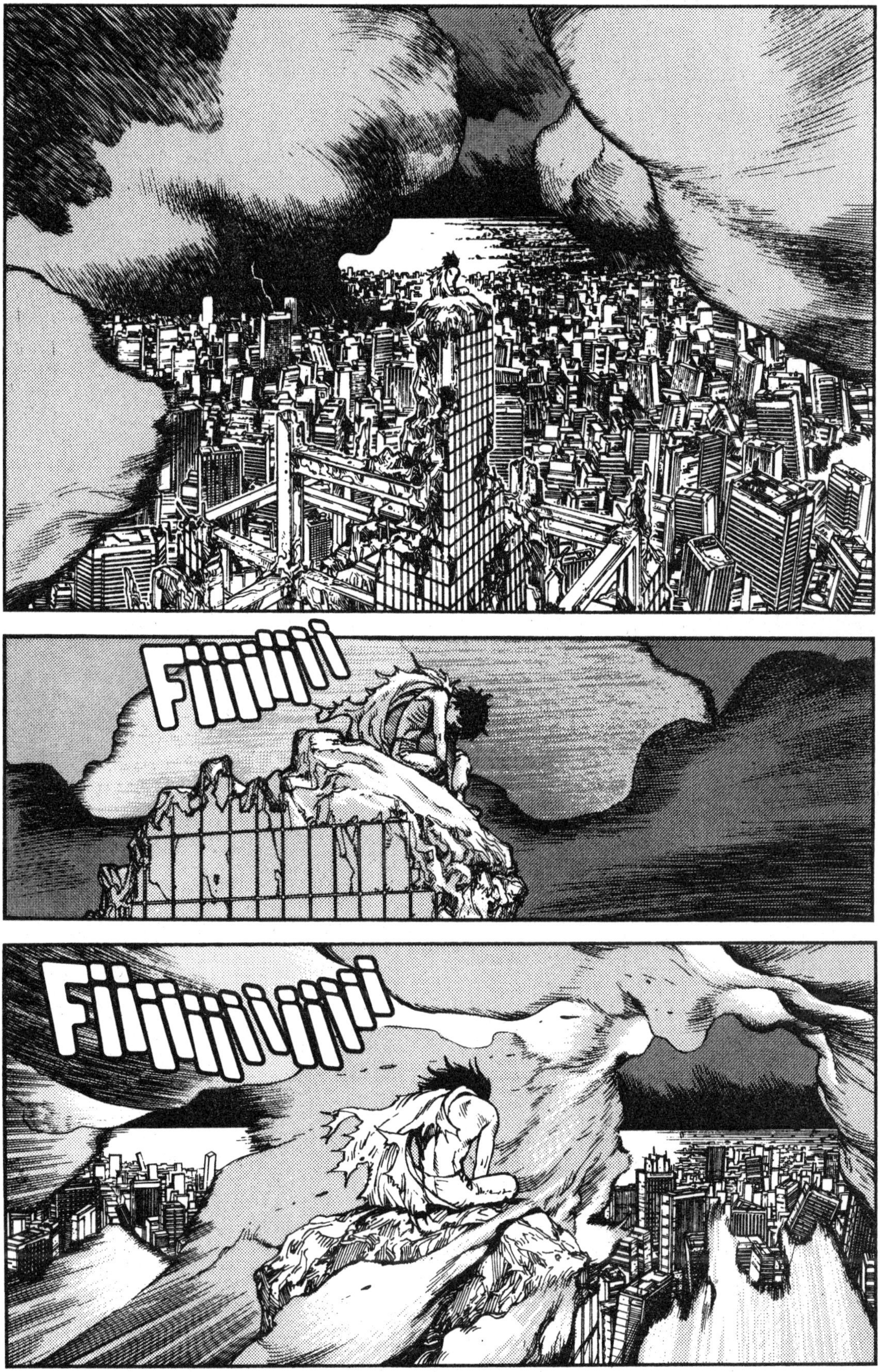
Fiiiiiii
Fiiiiiiiiiii

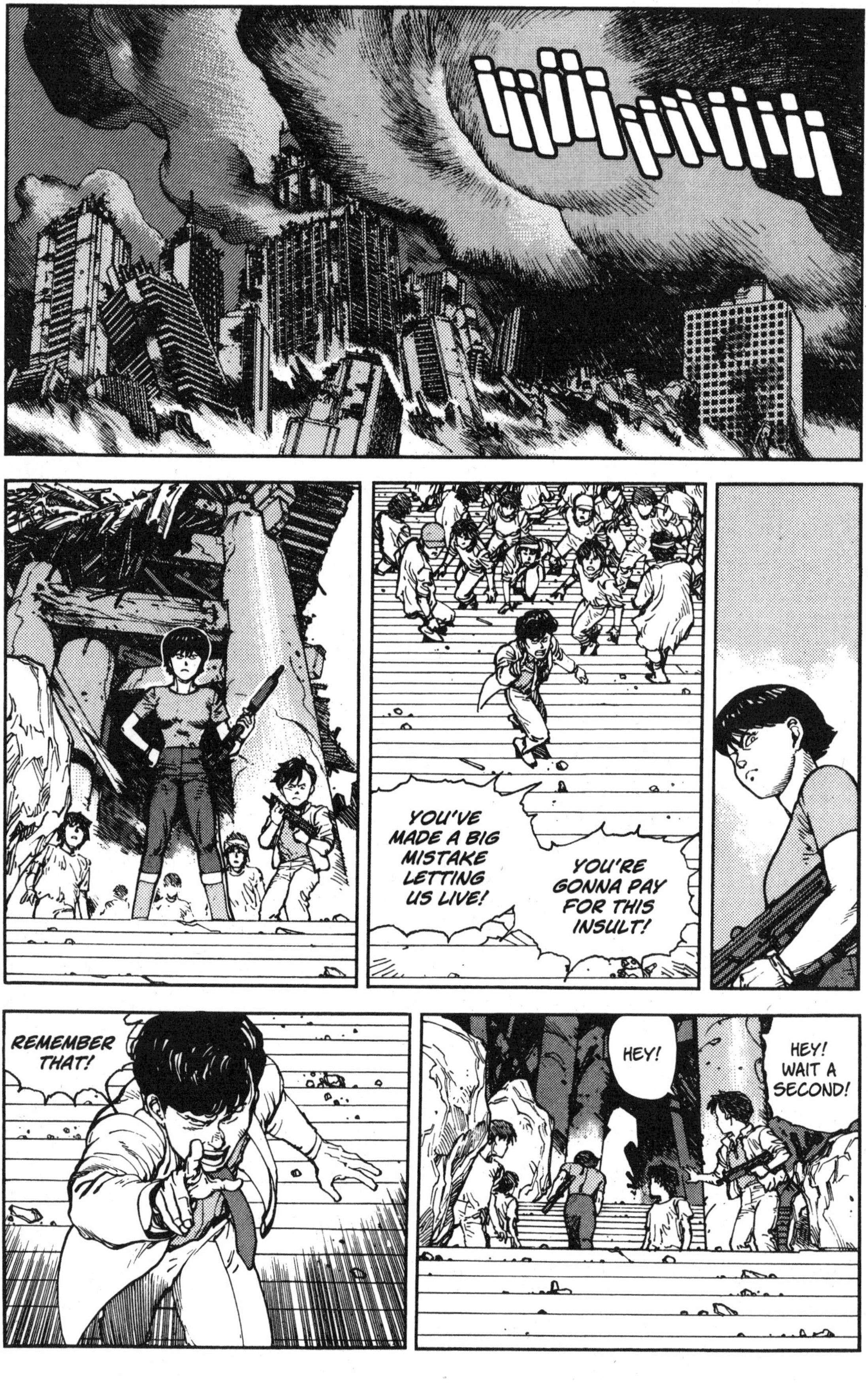
YOU'VE MADE A BIG MISTAKE LETTING US LIVE!
YOU'RE GONNA PAY FOR THIS INSULT!
REMEMBER THAT!
HEY!
HEY! WAIT A SECOND!

I HAVE TO TALK TO YOU.

...BUT THAT'S NOT MY...

NEVER MIND THAT! DON'T YOU RECOGNIZE ME?

I KNOW.

IT WOULD BE SAFER FOR US TO JUST KILL THEM..

AREN'T YOU THE GIRL WHO WAS AT HARUKIYA WITH KANEDA?

?

OH!

I WAS THERE TOO, WITH YAMAGATA AND SOME OF THE OTHERS.

YOU'RE ALIVE!

SO ARE YOU!

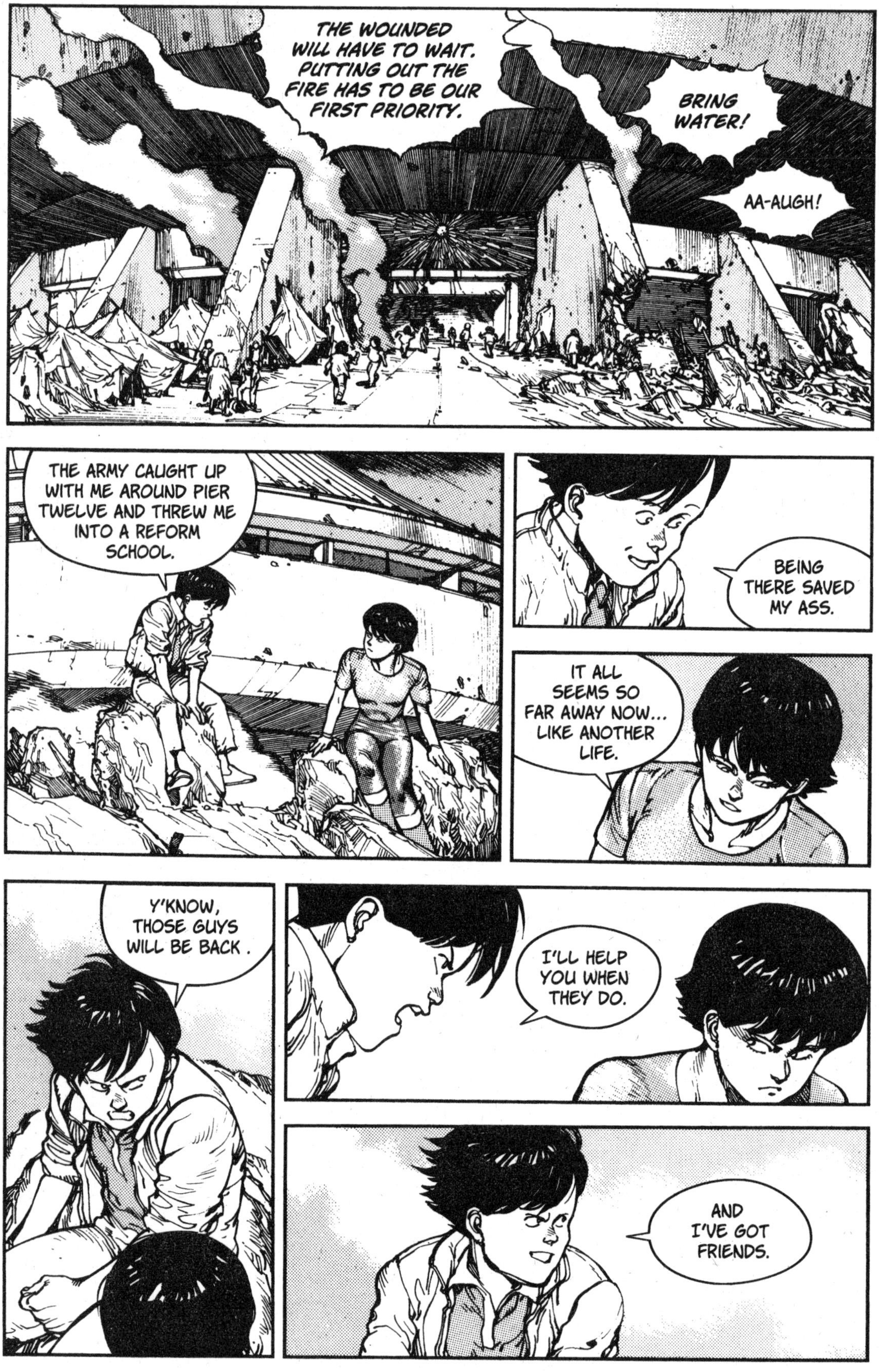
THE WOUNDED WILL HAVE TO WAIT. PUTTING OUT THE FIRE HAS TO BE OUR FIRST PRIORITY.
BRING WATER!
AA-AUGH!
THE ARMY CAUGHT UP WITH ME AROUND PIER TWELVE AND THREW ME INTO A REFORM SCHOOL.
BEING THERE SAVED MY ASS.
IT ALL SEEMS SO FAR AWAY NOW... LIKE ANOTHER LIFE.
Y'KNOW, THOSE GUYS WILL BE BACK.
I'LL HELP YOU WHEN THEY DO.
AND I'VE GOT FRIENDS.

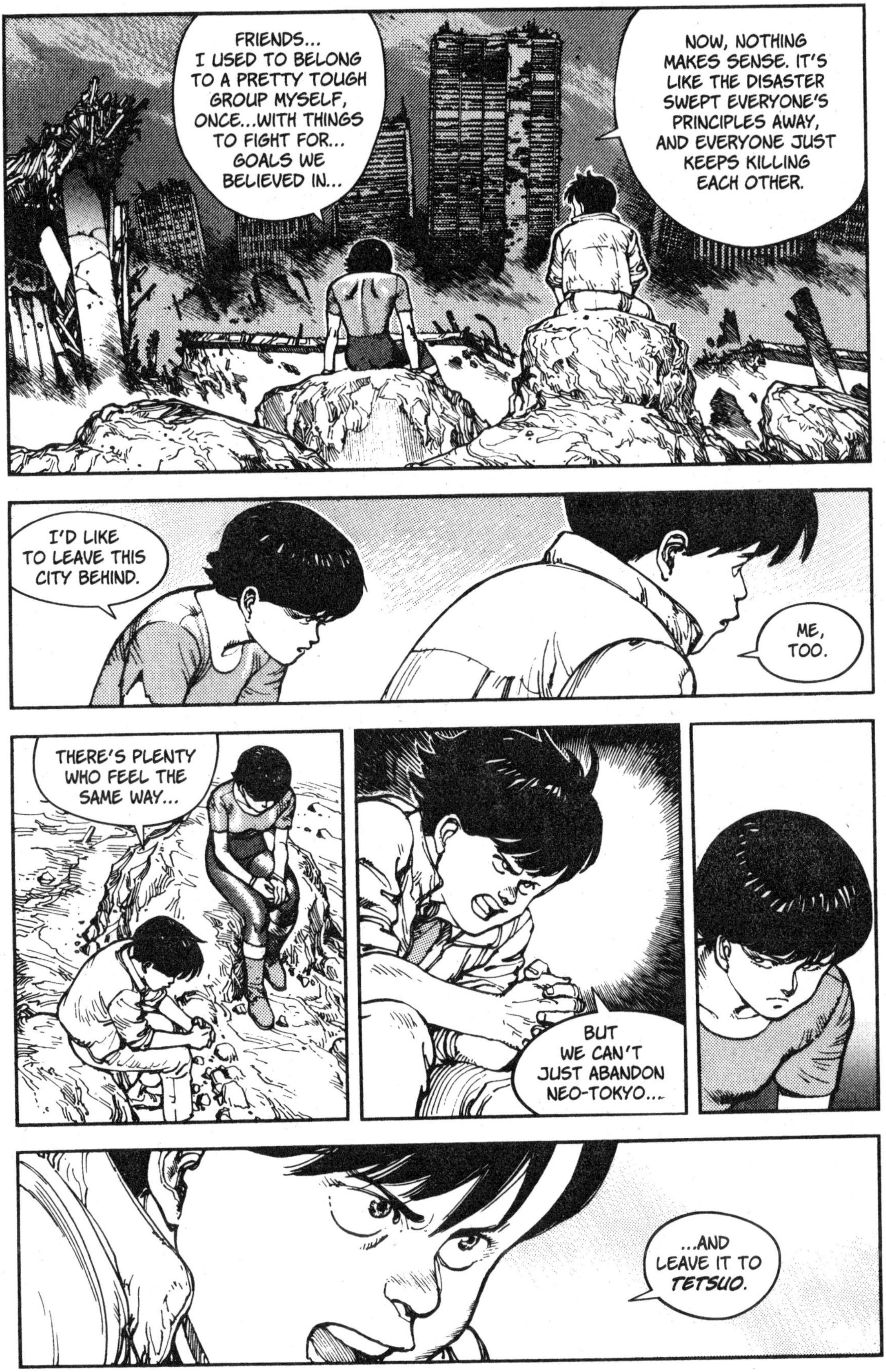
FRIENDS... I USED TO BELONG TO A PRETTY TOUGH GROUP MYSELF, ONCE...WITH THINGS TO FIGHT FOR... GOALS WE BELIEVED IN...
NOW, NOTHING MAKES SENSE. IT'S LIKE THE DISASTER SWEPT EVERYONE'S PRINCIPLES AWAY, AND EVERYONE JUST KEEPS KILLING EACH OTHER.
I'D LIKE TO LEAVE THIS CITY BEHIND.
ME, TOO.
THERE'S PLENTY WHO FEEL THE SAME WAY...
BUT WE CAN'T JUST ABANDON NEO-TOKYO...
...AND LEAVE IT TO *TETSUO*.

WE CAN'T GO ANYWHERE UNTIL WE TAKE CARE OF HIM!

WE HAVE TO SETTLE THE SCORE!

HUHN?

UH... BY THE WAY... WHAT BECAME OF KANEDA?

HE... DIDN'T MAKE IT TO SHELTER.

I DON'T THINK HE...

I ALWAYS THOUGHT HE WAS IMMORTAL, THAT GUY.

UH...

YOU TWO EVER DO IT?

OH, COME ON! NOT YOU, TOO?

WHAT?

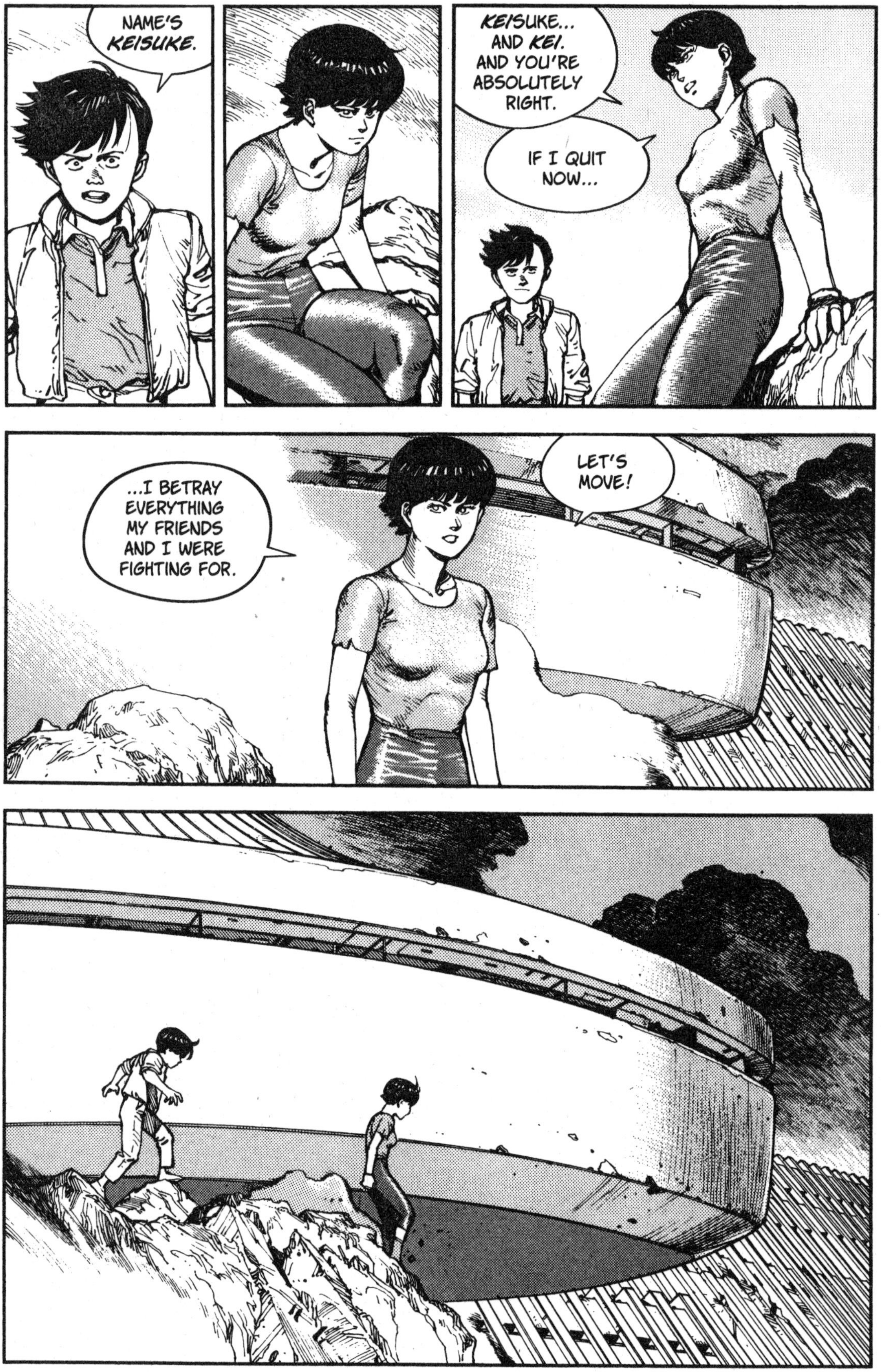
NAME'S *KEISUKE*.
*KEI*SUKE... AND *KEI*. AND YOU'RE ABSOLUTELY RIGHT.
IF I QUIT NOW...
...I BETRAY EVERYTHING MY FRIENDS AND I WERE FIGHTING FOR.
LET'S MOVE!

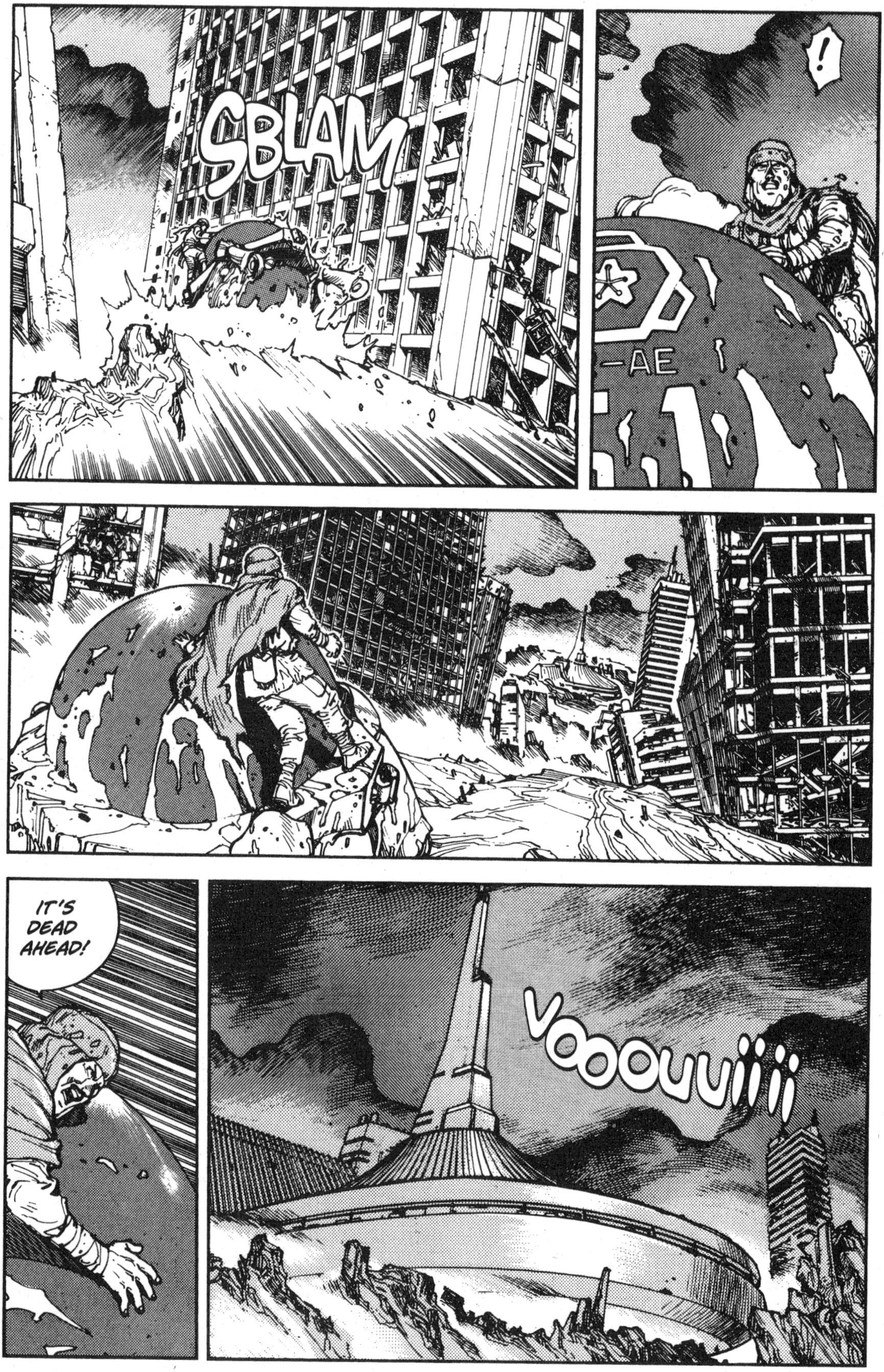
SBLAM
!
-AE
IT'S DEAD AHEAD!
VOOOUUIIII

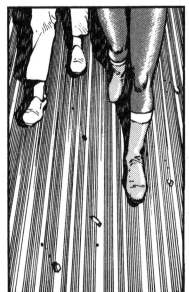

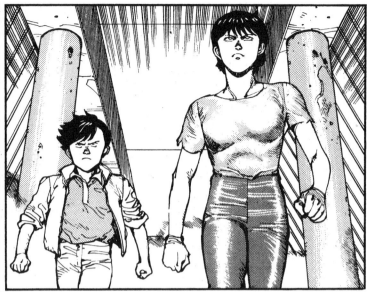

GET THE FIRE OUT!

WE NEED MORE WATER!

GET A STRETCHER OVER HERE!

OUT OF THE QUESTION!

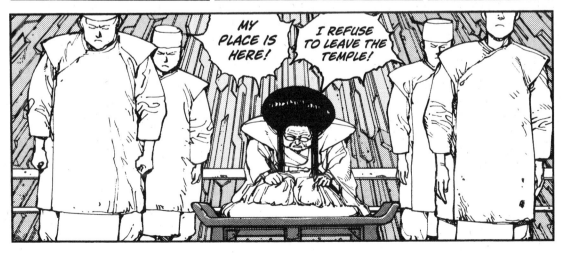

MY PLACE IS HERE!

I REFUSE TO LEAVE THE TEMPLE!

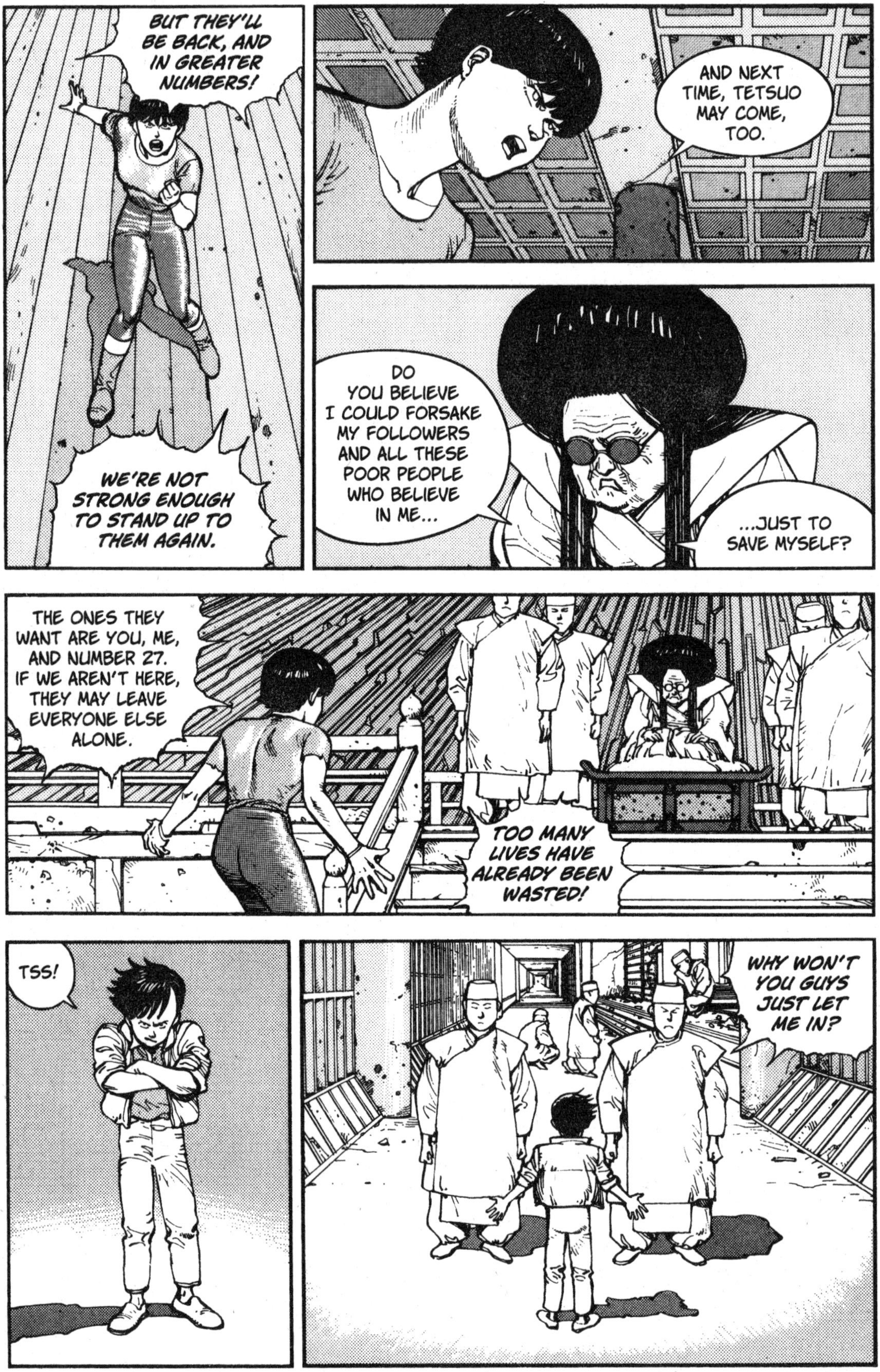
BUT THEY'LL BE BACK, AND IN GREATER NUMBERS!
WE'RE NOT STRONG ENOUGH TO STAND UP TO THEM AGAIN.
AND NEXT TIME, TETSUO MAY COME, TOO.
DO YOU BELIEVE I COULD FORSAKE MY FOLLOWERS AND ALL THESE POOR PEOPLE WHO BELIEVE IN ME...
...JUST TO SAVE MYSELF?
THE ONES THEY WANT ARE YOU, ME, AND NUMBER 27. IF WE AREN'T HERE, THEY MAY LEAVE EVERYONE ELSE ALONE.
TOO MANY LIVES HAVE ALREADY BEEN WASTED!
TSS!
WHY WON'T YOU GUYS JUST LET ME IN?

WE WILL REMAIN HERE, NUMBER 27 AND I...

IT WAS NO SERIES OF RANDOM ACCIDENTS THAT BROUGHT US ALL TOGETHER HERE.

WE MUST PERMIT DESTINY TO FOLLOW ITS COURSE, AND HERE IS WHERE THAT MUST BE ACHIEVED.

BUT WHAT POSSIBLE GOOD WILL YOUR DEATH DO?!

THAT IS NOT THE QUESTION...

THIS IS WHY I CAN'T STAND FANATICS...

...THEY'RE ALWAYS SO SURE THEY'RE RIGHT!

HUNH?

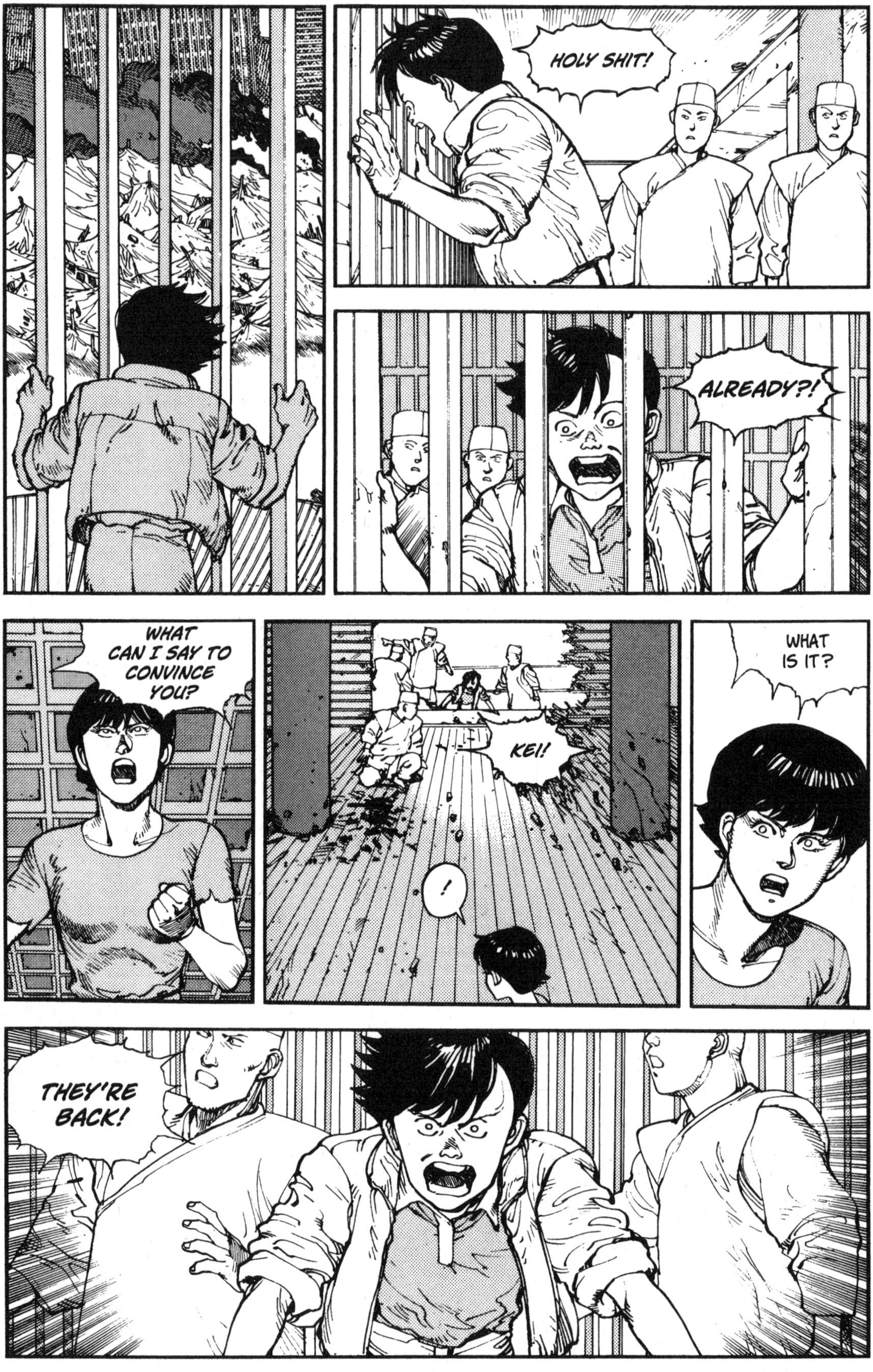
HOLY SHIT!
ALREADY?!
WHAT CAN I SAY TO CONVINCE YOU?
KEI!
!
WHAT IS IT?
THEY'RE BACK!

FWiiiSH

THE WIND IS WITH US! SET FIRE TO EVERY-THING!

BURN IT! BURN IT ALL! DON'T HOLD BACK!

WHERE'S THE EXTRA GUNS AND AMMO?

AND THE REINFORCE-MENTS?

HURRY!

FORWARD, PROUD WARRIORS! THE FATE OF THE EMPIRE IS IN YOUR HANDS!

WHAT IS THIS?

BROOO

EH?

BROOBRO

WE CAN MAKE IT! KEEP GOING!

KSHAK

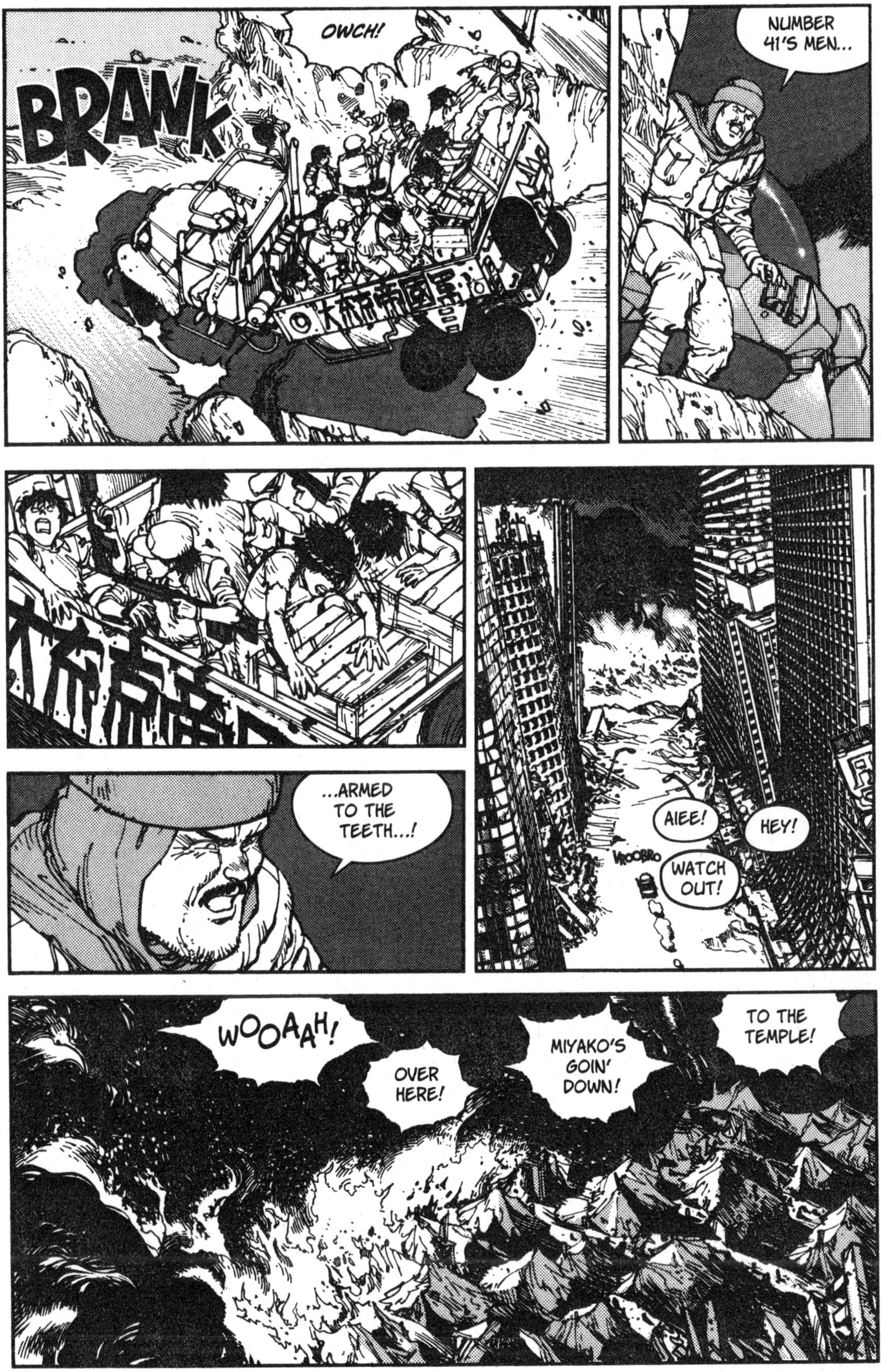
BRANK
OWCH!
NUMBER 41'S MEN...
...ARMED TO THE TEETH...!
AIEE!
HEY!
VROOBRO
WATCH OUT!
WOOAAH!
OVER HERE!
MIYAKO'S GOIN' DOWN!
TO THE TEMPLE!

SKORCH

GETCHA AMMO RIGHT HERE, BOYS!

HEY! DON'T THROW THE BOXES, YOU MORON!

HERE!

ARE THERE MEN POSTED AT THE BRIDGE?

YESSIR! AND WE PLACED EXPLOSIVES ON THE CENTRAL PILLAR!

TAKE A LOOK AT THIS, COMMANDER!

WE FOUND A BUNCH OF THESE.

THEY FIRE HEAT-SEEKING MISSILES!

PERFECT.

TIME FOR ROUND TWO.

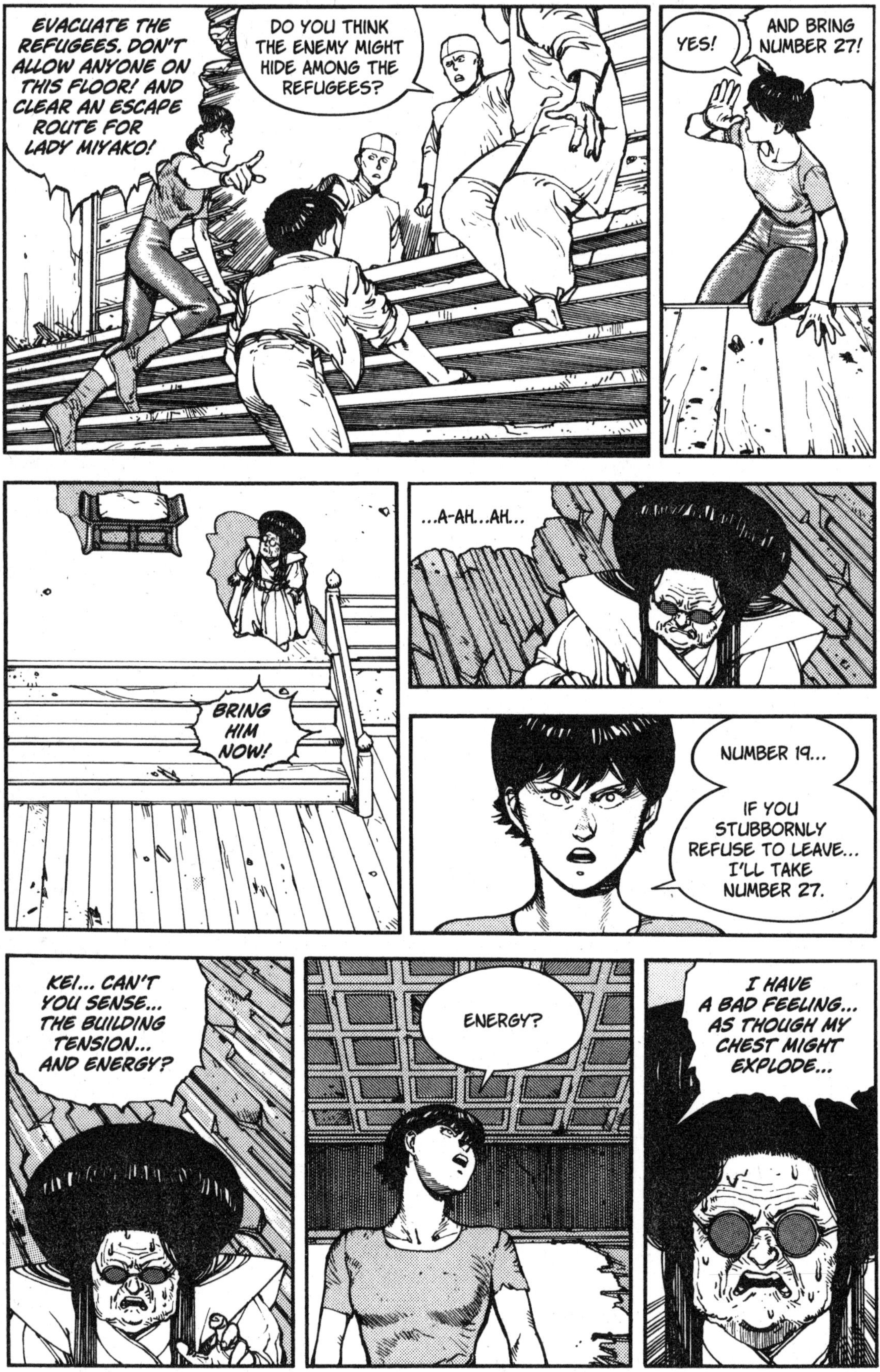
EVACUATE THE REFUGEES. DON'T ALLOW ANYONE ON THIS FLOOR! AND CLEAR AN ESCAPE ROUTE FOR LADY MIYAKO!
DO YOU THINK THE ENEMY MIGHT HIDE AMONG THE REFUGEES?
YES!
AND BRING NUMBER 27!
BRING HIM NOW!
...A-AH...AH...
NUMBER 19...
IF YOU STUBBORNLY REFUSE TO LEAVE... I'LL TAKE NUMBER 27.
KEI... CAN'T YOU SENSE... THE BUILDING TENSION... AND ENERGY?
ENERGY?
I HAVE A BAD FEELING... AS THOUGH MY CHEST MIGHT EXPLODE...

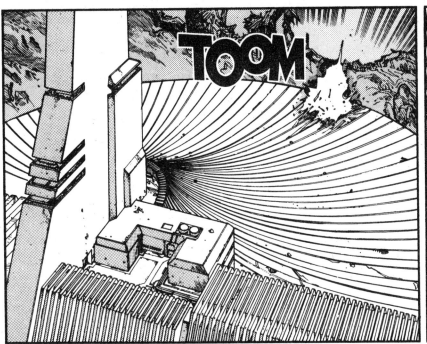

THIS IS GETTING SERIOUS!

WHAT'LL WE DO?

DOWNSTAIRS IS A ZOO. IF WE TRY TO GET OUT THROUGH THAT PANIC WE COULD GET TRAMPLED.

THEY'RE ATTACKING, AND THE REFUGEES ARE ALREADY ON THE RUN.

IT'S IMPOSSIBLE TO HOLD THEM BACK NOW, THEY COULD BE HERE ANY MINUTE.

GETTING OUT WILL BE TOUGH.

WE DON'T HAVE MUCH TIME.

AS SOON AS THEY BRING NUMBER 27 IN, WE'LL MAKE OUR MOVE.

WHERE TO?

FROM THE TOWER...

UP.

...WE'LL HAVE A BETTER CHANCE OF STOPPING ANYONE COMING FROM BELOW.

NUMBER 19 SHOULDN'T BE ABLE TO BITCH ABOUT THAT...

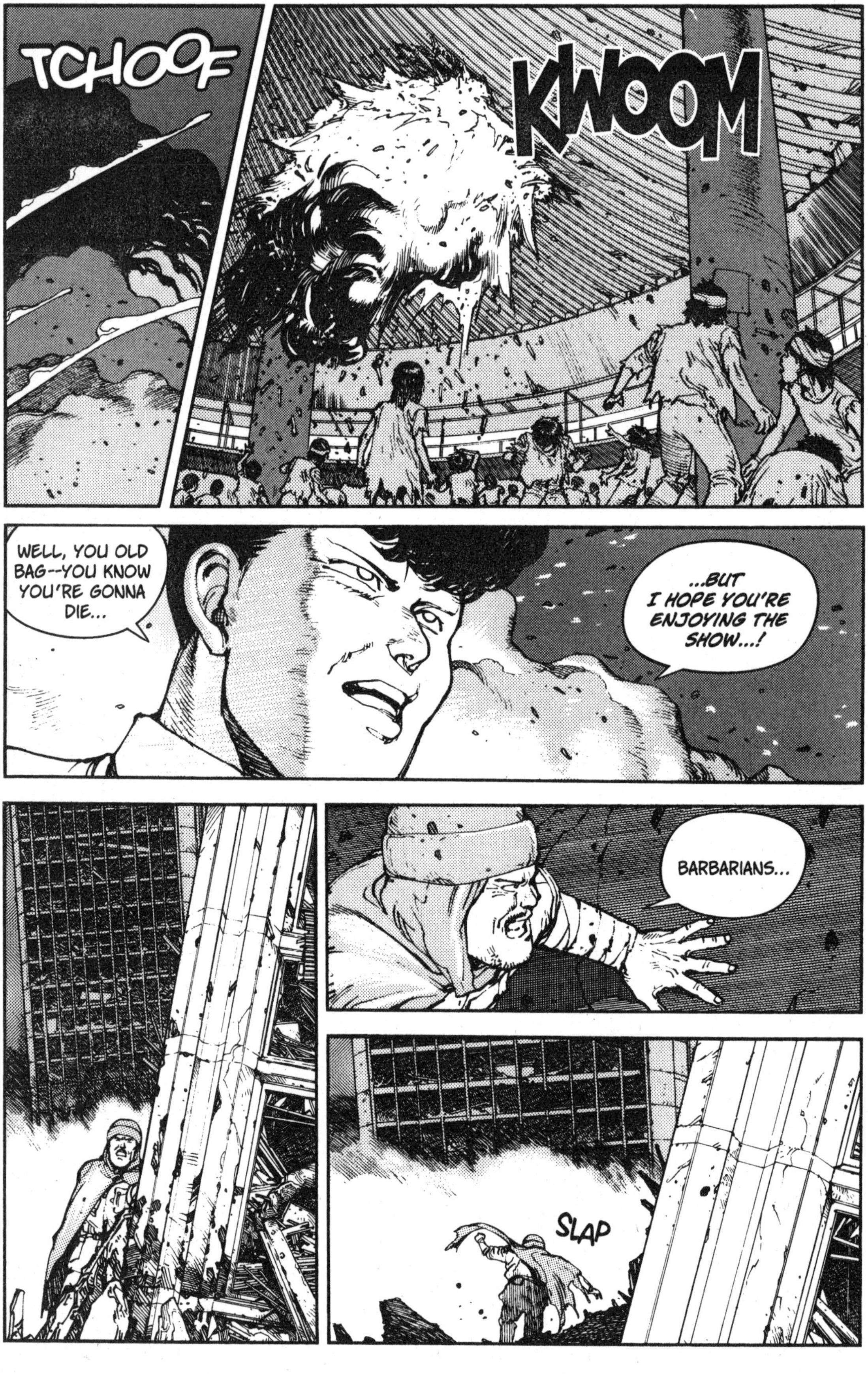
TCHOOF
KWOOM
WELL, YOU OLD BAG--YOU KNOW YOU'RE GONNA DIE...
...BUT I HOPE YOU'RE ENJOYING THE SHOW...!
BARBARIANS...
SLAP

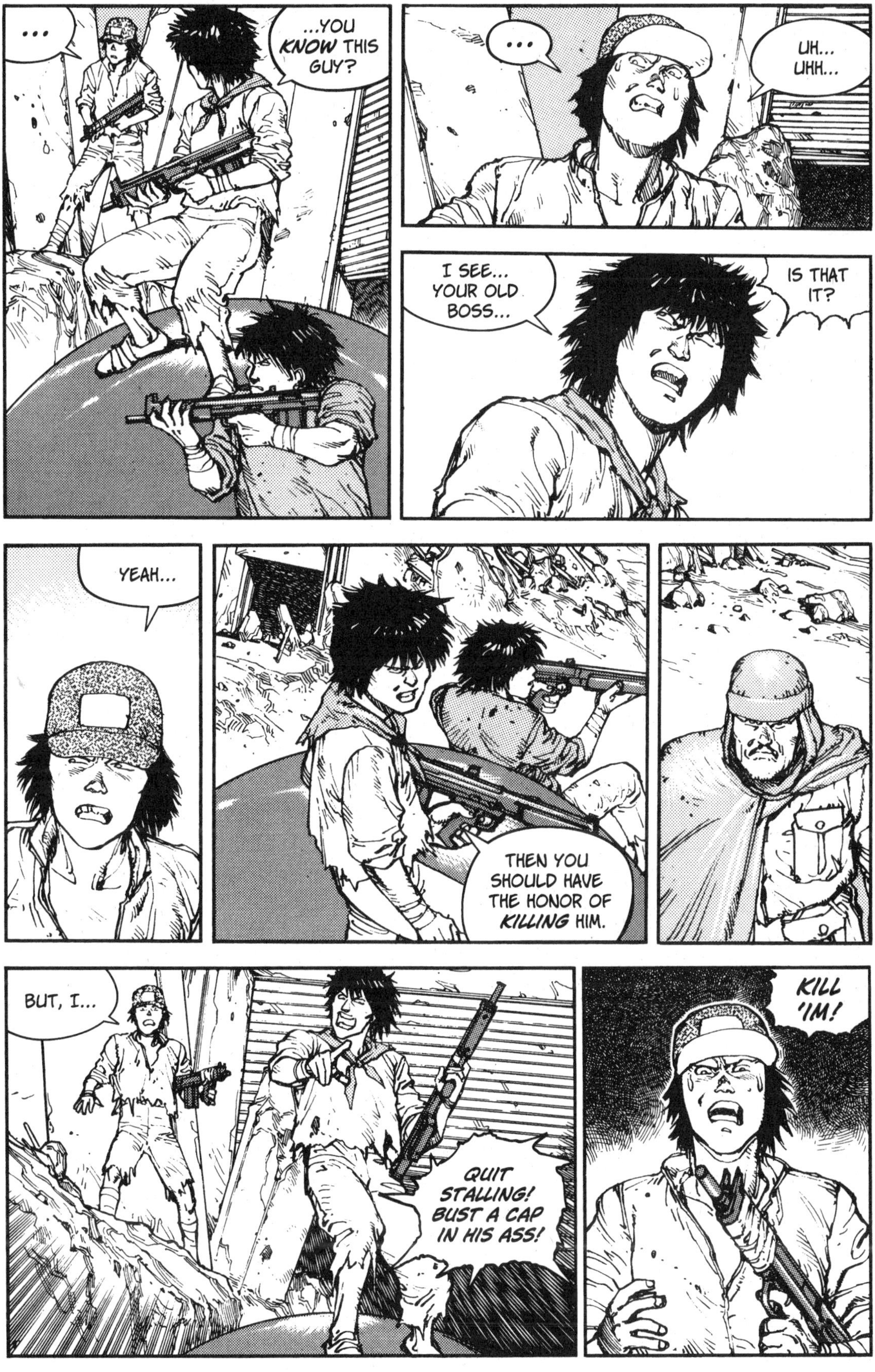
...
...YOU KNOW THIS GUY?
...
UH... UHH...
I SEE... YOUR OLD BOSS...
IS THAT IT?
YEAH...
THEN YOU SHOULD HAVE THE HONOR OF KILLING HIM.
BUT, I...
QUIT STALLING! BUST A CAP IN HIS ASS!
KILL 'IM!

KSHAM

AAGH!

THEY'RE GETTING CLOSER WITH EVERY SHOT...

MAYBE THE TOWER ISN'T SUCH A GREAT IDEA...! WE'D BE SITTING DUCKS!

NUMBER 27!

THIS SHRINE IS STRONGER THAN YOU THINK.

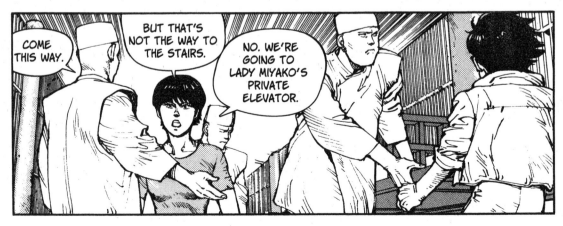

COME THIS WAY.

BUT THAT'S NOT THE WAY TO THE STAIRS.

NO. WE'RE GOING TO LADY MIYAKO'S PRIVATE ELEVATOR.

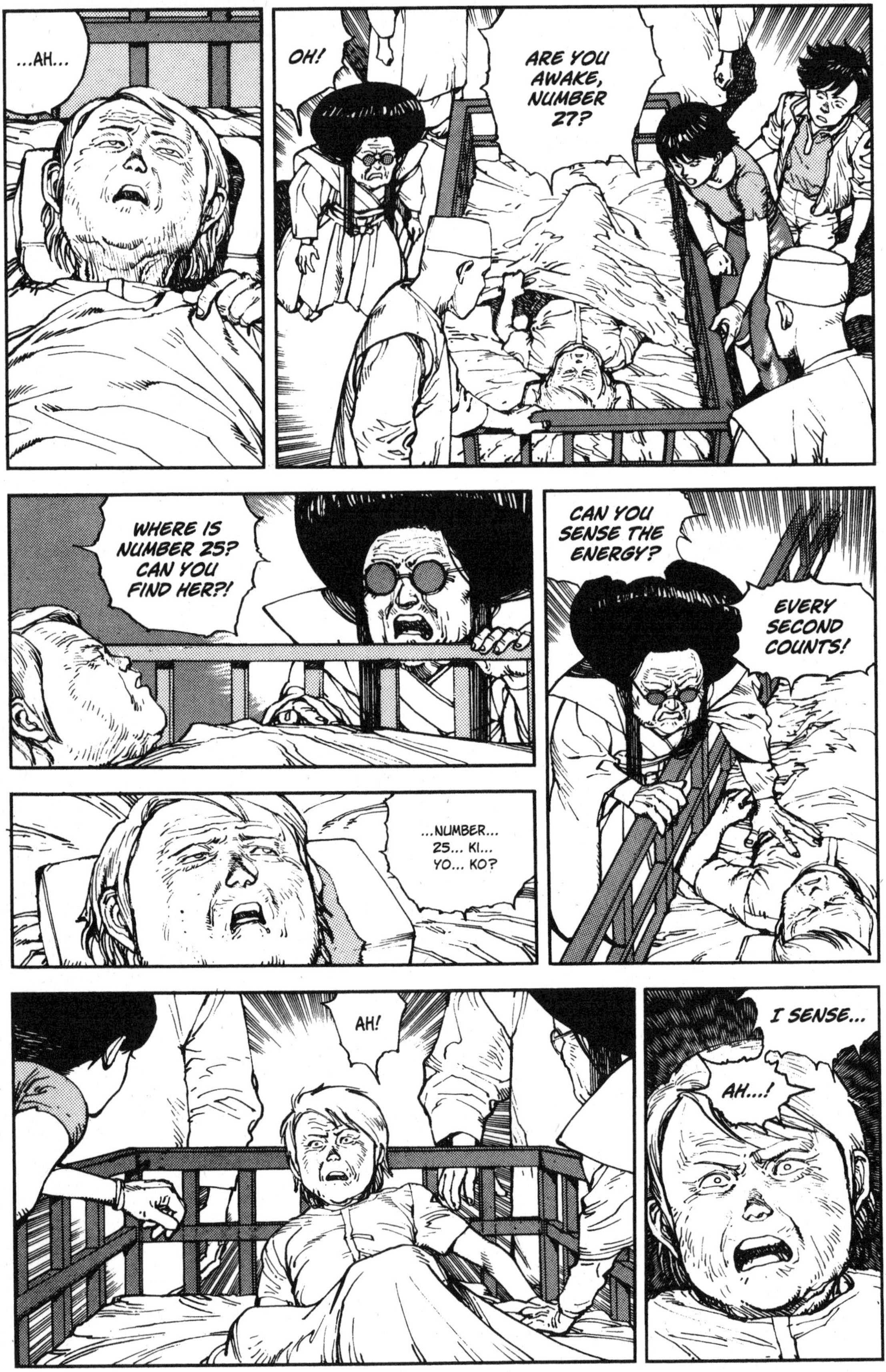
...AH...
OH!
ARE YOU AWAKE, NUMBER 27?
WHERE IS NUMBER 25? CAN YOU FIND HER?!
...NUMBER... 25... KI... YO... KO?
CAN YOU SENSE THE ENERGY?
EVERY SECOND COUNTS!
AH!
I SENSE...
AH...!

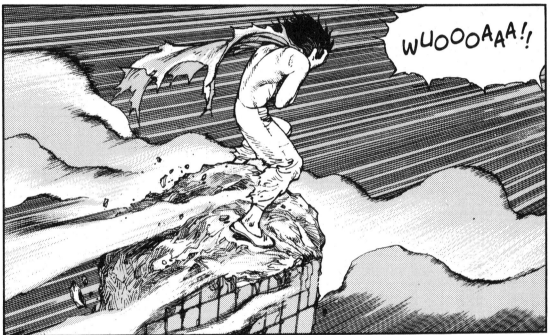

WUOOOAAA!!

MASARU!

CAN YOU FIND KIYOKO?!

KI... YO...KO... KIYOKO IS...

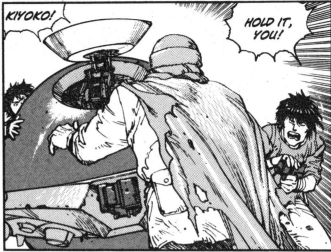

THAT TOWER?

I WARNED YOU!

BANG BANG BANG

COLONEL!

AGH...!

I TOLD YOU YOU'D SUFFER...

POUM

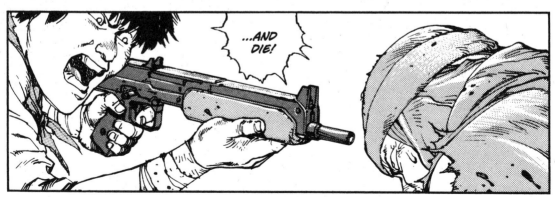

...AND DIE!

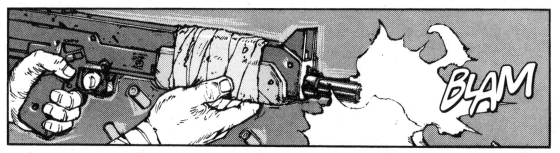

...ARGH!

YOU... TRAITOR...

BAOF.

MY COLONEL!

HURRY...

351

ARE YOU SURE IT'S THE SAME LITTLE GIRL?

A STRANGER HAD HER HIDDEN IN ONE OF THOSE CARE-TAKER ROBOTS.

SHE LOOKS JUST LIKE THE KID WE'VE BEEN SEARCHING FOR.

GOOD!

ALL THE PRETTY FLOWERS...

...FINALLY TOGETHER IN ONE BIG BOUQUET!

THERE ARE TWO MEN GUARDING THE STRANGER, BUT HE LOOKS PRETTY TOUGH.

HEY, YOU GUYS!

...I DON'T WANT HER TOUCHED!

LISTEN UP!

TAKE FIVE OR SIX MORE WITH YOU.

IF HE GIVES YOU ANY TROUBLE, KILL HIM! BUT LEAVE THE GIRL ALONE.

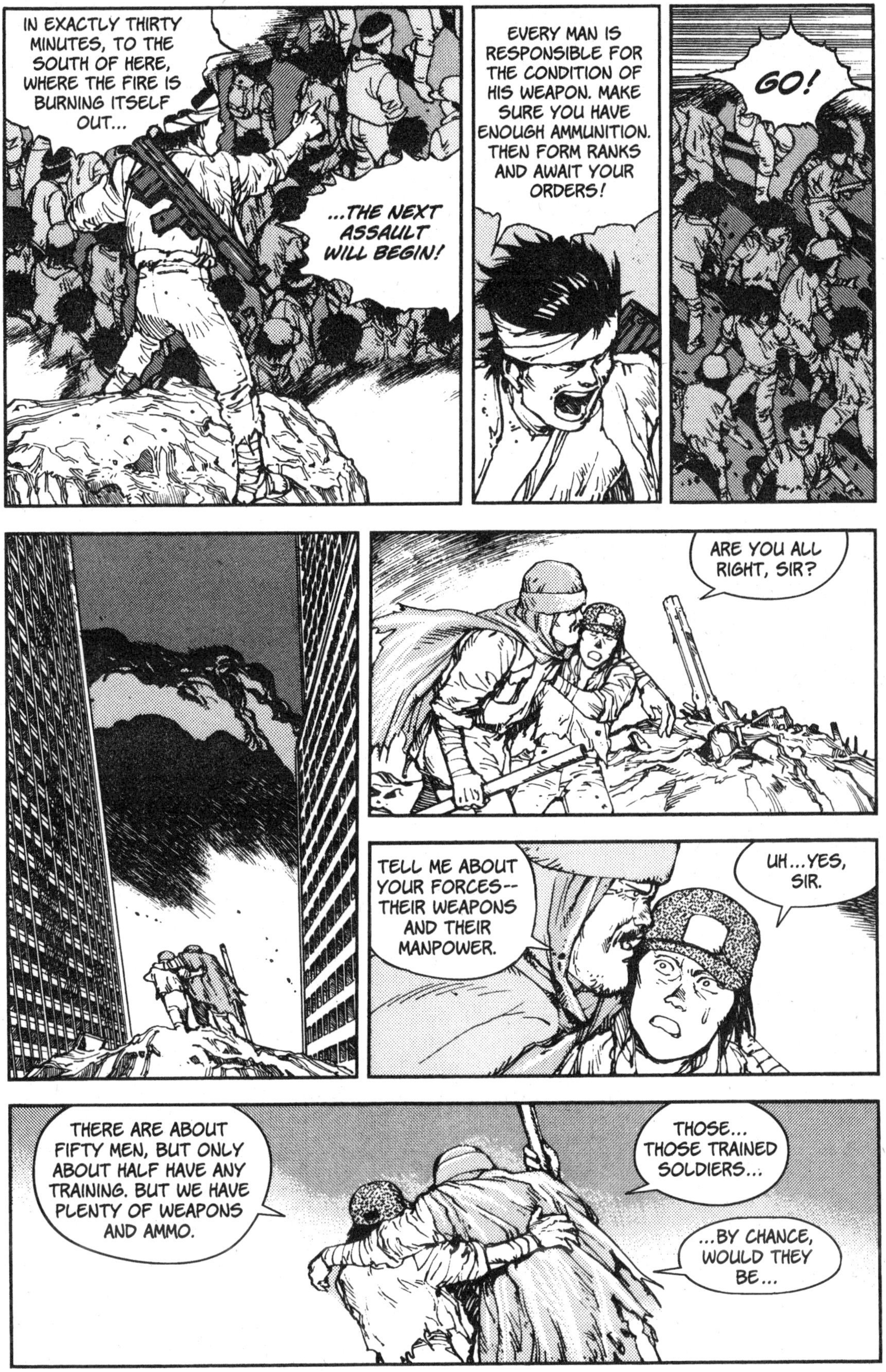
IN EXACTLY THIRTY MINUTES, TO THE SOUTH OF HERE, WHERE THE FIRE IS BURNING ITSELF OUT...
...THE NEXT ASSAULT WILL BEGIN!
EVERY MAN IS RESPONSIBLE FOR THE CONDITION OF HIS WEAPON. MAKE SURE YOU HAVE ENOUGH AMMUNITION. THEN FORM RANKS AND AWAIT YOUR ORDERS!
GO!
ARE YOU ALL RIGHT, SIR?
TELL ME ABOUT YOUR FORCES-- THEIR WEAPONS AND THEIR MANPOWER.
UH...YES, SIR.
THERE ARE ABOUT FIFTY MEN, BUT ONLY ABOUT HALF HAVE ANY TRAINING. BUT WE HAVE PLENTY OF WEAPONS AND AMMO.
THOSE... THOSE TRAINED SOLDIERS...
...BY CHANCE, WOULD THEY BE...

354

WHATEVER YOU DO, DON'T HURT THE KID!

FROP

DOWN THERE!

HNN
HN

YOU CAN RUN, BUT YOU CAN'T HIDE, PAL!

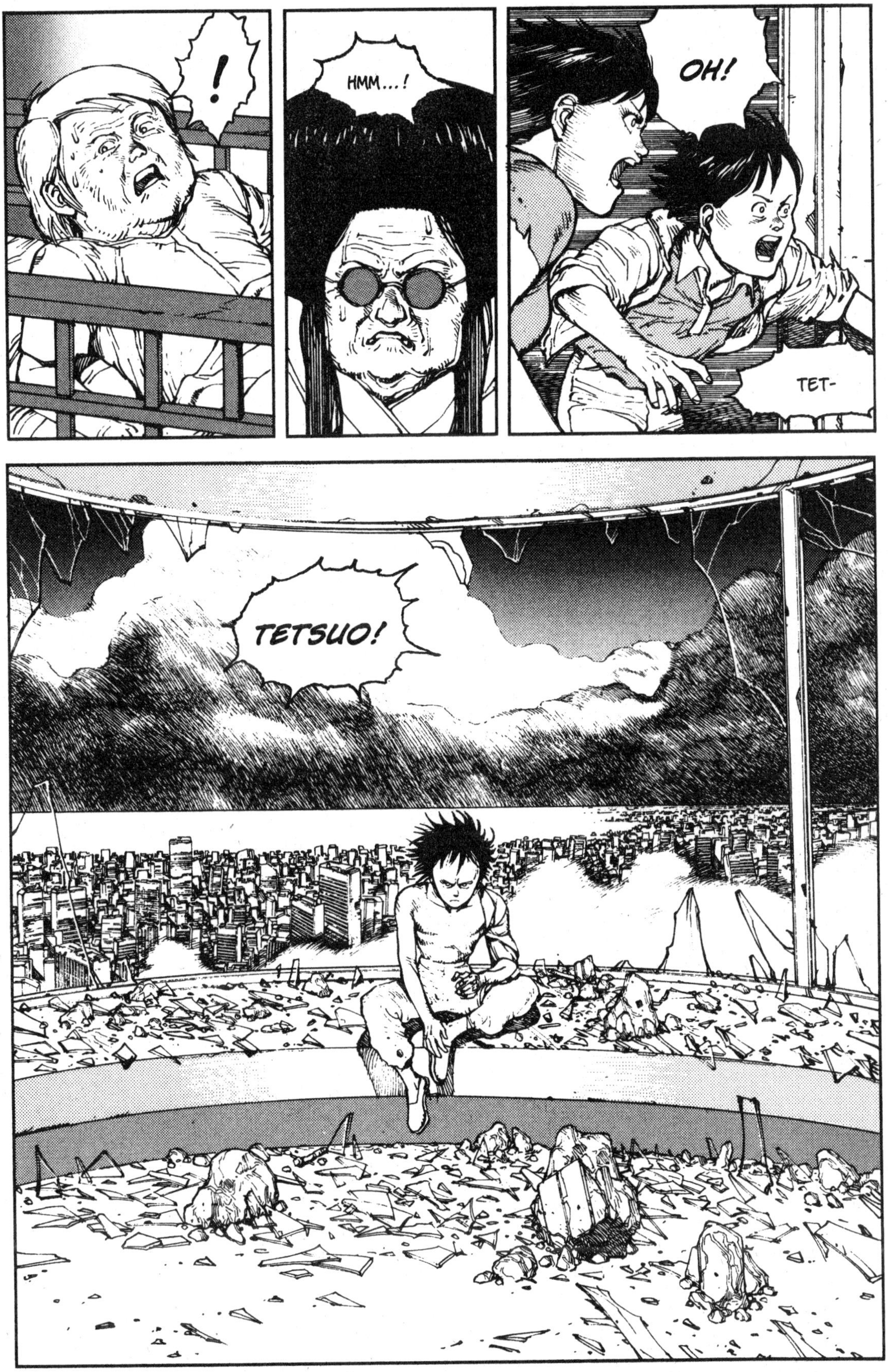
!
HMM...!
OH!
TET-
TETSUO!

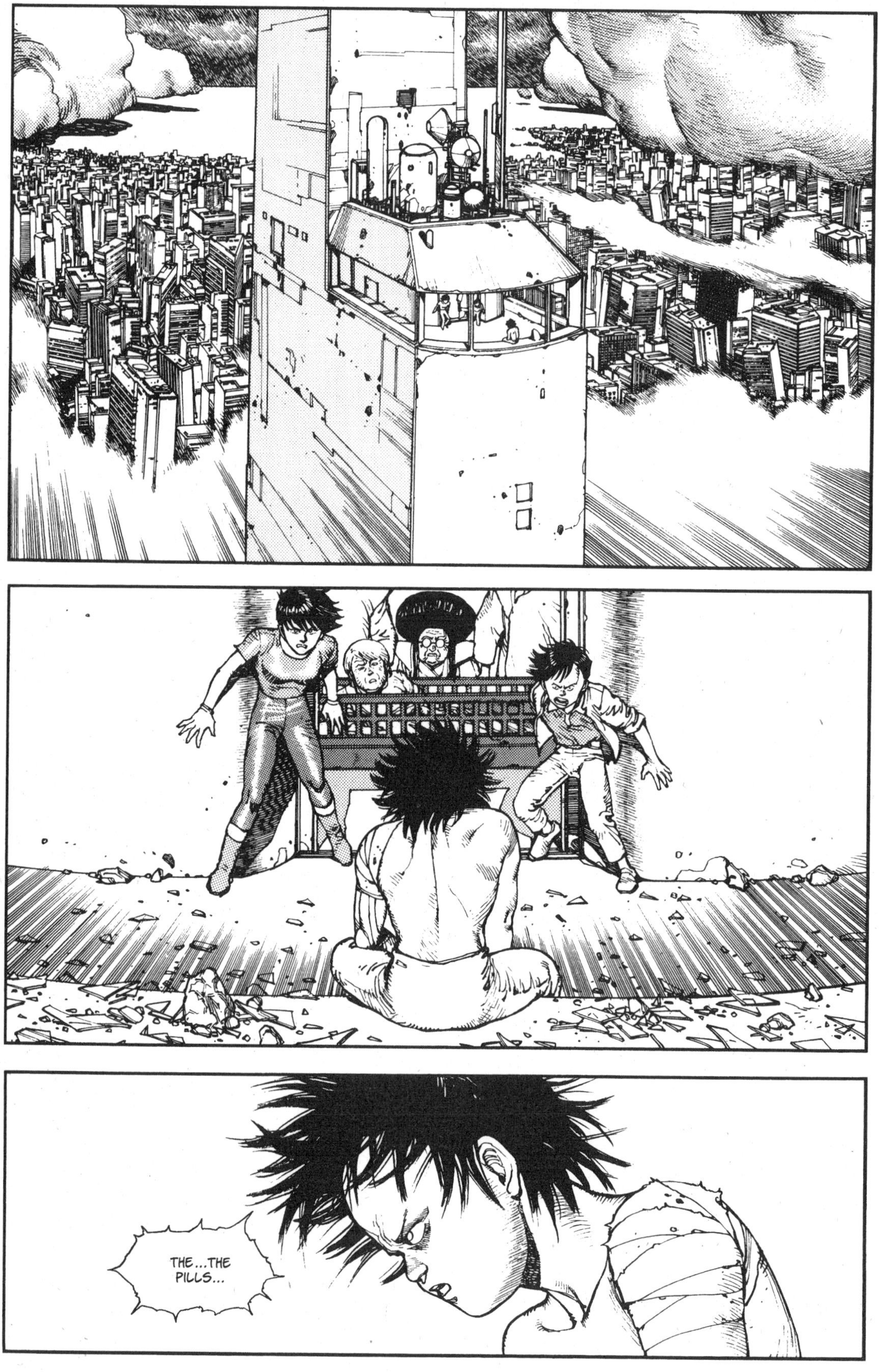
THE...THE PILLS...

NUMBER 41! HAVE YOU NO SHAME?!

GIVE... ME...THE... PILLS...

ACCEPT THE PAIN AND FACE YOUR DESTINY!

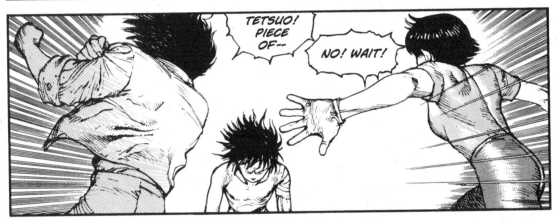

TETSUO! PIECE OF--

NO! WAIT!

SOMETHING'S WRONG WITH HIM...!

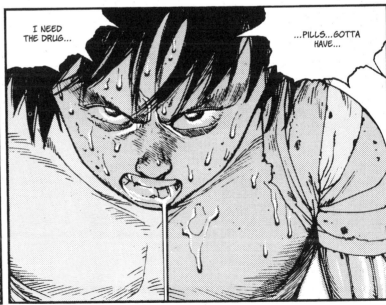

I NEED THE DRUG...

...PILLS...GOTTA HAVE...

"RAKAKA RAKAKA

SO... CHANGED YOUR MIND, EH? YOU WON'T BE MISSED!

GONNA SMOKE YOU, YOU SON OF A--

?!

WANT TO DIE LIKE A HERO WITH YOUR SHITTY LITTLE GUN!?

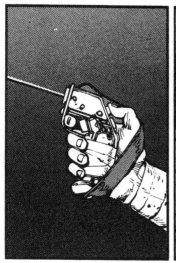

WHAT IS THIS BULLSHIT?!

A LASER?

GHH... GNN...
KILL HIM!
YEAH!
TWIT

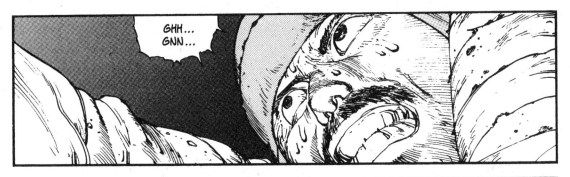

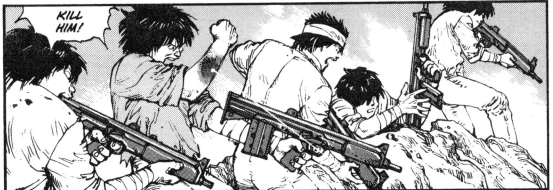

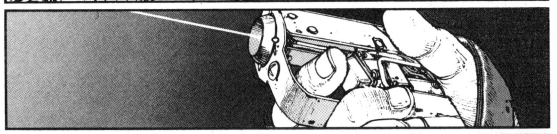

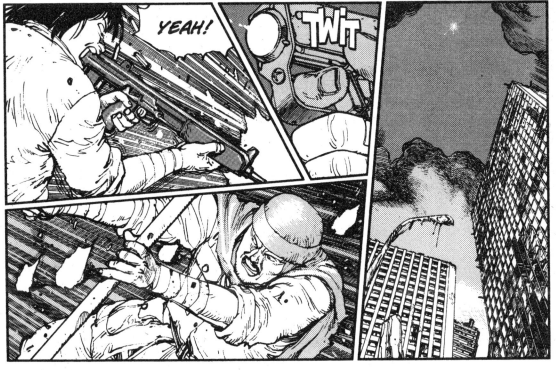

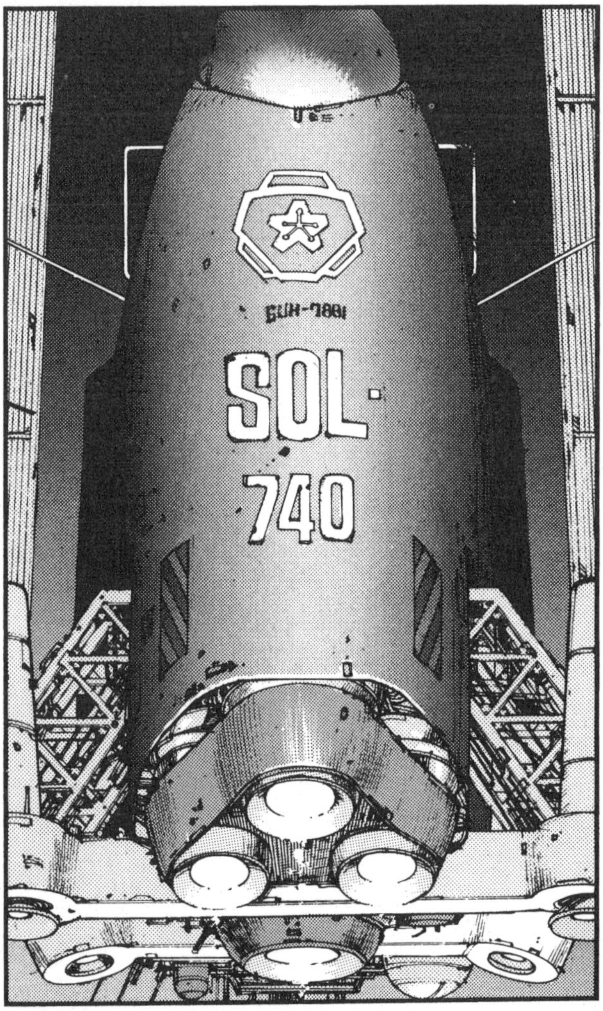
SOL·
740
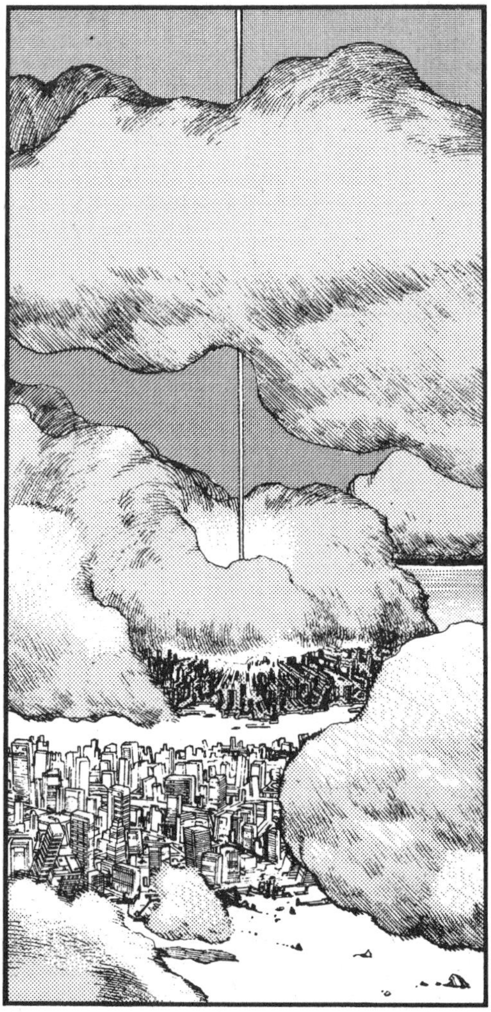
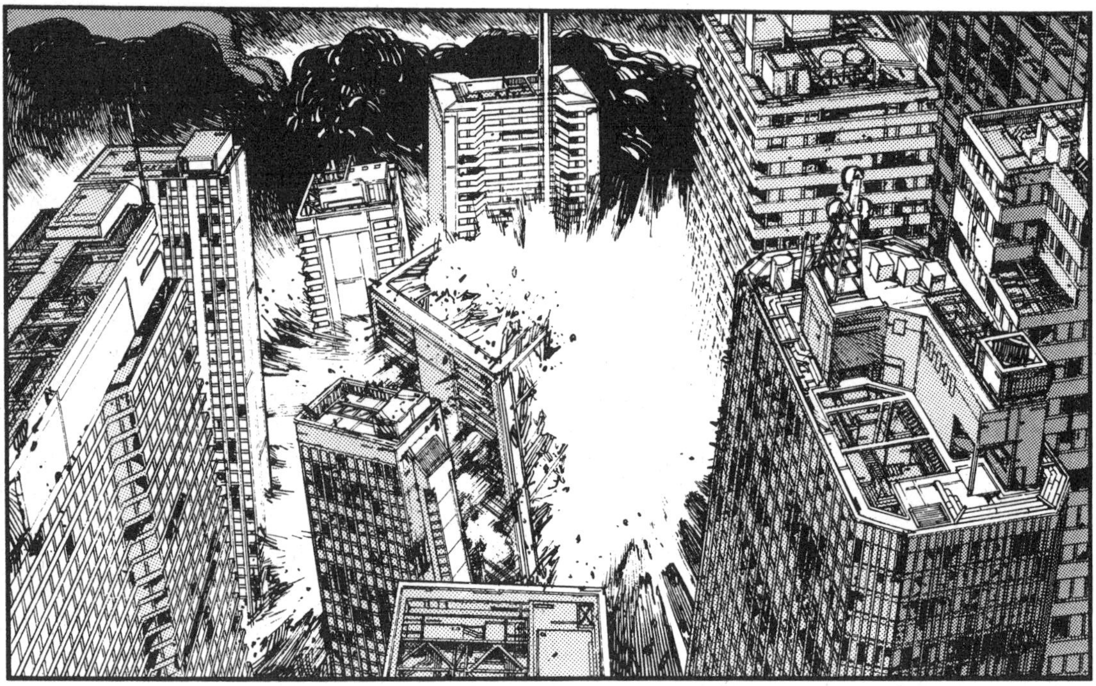

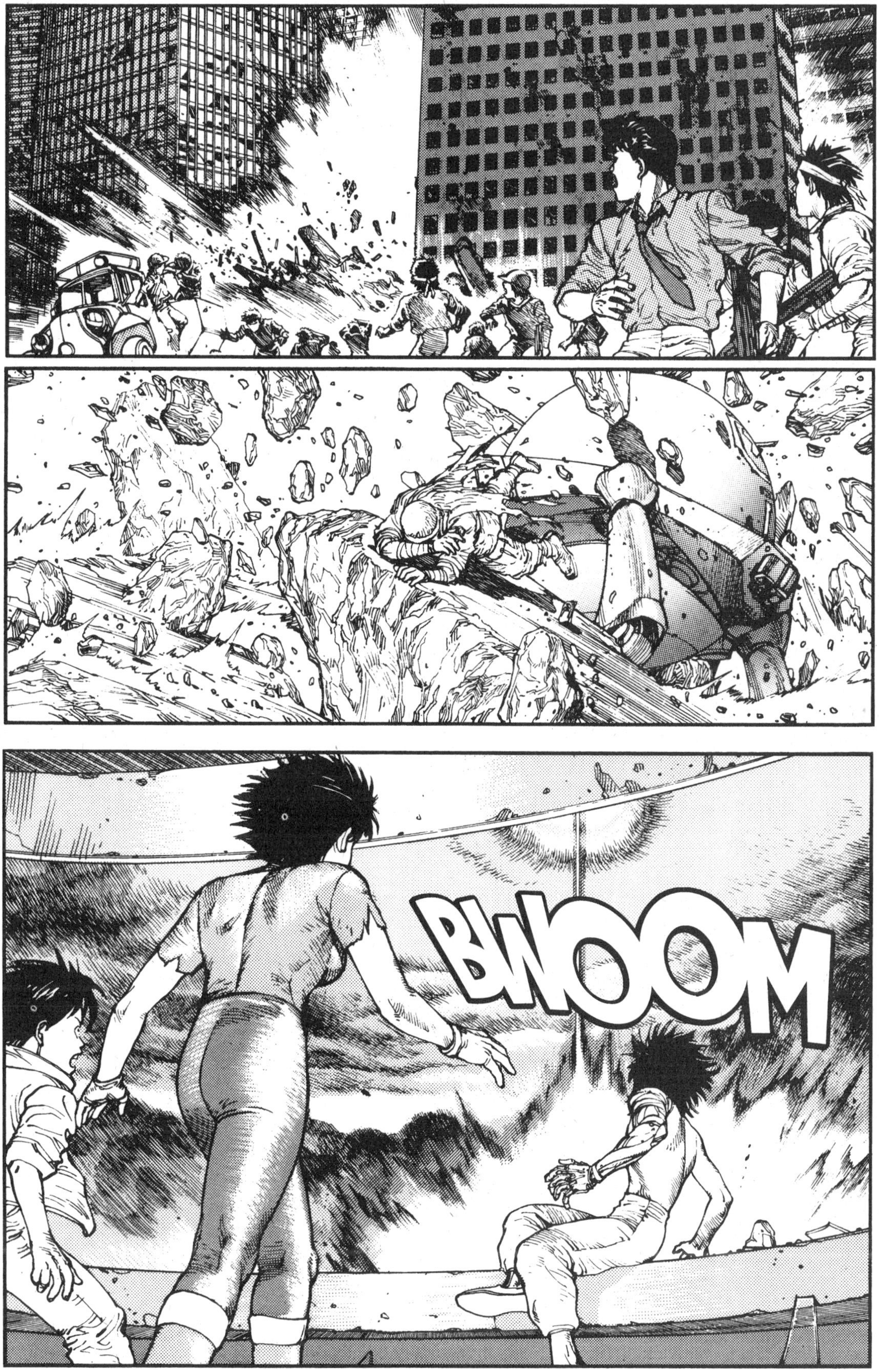
BWOOM

THAT
LIGHT...?!
WHAT--

...OH...

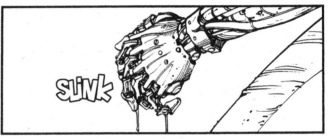

SLINK

OOOH...

...OOOOHHHH!

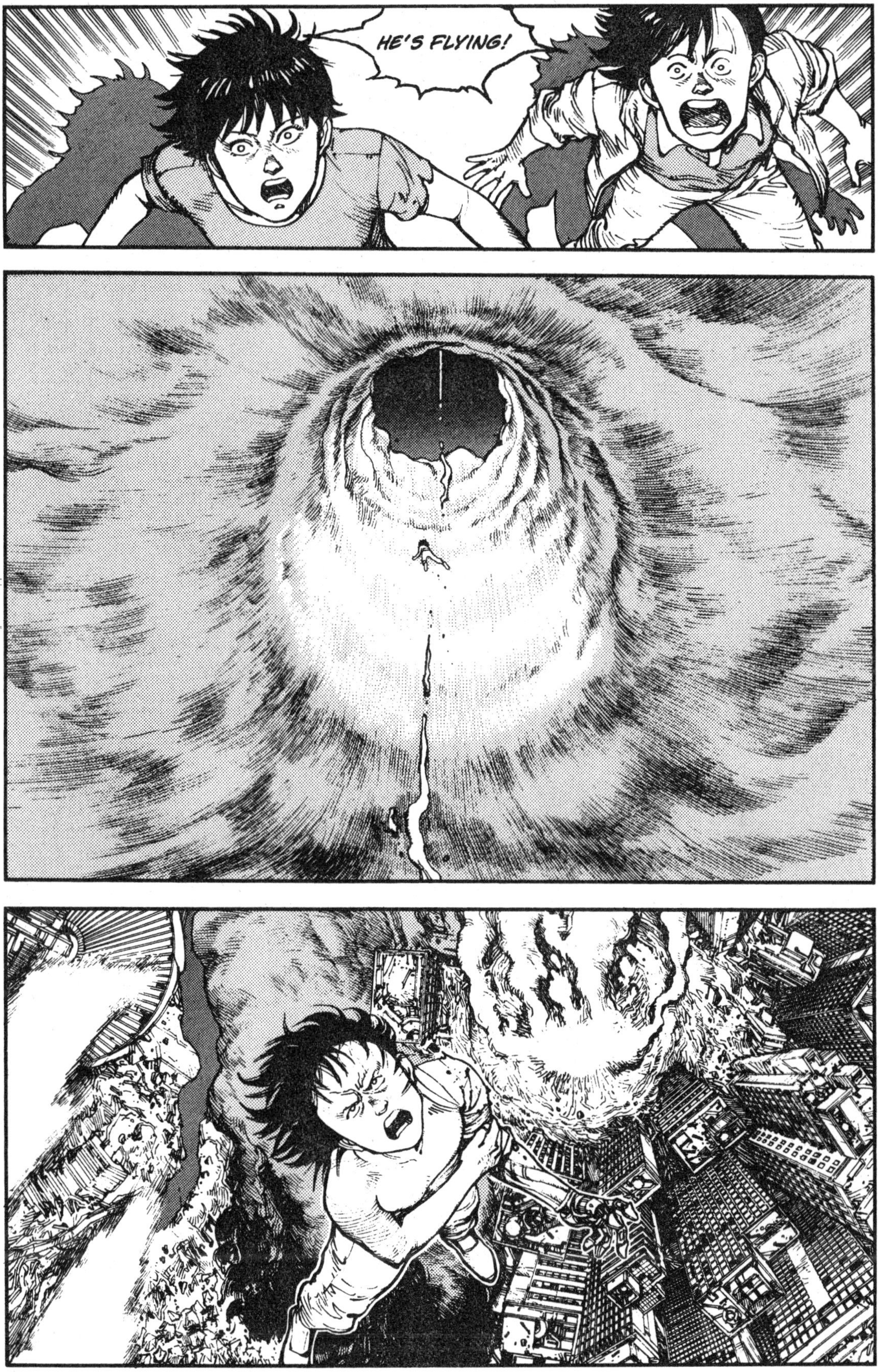
HE'S FLYING!

TLING

?

AKIRA... YOU'RE NOT EATING...

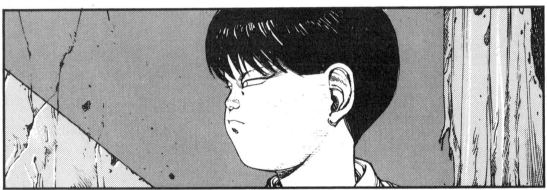

WOOOOAA!

OOOH!

LADY MIYAKO!

ANSWER ME, KIYOKO!

KIYOKO!

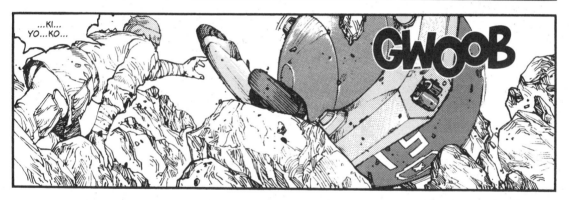

...KI...
YO...KO...

GWOOB

UP THERE ...!

WHAT ...?

DO YOU THINK...?

NO... IT'S NOT POSSIBLE...

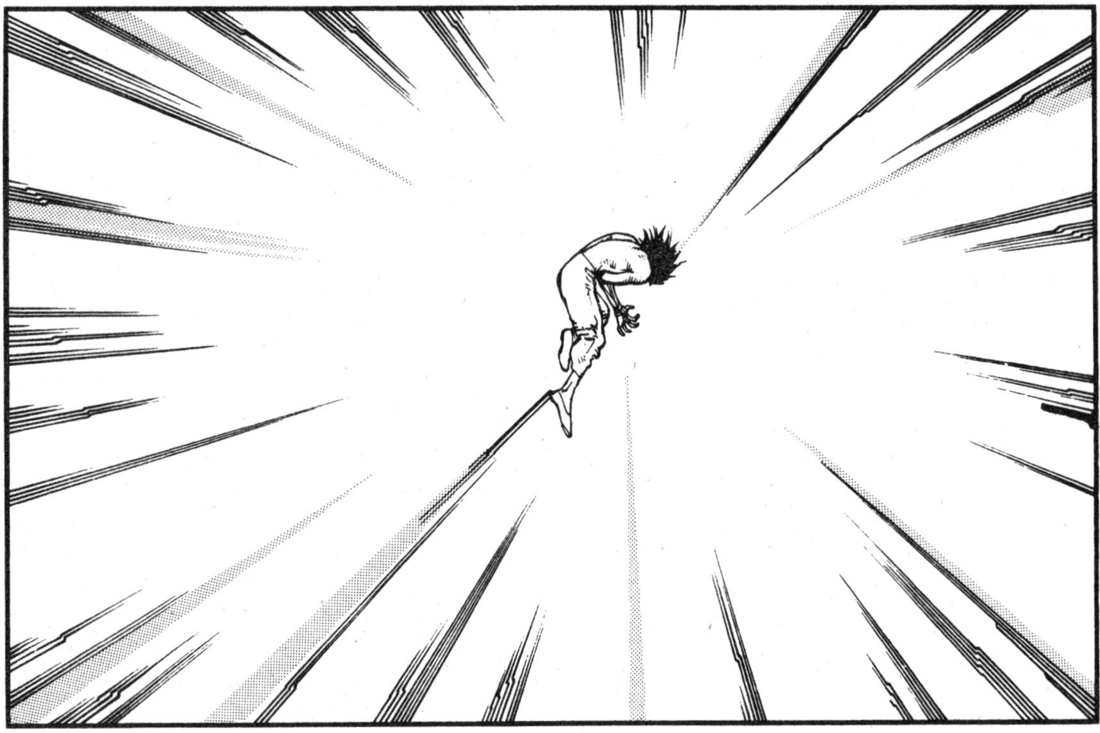

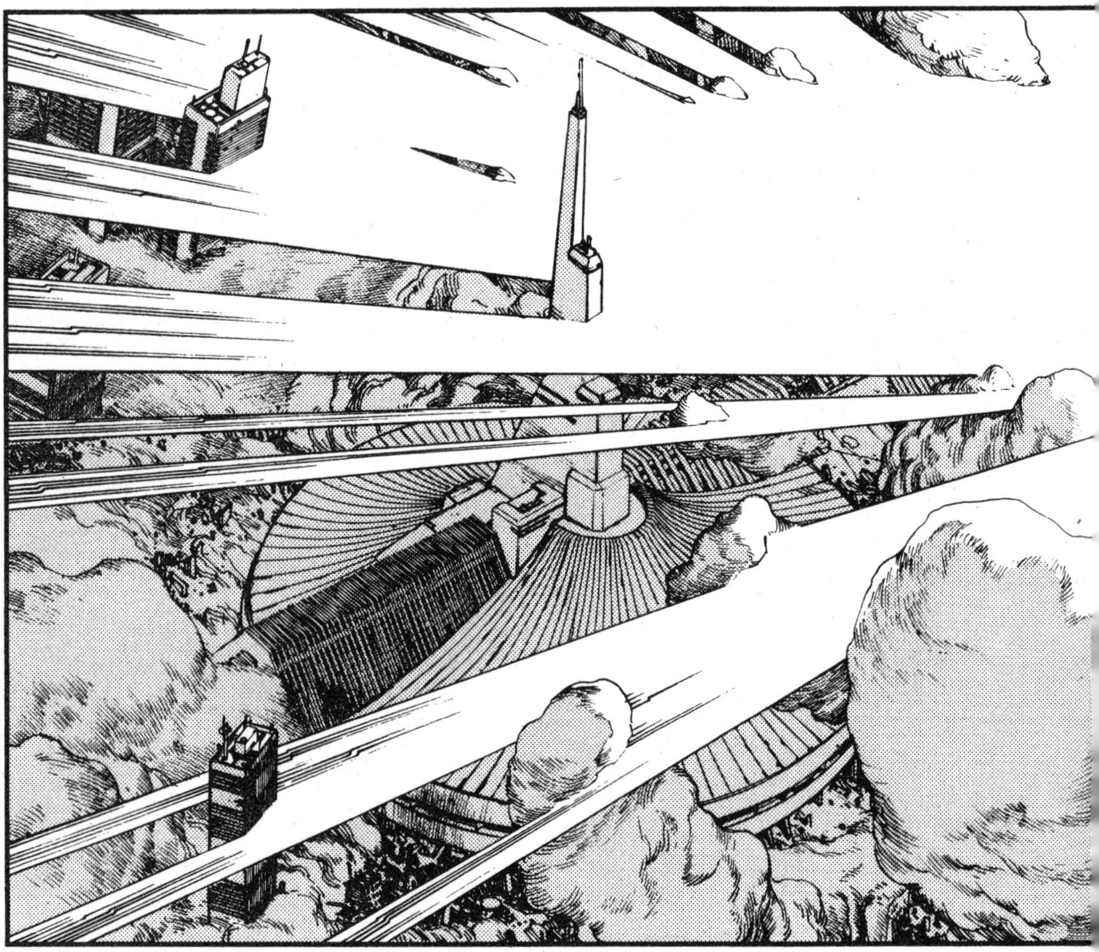

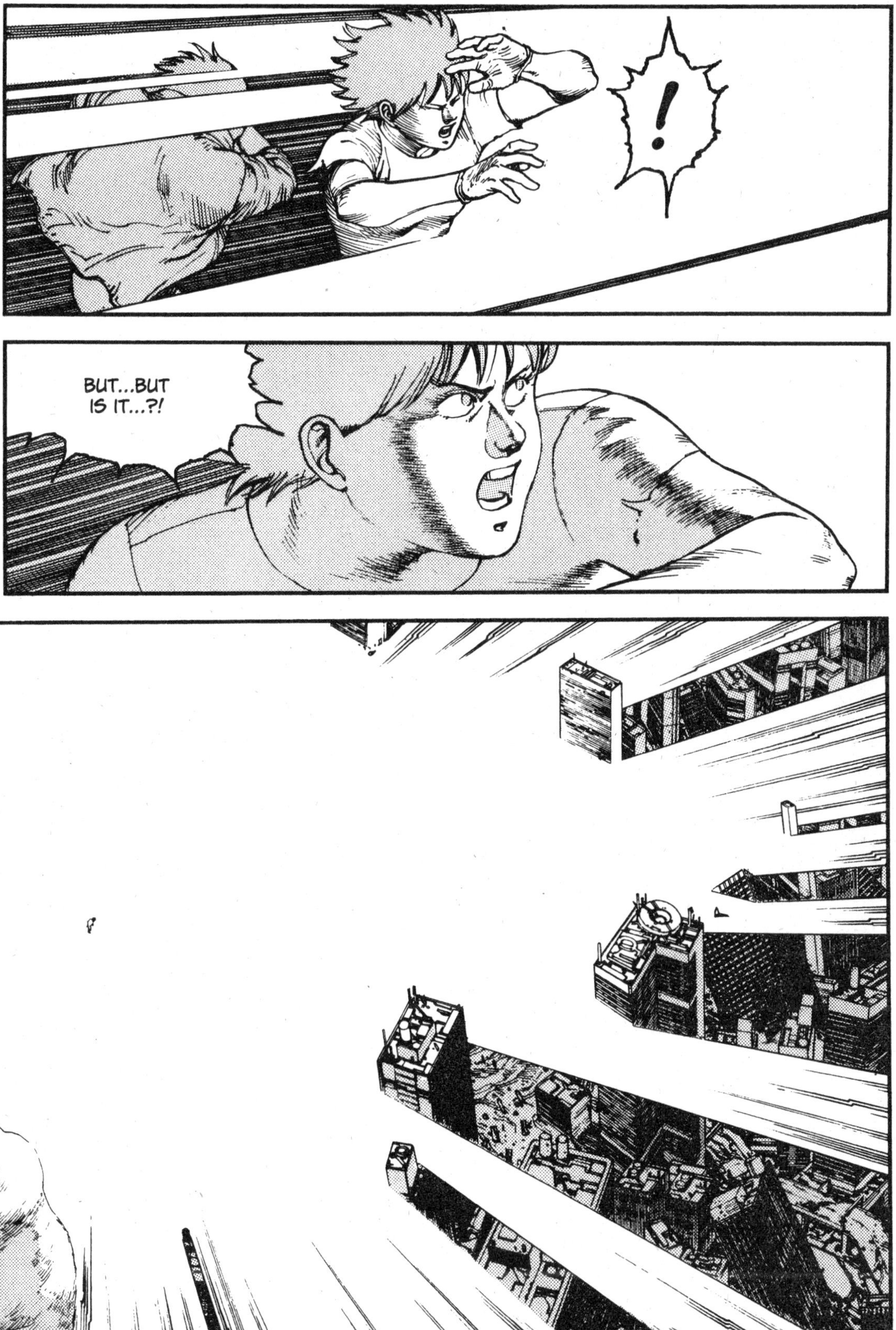
!
BUT...BUT IS IT...?!

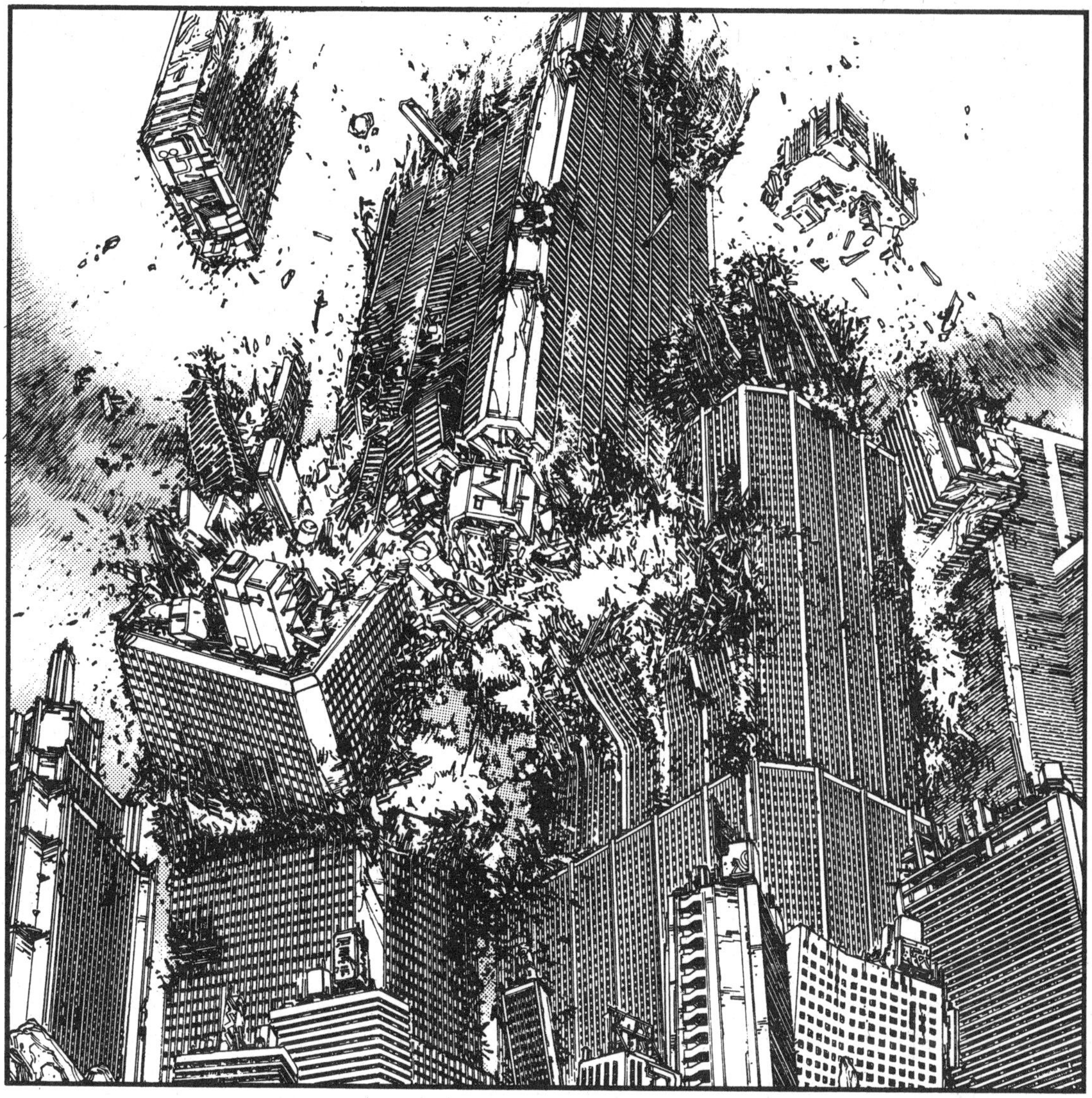

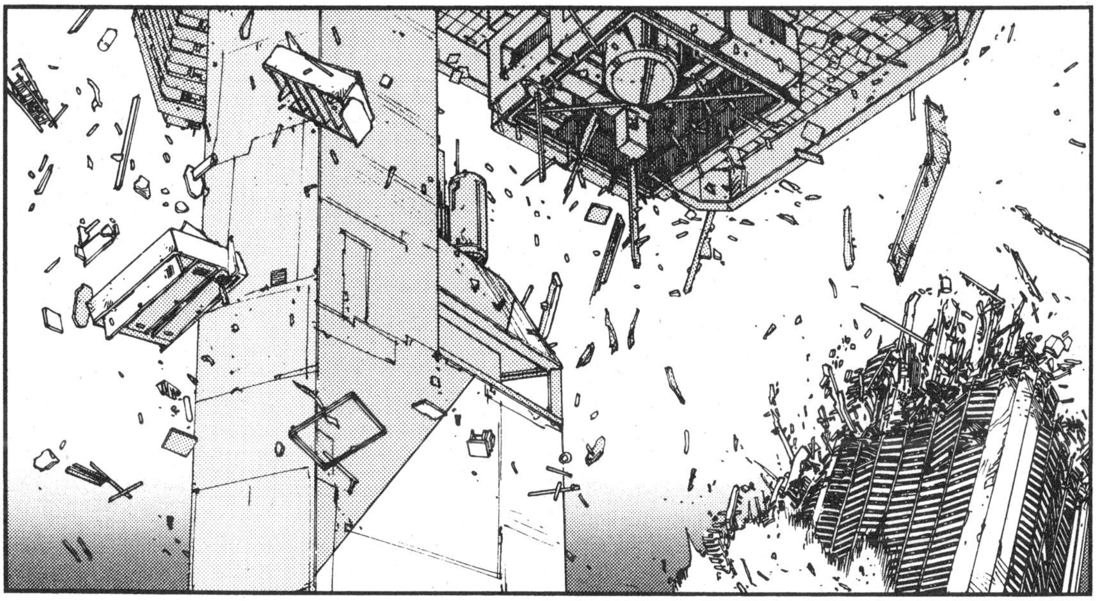

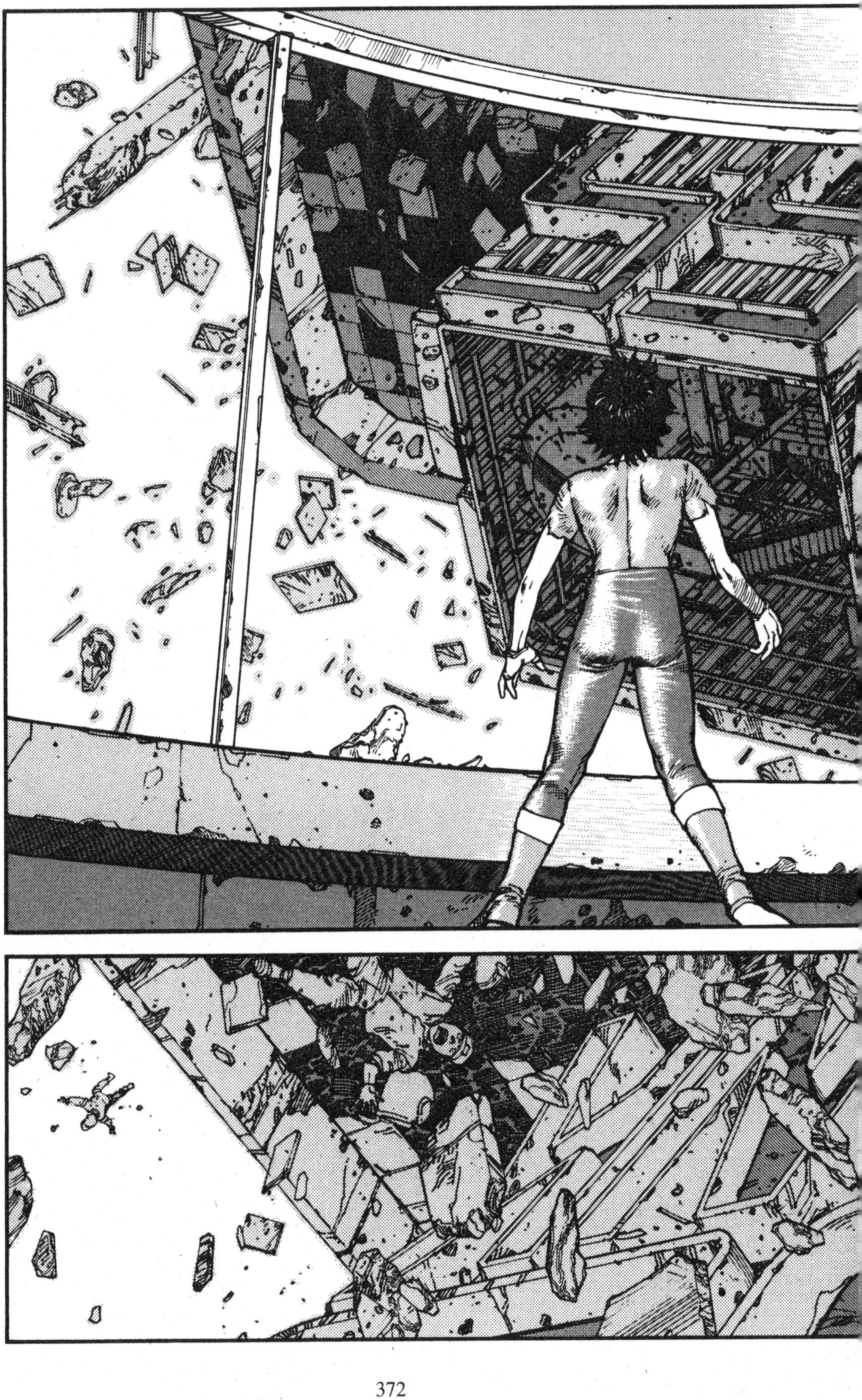

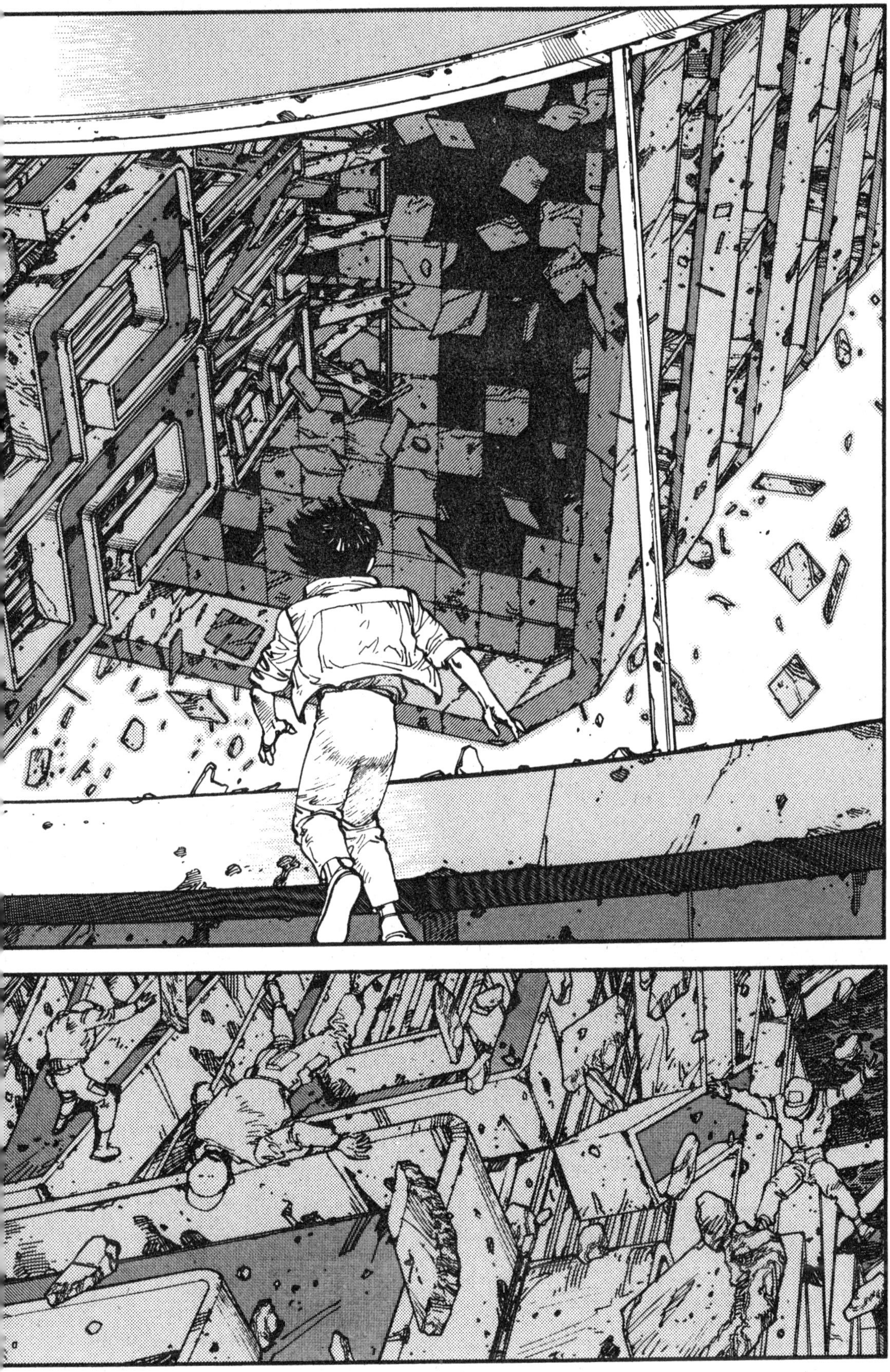

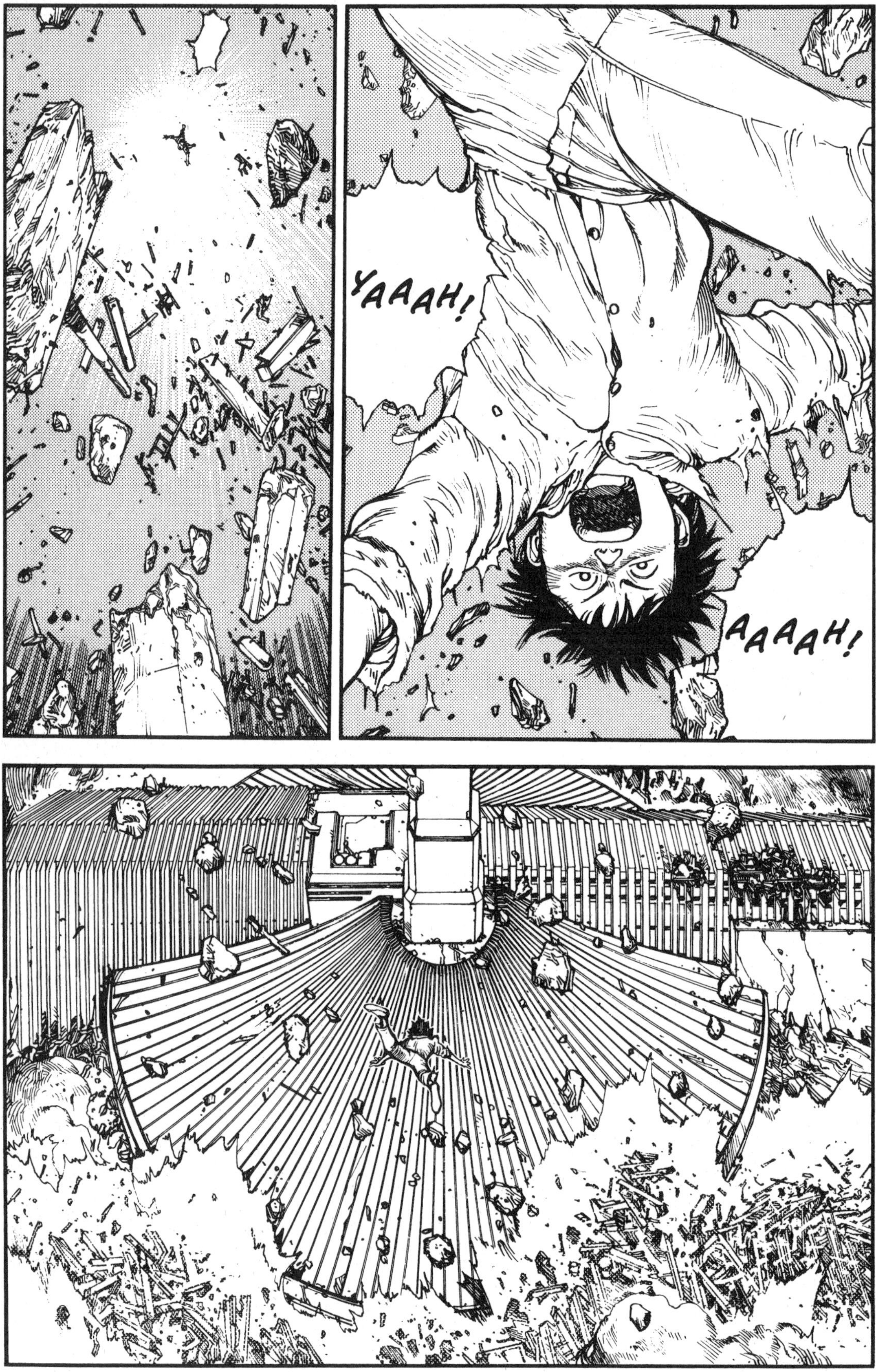
YAAAH!
AAAAH!

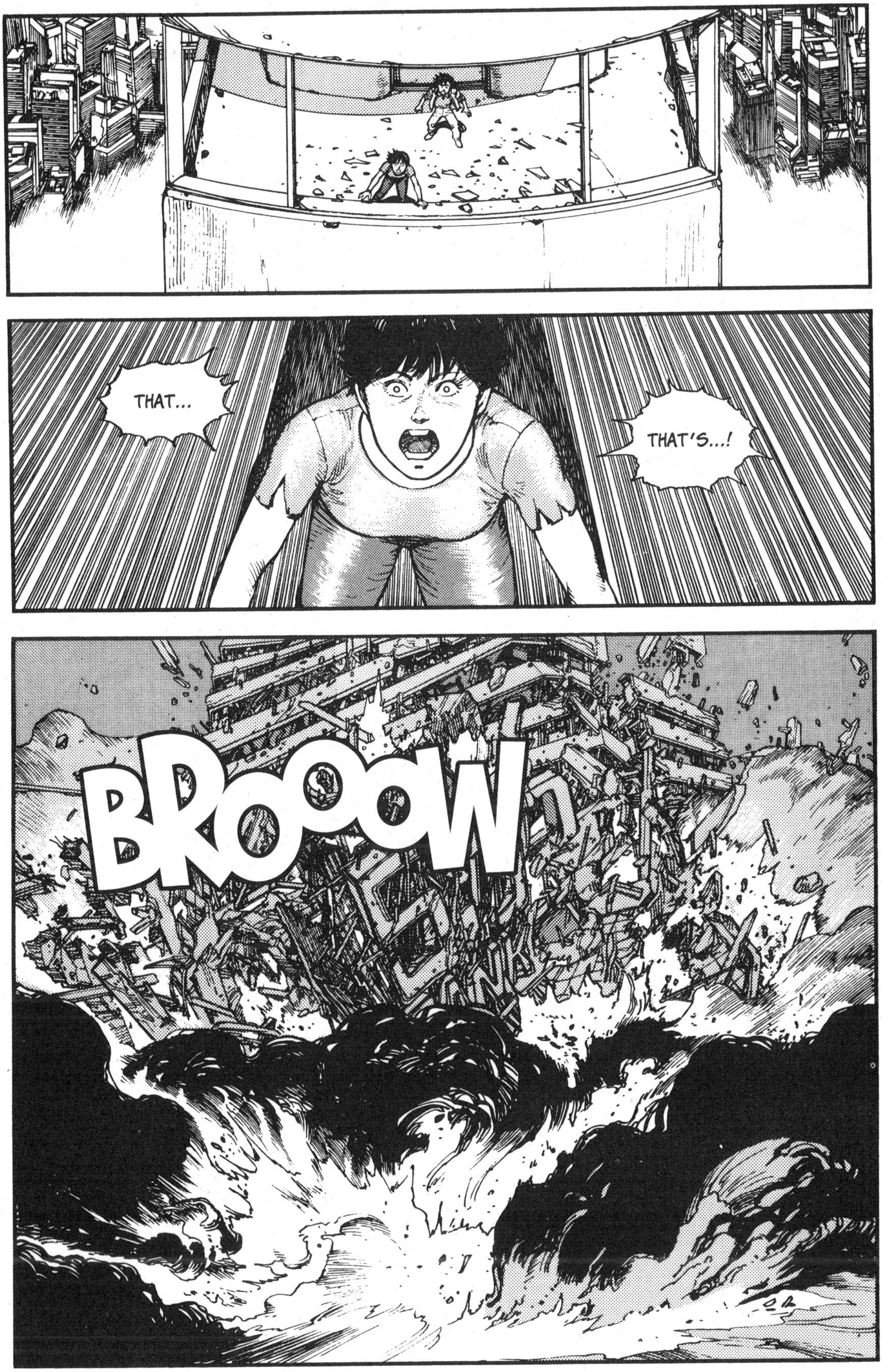
THAT...
THAT'S...!
BROOOW

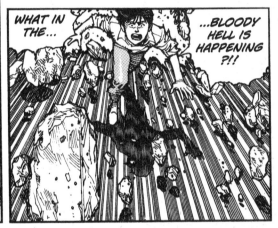

WHAT IN THE...

...BLOODY HELL IS HAPPENING ?!!

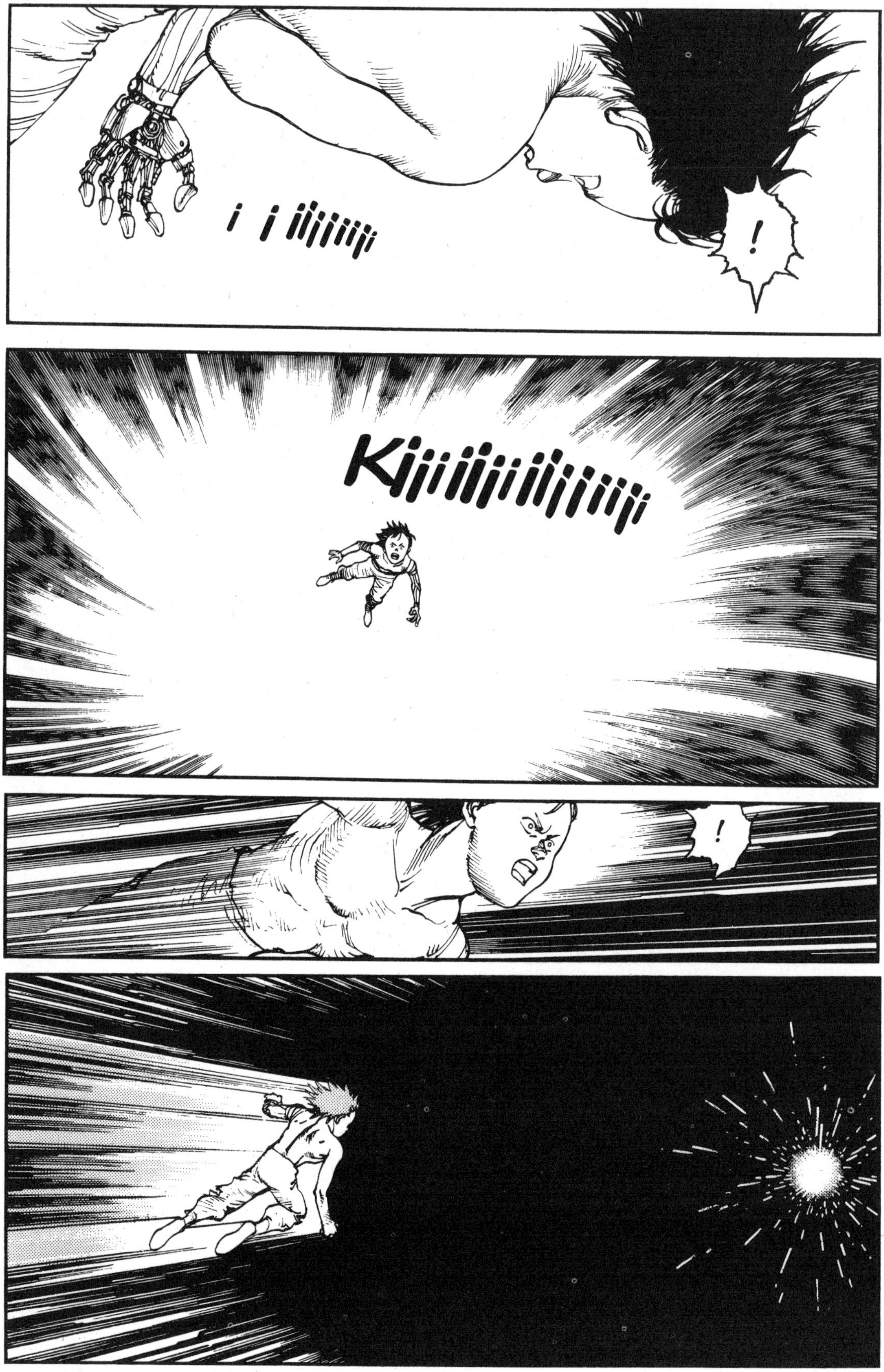
i i iiiiiiii
!
Kiiiiiiiiiiii
!

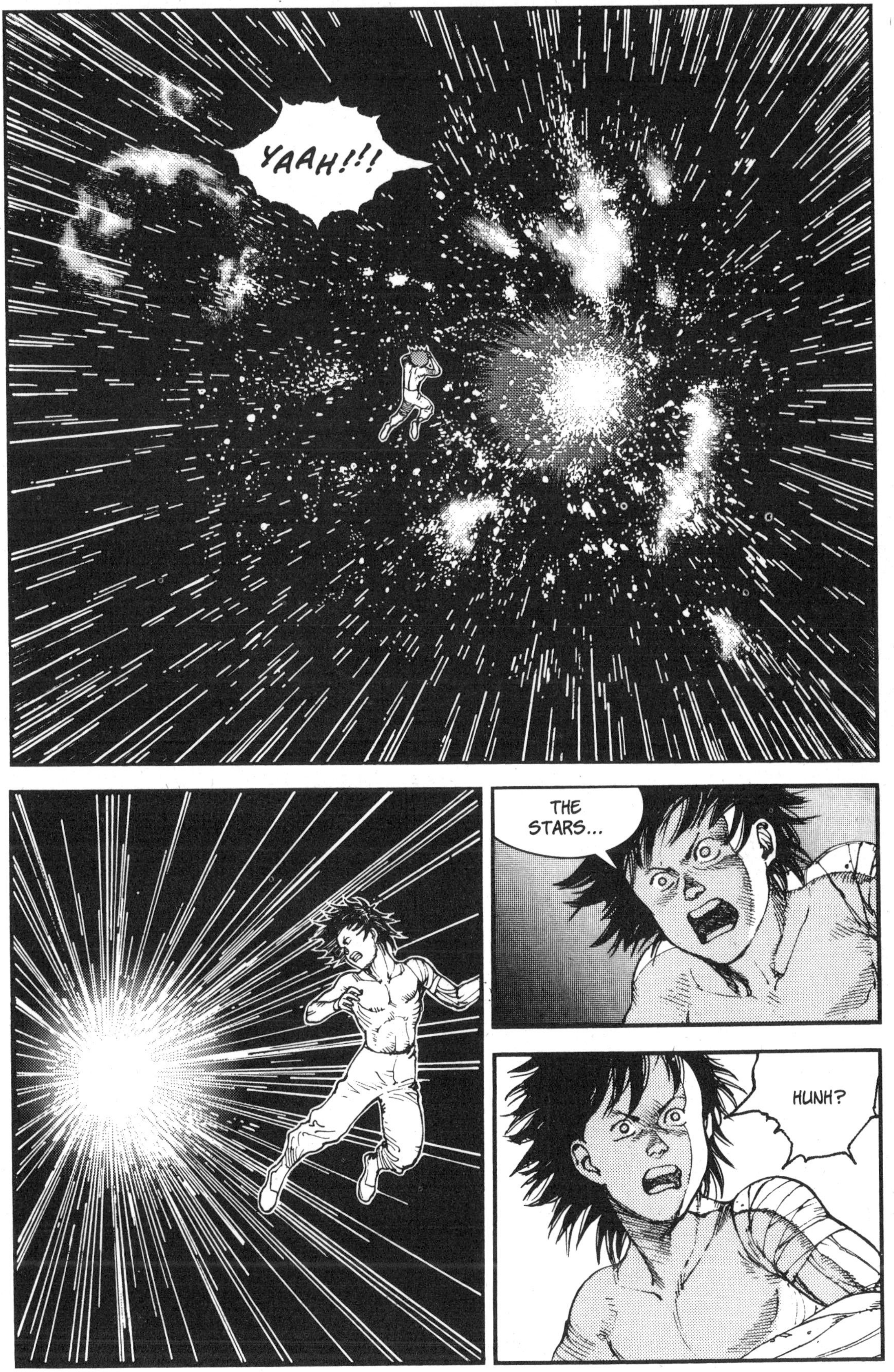
YAAH!!!
THE STARS...
HUNH?

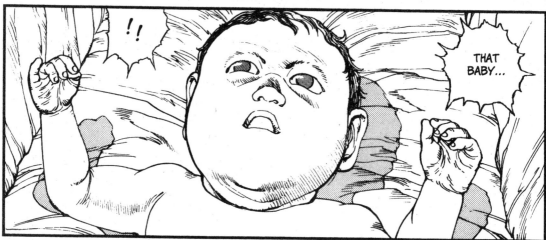

THAT BABY...

IT'S ME!

AND THERE... ARE THOSE MY ...*PARENTS*?!

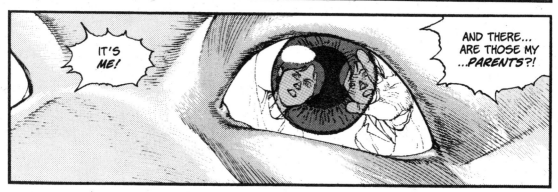

381

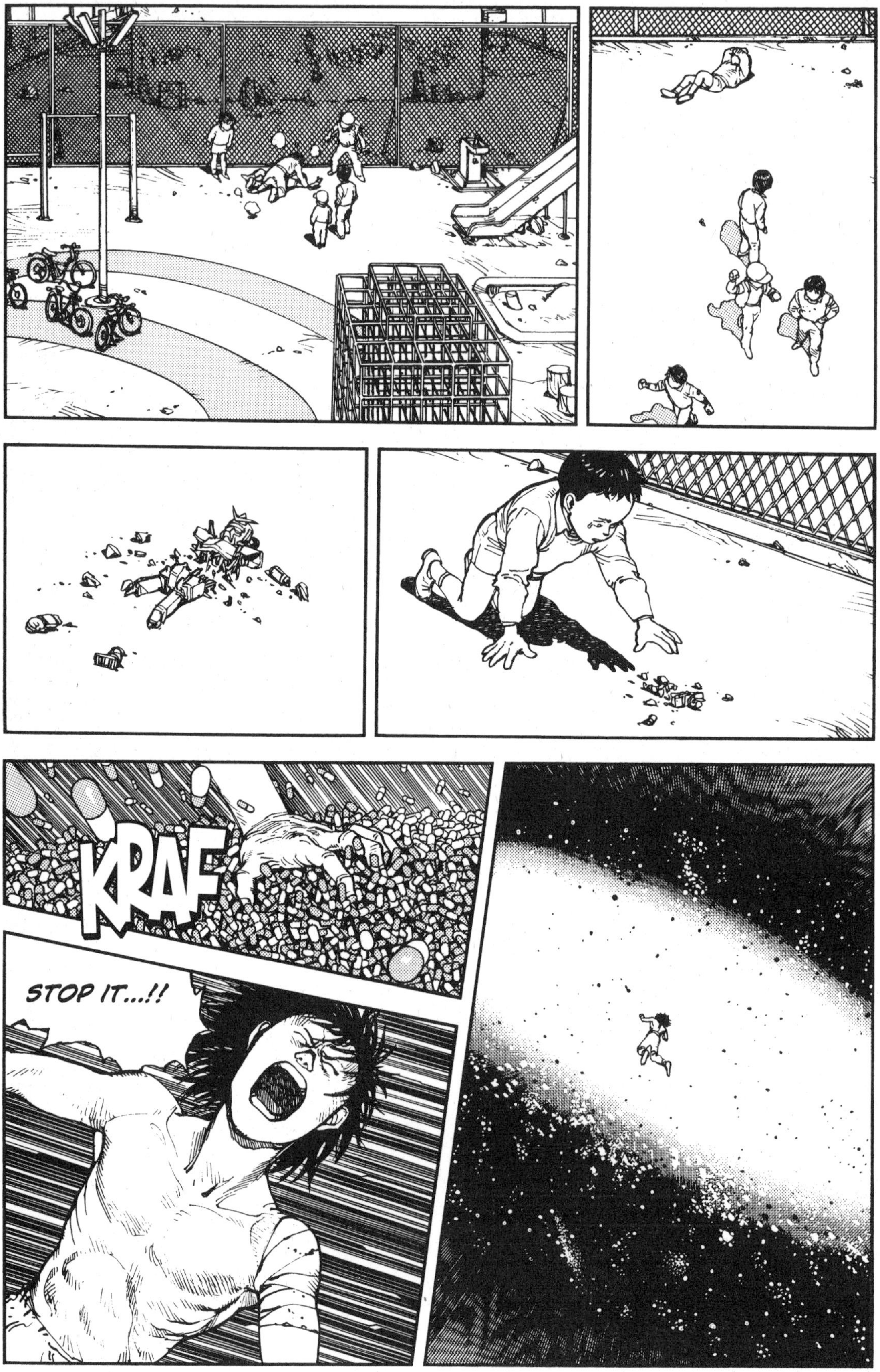
KRAF
STOP IT...!!

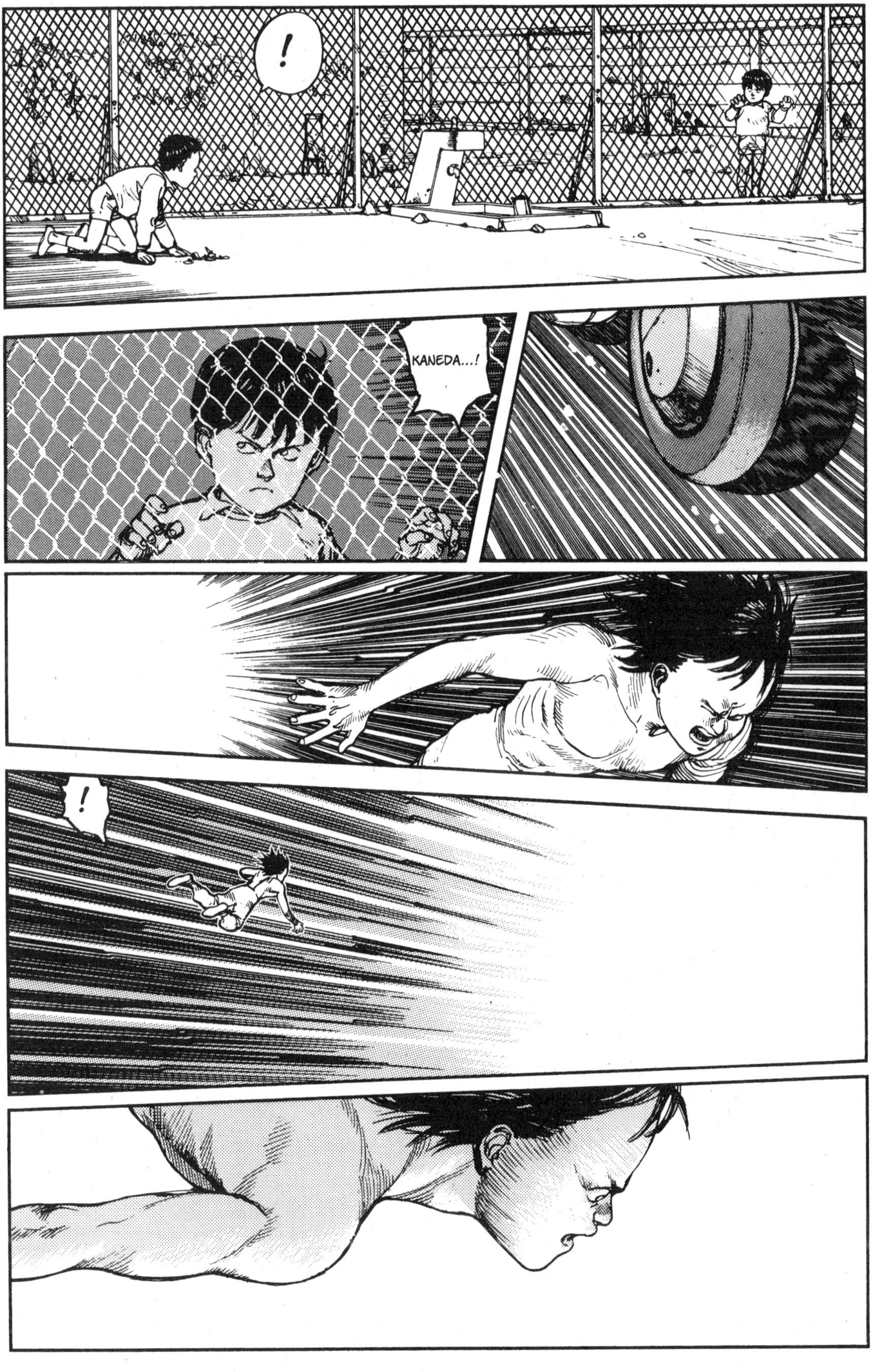
!
KANEDA...!
!

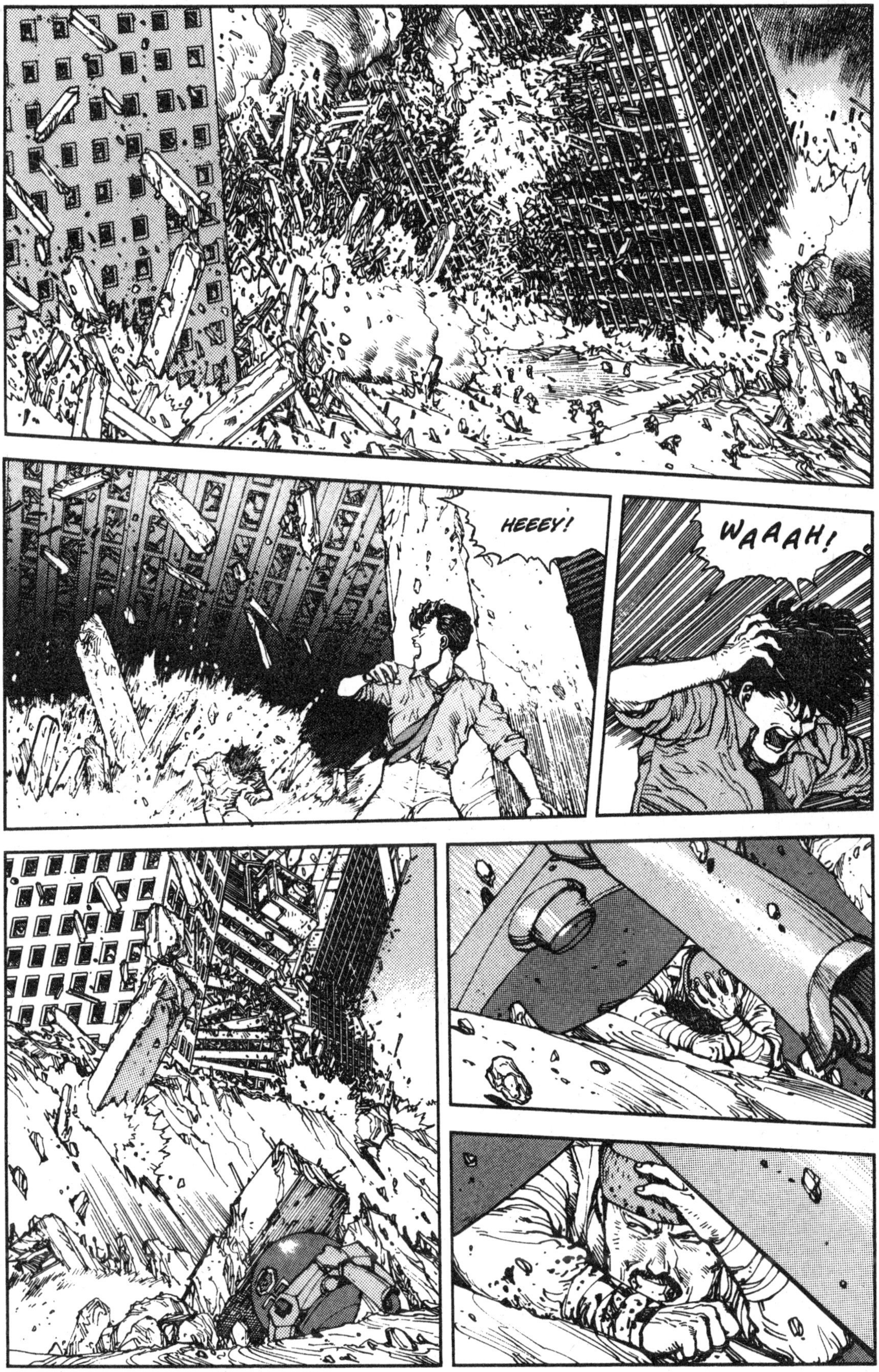
HEEEY!
WAAAH!

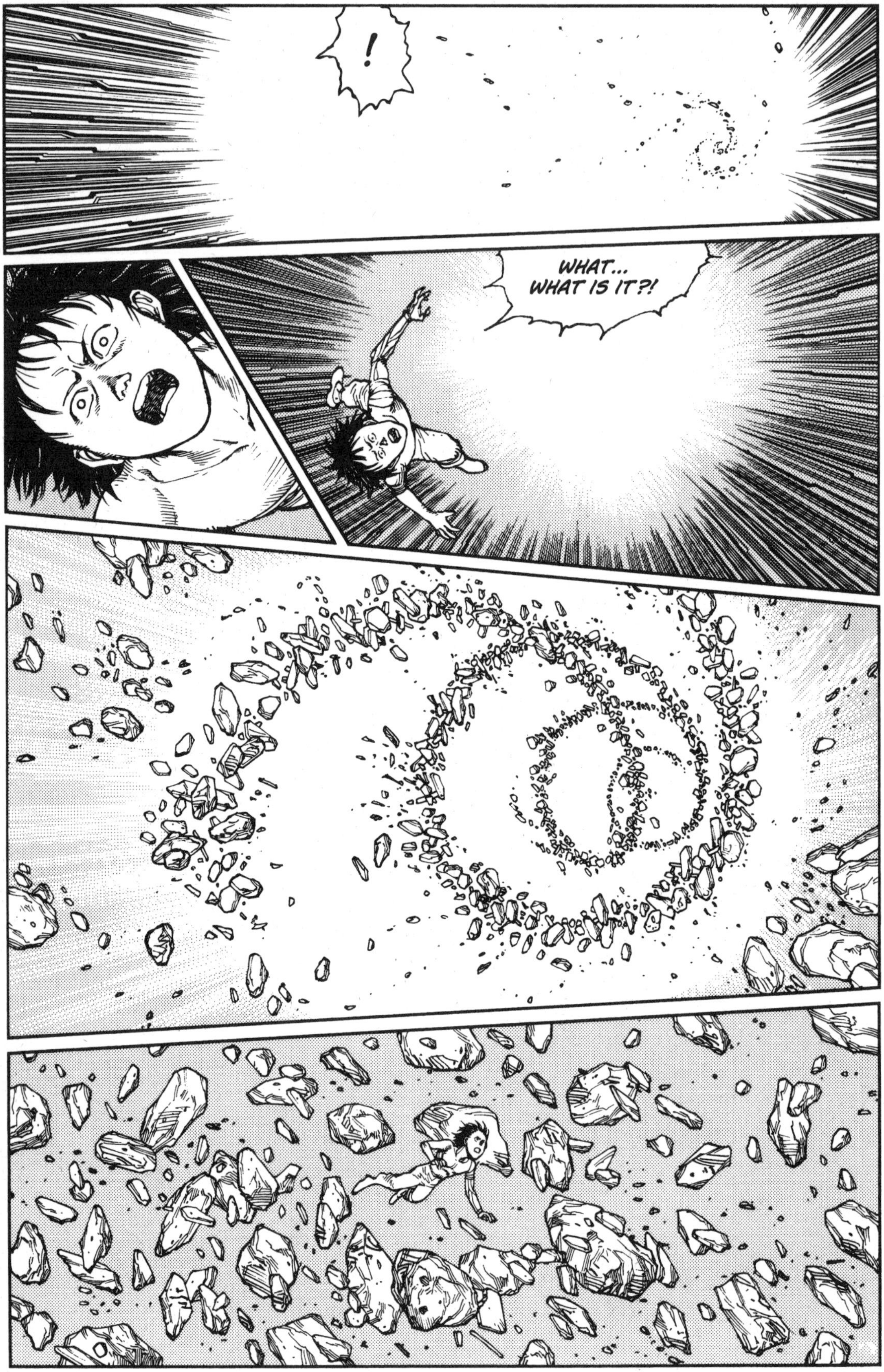
!
WHAT... WHAT IS IT?!

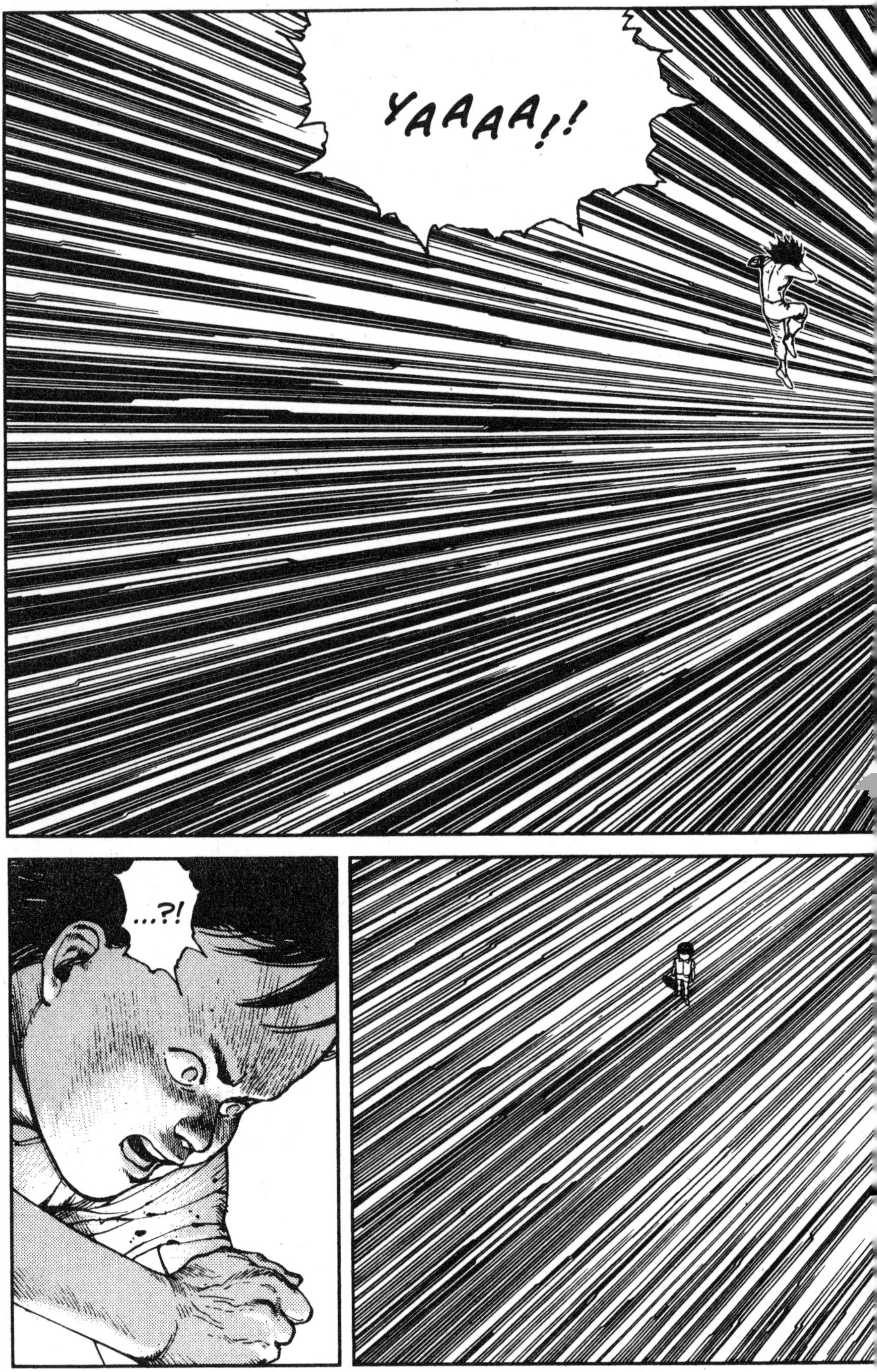
YAAAA!!
...?!

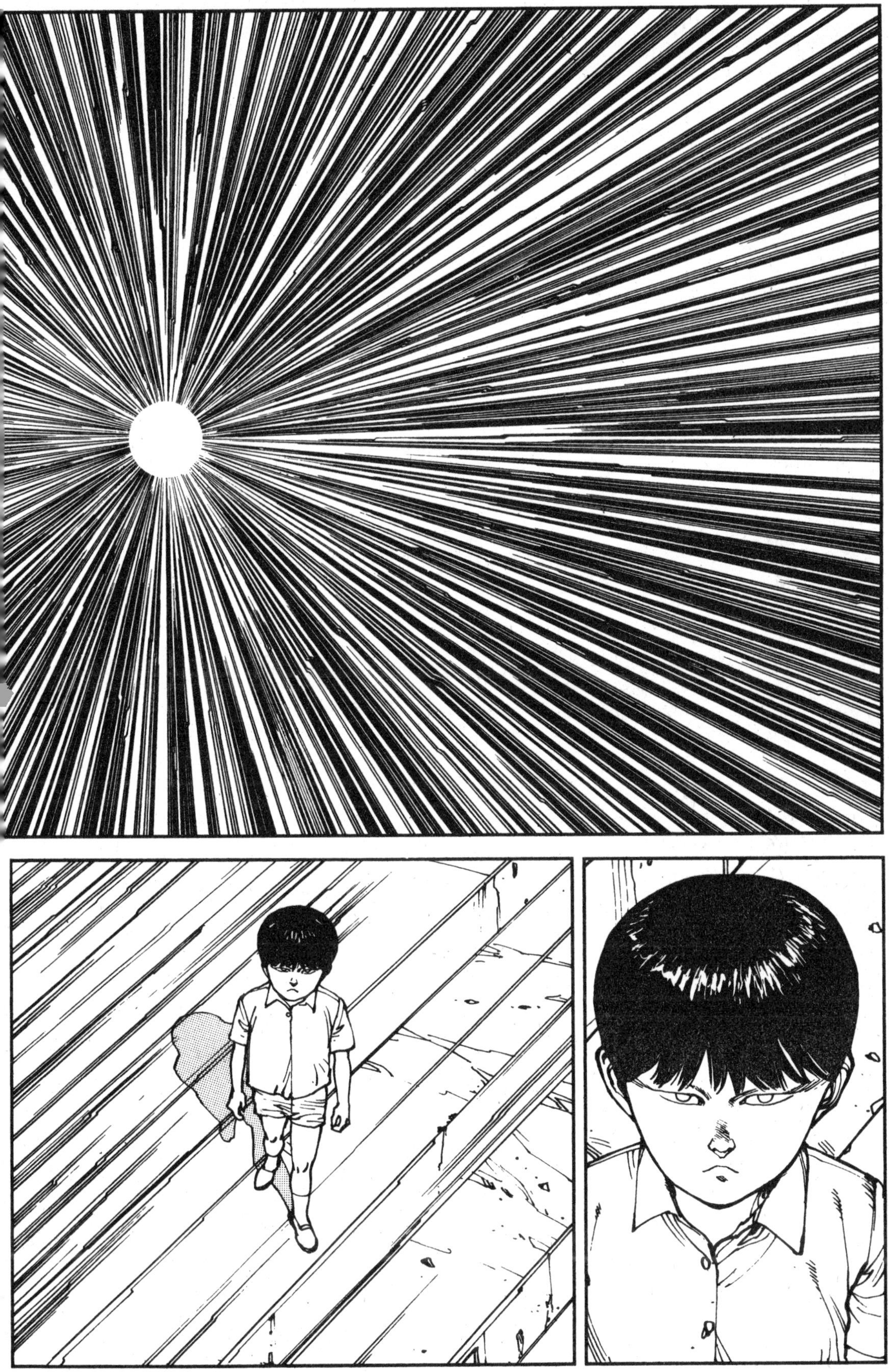

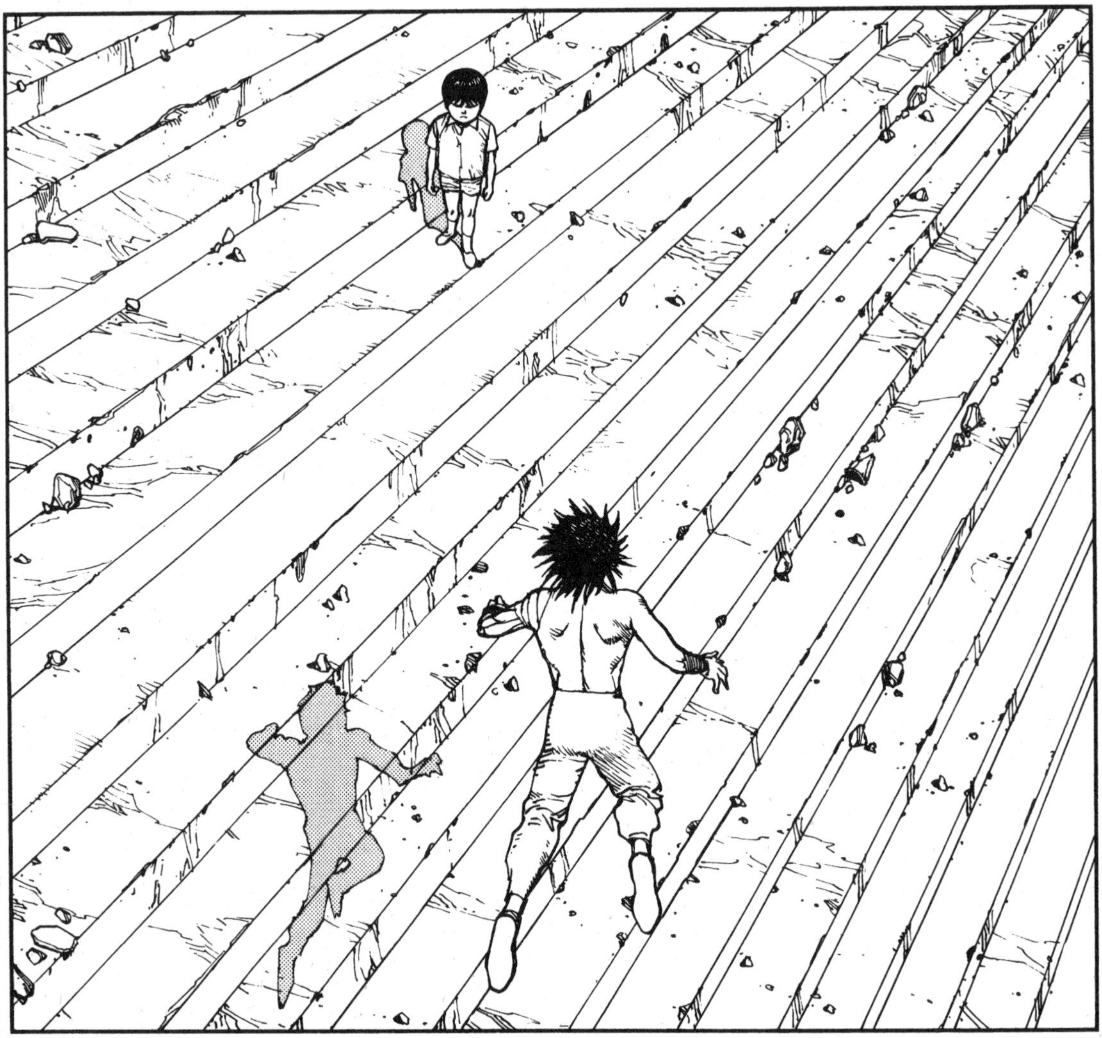

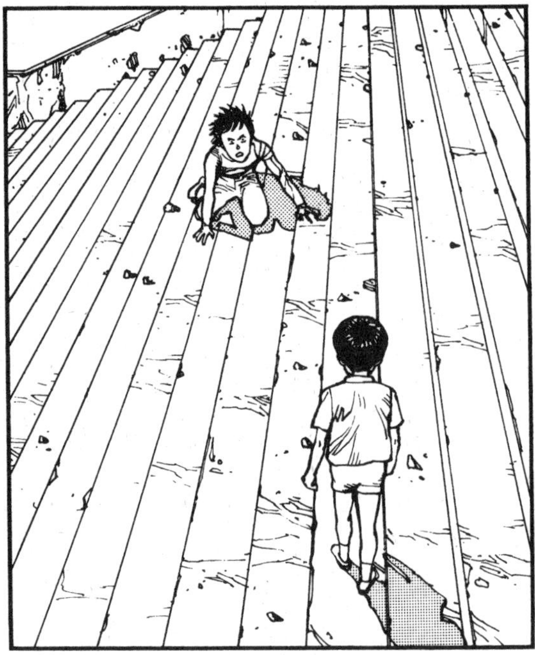

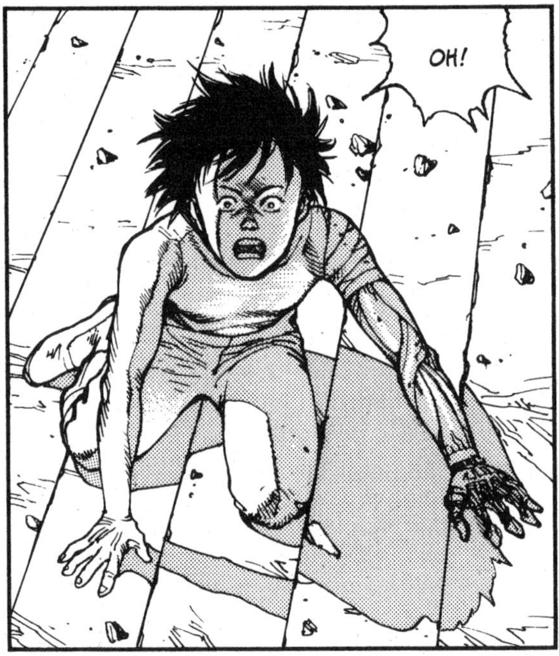
OH!

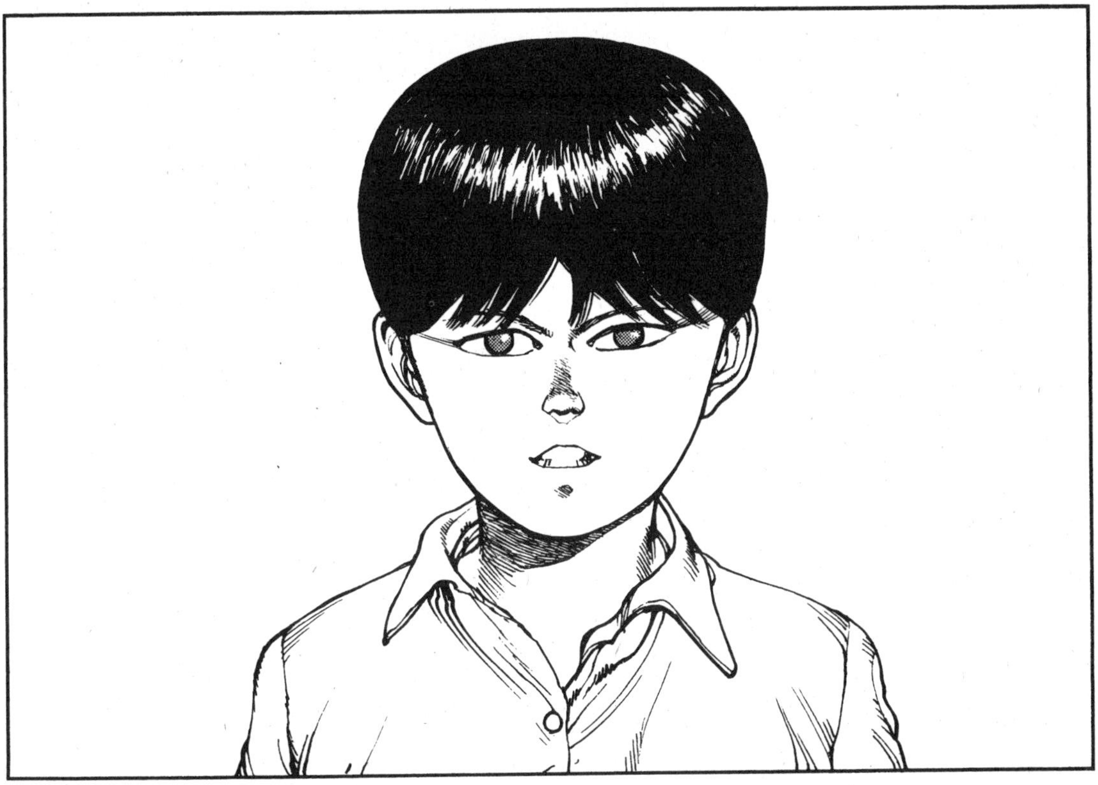

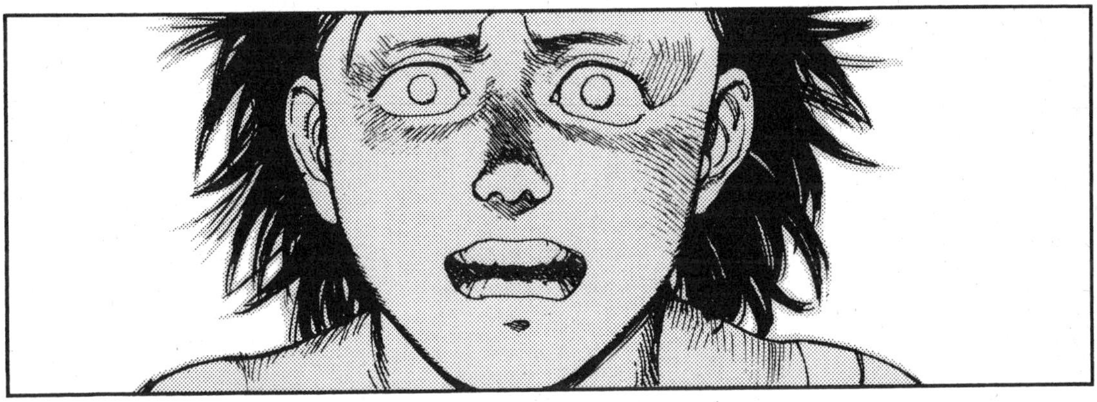

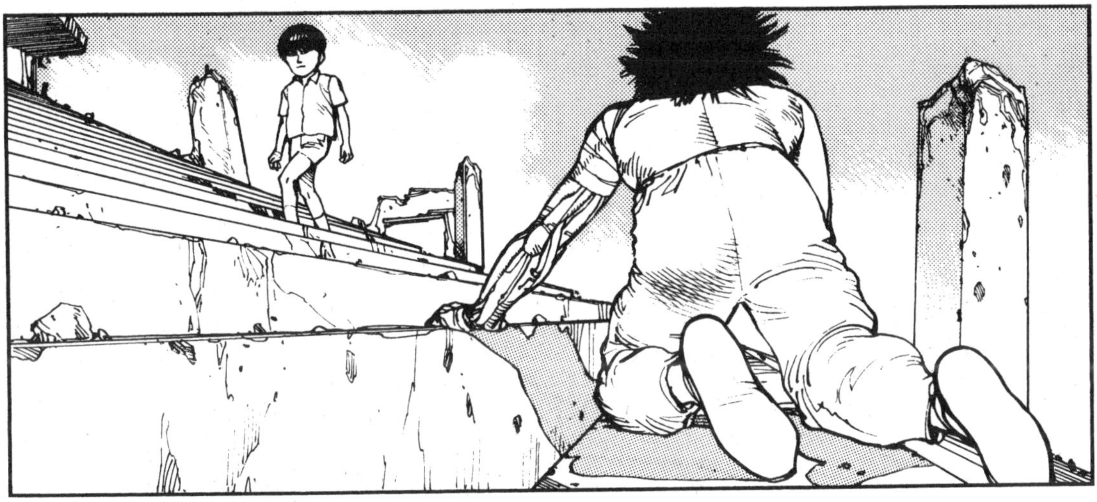

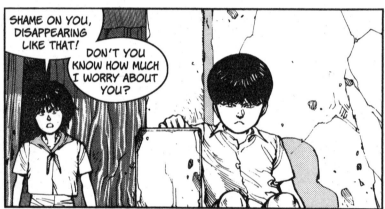

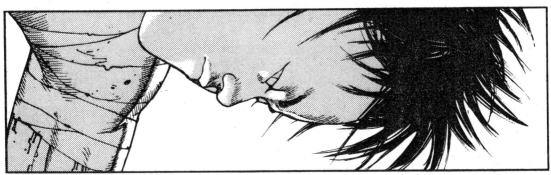

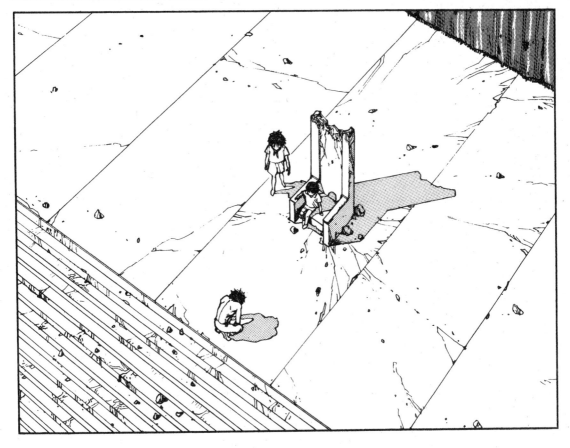

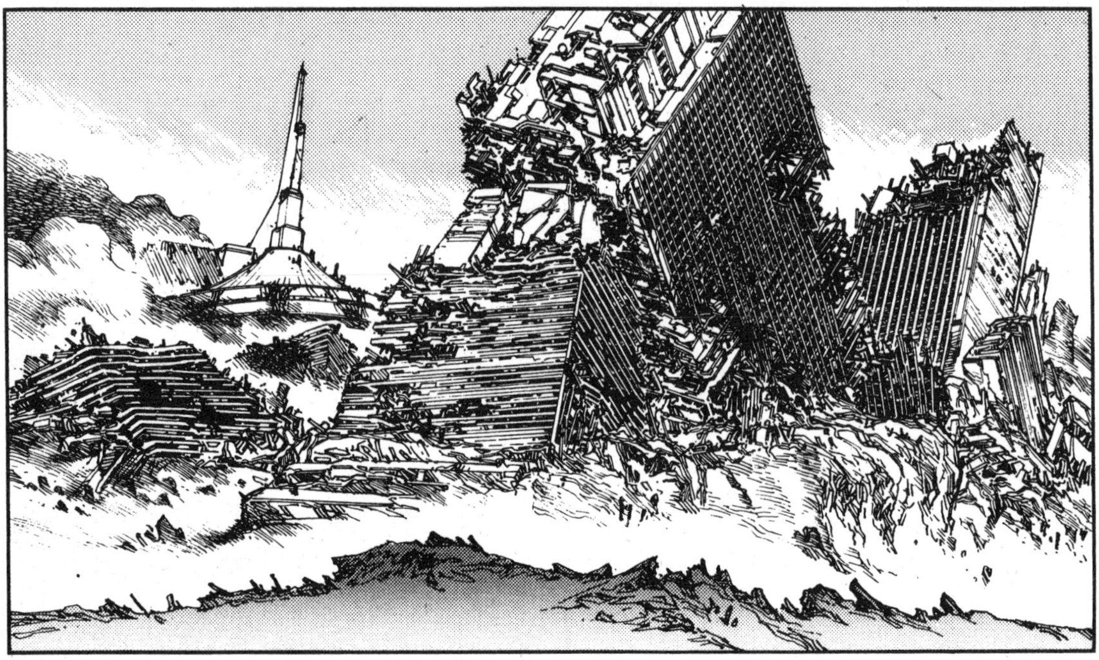

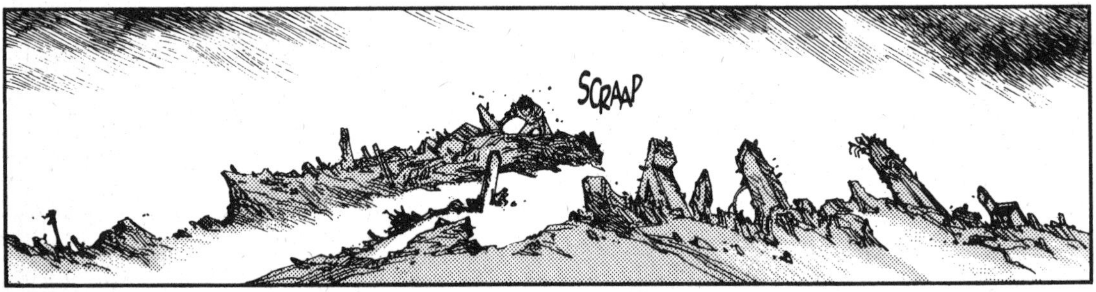
SCRAAP

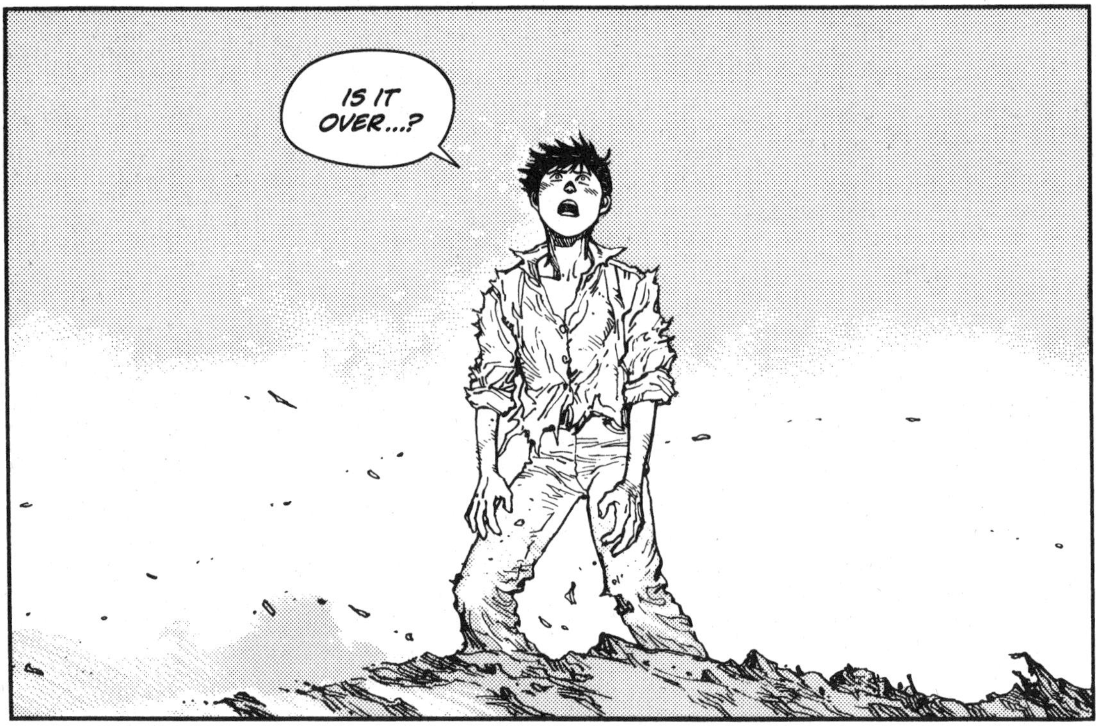
IS IT OVER...?

PART 4 ケイI 完 KeiI -END-

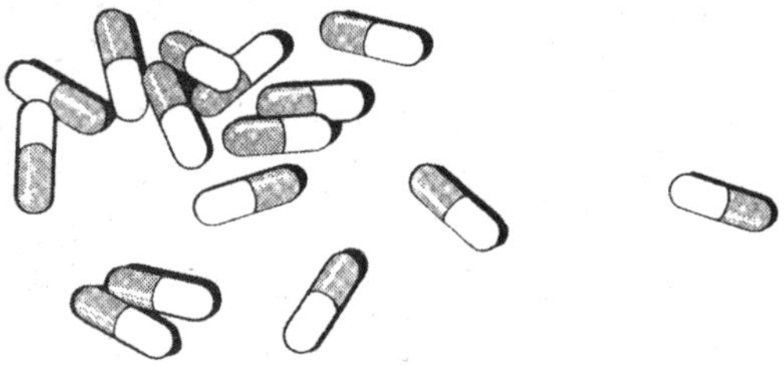

KATSUHIRO OTOMO

Katsuhiro Otomo was born in 1954 in Japan's Miyago Prefecture, a rural province some 300 miles northeast of Tokyo. While in high school, Otomo became, in his own words, "crazy about the movies." The young artist often traveled three hours by train just to see films, and the influence of cinema is a constant thread that runs through Otomo's work.

Soon after graduating high school, Otomo moved to Tokyo with the goal of becoming a comics artist. His first professional work was *Jyu-sei (A Gun Report)*, an adaptation of the Prosper Mérimée novella *Mateo Falcone*, which appeared in the weekly magazine *Action*. Otomo went on to create a series of short stories, usually twenty to thirty pages, challenging works that captured widespread critical acclaim in Japan. A 1980 review in the *Asahi* newspaper said, "Just as the New Cinema movement had demolished the old style of Hollywood filmmaking to usher in a fresh style of movie production in America, Katsuhiro Otomo…came to Tokyo to create a new comics style and shattered the conventions existing in manga."

In 1979, publication began on Otomo's first serialized work, *Fireball*, a story built around a "man versus computer" theme. Though the series was never completed, *Fireball* marked the beginning of Otomo's interest in science-fiction themes and was the forerunner of future work that would define his comics career and firmly establish him internationally as one of the acknowledged masters of the comics medium. *Domu*, first serialized in 1980 and collected in 1983, became a best seller and was the first manga to win the coveted Science Fiction Grand Prix Award, Japan's equivalent to America's Nebula Award. The media attention gained from this landmark achievement made

Otomo one of the best-known comics authors in Japan. Critics raved about *Domu*, a story that combined terrifying paranormal genre elements with poignant observation of urban life in modern Japan. From the *Yomiuri* newspaper: "The weirdness that lurks in the seemingly peaceful living environment of a huge housing complex symbolizes the precariousness hidden at the bottom of today's living conditions in Japan."

Upon completion of *Domu*, Otomo began work on *Akira*, a two-thousand-plus-page epic of staggering illustrative virtuosity and gut-wrenching thematic power. Ten years in the making and eventually collected in six volumes, *Akira* went on to win every possible award and spawned video games, an animated feature film directed by Otomo himself — compared favorably by critics to science-fiction masterpieces such as *Blade Runner* and *A Clockwork Orange* — and a blizzard of merchandise. *Akira* has been published in virtually every language and stands not only as one of the crown jewels of manga, but is regarded by many as the finest work of graphic fiction ever created, anywhere. While the completion of *Akira* marked the beginning of Otomo's moving away from comics — his only major comics work since *Akira* has been the writing of *The Legend of Mother Sarah* — it began his odyssey as a filmmaker. After completion of the animated *Akira*, Otomo has gone on to work on a variety of animated films, including *Labyrinth Stories*, *Robot Carnival*, *Roujin Z*, *Spriggan*, and *Memories*, an anthology of adaptations of earlier Otomo comics stories. Otomo also directed the live-action *World Apartment Horror* as well as television commercials for Honda, Suntory, and Canon. Otomo lives and works in Tokyo.

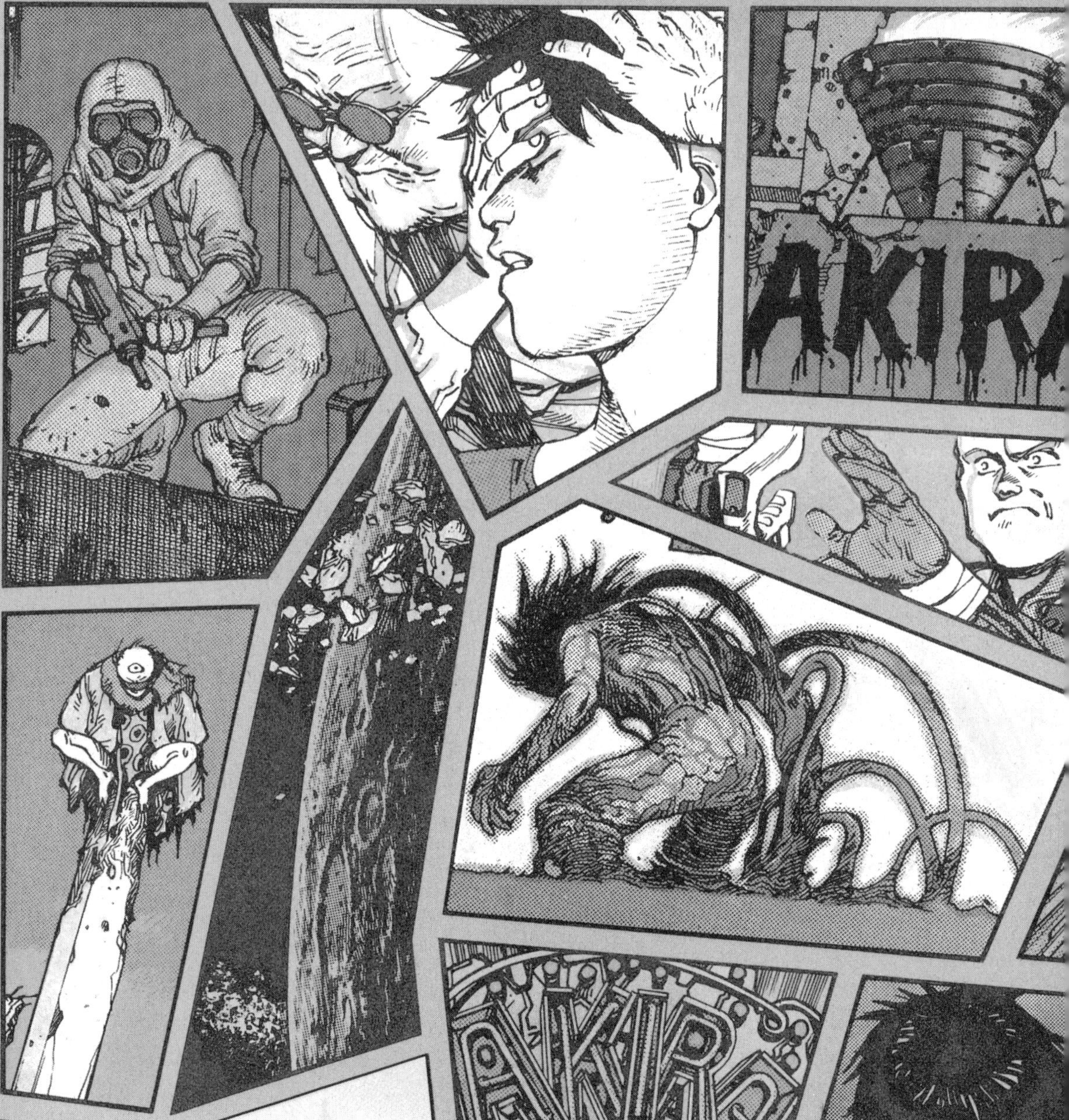

The twisted ambitions of super-being Akira and his partner-in-terror, Tetsuo, continue to dominate Neo-Tokyo. But the planet at large will not take this threat lying down, and the might of the world is ready to take on Akira's Great Tokyo Empire. But will the technologically advanced weaponry of the resistance fighters be enough to defeat Akira and Tetsuo?

Look for AKIRA Volume 5 in 2011, wherever books are sold!

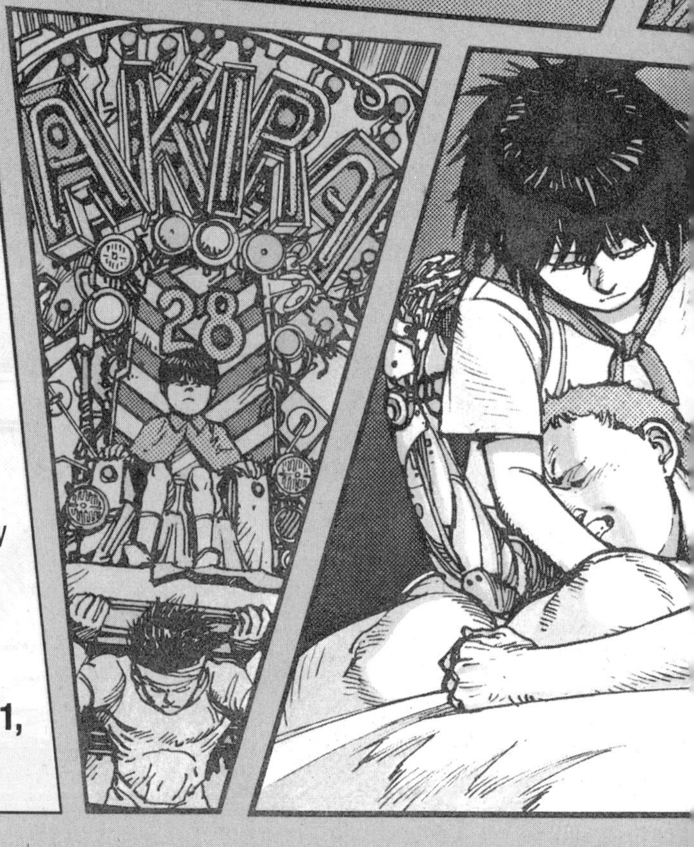
AKIRA
28